BUILDING A CIVIL SOCIETY

Associations, Public Life, and the Origins of Modern Italy

STEVEN C. SOPER

Building a Civil Society

Associations, Public Life, and the Origins of Modern Italy

UNIVERSITY OF TORONTO PRESS
Toronto Buffalo London

ISBN 978-1-4426-4503-5

Printed on acid-free paper
Toronto Italian Studies

Publication cataloguing information is available
from Library and Archives Canada.

This book has been published with the help of a grant from the Willson
Center for the Humanities and Arts at the University of Georgia.

University of Toronto Press acknowledges the financial assistance to its publishing program of the Canada Council for the Arts and the Ontario Arts
Council.

University of Toronto Press acknowledges the financial support for its publishing activities of the Government of Canada through the Book Publishing
Industry Development Program (BPIDP).

Contents

Acknowledgments

My work on this project began at the University of Michigan, under the guidance of two great scholars, Raymond Grew and Geoff Eley, whose encouragement and friendship have stood the test of time, and then some. Julia Adams, Kathleen Canning, and Sonya Rose provided advice and support as members of my dissertation committee. So many other professors and friends made my years in Ann Arbor a pleasure, including, in rough order of acquaintance, Nancy Carnevale, Jay Smith, Amy Nelson, Corinne Gaudin, Bill Sewell, Bill Shea, Michael Kwass, Tom and Sue Schrand, Dennis Sweeney, Peggy Somers, Jon Mogul, Rebecca Friedman, Dave Anthony, Erin Desmond, Liz Horodowich, and Chris Schmidt-Nowara. I would also like to pay my respects to a special teacher, the late Marvin Becker.

I have enjoyed the friendship and support of colleagues at Virginia Tech, Loyola University of Chicago, and the University of Georgia, in particular the following generous readers and critics of my work: Tony Cardoza, Suzanne Kaufman, Bill Sites, Michael Kwass, Laura Mason, Claudio Saunt, David Roberts, Stephen Mihm, Reinaldo Roman, and Aidan Wasley. I owe special thanks to Claudio Saunt for producing the two maps that appear in this book, to David Roberts for his steady fellowship and encouragement, and to the many other friends who have made living in Athens so enjoyable, including Bryant, Ann Marie, Rachel, Akela, Kim, Cori, Jay, Brett, April, Andrew, Sandrine, Ed, Stacey, Adam, and Panda. My collective thanks go out to the talented and good-natured undergraduate students at the University of Georgia, who will be surprised to learn that this book is not about Giuseppe Garibaldi:

In Italy, I benefited from the help of archivists and librarians at the following institutions: in Padua, the Archivio di Stato, the Biblioteca Civica (special thanks to Ugo Culocchi), and the Biblioteca Universitaria on via S. Biagio; in Vicenza, the Archivio dell'Accademia Olimpica and the Biblioteca Bertoliana; in Venice, the Biblioteca Nazionale Marciana and the Archivio Luzzatti at the Istituto Veneto di scienze, lettere ed arti (under the exceptional direction of Sandro Franchini); and in Schio, the Biblioteca Civica "Renato Bortoli." Early in my research, I had the great fortune to meet Italy's leading historian of associational life, Marco Meriggi, who provided invaluable advice, support, and friendship. In Vicenza, I met another good friend and talented scholar, Renato Camurri. I would also like to extend much-belated thanks to my kind co-participants in a conference held in Vicenza in November 1999 on the revolutions of 1848, in particular Massimo Baioni, Renato Camurri, Tullia Catalan, Emilio Franzina, Gilles Pécout, Nina Quarenghi, Lucy Riall, Simonetta Soldani, and Fiorenza Tarozzi, More recently, Luca Mannori kindly read several chapters of my manuscript and offered helpful advice. Last but not least, heartfelt thanks to Alberto Garzotto and Francesca Gambarotto, Marina Pravato, and the social circle at Liuska and Serena's home on Riviera Ruzzante.

The original research for this book was made possible by a generous grant from the Gladys Krieble Delmas Foundation, and by additional support from the University of Michigan's Department of History and Horace H. Rackham School of Graduate Studies. Thanks also to the Society for Italian Historical Studies and its Helen and Howard R. Marraro Prize committee. At the University of Georgia, the Willson Center for the Humanities and Arts has generously assisted in the publication of the book. It has been a pleasure to work with the University of Toronto Press; many thanks to Ron Schoeffel, Shoshana Wasser, Ani Deyirmenjian, Terry Teskey, Anne Laughlin, the design team responsible for the cover of the book, and the two anonymous readers of my manuscript, who offered excellent advice.

Having spent such a long time with this book, I find it easy to appreciate the positive constants in my life: the love and support of my parents Richard T. Soper and Delyle Myers Soper, my brother Tony and sister Les, and the Rosenbaum and Vezu families; the good humour and sympathy of friends old and new, especially Mike and Dennis; the companionship of Mo, Ruby, Elsie, and Socks; and the fantastic voyage of life with Susan Rosenbaum and Natalie Margot Soper. In truth, my twenty-plus years working on this book have been a joy, not a burden, because I have spent those years with Susan, who is somehow able simultaneously to be funny, smart, beautiful, and loving. As for Natalie, she is just the greatest little girl I know.

BUILDING A CIVIL SOCIETY

Associations, Public Life, and the Origins of Modern Italy

Introduction

Italy's full-blown age of association began dramatically, with the creation of the Italian Kingdom. In one territory after another – first Lombardy in 1859, then the duchies, most of the Papal States, and southern Italy in 1860, and finally the Veneto in 1866 and Rome in 1870 – citizens promptly celebrated their liberation from oppressive rulers by creating a spate of new associations: political associations, workers' mutual aid societies, veterans' groups, social clubs, agrarian associations, music bands and drama clubs, reading societies and night school programs, consumer cooperatives and credit unions, associations of wine producers, horse breeders, and beekeepers. These were not the first associations ever to form in Italy. Nevertheless, the spread of legally constituted associations before unification was fitful and uneven, confined for the most part to aristocratic and bourgeois elites in major cities, and it was poorly publicized by the periodical press. Reactionary governments were partly to blame, for they restricted citizens' right to form associations and print newspapers. But association organizers were also frustrated by the general population's apparent lack of civic initiative. As a result, for most Italian proponents of association, unification was doubly dramatic. On the one hand, it promised to bring about a great change, the birth of freedom and a bold new age of association. On the other hand, it was a daunting and uncertain moment of truth, a test of the power of freedom to inspire a downtrodden people. Would ordinary Italians overcome their inertia and build a new civil society? This open question profoundly shaped the history of associational life in Italy.

The men who dominated Italian politics and associational life after unification were not inclined to wait around for an answer. They were, for the most part, bourgeois professionals and aristocratic landowners with a shared commitment to the ideals of nineteenth-century European liberalism: constitutional law, parliamentary government, secular education, economic progress, and a sexual division of public (male) and private (female) spheres.[1] As educated elites, they were convinced that they alone knew how to govern associations properly – how to draft statutes, conduct meetings, balance budgets, and hold elections – and, just as important, which types of association a poor and illiterate society needed most. In their view, it was not enough to expand the bases of associational life to include a slightly larger section of the bourgeoisie, or to enjoy new forms of political and recreational sociability; rather, what Italy urgently needed were economic and educational associations – mutual aid societies, credit unions, cooperatives, and adult education programs – that could increase productivity and instil new habits of self-discipline in the lower classes. They expected to meet resistance from conservative defenders of the status quo, from republican and socialist rivals, and possibly even from the very people they were trying to help.

In the Veneto, which is the focus of this study, the sense of urgency attached to the creation of new associations after unification was especially great. From 1859 to 1866, Venetian liberals watched as their counterparts in the already united regions of the Italian Kingdom started newspapers, formed associations, and held free elections. They corresponded with the founders of new associations in united Italy, gathering practical advice and requesting copies of official statutes and publications. Some tried to convince the ruling Austrian government to ease its restrictions on freedom of the press and association, with limited success. Others grew impatient and left the Veneto to try their hand at starting associations in the neighbouring regions of Lombardy and Emilia-Romagna. Thus it was no surprise that the first newspapers to appear in the Veneto after the departure of the Austrians, in the summer of 1866, immediately set about promoting and celebrating associations.

At that moment, Italy needed something to celebrate. In the years preceding the war for Venetia, the Italian army had been fighting a bloody civil war in the south of Italy, ostensibly to root out brigands but also to impose the new Piedmontese political and legal order on a resentful population. Other discouraging news concerned the peninsula as a whole: the first government-sponsored surveys of social and economic conditions in Italy confirmed that Italy lagged behind the leading European states in a number of areas, from literacy and per capita income to the establishment of public libraries and workers' mutual aid societies.[2]

Critics of Italy's terrible military performance in 1866 – for it was Prussia, not Italy, that turned the war against Austria – drew upon this broad profile of civil and institutional backwardness to explain what had gone wrong and how to fix it, arguing that Italy needed a stronger army but also more (and better) schools, banks, industries, and associations. The most famous of these critics, the Neapolitan liberal Pasquale Villari, issued a call for a "new war of internal conquest."[3] The leading Venetian proponents of association echoed these remarks, in the summer and fall of 1866 and for several years to come. Luigi Luzzatti, a tireless promoter of credit unions, likened himself to a general heading into battle. Alberto Errera compared the supporters of a new library for workers in Venice to a cadre of talented revolutionaries, who dared to "stir an impoverished civilization from its perpetual drowsiness."[4]

We are not accustomed to dramatic, uncertain, or embattled histories of associational life. Few historians of associational life in eighteenth- and nineteenth-century Europe feature bold leaders or pivotal events because they are more concerned with collective action and broad processes of historical change – in particular, the emergence of civil society and the making of the middle class. From Tocqueville to Habermas to Robert Putnam, writers have described the spread of associations in Europe and the United States in terms of the self-motivated actions of "joiners." In Tocqueville's *Democracy in America*, civic-minded Americans of the early nineteenth century do not need to be stirred; rather, they are simply "forever forming associations." In *Making Democracy Work*, Robert Putnam implies that the same is true of contemporary northern Italians, who can trace their civic culture back to the medieval period. Less civic-minded, perhaps, but no less confident, the eighteenth-century Europeans described by Habermas (and many historians after him) rush to fill the new institutional spaces of an emergent "public sphere." They might struggle against overbearing states and retrograde aristocracies but not against an impoverished civilization, for history was on their side: the spread of print culture and literacy; the growth of commerce and the professions; the emergence of new conceptions of privacy, sociability, and sovereignty – all of these conditions favouring the emergence of a vibrant civil society and a proactive bourgeoisie had been gathering force since the seventeenth century. By the early nineteenth century, in Europe and the United States, a widely diffused pattern of wilful, if not spontaneous, action was set: men and women *organized themselves* in associations, and associations *responded* to the needs of a rapidly changing society.[5]

The first generation of political and civic leaders in the Veneto regarded associations in very different terms. Although in theory they embraced the principles of voluntary association and individual self-help, in practice they treated the association as a means by which a small group of enlightened organizers might intervene to transform a backward society. Late unification and the damaging effects of economic and civic decline convinced most Venetian liberals that, at least in Italy, a civil society could not be taken for granted, but rather had to be encouraged, awakened, educated, organized, even created anew. Even in the region's main urban centres – Venice, Padua, Vicenza, and Verona – only a small percentage of the population could be expected to understand what a voluntary association was, let alone how it functioned. Ordinary Venetians might easily confuse modern mutual aid societies with outdated religious confraternities and restrictive guilds; or, worse, they might be lured by republicans into joining political associations and jeopardizing the constitutional order that the ruling liberals had striven to create. (Republicans countered that liberals cared too much for their own power, too little for freedom.)

The educated and propertied men who founded most of united Italy's first mutual aid societies, savings banks, evening schools, and agrarian associations assumed that they would have to prepare the way for inexperienced and ignorant joiners. Fearing that reluctant workers and traditional farmers might not rush to join these new organizations, Venetian liberals made what they thought were necessary adjustments, lowering dues and making meeting times and places more convenient. They also assumed that most new members would be unfamiliar with the basic procedures of orderly assembly, so they heavily publicized meetings and contrasted the tranquility and harmony on display at these events with the ritual excesses of large public gatherings and political demonstrations. In short, more than an expression of individual freedom, civic autonomy, or bourgeois ascendancy, to Italian liberals the association was both a model of constitutional government and a practical instrument of civic education: a place where responsive citizens might gather but also where responsible citizens could be formed.[6]

This tutelary vision of associational life was beset with tensions and contradictions. After unification, Venetian liberals proudly noted the democratizing effects of "popular association," but they excluded women from most new associations and made little effort to reach the very poor. At the same time, they were unable to exercise complete control over the associations they created. No matter how hard they worked to promote procedural order and discourage political conflict, they could not prohibit members from speaking up at meetings or prevent them from leaving to form rival associations. In fact, the statutes and regulations Venetian liberals drafted (for all sorts of associations) encouraged ordinary members – including unenfranchised workers – to value the participatory acts of public assembly, discussion, and voting.

Within popular associations, in particular, liberal founders' promise of dramatic social and economic change proved hard to live up to, and even harder to reconcile with a fundamentally paternalistic approach to governance. Critics doubted whether elite-led workers' associations were consistent with the principle of self-help, and the leaders themselves struggled to make the ongoing patronage of wealthy, honorary members seem modern rather than conservative. In other respects, these associations became modern to a fault: joined together in increasingly large and complex networks – linking mutual aid societies and food stores to credit unions and housing projects – they began to seem more like impersonal institutions than associations, making it a challenge both to recruit new members in search of fraternal sociability and to uphold the leaders' personal, charismatic authority.

Such dilemmas were hardly unique to Italy. Even in Britain, where the myths of individual self-help and *laissez-faire* government were especially strong, voluntary associations were sites of masculine exclusion, bourgeois paternalism, and bureaucratic organization, operating in the shadow of an increasingly interventionist state.[7] In terms of the number, variety, and size of associations, by mid-century Italy lagged behind Britain but was keeping pace with most other countries in Europe. Recent historians have drawn attention to the dramatic proliferation of associations in France, Germany, Austria-Hungary, and Russia at the same moment as it occurred in Italy, in the 1860s and 1870s, and in similarly dramatic circumstances of political change, state-building, and constitutional reform. "In all these instances of state-making and remaking," Philip Nord has written, "at issue were major institutions of public life – representative bodies, schools, armies – and how they were best constituted."[8] Also at issue, one might add, was the capacity of voluntary associations to contribute to this project of "wide-ranging institutional redesign": not simply as an external voice of public opinion (representing civil society to the state), but as another proactive site of reform, another arena in which to promote civic rights and duties, secular education, patriotism, and economic progress. Viewed in light of this mid-century conjuncture – an energizing moment of political opportunity, ambition, and uncertainty throughout Europe – the Venetian approach to associational life seems anything but peculiar.

It took the "democratic transitions" of the 1970s and 1980s in southern Europe and the "velvet revolutions" of 1989 in Eastern Europe to draw scholars' attention to a more eventful and geographically diverse history of associations.[9] For years, the leading European historians of associational life focused on the British and French experience of the long "age of revolution" (1750–1850) and a process of steady associational growth that peaked in the 1830s and 1840s. By comparison, the period after 1848 was the subject of far less research, and the main theme was one of crisis rather than triumph: challenged "from above" by an interventionist state and "from below" by a fragmented consumer culture, associations in *fin-dè-siecle* Europe lost their sense of civic identity and purpose and began a slow decline.[10]

The same periodization and themes also characterized many of the first Italian histories of associational life. In part, this can be attributed simply to Italian scholars' accurate reading of the impact developments in other European countries had on Italy. The effects of the French Revolution, of course, were especially profound. By abolishing guilds and corporations, praising the virtues of civic action and political participation, and promoting constitutional government – not simply in France but throughout the Napoleonic Empire – the French gave the voluntary association new meaning and importance. In addition, the proliferation of associations with social reform aims in the 1830s and 1840s, notably in Britain and the United States, inspired talk in Italy of a new "spirit of association" and a concerted effort to study and compare the variety of associations forming throughout Europe.[11]

Most historians of modern Italy were already inclined to think in terms of gradual rather than dramatic change. After the Second World War, revisionists exploded the myth of Italian unification as a heroic watershed. And the shift towards social history in the 1960s further strengthened a long view of the nineteenth century. Each new topic of study – agricultural capitalism, the bourgeoisie, industrialization (including the fateful dualism between North and South), state formation, and so on – appeared to confirm that the roots of modern Italy lay deep in the pre-unification period. Thus, by the time scholars in Italy turned their attention to the history of associations, in the 1980s, a broad continuity thesis had been established.[12]

The first wave of research on Italian associations grew out of a larger re-examination of the Italian bourgeoisie. Scholars revised the traditional view of the nineteenth-century Italian bourgeoisie as numerically small, politically weak, and socially and culturally beholden to the landed aristocracy. Their work was explicitly international and comparative: new evidence of the lasting power of the landed aristocracy in England, and of the modernity of the German bourgeoisie, encouraged scholars in Italy to rethink the models and measures used to assess the Italian bourgeoisie, and thus also to challenge the assumption that Italy's "path to modernity" was inherently flawed.[13] Mounting this challenge entailed a creative search for new evidence, methods, and conceptual tools. Probate records allowed scholars to produce a far more detailed and nuanced profile of bourgeois (and aristocratic) wealth. Family histories of Italy's first industrial entrepreneurs revealed a mix of modern production strategies and conservative labour relations. And the history of associations offered fresh insight into the Italian bourgeoisie's social habits and ties, in particular its interaction with nobles in a small cluster of clubs and cultural societies. Although each of these lines of inquiry yielded distinct results, they tended to converge around a central theme: the gradual fusion of aristocrats and bourgeois into a new, ambivalently modern elite. But the study of associations, which did not gather full steam until the early 1990s, promised something more than a new angle on the Italian bourgeoisie: namely, the chance to move beyond the conventions of socio-economic analysis, to consider new ways of combining social, political, and cultural history.

Maurice Agulhon's studies of sociability in southern France provided an inspiring model. Agulhon conceived of sociability in broad ethnographic terms, as a mix of formal and informal activities, habits, needs, and relations. Thus, to capture the unusual vibrancy of *sociabilité* in the south of France, he studied the records of legally constituted associations but also any evidence he could find of traditional celebrations and games, family gatherings, conversational rituals, and political demonstrations.[14] This approach is well suited to the study of places and periods, such as continental Europe before 1789 and from 1815 to 1848, when government restrictions led people to gather in spaces that offered a measure of protective privacy or anonymity, including salons, Masonic lodges, cafes, theatres, and large public squares. It also has the advantage of taking into consideration groups that were generally excluded from formal associations, above all women and peasants but also religious and ethnic minorities. Agulhon was especially interested in the social transmission of associational practices, whereas recent historians have tended to emphasize the construction of social boundaries along the multiple lines of class, gender, race, religion, ethnicity, and nationality. But they all share a strong interest in Europe's complex shift, across the revolutionary divide of 1789, from a corporate society of "orders" to a more open and individualistic society of "classes."[15]

It is easy to understand why Agulhon's broad conception of social forms and relations was attractive to Italian historians of the pre-unification period, when informal sites of private and public encounter far outnumbered formal, legally constituted associations. Thus, it inspired Philippe Boutry to challenge the standard view of Rome's barren social scene during the Restoration by noting the existence of various confraternities, salons, circles and academies, institutions that had escaped the attention of oft-cited contemporaries like the poet Giacomo Leopardi (and many historians since) because they did not meet their expectations of "dense and binding structures of sociability."[16] Likewise, Maurizio Ridolfi has shown how republicans in Emilia-Romagna used ostensibly non-political forms of sociability to strengthen their movement in the face of government persecution.[17] And numerous scholars have demonstrated the pivotal role social clubs (*casini*) played in the formation of new ruling elites. In these clubs, the quintessentially sociable pursuits of conversation, games, and dancing gave nobles and bourgeois a unique opportunity to gather together in a regulated yet intimate setting. At a time of limited public freedom and civic action, the *casino* stood at the centre of associational life in most Italian cities.[18]

But what about the period after unification, when legally constituted associations proliferated for the first time; when the line separating formal and informal associations became more pronounced; above all, when the elusive combination of public enthusiasm (the "spirit of association") and public freedoms (of assembly, speech, and the press) was finally achieved? In the summer and fall of 1866, the founders of new associations in the Veneto frequently claimed to be making a break with the past: mutual aid societies and credit unions, they stated, would render obsolete the Catholic Church's vast network of charitable institutions, and new schools and libraries for workers would put an end to the narrow elitism of centuries-old academies. Constitutional freedoms suddenly cast a negative light on informal cafe gatherings and secretive political meetings, and the urgent tasks of economic and educational reform made the recreational focus of social clubs seem like an indulgence. Exclusive clubs continued to thrive after unification, but they no longer played a central role in associational life as a whole. New, more broadly based associations of merchants and artisans inevitably drew attention away from associations aimed exclusively at elites. Just as important, several of the key principles and goals informing associational life during the Restoration – secrecy, play, recreation, and entertainment – fell into disrepute, paving the way for a more sober, industrious, and disciplinary ideal, both in associations and more generally in public life. Privately, Venetian civic leaders may have continued to enjoy the balls held at the local *casino*, but in public they warned against the wasteful and damaging effects of festivities, whether at taverns, political rallies, associational banquets, or patriotic celebrations. In place of the fluid conviviality characteristic of early nineteenth-century clubs, liberals in united Italy promoted a more regulated and procedural model of assembly, complete with carefully prearranged agendas and designated speakers.[19]

Venetian liberals exaggerated the novelty of their efforts in 1866. They indulged the anti-Austrian sentiments of the moment, and tried to portray the act of founding a new association as yet another heroic contribution to Italy's rebirth. In this respect, they were no different than the other mythmakers of their era. For, as it turns out, social clubs were not the only associations to survive the transition from Austrian to Italian rule: reading rooms, agrarian associations, and a range of charitable and educational groups – many of them founded before 1848 – also stood alongside the new associations of the immediate post-unification period. In fact, Marco Meriggi has made a convincing case that the 1830s and 1840s marked a greater turning point in the history of Italian associations than did unification. It was during the former period, he argues, that the number and variety of associations increased; the method of admitting members began to shift from the cooptation of elites to voluntary subscription; and the creation of organizations aimed at aiding, if not enlisting, the popular classes marked the advent of more programmatic and less intimate types of association. The next major change, Meriggi and other historians argue, did not occur until the 1880s, well after unification, when the forces of political, economic, and cultural modernization initiated a new age of national, mass membership organizations (of workers, sportsmen, tourists, etc.).[20]

For all its strengths, this associational continuity thesis has obscured the true novelty of the post-unification period – not simply the successful creation of an unprecedented number and variety of associations, or the positive excitement felt by the leaders of this wave of activity, but also the dramatically fuller realization of two goals of special importance to Italian liberals: the creation of a public culture of association and the involvement in associational life of ordinary men and women. In most

Italian cities, it was only after unification that daily newspapers began to provide regular and detailed coverage of associational life; that associations themselves announced upcoming meetings in the press and on wall posters, and published the minutes of these meetings (along with itemized budgets) in annual reports; that delegates of multiple associations routinely stood alongside government officials at a variety of ceremonial events. No matter how removed ordinary citizens ("real Italy") felt from parliamentary elections and government ("legal Italy") – a common motif in histories of the post-unification period – it was hard to miss the ongoing display of procedural order and civic representation that countless local associations provided. Italy's ruling liberals tried to minimize the politicizing effects of these new ideals and practices, but to no avail. Opposition groups learned to make creative and critical use of their right to speak at meetings, form associations, and represent themselves at large public gatherings; over time, even the most heavily repressed "extremists" of the left and right – socialists as well as Catholics – adopted the liberal model of organizational publicity.[21]

Although the goal of reforming the popular classes was not new in the 1860s, the extensive use of large, socially inclusive voluntary associations to accomplish this goal was. Before unification, the target of most reform initiatives was not the popular classes but the poor, and the task of assisting and disciplining the poor rested primarily with a network of church- and government-run institutions: foundling homes, workhouses, asylums for women, and so on. A limited number of charitable associations formed to assist very specific groups – released convicts, for example, or the infants of working parents – without enlisting their beneficiaries as members. The mutual aid societies of professionals and artisans that formed before unification were different – their proponents called them institutions of welfare (*previdenza*), not charity (*beneficenza*) – but government suspicions of organized labour limited their spread. Unification brought immediate and dramatic change: the number of mutual aid societies in Italy tripled in little over a decade, joined now by a series of other, at least nominally "popular" associations: banks, libraries, schools, cooperatives, and so on. In reality, most of the new associations attracted a broad range of professionals, merchants, manufacturers, and landowners, and relatively modest numbers of workers or peasants; and their leaders were often local notables, just as the benefactors and administrators of charitable institutions had been before unification. But the appearance of institutional continuity and conservatism is deceiving. Unification created a new political and ideological framework for institutional reform, encouraging associational leaders and members to identify with the new state's secular, progressive, and constitutional ideals – its break with the church, its promise of economic improvement, its respect for publicity and procedural order – and challenging local elites to construct new relations with ordinary citizens and the poor, not to mention with the church and the state.[22]

Historians have been inclined to view the effort by liberal elites to form popular associations, before and after unification, as a half-hearted and short-lived prologue to the proliferation of truly independent, socialist trade unions.[23] There are good reasons, however, to put aside the long view of popular associations as failed instruments of bourgeois hegemony or modern labour organization, and examine more closely what was new and meaningful about them in the specific context of Italian unification. Italian liberals were not united in their enthusiasm for popular associations, but this is neither surprising nor sufficient to explain historians' relative neglect of the topic. Several types of popular association in Italy were initially concentrated in specific regions: thus, popular libraries first proliferated in Tuscany, a region with a strong tradition of popular schooling; and popular banks spread most rapidly through the north of Italy, following the Venetian Luigi Luzzatti's promotional trail. The leaders of these associations encountered resistance from political opponents but also from members of their own party. Official statistics appear to confirm this ambivalence, for the growth of popular associations during the first two decades after unification, when liberal dominance of associational life was greatest, pales in comparison to the figures for the late 1880s and 1890s, when Catholic and socialist organizers got involved. But there is a danger of letting the general pattern of fragmentation after 1880 confirm a more or less teleological story of liberal failure. Thus, the argument runs, if countless workers and peasants began to join Catholic and socialist cooperatives, mutual aid societies, and cultural organizations in the 1880s, the associations run by liberal elites must have been flawed – not genuinely inclusive, egalitarian, or democratic enough to last – and these flaws, in turn, must reflect the larger weaknesses of a conservative and insular ruling elite. At best, then, the liberal effort at creating popular associations becomes part of united Italy's long, dysfunctional history of unrealized reform initiatives (inside and outside of Parliament); at worst, it seems like a naked attempt at social control by an elite with little will or capacity for lasting hegemony. Indeed, given the narrow franchise before 1882, it is a wonder that Italy's ruling liberals bothered to appeal to the popular classes at all.

But they did bother (well before the 1880s), and this is reason enough to subject the standard narrative of liberal inactivity to new scrutiny. Venetian liberals may have been especially active, thanks in large part to the power and influence of men like Luigi Luzzatti, Emilio Morpurgo, and Fedele Lampertico. It is hard to say, because relatively few Italian scholars have studied the local politics of popular association. The leading historians of associational life routinely note the proliferation of mutual aid societies after unification but remain focused on elite clubs and sociability, or else they focus on the workers' associations founded by republicans and socialists rather than by liberals. Important studies of the parliamentary politics of welfare reform necessarily leave out the local dimension, and studies of local mutual aid societies and cooperatives generally do not put their findings in a larger context.[24] Government statistics offer a partial snapshot of associational activity at the provincial and regional levels, but cannot provide an accurate reading of the strength of associational ties or the nature of associational governance.

Did liberal enthusiasm for popular associations wane in the 1880s, in the face of Catholic and socialist competition? In the Veneto, local records indicate that liberals actually intensified their efforts in the 1880s, founding a greater variety of associations in dozens of new towns. In some respects, Venetian liberals' response to the new challenges of the late nineteenth century failed, but their efforts were successful enough to prolong (into the twentieth century) and extend (to small provincial towns) their dominance of local politics and government. After all, the definitive crisis of Italian liberalism did not occur until after the First World War.

To study local institutions and liberal ideology during the middle decades of the nineteenth century is to cut against the grain of much recent Italian scholarship, which has focused on the history of national identity during the Risorgimento. Take, for example, Alberto Banti's path-breaking study *La nazione del Risorgimento* (2000). In it, Banti analyzes a "canon" of patriotic texts (including works of literature and history as well as paintings and operas) and traces their impact on a sample of memoirists in order to identify the images and themes that defined Italy's emergent national discourse. The chronological focus of Banti's book (and many studies since) is the first half of the nineteenth century, the age of revolutionary Romanticism. It is during this period that a profoundly historical, emotional, and intimate "idea" of Italy, grounded in traditions of Christian sacrifice and family honour, took hold. The developments of the 1850s (the nationalist movement's turn towards Piedmont, the

political ascendancy of moderate liberals) hardly matter; Banti implies
that the liberal rulers of Piedmont after 1848 and united Italy after 1860
effectively inherited the Romantic idea of the nation, and struggled to
fulfil its promise. Banti's main protagonists are not the "great men" and
institutions of traditional political history, nor the impersonal structures
and classes of revisionist social history, but rather the relatively ordinary
men and women who risked their lives to create Italy. Their stories demonstrate that Risorgimento Italy's most talented writers and propagan-
dists succeeded in creating a "mass" movement of patriotic nationalists
before the political unification of the country occurred.[25]

In fact, the new history of Risorgimento nationalism sheds considerable light on the story I propose to tell in this book. First, the powerful
emotional register of Risorgimento culture helps explain why many Venetian liberals tried so hard to dramatize the process of forming associations immediately after unification. Addressing audiences raised on a
steady diet of patriotic tales that were, as Banti and Paul Ginsborg put it,
"capable of making the heart beat, capable of making the blood boil in
the veins,"[26] the moderate liberal founders of new associations routinely
indulged in a rousing rhetoric of heroic "civil" action in the face of government oppression, of epic social battles to end poverty and illiteracy,
and of daring, even transgressive experiments in popular assembly. Second, the successful establishment of Italian national identity by the 1860s
helps explain why Venetian liberals spoke and wrote with such confidence, immediately after unification, about the need to focus on social
and economic problems. Massimo d'Azeglio, it turns out, never uttered
the famous words "Now that Italy is made, we must make Italians";
rather, he said that, in order to reform Italy, "it is necessary for Italians to
reform themselves."[27] Venetian liberals were convinced that associations
were a crucial part of that self-help process, an institutional means of
teaching ordinary Italians to be responsible, productive, law-abiding citizens. In other words, associations were a way to "make" not flag-waving
Italians but liberal subjects.

The primary setting for this reforming impulse was local and urban,
a fact reflected in the historiography of associational life in nineteenth-
century Europe. There are a host of studies of single cities, including
R.J. Morris's book on Leeds, England, Rudy Koshar's book on Marburg,
Germany, and Marco Meriggi's book on Milan; and a smaller group of
provincial and regional studies, including Carol Harrison's examination
of three cities in eastern France and Ludwig Stefan Hoffmann's study
of masonic lodges in Prussia and Saxony, as well as Maurice Agulhon's

remarkable books on the department of the Var in Provence. In nine-teenth-century Italy, the vast majority of associations were local or pro-vincial. After unification, the average Italian city might have one or two district branches of national organizations such as the Italian Medical Association or the Italian Alpine Club, but it would almost certainly have several dozen local associations: social clubs, reading groups, agricultural associations, mutual aid societies, political clubs, cooperatives, veterans' organizations, choral groups, gardening associations, sharpshooting so-cieties, and many more. Only a close, detailed examination of specific communities can capture the breadth of associational life and the density of associational networks.

A focus is not the same thing as a boundary, however. The liberals who dominated associational life in the Veneto belonged to a regional ruling elite that was forged by a variety of extra-local experiences: attendance of the region's one and only university in Padua, participation in the rev-olutions of 1848–49, voluntary or involuntary exile (especially to Pied-mont), and fighting in one or more of Italy's wars of independence. Many of these men travelled outside of the Veneto, and welcomed visitors from other Italian regions and European nations to their homes. More than just a story of privileged sociability, these encounters profoundly shaped the history of associational life in Italy, leading to the introduction of new associational forms and practices – English clubs, French library associations, and German credit unions – and forming the basis for pa-triotic demonstrations of civil progress at international exhibitions and congresses. At the local level, too, associations interacted with a range of institutions with complex and cosmopolitan ties of their own: museums and libraries, businesses and banks, church organizations and govern-ment agencies. In short, the local study is especially well suited to capture the multiple and shifting boundaries of associational life as it related both to civil society and the state, the nation and Europe, within but also well beyond the geographical limits of the locality itself.[28]

The focus of this study is a pair of provincial cities, Padua and Vi-cenza. Historians have aptly described the Veneto as polycentric, for by the nineteenth century the city of Venice had already ceased to function as a strong regional capital, unlike Milan (in Lombardy), Florence (in Tuscany), or Naples (in Campania), to name just a few examples.[29] The provincial capitals dotting the Venetian hinterland – Padua, Vicenza, Ve-rona, Treviso, Rovigo, Udine, and Belluno (see Map 1) – possessed their own, relatively distinct identities. For example, Padua, which came clos-est to replacing Venice as a regional centre in the nineteenth century, was an important commercial and intellectual centre, had the largest Jewish population outside of Venice, and served as a base for several of the region's most active and influential politicians, including Luigi Luzzatti and Emilio Morpurgo; whereas Vicenza was a smaller, more traditional and devoutly Catholic city, in a province with a conservative landowning elite but also two of Italy's largest factory towns (Schio and Valdagno). Venetians across the region had a number of things in common, including the experience of Austrian rule, late annexation to the Italian Kingdom, close proximity to the "unredeemed" lands of Trent and Trieste, and an unusually active Catholic laity. And to this list we should add the network of associations and institutions that liberal political and civic leaders throughout the region created soon after unification.

Venetian scholars came to the topic of associational life relatively late. In Vicenza in 1988, a conference organized around the political and intellectual career of Fedele Lampertico, the city's leading liberal politician, featured a handful of papers on the subject of "associationism and mutualism in the Veneto."[30] The same year, one of the region's leading historians, Emilio Franzina, published a collection of writings by the renowned Vicentine poet and priest Giacomo Zanella, which included a series of speeches Zanella delivered to the members of Vicenza's large mutual aid society of artisans. For the volume, Franzina wrote a hundred-page essay that, in addition to providing an invaluable introduction to Zanella's life and writings, offers an insightful account of Venetian associational life during the final years of Austrian rule.[31] Until very recently, the only scholar to attempt a comprehensive analysis of Venetian associations has been Renato Camurri, in a series of essays that focus on mutual aid societies but address much wider themes. No Venetian study comparable to the work of Meriggi (on Milan), Ridolfi (on Emilia-Romagna), Soldani (on Tuscany), or Caglioti (on Naples) exists.[32]

It is interesting to consider Venetian liberals' rhetoric of backwardness and modernization in light of the recent scholarship on Italian regionalism. If anything, the Veneto would appear to be one of Italy's historically charmed regions. It scores well in Robert Putnam's influential study of civic engagement, *Making Democracy Work*, and for the past twenty years it has been one of Italy's economic success stories – part of the so-called "Third Italy," an area known for strong traditions of handicraft production and family enterprise, stretching from Tuscany in central Italy to Friuli in the northeast.[33] The Veneto was significantly poorer in the nineteenth century. Even so, we expect nineteenth-century Venetians to

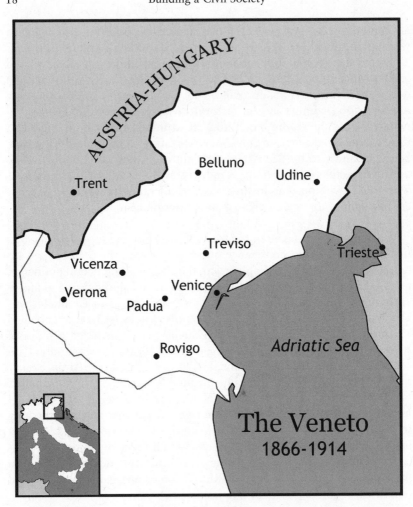

Map 1

define themselves as advanced – civilized, bourgeois, progressive – in contrast to southern Italians. As an impressive group of studies have shown,
northern Italians' stunning ignorance of the south during the Risorgimento quickly turned into disdain and bitter resentment after unification.[34] My study offers a different angle on this question. In the speeches
of leading Venetian liberals, there are scattered references to southern

backwardness, but just as many to southern progress; above all, there are countless, largely unfavourable comparisons between the Veneto and northern Europe. Unflattering character assessments of the Venetian people were not necessary because it was far more expedient to blame their defects on the old regime of Austrian oppressors, and to disregard the past in order to emphasize the benefits of the new associations forming everywhere in Europe. The main point was critical but hopeful: Venetians were behind but that did not mean they were fated to stay behind. Towards that end, the first and often humbling order of business for associational leaders – whether liberal, republican, Catholic, or socialist – was to determine the actual conditions in which Venetians lived, worked, and assembled. In this respect, there was a "Venetian question" in the Veneto – and, I suspect, a "Lombard question" in Lombardy, a "Tuscan question" in Tuscany, and so on – a good decade or two before there was a "southern question."

Venetian historians have written extensively on the themes of backwardness and modernization. In a famous essay from the 1960s, entitled "Venetian Civil Society from 1866 to the Advent of the Left," the Catholic historian Gabriele De Rosa presented the Veneto as a "static" society, closer to the regions of southern Italy than to those of northern Italy in terms of social and economic development; "in sum, a small peasant society, without modern economic impulses, poor, sleepy." Venetian society only began to break out of this depressed mould in the late nineteenth century, De Rosa argued, largely thanks to the energy, strength, and determination of the region's Catholic movement.[35] Against this view, during the 1970s and 1980s a second group of historians – sometimes referred to as the "Veneto school" – emphasized the co-existence in the region of a dynamic capitalist economy and a conservative ruling elite (with strong ties to the Catholic movement).[36] Both groups of scholars, however, agreed that during the nineteenth century a vibrant civil society or public sphere failed to emerge, let alone function as a key site of modernization.[37] But as Venetian scholars have delved deeper into the history of leading Venetian liberals – making greater use of the Fedele Lampertico archive in Vicenza and the Luigi Luzzatti archive in Venice – the importance of associational life has come into sharper focus, inspiring new questions about the pattern of modern historical development in the Veneto.

It is no accident that the names Lampertico, Luzzatti, and a handful of others (Errera, Morpurgo, Lioy, and Tolomei) recur throughout this book. They were friends and allies, and they all shared a passionate

interest, faith, and involvement in associational life. They were true protagonists, determined to put their stamp on public and political life. And
therefore we should not regard them as typical or presume that they were
representative of a much larger politics or culture of association in the
Veneto, let alone all of Italy. Nevertheless, their *protagonismo* in letters
and in print makes it possible to look beyond them and see much larger
local networks of associational leaders, administrators, and members.
Tensions and conflicts emerge from the records of the largest associations, such as the mutual aid society led by Lampertico in Vicenza or
Luzzatti's popular banks, which drew the attention of political rivals and
frustrated job-seekers. The records of countless weak or failed initiatives
reveal the practical challenges confronting organizers and the hesitations
of humble joiners. In short, the many associations at the centre of this
study brought a relatively small and homogeneous group of protagonists
in contact with a diverse group of citizens, who were actors in their own
right. Throughout these personal and institutional networks, at various
centres and peripheries, the drama of unification and the promise of a
great transformation unfolded.

1

In Search of Associational Life

In September 1842, Padua hosted the fourth annual Congress of Italian Scientists. Italy was still a peninsula occupied by eight different states, and Italians still suffered the isolating effects of internal trade barriers, poor transportation, and restricted civil liberties. Narrowly technical in appearance, the congresses of Italian scientists were in fact a highly anticipated experiment in national assembly and discussion. The first three congresses had met in Pisa, Turin, and Florence; thus, the fourth congress in Padua was the first to be held in the Veneto, the first, for that matter, to take place anywhere in the Austrian Lombard-Veneto kingdom (see Map 2). This fact only added to the local excitement surrounding the event. For two weeks the provincial city of Padua was the very centre of intellectual life in Italy. Hundreds of visitors from all parts of Italy came to the city: professors, academicians, journalists, and statesmen. Many more followed the events from afar. As was to be expected, geography favoured the participation of Venetian scholars, who made up close to half of the 514 congressional members. And ceremony dictated that Padua's social and cultural elite serve as the event's organizers. Thus, the president of the congress was Andrea Cittadella Vigodarzere, one of the wealthiest landowners in the province, and the secretary general was Roberto de Visiani, an acclaimed botanist and professor at the University of Padua. In the annals of local history, it was one of the most celebrated events of the entire Risorgimento period.[1]

For the occasion, Cittadella Vigodarzere, de Visiani, and several other local notables prepared a guide to the city of Padua. The guide was aimed at the city's distinguished "foreign" visitors, Italian and European scholars who had travelled to the congress from as far away as Scotland and as close by as the Duchy of Parma. These were not typical tourists. Pietro

Italy in 1842
showing host cities of the
Congresses of Italian Scientists
(1839-1847)

Map 2

Selvatico, author of the chapter devoted to Padua's artistic attractions, made sure to highlight only the city's very best sights. "To men of great talent more than to others," he explained, "time is a very precious treasure, to take it from them is a crime."[2] The guide also had to match the wide range of the congress participants' interests and expertise. In this respect, it departed from most early-nineteenth-century Italian city guides, which were primarily art-historical in nature. Typical of the older genre was Giannantonio Moschini's *Guide to the city of Padua for the friend of the arts*, published in 1817. Dividing Padua's artistic "sites" into two categories, the sacred and the profane, Moschini made little effort to supplement his aesthetic commentary with information on the city's civic or social life. Even the university, Padua's intellectual centre, appears in Moschini's guide as little more than a collection of scientific and architectural curiosities, one of many profane stops on the tourist's itinerary.[3]

The guide prepared in 1842 was different. In addition to the requisite historical and art-historical chapters, and a chapter on the rural towns surrounding the city, there were three topical chapters: one on "public education," one on "charitable institutions, convents, theaters and prisons," and one on "geology, hydrography, agriculture, commerce and industry." In part, these new subjects simply addressed the congress participants' intellectual and administrative interests; however, they also reflected a more specific, local desire: to provide a comprehensive portrait of the city. For the first time in Padua, the authors of a guide described not only where the occasional visitor might go in search of beauty, entertainment, or relaxation, but also where the typical resident *routinely* goes – or, in the case of the less fortunate, turns – to study, converse, work, pray, borrow money, or recover from an illness. The result is a partial, preliminary sketch of the city as a complex social organism.

Conspicuously absent from this urban portrait is a discussion of associational life. There is no separate section of the 1842 guide dedicated to associations, no place for them even in the chapter that leaps, topically, from convents to theatres to prisons. However, it is not only the *category* but the very *language* of associational life that is missing here. "Association," "society," "club," "circle" – practically the entire nineteenth-century lexicon referring to associational life is nowhere to be found in the text. There were only a few exceptions. In his chapter on the city's profane sites of artistic interest, Selvatico noted that the second floor of the renovated Caffè Pedrocchi housed an informal social club (*casino*), complete with a dance hall and a series of thematically decorated rooms for smaller gatherings. At the end of the long chapter on public education, another contributor mentioned the *Gabinetto di lettura*, or Reading Room, an association that gave its 187 members access to a variety of Italian and European newspapers, periodicals, and books.[4]

Instead of associations, the *Guida di Padova* presents an impressive array of institutions: the university and the seminary, public and private schools, a pawnshop (*monte di pietà*) and savings bank (*cassa di risparmio*), hospitals, convents, and prisons. All of them had fixed, salaried personnel rather than open memberships, and appointed as opposed to elected administrations. As a group, they reflected not the civic process of private individuals coming together to form a public body, but rather the recruitment and segregation of specific groups: school-age children, the clergy, criminals, the ill. They also testified to the prominence of the Catholic Church, second only to the Austrian government as a locus of institutional authority, especially in the areas of education and charity. In the city featured here, institutions do not simply overshadow associations, they overshadow public life as a whole. Theatres and piazzas are listed, but with a bare minimum of commentary; cafes are barely mentioned, taverns not at all.

This portrait of civic and public emptiness is surprising for two reasons. First, the 1840s seemed to mark a turning point in the history of Italian associational life. It was precisely during the early 1840s that specific reports about the formation of new associations, and general excitement about the spread of a new "spirit of association," filled Italian newspapers and periodicals. Not only was the number of associations in any given city increasing, but new kinds of associations were forming: agrarian associations, mutual aid societies, groups for the promotion of infant nursery schools or for the relief and reform of prisoners. To this group of organizations Italians would add yet another type, the political club, during the revolutions of 1848.[5] Second, even in the smallest of Italian towns, public life outside of associations and state- and church-run institutions was much more vibrant and diverse than the *Guida di Padova* makes it appear. Operas, plays, concerts, fairs, saint's day celebrations, and *Carnevale* were all staples of urban life in Italy long before anyone thought to organize a congress of Italian scientists or prepare a new kind of city guide. Why were these two dimensions of public life, the older one of popular recreation and the newer one of civic association, missing from the *Guida di Padova* of 1842?

It is tempting but ultimately misleading to argue that the *Guida di Padova*'s neglect of associations was due to bad timing. It is true that shortly after the Fourth Congress of Italian Scientists began, in September 1842, the members of the agronomy and technology section heard Pietro Selvatico, co-author of the *Guida di Padova*, promote the creation of "societies for the encouragement of agriculture" in every Italian province; and that, a week later, a special commission announced plans to form one in Padua. Over the next few years, more new associations took shape in Padua, including a Society for the Promotion of Gardening (1846); a mutual aid society for doctors, surgeons, and pharmacists (1846); and a horse-racing club (1847). In the same period, two local newspapers, the *Giornale Euganeo* (1844–47) and the *Caffè Pedrocchi* (1845–48), enthusiastically charted the activities of associations outside of Padua and the Veneto, heralding the presence of a new, transcendent spirit of association in Italy. And when the revolution of 1848 began, the citizens of Padua formed the city's first political clubs since the Napoleonic era.

All of these positive developments, however, were contingent on the policies of the Austrian government, and thus subject to sudden interruptions and reversals. Tight restrictions on freedom of the press and association were the norm everywhere in Italy before 1848, and everywhere except the Kingdom of Piedmont-Sardinia before 1859. Contrary to a remarkably persistent "black legend" about the severity of Austrian rule, conditions were not particularly bad in Venice, at least prior to 1848; nor were the Austrian government's limits on the press and association continuous.[6] For discrete periods of time – 1815–21, 1835–48, 1855–59, and 1864–66 – the Austrian government tolerated a significant amount of journalistic and associational activity in its Italian territories. Nevertheless, each of these phases of Austrian liberalization ended suddenly and violently in revolt (1821, in Lombardy), revolution (1848), and war (1859 and 1866). The second phase, 1835–48, was longer than the others but no less finite. Thus, when the Austrians defeated the revolution of 1848 in Padua and returned to power, both the publication of *Il Caffè Pedrocchi* and all talk of forming new associations stopped dead. Can we say, then, that the 1842 *Guida di Padova*'s civic profile was deceivingly slim? If it had been published in 1847 rather than 1842, it might have contained a separate section or chapter on the city's associations, but not if it had been published in 1849.[7] In fact, it would never have occurred to the dejected citizens of Padua to produce a guide to their city in 1849. In short, as far as the history of associations in Risorgimento Italy is concerned, it is difficult to speak of turning points or take-offs, and more appropriate to speak of a series of false starts. Progress was not simply halting but pendular: proponents of associations started and stopped, organized and waited.

The evidence historians typically use to document the *growth* of associational life in Risorgimento Italy is marked with voids, interruptions, and delays. Associational statutes from the 1830s, newspapers from the 1840s, diaries and academy reports from the 1850s, and letters from the 1860s reveal positive changes in Venetian associations, but they also reveal a surprising degree of negative continuity: decades pass and still – in

1850, 1856, 1863 – Venetian liberals talk about how difficult it is to find the spirit of association, and look forward to the day when an age of association will begin in earnest. In most of Italy, and especially in provincial cities like Padua, right up until unification associations remained few in number and slow to develop a public personality of their own.

The 1842 *Guida di Padova*'s neglect of popular recreation demands a different, more specifically ideological, explanation. The authors of the guide knew perfectly well how numerous and important theatres, cafes, taverns, fairs, and festivals were; they simply chose to ignore this fact. Their aim was to prepare a serious liberal guidebook for serious liberal visitors, which is to say, for men who were at once loath to waste time themselves and committed to reforming society in their own productive image. These were not puritans. During their stay in Padua, congressional visitors were treated to dinners, parties, and horse races. Back home, most of them probably belonged to an elite social club dedicated to the enjoyment of music, games, dances, and conversation. Nevertheless, by the 1840s these same men were beginning to develop a critical view of "idle" recreation and entertainment. Gala parties and popular spectacles began to seem like a luxury Italy could ill afford; "useful" institutions and reforms became a priority.

In Italy, as elsewhere in Europe, this critique of idleness was at least as old as the eighteenth-century Enlightenment, but several developments during the 1830s and 1840s conspired to give it new importance for Italian liberals. First, years of European-wide debate about poverty and poor relief led many Italian reformers to critically examine the work and leisure habits of the lower classes, and to question the larger culture of recreation. Second, Italian liberals' increasing faith in associations, in particular those new types of association that promised to reform and modernize society, inevitably cast a negative light on older and "merely" recreational institutions. Third, the defeat of the revolutions of 1848–49 convinced many Venetian liberals that a new seriousness was called for in order to end Austrian rule, and that one step in this direction would be for all Venetians to refrain from attending theatres and festivities, thus demonstrating to the world that life under the Habsburgs was unquestionably joyless.

Unlike new associations, which came and went during the Risorgimento, such new *ideals* of associational and public life were not easily delayed, interrupted, or repressed. Gradually, over the course of the 1840s and 1850s, leading Venetian liberals turned away from the primarily recreational practices of elite social clubs, bourgeois cafes, and popular

theatres, and embraced a new model of association: more inclusive, socially and geographically, in its membership and activities; more practical and reformist in its aims; more administrative and hierarchical in its
basic operations. It was a change without clear turning points, but a great
change nonetheless. In 1830, associational life in the Veneto was practically synonomous with the intimate pleasures of sociable encounter: over
a billiard table, in a reading room, at an opera. By the early 1860s, the
leading proponents of associational life in Venice had little or nothing to
say on the subject of sociability and its everyday pleasures. Anticipating
the transition from opposition movement to ruling elite, Venetian liberals got serious.

1830s: Rules of Recreation

Slightly smaller and more provincial than Padua, the city of Vicenza led a
more typically quiet existence during the Restoration. It did not play host
to a congress of Italian scientists. It did not inspire anyone to prepare a
civic guide comparable to the *Guida di Padova* until after unification.
No newspapers of note were published there until the late 1850s, and it
was at about the same time that the first significant changes in local associational life occurred. The excitement produced by these changes led
more than one local writer to reflect back on the years before 1848 as a
period of uneventful "silence" in the city.[8]

A document from 1834 offers a glimpse into this sleepy, unmemorable
period in Vicenza's history. It is the published list of rules and regulations
pertaining to the Duomo Club (Società del Casino al Duomo), an elite
social club and one of the few formal associations in the city at the time.
The opening lines of this *Regolamento* draw attention to the minimal
outlines of social life in Vicenza:

> The goal of the Society is to have a statutory Conversation with games every
> evening from 26 December to 31 March, and, during the rest of the year,
> every evening in which the Eretenio Theater is not open with an opera or
> play; and also, when the time is right, to have dance parties, musical acad-
> emies, and other entertainments.[9]

Vicenza apparently had two social seasons, the one provided by the
Eretenio Theatre and the long, dull void of a winter that followed it.
On paper at least, Vicenza had two other associations – a reading room
(founded in 1830, the same year as the one in Padua) and the Olympic

Academy of arts and sciences – but the fact that the Duomo Club made newspapers as well as nightly conversation available to its members suggests that both institutions were essentially dormant in the 1830s.

Peculiar as its rules and regulations may seem, the Duomo Club in Vicenza was actually characteristic of associational life in Italy prior to unification. In many cities, social clubs were the largest and most successful associations; for long periods of time, as in Vicenza during the 1830s, they were among the few associations to exist at all. The activities which the Duomo Club sponsored – conversation, games, reading, concerts, and dances – were the main focus of associational life throughout Italy, especially prior to the 1840s. Supplementing local theatres and cafes, social clubs offered traditional forms of recreation in a structured setting, using formal rules and regulations both to satisfy the requirements of government authorities and to negotiate old and new social relationships. But creating clubs and other associations was no easy matter, and not simply because of Austrian restrictions. While Italian proponents of associations struggled with the local population's poor spirit of association, the Austrian government developed its own appreciation for the existence of a regulated and identifiable associational public in Italy.

When the Duomo Club was first created in 1808, the city of Vicenza already had one social club, the Nobles' Club (Casino dei Nobili), which dated back to the seventeenth century, according to one local writer, and folded in the 1820s.[10] It is tempting to treat the fall of the Nobles' Club, and the rise of the nominally more inclusive Casino al Duomo, as evidence of the fusion of Vicenza's aristocracy and bourgeoisie. Working with better evidence than the city's two social clubs provide, historians have made a more compelling case for intermarriage and the expansion of the landowning class following the Napoleonic seizure and sale of church property, as the keys to the creation of a new elite in Vicenza. The social composition of Italian clubs varied. At one extreme, the Società del Casino in Bologna welcomed teachers, civil servants, and shopkeepers during the final years of Napoleon's rule, and went on to test the limits of papal restriction during the 1830s and 1840s. At the other extreme, Turin's Società del Whist remained a predominantly noble club from its inception in 1841 right down to the start of the First World War. On the whole, though, the trend was clear: following the era of the French Revolution and Napoleon, when privilege ceased to be a birthright, it became not just possible but necessary for urban elites to redefine social boundaries and identities in Italy, and social clubs were one means of doing so.[11]

Some clubs made a precise definition of social boundaries an explicit goal, but most let high membership dues and restrictive rules for admission limit the range of social mixing. Vicenza's Duomo Club put the admission of new members to a secret-ballot vote by the group's leaders, whereas admission to the club that met above the Caffè Pedrocchi in Padua centred on an extended, collective ritual of review, in which the name of the prospective member (and his promoters) was "exposed" to all existing members, who could privately communicate their opinions to the club's leadership.[12]

Club memberships reveal distinctions and ties between groups other than the aristocracy and bourgeoisie. Social clubs had unusually *large* memberships; for example, the Pedrocchi Club in Padua, with its 476 members in 1858, was nearly three times larger than any other association in the city. Can one see the intersection of local aristocracy and bourgeoisie in the club's official membership list for 1858? Absolutely: 108 of the members were listed with the professional titles of *Dottore* or *Professore* alongside their names; 93 had noble titles (*Nobile, Conte, Barone*, etc.); and another 18 had Austrian-conferred titles of one kind or another (*Cavaliere*, above all, but also Imperial Royal Engineer, Imperial Royal Delegate, etc.). But that meant that over half of the club's 476 members did not report a title of any kind, and only one in five claimed to be of noble status. Perhaps the most impressive sociological fact about the membership was the percentage of University of Padua faculty who belonged: 25 per cent (17 of 69) of the total faculty and 56 per cent (13 of 23) of the law and mathematics departments.[13]

The most distinctive feature of the *casino* as an associational form was its inclusion of women. Of course, inclusion is a relative term. On the one hand, clubs were more inclusive than reading rooms and academies, the two other most common associations in Risorgimento Italy, which typically did not allow women at all.[14] On the other hand, compared to the models of sociability provided by old regime courts and salons, the nineteenth-century social club was an exclusive male preserve. It is odd, for example, to find a reference to "Lady Members" in the 1858 statute of the Duomo Club in Vicenza, for social clubs generally did not admit women as members but rather as guests, in particular when a club held a dance or party. This was almost certainly also true of the Duomo Club, as only two of the seventy-eight articles in its 1858 statute refer to women, the first time in Article 30, from the section "On Entertainments [*Dei Trattenimenti*]," and not again until Article 45, from the section "On the Society's Meetings," which states, "Lady Members are excused from the leadership and Administration of the Society." The first of these two articles was much more detailed, revealing that the true reference point for the inclusion of women was not the honest and well-mannered individual who happened to be female, but the family and, more specifically, the home:

> [Art.] 30. Admitted to entertainments are, in addition to the mothers and the wives of Members, their sisters and children of either sex no less than 14 years of age, [if] unmarried and living with their families.
>
> This accomodation is not available to male sons who are 21 years old. The male sons of Members who are above this age, single, and living with their father[s], may become special Members by paying half the annual fee of 48 Aust. [Austrian] L. [lire].

Whereas the adult sons of members had to join the club if they wanted to go on attending its parties and concerts, the adult daughters of members were welcome for as long as they remained single and dependent. Manhood provided a direct link to membership, womanhood only indirectly, through fathers or husbands.[15]

One exception to this rule, which appears in the 1834 statute of the Duomo Club, reminds us of a more awkward function of social clubs during the Restoration: the entertainment of Austrian authorities stationed in Italian cities. According to the 1834 statute, for all performances (*spettacoli*) the leadership of the Casino al Duomo was required to invite the city's leading civil and military authorities and their families. The top military commander of the city could also expect to distribute anywhere from six to ten of his own invitations. Immediately following these requirements was an additional provision regarding invitations: so as to render special events more decorous, the leadership could also invite some ladies who resided in Vicenza, and with them one or more of their relatives, by whom they may be accompanied. It may be significant that this set of rules pertaining to special invitations did not appear in the reformed statute of 1858.[16]

The production of elaborate rules of recreation is not itself proof of government oppression. After all, dating back to the early eighteenth century, one of the main reasons why the much admired citizens of England began to form associations was, precisely, to bring order to an increasingly popular and commercialized set of leisure activities. Musical and theatrical societies had order and decorum in mind when they raised money to build or rent suitable performance spaces, and horse-racing

clubs did their best to regulate both the races and the betting that accompanied them.[17] The Società del Casino in Bologna not only determined the precise number of concerts, poetry readings, and balls it would
sponsor each year, it regulated in great detail the forms of dress it would
allow: when dancing, wearing gloves was required while wearing a hat or
boots was prohibited; at balls, guests were forbidden to wear overly long
or short overcoats, to dress up like warriors or Turks, to sport coloured
or black neckerchiefs, or to tuck their pants into their shoes.[18]

Long after the Austrians departed northern Italy, social clubs continued
to discipline members' behaviour at the billiard table or during masked
balls.[19] And yet the imprint of Austrian power on these social clubs is
unmistakeable. Article 1 of the 1834 statute of the Casino al Duomo indicates that social activities in Vicenza were lacking, but it also specified
that club-sponsored dances would only be allowed on certain days, and
only in between certain hours of those days ("fixed by the Government
Notification of 3 July 1827 N. 20721-1754"); that conversations had
to be "statutory," which is to say, consistent with the Austrian government's general restrictions of free speech; that only "the most accredited
newspapers" would be permitted in the conversation rooms, and never
outside of the building.[20]

The greatest expression of Austrian control over Venetian associations
appears not in a statute's detailed contents but, before that, on its cover
page, in the subtitle: *Regolamento della Società del Casino al Duomo in
Vicenza: Approved by the Eccelso I.[Imperial] R. [Royal] Government
with the Decrees [of] 2 May 1834 N. 14999–1559, and [of] 18 September the same year N. 34031.*[21] Everywhere in Italy from 1814 to 1848,
and everywhere except Piedmont right up until unification, proponents
of new associations had to request government permission. Official approval could be delayed for years, when it was not denied outright. In
Genoa, Piedmontese officials denied elite citizens' requests to form an
academy of sciences (on two occasions, in 1820 and again in 1837) and
a reading room. In Catania, Bourbon officials advised a group promoting a "Civil Society or Civil Meeting" to adopt the more acceptable name
of "Civil Conversation Room." In Turin, the government intervened to
settle a dispute within the Subalpine Agrarian Association in favour of
the group's more moderate faction, led by Cavour.[22] It did not take Venetian elites long to understand that a prospective association's chances of
approval depended on certain limiting factors: the adoption of a bland,
apolitical goal or program for the association; the restriction of the membership to a small, socially elect group; and, perhaps most important of

all, the inclusion on the list of founding members of at least one person looked upon with favour at the royal court in Vienna. A case in point is Padua's Reading Room, which was approved without much delay in 1830. The founder and first president of the new association was Francesco Maria Franceschinis, a university professor with close, long-standing ties to the Austrian government.[23]

The Austrian government also looked with relative favour upon the clergy. Although the Habsburg rulers did not try to undo the extensive damage caused to the Catholic Church by Napoleon (the seizure of property, the suppression of religious orders, etc.), they restored the clergy's considerable powers of local administration. Throughout the Lombard-Veneto Kingdom, the parish served as the primary unit for the registry of births, deaths, and marriages; for military recruitment and tax collection; for the provision of health and veterinary services; for the administration of pensions and poor relief; and last but not least, for schooling.[24] Priests and lay activists received permission to create new charitable institutions, schools, confraternities, and assorted other associations. In the otherwise sleepy city of Vicenza, the future bishop Giovanni Antonio Farina (1803–88) followed his seminary training with a burst of public activity: in 1828 he joined the short-lived Academy of Sacred Eloquence, in 1836 he established a local order of the Teaching Sisters of Saint Dorothy, in 1841 he helped found a mutual aid society for poor priests, and in 1844 he joined the city's historic and newly revived Olympic Academy of arts and science.[25] Another young seminarian, Giuseppe Fogazzaro (1813–1901), founded the city's first infant nurseries in 1839. The clergy's involvement in the revolutions of 1848 caused a serious breach in the Austrian government's trust, but as long as Catholic activists stayed within the traditional domains of charity and education, they continued to enjoy considerable latitude.[26]

Most other associational initiatives ran into some kind of trouble. Permission to form the Society for the Encouragement of Agriculture, which aimed "to promote and stimulate agricultural progress in the Province of Padua," was denied several times over a four-year period before it was finally granted in 1846. For its time this association was new and ambitious. Its physical boundaries were not the meeting rooms of a specific building but the province of Padua, and its social boundaries – or, rather, lack of them – were even more troubling: to improve agriculture, even if only by "holding competitions, awarding medals, and giving away prizes and money," threatened to bring the elite members of the association into frequent contact with a variety of non-elite groups, including more or less immiserated peasants. There was nothing bland about the prospect of an anti-Austrian Fronde. Needless to say, whenever the threat of political action became a reality, as in the Milanese insurrection of 1821 and the revolutions of 1848, the Austrian government suspended its Italian subjects' already limited rights of association.[27]

It would be a mistake, however, to attribute the weakness of associational life in the Veneto entirely to a repressive Austrian regime. Venetian elites themselves were aware of a different, if related, problem: the poor spirit of association in the region. Even with the Austrian government's blessing, new associations often failed to attract enough interested people to get off the ground. The more provincial a city was, the more likely it was to suffer from these problems. In *Terra e Denaro*, Alberto Banti recounted the story of Pietro Giordani's efforts to get a reading room started in Piacenza. In 1819, after a stay of several years in Milan, Giordani experienced a traumatic return to his native city. "In this town of mine," Giordani complained, "one cannot do anything." To help rectify the problem, the following year Giordani promoted the creation of a reading room. In Piacenza, he explained to the new group's founding members, "there are no opportunities for studious conversation; and generally speaking there is a lack of urban sociability."[28] The social and intellectual habits that seemed to take root naturally in a large city like Milan had to be tirelessly promoted in provincial cities like Piacenza, Padua, or Vicenza. Nevertheless, even in large cities critics sometimes found the spirit of association wanting. Thus, several months before the sixth Congress of Italian Scientists was to take place in Milan, Carlo Cattaneo presented the readers of the liberal newspaper *Il Politecnico* with some painful questions regarding the city's civic profile:

> why does a city that has four hundred doctors and surgeons not have a medical association, a surgeon's association, a depository of pathology preparations, of instruments, of books at least; ... why does an area which lives from agriculture above all else, and which trembles constantly over the unstable worth of the mulberry tree, not have in its splendid capital a botanical garden, nor an agrarian association ...?

The congress, Cattaneo added, presented an occasion to "shake up the old Castilian lethargy."[29]

As often as not, when elites successfully overcame the forces of lethargy and formed an association, the results were short lived. Frequently the problem was financial. The Duomo Club in Vicenza required a five-year commitment of all new members in 1834, and a ten-year commitment beginning in 1858.[30] Rules pertaining to dues varied from one association to the next, but the effort needed to collect dues was a constant: the "member in arrears" (*socio moroso*) is a figure to whom entire boxes of associational records are dedicated. Indeed, the leaders of associations often had to make a conscious effort not to throw out non-paying members. Likewise, the period that followed the annexation of the Veneto to the Italian Kingdom in 1866 was marked not only by the formation of many new associations but also by the reform or consolidation of several older, financially unsound institutions.[31] As a result, from one period to the next there was not much continuity in associational life. In most cities, for every social club or reading room that survived there was a long roster of associations that barely left a trace on the historical record, from the Euganean Society for the Utilization of Peat in Padua to Vicenza's intriguing Chameleon Society.[32]

Beyond its power of initial approval, the Austrian government always reserved the right to attend an association's meetings, review its records, and approve or deny subsequent changes in its constitution.[33] The "political delegate" who reported to the government on all associational activities was a Napoleonic, not an Austrian, invention, but like the gendarme it was a revolutionary invention that the conservative Austrian government chose not to abolish.[34] Whether or not the Austrian authorities routinely supplemented these delegates with paid informants, it is easy to see the political utility of associations. Not only did they tend to bring together the most active (and therefore potentially troublesome) members of local society, but they did so within a structured setting.[35] It proved far easier for the Austrian police to monitor the official and unofficial proceedings of an association than to infiltrate several other, more unruly arenas of public life, including cafes, piazzas, and theatres.

1840s: Historic Centres – Cafes, Piazzas, Theatres, Streets

Il Giornale Euganeo had been in publication in Padua for little over a year when, in January 1845, it announced that it had received permission to publish a "weekly fly sheet of Literature, Theaters and Variety," entitled *Il Caffè Pedrocchi*.[36] Seven months later, in a special advance issue of the new paper, the editors-to-be explained their choice of titles: the Caffè Pedrocchi, they wrote, was "the marvel of Padua," the first stop on every tourist's itinerary, ahead of the great medieval city hall building

or the frescoes by Giotto and Mantegna. It was both the most beautiful
work of modern architecture in the city and the most celebrated example
of that equally modern phenomenon, the cafe as "grand social center."
More than just a meeting place, however, the Caffè Pedrocchi was a force
of "centralization." It drew together "the great man, and the great idler,
the galant woman and the numbskull and the swindler," with luck even
the honourable man, not to mention professors, merchants, and doctors
– "such diverse elements" – all in one place.[37] Continuing in this mildly
democratic vein, the editors of Il Caffè Pedrocchi directed the reader's attention to the new publication's masthead, a "prospect of the great building, not as it is now, with its semi-circular plaza [piazzale], but instead
closed [off] with elegant gates," according to an early design by the cafe's
architect, Giuseppe Jappelli. Like Jappelli, who eventually opened up the
cafe-plaza area, Il Caffè Pedrocchi would, by covering a wide variety of
topics – the arts, literature, science, current events, etc. – "aim to break
the gates and tear down the impediments."

One historian has called Il Giornale Euganeo "the most important
Venetian periodical of the entire second period of Austrian domination
[1814–48]" and "the most advanced expression of Venetian culture in
the 1840s."[38] With its serious tone and national focus, it was the perfect
journalistic extension of the movement of ideas taking place simultaneously at the congresses of Italian scientists. Il Caffè Pedrocchi, by comparison, was provincial and light-hearted. While Il Giornale Euganeo
printed essays on feudalism and popular botany, Il Caffè Pedrocchi reported on local concerts and lottery drawings, and presented humorous
as well as serious thoughts on a variety of more general topics. Nevertheless, precisely because it was more local in orientation and appeared
weekly instead of monthly, Il Caffè Pedrocchi offers a better view of public life in Padua during the 1840s than its sponsor. What it reveals is the
limited presence of the association in the public imagination, the association's relative weakness as a force of "centralization." In this unusual
source, and also in an important diary from the period, it is cafes, piazzas, theatres, and streets, rather than associations, that seem to attract
and define the local public.

Although its coverage of local, everyday life in Padua was limited, Il
Giornale Euganeo was filled with news about associations. Issues from its
first year of publication, in 1844, include reports on a public exhibition
put on by Turin's Society for the Promotion of the Arts; a plea by a man in
Verona for an organized network of provincial "encouragement societies"
to protect and promote the inventions of Italian scientists; a long letter by

Giovanni Berselli, the eventual founder of Padua's mutual aid society for doctors, surgeons, and pharmacists, explaining the merits of such "medical unions"; and a pair of articles on "the clubs and gaming houses in London." One of the most exciting features of the association was its capacity to transcend local boundaries. News about associations in Milan, Florence, Modena, and outside of Italy easily invited local comparisons, not to mention calls to action: The Society for the Encouragement of Agriculture in Milan is proceeding well, so why has our own Society for the Encouragement of Agriculture in Padua not yet been approved by the Austrian government? We Italians should follow the example of the Germans and form societies for the preservation of local monuments. Taken together, these items seemed to demonstrate that the spirit of association had spread far and wide in Italy, enough so that the more light-hearted writers at *Il Caffè Pedrocchi* began parodying the phenomenon, "reporting" on a mutual admiration society of composers who had been booed by their audiences, a society for the prevention of the spread of bad literary concepts, even a society to help support people who had joined too many societies.[39]

The excitement generated by a transcendent print culture can be misleading, however. Writers for *Il Giornale Euganeo* and *Il Caffè Pedrocchi* literally made it appear that Padua was participating in a national movement of associational activity, but in fact the evidence of local progress was uneven at best. For every association in Florence, Turin, or Milan that had (or inspired) a counterpart in Padua, there were four or five others that did not. A society for the preservation of local monuments did not form in Padua in the 1840s, nor did a society for the prevention of cruelty to animals or a mutual aid society of typographers, despite the fact that readers of *Il Giornale Euganeo* and *Il Caffè Pedrocchi* were exposed to the benefits of all three. In May 1846, a writer for *Il Caffè Pedrocchi* ended a report on the first meeting of the Society for the Encouragement of Agriculture in Padua by noting that "in just a few months time we have seen three beneficial Societies come together in Padua" before declaring: "May the spirit of consociation spread, burn, grow, intertwine and prosper variously in every part of Italy." Of the three local associations in question, however, only one – the Society for the Promotion of Gardening – formed without difficulty; it took a few years, not a few months, to get the Society for the Encouragement of Agriculture in Padua started, and even longer – seven years: 1845–52 – to create a joint-stock company (*società per azioni*) for the production of iron. The Austrian government alone could not be blamed for these delays. The same *Caffè Pedrocchi* writer who wished for the rapid spread of the spirit of consociation in Italy admitted, at the start of the same article, that in Padua one obstacle to progress was "the cold and sometimes damaging habit of waiting." Others spoke in more frustrated terms of unfounded "fears" and "prejudices," of sceptics and opponents, of "the lethargy of the times." As one writer put it, so many of the ideas that made it into books and newspapers "stay in a state of embryo; die stillborn."[40]

The tempo of activity by the small number of associations that did come to life in Padua is easier to gauge from reading the weekly *Caffè Pedrocchi* rather than the monthly *Giornale Euganeo*. Not counting two brief announcements of upcoming meetings, only five out of fifty-two issues from the first year of *Il Caffè Pedrocchi* (1846) contained news regarding the city's active associations. The following year the number increased to six out of fifty-two. Significantly, most of these references (eight out of eleven) were not to meetings, the standard associational event of the post-unification period, but to public festivities and concerts, which local associations participated in or organized. Whether you belonged to one of Padua's few associations or not, you went to the large piazza known as the Prato della Valle to see a horse race, or to the Caffè Pedrocchi to hear music.[41] Rather than carving out their own place within Risorgimento Italy's public sphere, associations joined the crowds of people who gravitated to Padua's historic and modern centres, the piazzas and the Caffè Pedrocchi.[42]

Newspapers are not the only source from the period to identify "society" or sociability with piazzas, cafes, theatres, and streets rather than associations. Take, for example, Carlo Leoni's diary. A scholar and writer who made his name as a composer of epigraphs, Leoni (1814–1874) was also a contributor to *Il Giornale Euganeo* and *Il Caffe Pedrocchi* and a member of Padua's provisional government during the Revolution of 1848. In his "secret chronicle" of Padua from 1845 to 1874, Leoni attempted not only to record the main political events of the Venetian Risorgimento but also to provide a detailed description of the institutions, manners, and mores of Paduan society. Over half of Leoni's 725-page document is dedicated to the years 1848–51, recounting the transition from revolution to Austrian repression. In this respect, what Leoni describes is not so much Paduan society as its shadow or shell. It is a portrait of the city's "dissociability."

[1849, December] 17. The city especially during the evening continues to be solitary indeed: it seems like a large convent, the cafes sparse on account of the spies and after said intimations even the very few private conversations are breaking up. On the street we greet each other, gloomy and reserved, not having anything comforting to share, just misfortunes: many agree to avoid each other and we hardly pay each other visits any more: society in dissolution.

[1850, January] 2. ... Fear is growing in many, such that there are no conversations and rarely visits. In short, here there is no longer society.

[1850, February] 3. ... At 9 in the evening the streets are already deserted. A dark and melancholy silence reigns over them, alone, taciturn passersby quickly move along. People avoid approaching each other: no more songs, the theater and the cafes deserted and under control, general the bad mood and the mourning.

[1850, April] 15. The dissociability and the weakness [atonia] are such that [the] letters, sciences and arts seem dead. As far as letters are concerned, with the exception of five or six bad newspapers throughout the kingdom the press is silent, to the great damage of everything and everyone.

Reports from newspapers, as well as from visitors, gave Leoni a similar impression of the region as a whole:

[16 June 1849] The cities squalid and deserted, the cafes abandoned, theaters and the University closed; many people for a year now exiles from the disastrous reoccupation. No sociability, everyone suspicious of his neighbor, the cities placed in a state of siege under military despots with summary justice.[43]

The temptations of heroic anti-Austrian melodrama aside, these are fascinating comments. And it is significant that Leoni does not mention the conditions of local associational life in these disconsolate pages.

On the one hand, during the years 1848–50 there was little in the way of associational activity to record: the few associations that existed in Padua suspended activity during the revolutionary events of March–June 1848, and then fell victim to the broad crackdown on public freedom that followed the return of the Austrians to power. On the other hand, given that Leoni himself was a vocal proponent of associations prior to the Revolution of 1848, it is odd that he did not comment on their disappearance, nor, for that matter, on their revival after 1850. In two brief entries from 1851, Leoni praised the newly reconvened Society for the Encouragement of Agriculture in Padua, and in 1856 he noted the creation of two new associations, the Pedrocchi Club and the

Philarmonic-Theatrical Circle. Finally, in January 1869, over two years after the annexation of the Veneto to the Italian kingdom, Leoni made a point of listing ten of the city's "many important associations and daughters of liberty."[44] In general, however, what concerned Leoni was freedom of the press, of speech, of assembly, even of dress, more than freedom of association. Again and again, Leoni's thoughts on social and political life in Padua turn to theatrical performances, Carnevale celebrations, funeral processions, wall grafitti, cafe closings and raids, and gatherings at Prato della Valle, not to mention demonstrations and arrests.

1850s: The Limits of Leisure

In Carlo Leoni's view, the deserted theatres and melancholy streets of Padua after 1848 were both regrettable and necessary. Regrettable above all because of the corrupting effects of a world without culture or society, "in which only material life is free." Necessary because it was the patriotic duty of Padua's citizens to demonstrate that a return to life under the repressive Austrian regime was not normal but tragic, and thus incompatible with a lively theatre season or Carnevale celebration. The ideal response would have been to subvert all grand cultural events with acts of protest, as when, in July 1854, much to Leoni's pleasure, a University of Padua student at the Duse Theatre shouted, "Goodbye O sun of Italy." Short of such heroic gestures, the only acceptable action was to refuse to attend theatres, dances, and horse races, and to avoid donning masks for Carnevale. In several diary entries, Leoni notes that the Austrian police forced local proprietors (and city governments) to keep theatres open, paid individuals to put on masks and congregate in the city's main squares during Carnevale, and had newspapers report false accounts of high local turnouts at these events. Conversely, whenever theatres and squares really did fill up, he expressed his disgust with the local population, as in this entry from June 1850: "[It is] proof of the weakness of these people, who are now taking up again the old habits of servitude in too many things. The five hundred subscriptions to the theater are a scandal."[45]

Leoni's disapproval of local theatregoers and revellers is a symptom of something more than just the politics of symbolic protest against Austrian rule. Along with many other liberals at the time, Leoni was also articulating a more general critique of idle recreation. An exact chronology of this particular strand of liberal ideology is difficult to establish, although it certainly dates back to the eighteenth-century Enlightenment, and just as certainly gathered momentum in the 1820s and 1830s, when more and more Europeans began to investigate the moral and behavioural roots of pauperism. By the 1840s, special praise for all things useful or productive – including "useful associations" – had become a standard feature of the Italian press. Among the leading Italian proponents of association, gradually, between the 1840s and 1850s, attention shifted from the more or less serious, but certainly intimate, pleasures of elite social clubs and reading rooms to the organizational and administrative challenges of "popular," reform-oriented agricultural associations and mutual aid societies.[46]

For Carlo Leoni, the experience of revolution in 1848–49 provided its own valuable lesson in behavioural reform. Among the changes in local customs that took place during the Revolution of 1848, Leoni noted that "even boys dress in military style and no longer speak of theaters, singers, and ballet dancers." And at the end of 1849, after the return of the Austrians to power but before the scandalous signs of weakness began to reappear, he declared: "How our society has changed in these past few months! I believe that never again in so brief a period of time will such a profound social change occur. From luxury, epicureanism, frivolity, we have passed perfectly to their opposites. Now one thinks, one meditates and with dignity one suffers, hopes and waits!"[47] Other liberals, less convinced perhaps by the social and cultural benefits of revolution, also endorsed this turn away from idle pasttimes. In May 1855, the president of Padua's Academy of Science, Letters and the Arts, Giovanni Cittadella, began a talk entitled "Considerations on the Current Progress of Civilization in Padua" by defining what he meant by civilization:

> To the person who might want to locate it in the ease of a courteous smile, in graceful manners, in the nimble disposition to improvise ties of unaffected friendship, in the squandered lavishness of banquets, in the fickle pomp of carriages, in the attendance of indolent clubs, in the idle protraction of night life and the shortening of days; to the person who sees civilization as insincere protests and empty promises I would not know how to respond, because I lack the ability to understand the word in these terms. Rather I hope to make myself understood to all those who think that civilization means progress, the inclination of a nation, a people, a city to perfect its civil life, to broaden the relations between men, to increase the means of common prosperity and to see that they spread as far as possible, to elevate the life of the individual, private life, the life of man in his ideas, his sentiments, his abilities.[48]

What we have here is not simply the familiar theme of a liberal-bourgeois elite's disapproval of plebeian leisure. It is true that, in his *Letter of a galant'uomo to the Lombard-Venetians*, composed and circulated in 1847, Carlo Leoni called for the creation in Padua of night schools, arguing that they would help "refine our depraved and epicurean people." The same year, however, in the pages of *Il Caffè Pedrocchi* Leoni proposed to end the "plagues" of "discouragement, frightening softness, epicureanism, sloth and a drowsy slowness" by promoting mutual aid societies – not just, or primarily, artisanal organizations, but "unions" of doctors and lawyers as well. Other than peasants ("always apathetic and drunk"), the group that inspires the harshest words in Leoni's diary is not the working class but the students attending the University of Padua.[49] Even less plebeian were the false signs of civilization that Giovanni Cittadella singled out for criticism: the physical gestures reminiscent of a courtier, the excessive display and dissipation of the idle rich. Leoni evoked the Greco-Roman past when he contrasted epicureanism with martial (masculine) virtue, whereas most of his contemporaries, including Cittadella, favoured the more modern opposition of idleness and usefulness. But what they shared is more important: a critical view of recreation *in general*, and a growing appreciation of the urgent need for social reforms in Italy.

The combined journalistic and institutional vogue of *utilità* did not reach provincial cities like Padua or Vicenza until the 1840s, and even then did not imply a clear disavowal of recreation or sociability. Contributors to *Il Giornale Euganeo* took Padua's students to task for wasting time in cafes and exposed the decadence of London's clubs and gambling dens. But *Il Caffè Pedrocchi* defended the shows that the Venetian hosts of the ninth congress of Italian scientists put on for visitors in September 1847, and made a point of praising gala concerts or horse races if they benefited one of Padua's "useful institutions."[50] The Catholic clergy was far more consistently critical of urban sociability. Before and after unification, pastoral visitation records obsessively identify the many "dens of unbelief" to be found in small and large city centres: taverns, of course, but also clubs, cafes, restaurants, dance halls, barbershops, even the homes of local elites. The decadent urban mentality threatened parishioners everywhere; the declining rates of church attendance and confession were evidence of that. But priests, too, had to beware. As one concerned bishop put it in 1860, it was fine for priests to pick up a newspaper, to drink an espresso or mineral water and eat an ice cream, but they should not be allowed to "spend a good part of the day" doing so, at the expense of their studies and duties.[51]

More than print culture, it is the new associations of the 1840s that reveal the beginning of a shift away from the pleasures of recreation and sociability. The Society for the Encouragement of Agriculture, in particular,
provided an impressive new model of associational activity. Above all, its
mission was expansive: to "promote and stimulate agricultural progress
in the Province of Padua" meant, quite literally, to leave the confines of
the city and investigate the practices of landowners in dozens of nearby
villages. Before the society could award prizes for the best silkworm co-
coon, plough, or olive grove, or for a specific combination or rotation of
crops, jury members had to make their way out to the contestants' farms
or estates. Metaphors of travel and transgression filled the speech given
by the society's president, Ferdinando Cavalli, at the first awards ceremony, held at the University of Padua's Grand Hall in September 1851.
By moving beyond the "strict limits" of the legal order and the sphere of
government action, he said, the "new power" of association "takes progress on otherwise inaccessible and untried roads"; and the Society for the
Encouragement of Agriculture, in particular, promised to spread wealth
and virtue "everywhere, into palaces and into huts." A year earlier, Cavalli's predecessor, Andrea Cittadella Vigodarzere, had noted the range of
social benefits produced by the personal, physical act of bringing useful
knowledge out into the countryside: it helped free the "rustic" from old
habits and prejudices, it encouraged the scholar of agricultural science to
be practical rather than abstract, and it took landowners away from "the
torpid idleness of the city."[52]

Humble rustics do not appear on the membership lists of the Society
for the Encouragement of Agriculture, but their place among the targeted
recipients of "encouragement" made the society not simply a useful institution but a *popular* useful institution; that is, along with infant nursery schools, savings banks and, somewhat later, mutual aid societies, it
aimed to assist and reform society's "popular," non-elite classes. When
its initial offer of prizes failed to inspire the participation of local peasants, the society stepped up its efforts to print and distribute a *Popular
Almanac* and an *Agrarian Catechism*. Preparation of the almanac was
actually part of the 1847 program of society-sponsored competitions;
contestants were required to provide news pertaining to local agriculture
and industry, discuss new and improved agricultural methods, explain
the advantages of savings banks, offer basic lessons in hygiene (including proper maintenance of livestock), facilitate a wider understanding of
the metric system of weights and measures, and give brief profiles of the
various charitable and educational institutions in the province. This list

of topics was expanded upon in another of the society's popular publications, *Il Raccoglitore*, a pocket-sized volume of about three hundred pages that came out once a year beginning in 1852. By the time the society held its first prize ceremony in 1851, it had been renamed the Society for the Encouragement of Agriculture and Industry, and thus the first few editions of *Il Raccoglitore* featured at least a few articles with an urban orientation: a profile of the great cafe owner, Antonio Pedrocchi; a discussion of mutual aid societies; an article on the new Benech-Rocchetti ironworks in Padua; and a fictional conversation between two artisans, in which the sins of foul language and drinking, among others, were confessed and condemned.[53]

Although mutual aid societies were also relatively new to Italy in the 1840s, they appeared to mark a less significant departure from the traditions of urban association. In contrast to the dynamic, mobile rhetoric of "encouragement," the language of mutual aid could be intimate and familial. "It is sweet for me to be surrounded by you, beloved colleagues," remarked a member of the Mutual Aid Society of Lawyers and Notaries in Venice, at the group's inauguration in August 1847, "very sweet to see all of you moved by the same sentiment ... insofar as this affectionate harmony is to me a secure guarantee that the ties of fraternal benevolence will become ever stronger."[54] In part, no doubt, the founders of the first mutual aid societies had in mind the sociable ideals of confraternities and guilds. At the same time, a mutual aid society was not to be confused with a social club or reading room. There were no sections on "entertainments" in mutual aid society statutes, no promises of comfortable rooms for conversation, games, or dances. Rather, statutes and speeches alike remained focused on the economic task of collecting and distributing funds so as to be able to help members in times of need. Concerned, perhaps, that the members of the newly formed Mutual Aid Society of Doctors, Surgeons, and Pharmacists in Padua might not understand the association's basic purpose, Giovanni Berselli told them, "Neither the nature, nor the number of our meetings allows us to turn our minds to the community of studies, [which is] the elect field of Academies and Athenaeums ..." Berselli had begun his speech by calling the members "brothers," but went on to give a sober account of the poverty and low social esteem to which many doctors fell victim, and to angrily reject the notion that an association that aimed to prevent such suffering might somehow further compromise the reputation of the medical profession. In mutual aid societies, the experience of brotherhood was secured not by daily encounters with fellow members, but by the essentially administrative, if "very noble," practice of helping fellow members preserve their own and their families' well-being.[55]

1860s: Association versus Sociability

Prior to the 1860s, the most prominent Venetian mutual aid societies were not "popular" but professional. In Venice as in many other large Italian cities, several associations of artisans formed during the 1840s and 1850s, but in provincial cities most of the mutual aid societies created prior to unification benefited doctors, priests, teachers, and musicians. How much this can be attributed to Austrian restrictions, rather than to the inertia or reluctance of local elites, is difficult to determine. In 1844, Padua's *Giornale Euganeo* printed enthusiastic reports by Gottardo Calvi and Giuseppe La Farina on artisanal mutual aid societies in other cities and regions, but several years went by before it (or *Il Caffè Pedrocchi*) returned to the topic, with a pair of brief and rudimentary articles. The article on mutual aid societies that appeared in the 1852 issue of *Il Raccoglitore* offered a more detailed analysis of "workers' associations" – stressing the importance of statistical tables and strict rules regarding the distribution of aid, answering critics' fears of social disorder and administrative failure – but it contained no hint of plans to create one in Padua.[56] Through institutions like the Society for the Encouragement of Agriculture and Industry in Padua and the Olympic Academy in Vicenza, local elites began sponsoring popular education programs in the early 1850s, but another decade would pass before they made a concerted effort to organize artisans in mutual aid societies. Ahead of most others by several years, in 1858 Fedele Lampertico and Giovanni Scola founded the General Mutual Aid Society of Vicentine Artisans (Società Generale di mutuo soccorso degli artigiani vicentini, hereafter to be referred to as the Società Generale). More typical, though, were the experiences of Emilio Morpurgo in Padua and Luigi Luzzatti in Venice. Like their friend Lampertico, both men took steps to create a mutual aid society of artisans in their native cities, but unlike him they failed to win the approval of the Austrian government.

The group of young men who led the effort to promote the first new "popular associations" in the Veneto is so central to this study that they deserve introduction. The son of a wealthy silk merchant turned landowner, Fedele Lampertico (1833–1906) became the unquestioned leader of Vicenza's ruling elite after unification. Although he was briefly a member of Parliament and for several decades a senator, Lampertico spent most of his time in Vicenza or at his family's estate in nearby Montegaldella. As a result, he was able to exert an extraordinary influence over local affairs: as an elected member of Vicenza's municipal and provincial councils, as a board member of countless charities and civic committees, and as the leader of numerous associations, including the city's prestigious Olympic Academy as well as the Società Generale of local artisans. Emilio Morpurgo (1836–85) and Luigi Luzzatti (1841–1927) also combined careers in national politics with a passionate involvement in local associational life. Both came from wealthy and cultured Jewish families, and both built their reputations as reformers dedicated to rescuing the working classes from poverty and ignorance. While still in their thirties, Morpurgo and Luzzatti were called to participate in a string of influential government committees, notably the industrial and agricultural "inquiries" of the 1870s. Morpurgo died young whereas Luzzatti went on to become the first Venetian (and second Jewish) prime minister of Italy, in 1910–11. Lampertico, Morpurgo, and Luzzatti all studied politics and law at the University of Padua, and through mutual mentors – in particular, the economist Angelo Messedaglia and the priest and poet Giacomo Zanella – they became close friends. From this base of extraordinarily active students and teachers, a wide web of friendships and alliances took shape across the region, including within it Paolo Lioy (1834–1911) in Vicenza, Antonio Tolomei (1839–88) in Padua, and Alberto Errera (1842–94) in Venice.[57]

In contrast to the shadowy presence of associations in documents from the 1840s, the successes and failures of Lampertico, Morpurgo, Luzzatti, and many others during the 1860s are recorded in a wide range of archival and published sources. Historians should be especially thankful that these individuals were living in different cities, because distance forced them to share news of their activities in a steady stream of private letters. Naturally, their letters cover a range of topics, from the joys and sorrows of family life to opinions and inquiries regarding recent publications or political events. But the topic they come back to again and again is associational life, in particular those forms of association, like the mutual aid society, that they believed were best suited to assist and reform the popular classes. Some of their letters contain first-hand accounts of their own experiences promoting or leading associations, while others discuss associations they had only heard about from friends or read about in periodicals. In either case, what is striking is how little attention they pay to the social or recreational dimension of associational life. The greater civilizing role of mutual aid societies or social clubs is not debated, the idle distractions of the city are not a subject of great concern. And yet no detail having to do with the forms, rules, and administration of a mutual aid society escaped their attention. It is as if they saw association and sociability as two completely different worlds, when only a generation earlier the two had been practically synonymous.

Of particular interest are the letters between Luzzatti and Lampertico. When Luzzatti began to get interested in creating a mutual aid society in Venice, in 1863, he bombarded the more experienced Lampertico with questions:

> What steps are necessary in Austria to found a mutual aid society? Do mutual aid societies do better with workers from the same industries or with workers from different industries? How, from this point of view, are your Vicentine societies organized? What is the minimum and maximum number of members a mutual aid society must have in order to succeed? What is the usual payment made by members, weekly, or monthly? How do they pay? How do you proportion payments with subsidies? Do they all have to pay the same amount? What purpose do the Vicentine mutual aid societies serve? How do you keep and invest the society's funds? In your societies is there an electoral system?[58]

Luzzatti did not ask: How do you go about attracting members to join the association? What are the best ways of instilling feelings of brotherhood, of giving the members a chance to get to know each other?

On those rare occasions when Luzzatti and Lampertico addressed the issue of sociability, they discussed it in negative terms. Unlike most liberal proponents of associations in Italy, Lampertico chose to give the Società Generale a strong religious imprint. Article I of the association's initial statute reads:

> The Mutual aid society of artisans has as its aim to bring them [the artisans] together in a Christian brotherhood in order to provide, in proportion to its means, for their needs in cases of sickness or disability.[59]

Lampertico also provided the association with a patron saint – San Giuseppe, "patron of every good worker" – as well as a religious calendar of events. The annual meeting of the Società Generale took place on the third Sunday after Easter, the day assigned to Giuseppe on the Catholic Church's calendar of saints, and featured an inspirational "sacred speech" by one of Vicenza's leading priests.[60] The religious content of the

Società Generale no doubt helped the fledgling organization win the approval of the conservative and pro-Catholic Austrian regime, but it went against the secular principles of many liberals. As a Jew, Luzzatti had additional reasons to oppose this feature of Lampertico's association. A conflict between the two men on the matter seemed inevitable. It came in April 1863 – early in their friendship – and is documented in an exchange of angry letters. Significantly, though, what began as a fight over the religious identity of the Società Generale, in general, turned into a debate over the value of religious *celebrations*, in particular. "On religious questions," Luzzatti told his friend,

> there is an abyss that separates us, a real abyss! It is better that I avoid a multitude of observations that might wound you to the quick in your faith; I know that your convictions are very pure and for this reason, while fighting them, I respect them. But what does the church have to do with mutual aid? That money, wasted on masses, couldn't it be used for a circulating library?[61]

Lampertico took offence:

> No: your letter was not bland at all, it did nothing to mitigate the wounds to the quick of my religious feelings. The usual claims of tolerance: but at the same time I do not know how you reconcile [them] with accusations, I must say, as bitter as they are unjust. I will not repeat those expressions that certainly must have escaped from you. I will only rectify the fact, repeating what has already been said other times, that we have only two masses each year, and that for the church where we meet not a penny of the members' contributions is spent.[62]

Profound religious differences aside, Luzzatti and Lampertico both managed to agree that social events and celebrations were, at best, marginally important to associations. Fiscal austerity alone made them a luxury: only two masses a year, Lampertico insisted, not a penny from the society's coffers. Moreover, even to Lampertico, who saw the Società Generale's meetings as a luxury worth having, the value of such events was not social but religious; they did not create a circle of friends so much as a brotherhood of "pious men." Beyond the valuable lessons of thrift and mutual aid, he wrote Luzzatti, there was "a great good which comes from remembering that we are all brothers, before God, and from being close to one another in a place of worship, where one ponders that life is fleeting, that the vanity of man accomplishes little, that we who are diffident of ourselves must be trusting of the Lord."[63] Nevertheless, what is most interesting about this exchange is its exceptionality. In public speeches and writings as well as private correspondence, few of the emerging leaders of public and political life in the Veneto ever discussed the social function of associations. During the last phase of the Venetian Risorgimento, it is not a particular language of sociability that stands out but a great silence.

On certain occasions, local elites proved to be very sensitive to the meaning and value of social interaction. This was especially true of gatherings or events that appeared to transcend class boundaries. In May 1862, Fedele Lampertico wrote to Luigi Luzzatti about an awards ceremony held for the students of the Olympic Academy's "popular" night schools, at which a young member of the academy, Paolo Lioy, gave a particularly moving speech:

> The gathering of students, artisans, and academics was beautiful: Lioy's words were most noble and rich in doctrine and in heart. In everyone emotions ran high; I won't speak of myself, to whom Lioy offered some very affectionate sentiments, such that I could not keep from crying. On that day the correspondence between the various orders of citizens was confirmed: more than on any other occasion they drew closer together and recognized each other: everyone felt a certain pride and dignity for the fulfilment of a sacred duty in he who gave and he who received education.[64]

Educators and artisans did not always mix so well. In Padua, an Arts and Crafts Room for "engineers, artists, and artisans" risked failure because its members found it difficult to get along with one another. When it first opened in 1858, a writer for a local newspaper expressed his hope that the "exchange and diffusion" of ideas in "friendly conversations" would educate the "less cultured" and encourage the "less enterprising." Six years later, however, another newspaper reported that "today the *studio* is deserted," and suggested why:

> Some declare that it was the reluctance of the engineers to accept the artisans as brothers during those hours of educational association which led the latter to abandon it; and others maintain instead that it was only the apathy of the artisans that caused [those with] the sincerest intentions to lose courage and be rendered useless.

Either way it was a "simple misunderstanding," noted the writer, who then proceeded to make a lengthy appeal to each of the opposing groups. (Artisans, "the engineers have too much good sense not to appreciate you." Engineers, "under the rugged surface of the artisan beats a generous heart.") Soon, it was hoped, "the rooms which are now deserted will be filled again with the sounds of fraternally loving voices."[65]

Luigi Luzzatti, too, sometimes found himself in the company of the "less fortunate classes," especially when he was travelling through Lombardy to promote the creation of credit unions. What he sought from the common man, however, was not friendship but affirmation. To Antonio Tolomei, in the summer of 1864, he wrote:

> I just finished my tour of Lombardy, wistful and conscious of the ritual's solemnity; I inaugurated many popular banks. The seed has sprouted very well; your friend, welcomed with enthusiasm, felt in his hand the honored hand of the worker and the peasant [colono] and was consoled ... I gave my speech in a theater, where there were thousands of people. I spoke, visibly moved, and the continuous applause interrupted me practically at every passage.[66]

The very excitement of coming into (physical) contact with "the people" belied Luzzatti's true goal: not social interaction between the classes but his own, privileged act of social observation. Writing to Lampertico from Venice, before his exile in Lombardy, Luzzatti unwittingly demonstrated his remove from the objects of his study:

> To think that in these past few days I have performed a true inquiry [inchiesta]; I spoke with many workers, with many boatmen and I found them all open to the idea of mutual aid; I obtained statutes of some obscure [mutual aid] societies, spoke with their administrators and today I seem to be purer after this affectionate contact with the people ...[67]

More than a purifying touch, what elites wanted from the popular classes was order and discipline. In a letter written to Luzzatti in March 1862, Lampertico mentioned taking a trip to Bassano, a small city to the north of Vicenza, to attend the inaugural meeting of a mutual aid society. By Lampertico's own estimate, the meeting drew "about 300 artisans," an impressive figure for a small city. Yet it was not the size or social composition of the gathering that captured Lampertico's interest, but the "supreme regularity with which the leaders were nominated by secret ballot, and the good order of everything."[68] Rarely did the elite leaders of a "popular" association recognize the members' need or desire to socialize with one another. As men like Fedele Lampertico and Luigi Luzzatti saw it, workers and peasants did not simply congregate and mix in the meeting hall of a mutual aid society; they were brought together – hailed and organized – by the society's leadership.

Of course, one group of Venetian liberals' lack of interest in the fraternal bonds of association should not be confused with a decline or disappearance of sociability in Italian associational life. After unification, social clubs continued to host games, dances, and parties; moreover, as the work of many scholars has shown, they continued to perform the crucial function of forging and negotiating relationships between local elites.[69] They were joined by new forms of festive or recreational association, including groups whose main purpose was to promote (not boycott) Carnevale celebrations. Local newspapers went on praising benefit concerts and balls. Vicenza's Società Generale continued to hold its patron saint's day celebrations; in Padua, the leaders of the Mutual Aid Society of Artisans, Merchants and Professionals organized a "festival of work" in 1869. Nevertheless, there is no mistaking either the displacement of recreational associations from the central position they occupied in the first half of the century, in favour of mutual aid societies and other forms of so-called productive association, or the more general, ideological turn against recreation by Italy's leading liberals. Emblematic of these changes was the anti-leisure message of Padua's festival of work. "This celebration," Emilio Morpurgo explained to the assembled crowd, "is not being held for the vain display of a fleeting satisfaction," or "to allow us to be transported by the enchantment of transient splendors." It was a serious and solemn event.[70]

How far the concept of sociability fell from favour during the second half of the nineteenth century can be gauged by subsequent attempts to rescue it. In an essay published in 1909, the German sociologist Georg Simmel felt compelled to remind his readers that the human impulse to socialize was not simply functional ("for the sake of special needs and interests") but also playful and "artistic." The challenge of regulating one's own behaviour – of being personable without imposing too much of one's personal character or mood, of keeping a conversation interesting without letting it become too serious – this was what made a gathering sociable. Whereas the concept of *association* derived from the concrete, "content-determined" actions of men, *sociability* evoked an "ideal sociological world" of "pure interaction," in which "the pleasure of the individual is always contingent upon the joy of others." Simmel recognized that this sociable democracy was artificial, "a game in which one 'acts' as though all were equal, as though he especially esteemed everyone." But he was also critical of the rationalist effort to "do away with sociability as empty idleness." Sociability might be "freed of substance" and "the seriousness of life," he noted, but it also possessed a symbolic importance that distinguished it from "pure pasttime."[71]

The members of social clubs in nineteenth-century Italy would have found plenty to agree with in Simmel's essay. Compared to the formal encounter between speaker and audience at the inauguration of a popular bank, or the explicit recognition of cultured difference at an awards ceremony, theirs was a world of pure interaction. Compared to an encouragement society's promotion of a new plough or a mutual aid society's annual review of sick-pay expenses, their daily encounters with one another were playful. When Simmel wrote his essay, new forms of leisure and political mobilization had already displaced both the elite social club and the liberal encouragement society as models of association. Cinemas and cycling clubs competed for the attention of a new, seemingly "mass" public of cultural consumers. Less artistic and sociable, perhaps, than Simmel's ideal, this new public also seemed to possess very little of the seriousness that had begun to imbue Italian associations towards the end of the Risorgimento. Playfulness, artistry, and recreation were not the order of the day in Italy during the 1850s and 1860s. Shortly before the revolutions of 1848, journalists in Padua could still pause to admire the shows taking place in Venice. Shortly before the liberation of the Veneto in 1866, a new generation of journalists declared, "The series of idle years has ended forever."[72]

2

Poetry and Prose in the Risorgimento

When the liberation of the Veneto began in July 1866, Luigi Luzzatti was in Lombardy. A native of Venice, graduate of the University of Padua, and, in the not so distant future, the leading political figure in the region, Luzzatti had left his homeland for Milan in 1863. Lombardy at that time was already part of the united Italian kingdom, and Milan was a vibrant centre of social and intellectual life. The contrast with the oppressive atmosphere of the Veneto under Austrian rule could not have been greater. Luzzatti was only twenty-two years old when he arrived in Milan, but he was bright, ambitious, and well connected. He quickly made a name for himself as the proponent of a new kind of institution, the savings and loan association or "popular bank." Modelled after a form of credit union that the Prussian magistrate Hermann Schulze-Delitzsch had introduced in the early 1850s, popular banks aimed to provide credit to small shopkeepers, artisans, and peasants, groups whose only recourse to capital had previously been the usurious moneylender or pawnshop broker. First in the small Lombard town of Lodi, then in Brescia, Asola, Monza, and Milan, Luzzatti assisted in the creation of Italy's first popular banks. Before long, his efforts took him beyond Lombardy to Piedmont, Emilia-Romagna, Tuscany, and finally, in the summer of 1866, to the Veneto.[1]

By the time Luzzatti returned home, as he recalled in his memoirs, the line separating the Veneto from Lombardy "was no longer a border."[2] The Austrians had already begun their retreat, clearing the way for the arrival of Italian troops in Rovigo, Padua, Vicenza, and Treviso. A witness to the liberation of Padua, Carlo Leoni, recorded the excitement of the event in his diary:

12 [July 1866]. ... Word having spread thoughout the city that at noon a van-
guard of the Cavalry would arrive, in an instant like a spark of electricity all
the houses were decked with flags. Incredible and stupendous! If I myself had
not seen the city I would not have believed it. There was an immediate and
portentous opening of hearts, faces, and voices which for so many years had
been buried and petrified. There was a flow of people and carriages, aristocratic and popular, all decked out and heading towards the Mezzavia. There
was kissing, yelling, a delirium, frenzy ... In short today, 12 July, the entrance
of the first Italian liberation troops, will be eternally memorable for Padua.[3]

Luzzatti made it to Padua less than a week later. He was not too late
to enjoy the many festivities surrounding Venetian independence, which
continued throughout the summer and fall. But there is little mention of
these events in his memoirs. After all, a post facto celebration did not
compare with the liberation itself; to the "eternally memorable" events
of 1866, Luzzatti was neither witness nor participant.

Nevertheless, Luzzatti had his own story to tell. Shortly after his arrival in the Veneto, he began what amounted to a promotional tour of
the region on behalf of popular banks. In August, after returning home to
Venice, Luzzatti travelled to Vicenza, invited by a group of friends there
to speak on the subject of popular banks. The response was enthusiastic; in early September the Popular Bank of Vicenza began its operations.
Towards the end of September, Luzzatti repeated his message before a
group assembled in the rooms of Padua's Society for the Encouragement
of Agriculture. A month later it was back to Venice and the halls of the
Venetian Academy (the Ateneo Veneto), where for two and a half hours
Luzzatti lectured the gathering – representing "all the classes of the Venetian public" – about the many issues raised by popular banks. Luzzatti
held off from visiting other cities in the region, waiting for friends and
contacts to prepare the banks' successful foundation. "In the autumn of
liberation," Luzzatti wrote, "Padua and Venice were my general quarters, the centres from which the idea of popular credit spread."

More than just a proponent of a new form of credit institution, Luzzatti saw himself as a field marshal leading a liberal crusade.

As I passed through the liberated cities I found that, with the widest possible
reach, everywhere the idea of constituting mutual aid societies was flourish-
ing, and with my popular banks I can claim to have followed the liberating
army. (p. 208)

Luzzatti did not begin writing his memoirs until late in life, over fifty years after the liberation of the Veneto; thus he had every opportunity to cast a heroic light on his activities during the summer and fall of 1866. Nevertheless, friends and allies at the time echoed Luzzatti's sentiments. Writing from Verona in October 1866, Angelo Messedaglia told Luzzatti:

> I am here only a short time before the arrival of our troops, which will happen today at 3 p.m. And does it not say something that on this very day I am writing to you about popular institutions, banks, etc.? ... The Luzzatti-system bank ... I believe will prevail decisively; its supporters are also the founders of the Political Circle which held its first meeting yesterday and probably, rather certainly, will remain the only [political association in the city]. For an organ it has the newspaper *L'Arena*, which is perfectly honest.[4]

Indeed, as Messedaglia's letter indicates, Luzzatti did not march into the Veneto unopposed. Local support for the popular banks had to be organized and publicized, because there was more than one "system" to choose from: throughout the region, Luzzatti faced a rival by the name of Gian Giacomo Alvisi, who was busy promoting a different type of small credit institution, which he called the "people's bank."[5] Alvisi was from Rovigo (just twenty-five miles south of Padua), a Venetian liberal with his own contacts and allies in the region, and for this reason alone he was a potential threat to Luzzatti and his popular banks. The result was a battle between the "Alvisian" and "Luzzattian" banks for the newly liberated Veneto region. Luzzatti's popular banks took shape fairly quickly in Vicenza, Padua, and Venice, but it was some time before the Popular Bank of Verona got on its feet, following months of "consultations and disputes." In Rovigo, on the other hand, it was Alvisi's bank that prevailed. Ultimately, as Luzzatti proudly recalls, Alvisi's Banca del Popolo ran into trouble – the branch in Rovigo, for example, went into liquidation in 1874 – while Luzzatti's popular banks continued to prosper and grow. "Victory for me," Luzzatti immodestly tells us, "was absolute."

Rival proponents of banks manoeuvring for position in the liberated cities of the Veneto? This is not the kind of heroic battle we normally associate with Italian unification. It is a far cry from the exploits of Cavour and Garibaldi in 1859–60, less impressive even than the relatively unsuccessful military campaigns of 1866. The circumstances that led to the annexation of the Veneto – namely, the defeat of the Austrians not in northern Italy but in Germany at the hands of the Prussian army – were cause as much for disappointment as for grateful celebration. Neverthe-less, the "patriots" who led the movement for Venetian independence, from exiled conspirators like Alberto Cavalletto and Giambattista Giustinian to local "secret committee" members like Ferdinando Coletti in Padua, provided the heroic template of patriotic, revolutionary action. They were the true "poets" of the Venetian Risorgimento. And Luigi Luzzatti's popular banks? Well, they would appear to be exemplary of the "prose" that followed unification, colourless in comparison to Italy's great fight for independence.

Luzzatti clearly disagreed. So did many of his friends and allies in the Veneto, including Angelo Messedaglia in Verona, Fedele Lampertico and Paolo Lioy in Vicenza, Antonio Tolomei and Emilio Morpurgo in Padua, and Enrico Castelnuovo and Alberto Errera in Venice. Several of them helped Luzzatti set up popular banks in their home cities. All of them shared Luzzatti's belief that "civil institutions" like the popular bank represented the key to Italy's future. Independently of their friend, they promoted a series of other associations as well: mutual aid societies and cooperatives, reading societies and agrarian associations, educational programs and business groups. Few of these men had as much experience as Luzzatti with the task of organizing new institutions; they could not have achieved in the Austrian-controlled Veneto what Luzzatti did in exile. Nevertheless, they had followed closely the progress made by Luzzatti and other Italian liberals, sharing information, devising model statutes and debating the details of each association's internal administration. By the time the liberation of the Veneto finally occurred, figures like Lampertico, Morpurgo, and Errera were just as eager as Luzzatti to begin forming associations.

In short, the excitement in Luzzatti's memoirs was real. What inspired it was a new understanding of Italy's "rebirth." After 1861, the goals and concerns of Italy's political leaders could no longer be reduced to the single issue of unification; now they included the institutional consolidation of the state, the codification of laws, the formation of local governments and, perhaps most challenging of all, the creation of a liberal civil society. Towards these practical ends, a lot more than heroic wars of liberation were required. This was essentially the point made by the Neapolitan liberal Pasquale Villari in his famous article, "Whose Fault Is It?," which appeared in the Milanese newspaper *Il Politecnico* in September 1866. Explanations for Italy's poor showing in the war against Austria, Villari insisted, must go beyond the mistakes made by a small group of generals or politicians.

Those who lay all the blame at the government's door must ask themselves whether local government is any better, whether private and public enterprise is doing all that we expect, whether industry, commerce and science have acquired from freedom and national unification the drive which might have been hoped.

... Every man of good will must therefore set his hand to a new war of internal conquest.

It had to be a war, Villari added, waged not with "political rhetoric" or a "magic elixir," but with "humility, good will and hard work."[6] The editors of the moderate *Giornale di Padova* echoed Villari's sentiments when they wrote:

Now truly the time has come to establish widely among us those institutions which elsewhere, having sprung up with liberty, are now its most solid guarantee.

... For this reason, over every popular meeting, over every tribunical harangue, over every bohemian verse here there will be a preference for the prosaic institution of mutual aid societies, popular banks, cooperatives and schools.[7]

This paradoxical rhetoric of institution-building – as prosaic yet urgent and patriotic – has been grievously overlooked by historians. On the one hand, scholars of the final period of Austrian rule in Venice (1859–66) have only recently begun to abandon a focus on militant patriots like Alberto Cavalletto, that is, on figures whose acts of resistance and subversion helped place the Venetian Risorgimento within a broader, heroic tradition.[8] On the other hand, this is not simply a Venetian or Italian problem. Institution-building is one of the defining features of nineteenth-century European history, yet the *culture* of institution-building – unlike, say, the culture of nationalism or revolution – has received relatively little attention from European historians. Long before the challenges of imperial rule and mass electorates led rulers to start "inventing traditions," European liberals found, but also created, countless opportunities to present the apparently sober and undramatic act of institution-building as a heroic enterprise. They celebrated the inauguration of insane asylums and orphanages, commemorated the founders of schools, prepared elaborate anniversary albums for banks, and put workers' associations on display at national and international exhibitions. This deceptively ordinary evidence of institutional celebration suggests that, all over nineteenth-century Europe, liberals aspired to turn prosaic initiatives into poetic events.

That Venetian liberals did this *during* their region's ongoing struggle for independence is especially interesting. At a time when the standard for heroic action was still set by surprise invasions and secret meetings, what could the proponents of a mutual aid society or popular bank possibly do to convince themselves, or others, that institution-building was exciting? First, as we shall see, faced with the Austrian government's restrictions on public freedom, they turned the creation of any new association into a *quest*, complete with obstacles and risks, strategies and deceptions. Second, they argued that this quest was part of a longer *history* of dramatic, even revolutionary change. Together, these two efforts resulted in a story not simply of progress but of epic achievement, an *institutional* mythology of battles won and destinies fulfilled.

The Generation of 1860

Before the summer of 1866, Venetian proponents of association had to live with Austrian government restrictions. Even well-connected moderates like Fedele Lampertico were not free to do as they pleased. Yes, in 1858 Lampertico won approval of a general mutual aid society of artisans in Vicenza. But in 1860 his request to open night schools for the association's members was denied, and when he went ahead with the project (under the cover of the city's prestigious Olympic Academy) the police launched a formal investigation of the group's activities. Fortunately, there were other, less risky ways to promote associations before 1866. One was to make them an object of study: to count and compare them, to trace their development over time and across regional and national boundaries, to review their statutes and regulations, but also to identify the limitations of existing institutions and assert the need for new ones.

In doctoral dissertations, statistical and historical journal articles, funeral orations, regional guidebooks, and works of political economy, not to mention countless private letters, Venetian liberals presented arguments rather than demands for the associations they desired. Thus, although it is true that Lampertico's practical experience as the leader of the Società Generale in Vicenza won him the admiration and envy of liberals throughout the region, the roughly fifty newspaper articles, essays, and books he published before 1866 tended to be works of scholarship. He explicitly documented the accomplishments of the Società Generale in a few brief articles for the local newspaper, *Il Berico*, and in a published report on the association's first year of operations; however, he also promoted the cause of popular association and education in a number of other, more general texts: in a 56-page pamphlet of his thoughts on the connection between poetry and political economy (1854); in the 330-page volume *Vicenza and Its Territory* (1861), which he and Jacopo Cabianca prepared for Cesare Cantù's *Grande Illustrazione del Lombardo Veneto* series; in the funeral commemoration of Valentino Pasini, which he delivered at Vicenza's Olympic Theater (1864); and in a review of publications on mutual aid societies in Italy (1865), to name just a few.[9]

Fedele Lampertico (1833–1906) was one of the oldest members of a generational cohort of Venetians who came of age in the late 1850s and early 1860s, and went on to become the most powerful politicians in the region after 1866. Others in this group included Luigi Luzzatti (1841–1927), a member of Parliament and the Senate and, briefly, prime minister during the Giolittian era; Emilio Morpurgo (1836–85), a respected member of Parliament and then rector of the University of Padua; Antonio Tolomei (1839–88), Padua's mayor in the early 1880s; Paolo Lioy (1836–1911), a popular nature writer and a member of Parliament and the Senate; Alberto Errera (1842–94), a teacher and author of several books on economics and statistics; and Enrico Castelnuovo (1839–1915), a popular novelist. Too young to have participated in the revolutions of 1848–49, these men became active public figures at a peculiar moment in Venetian history: from 1861 to 1866, they lived in a region that was ruled by the Austrian Empire but adjoined by a free and independent Kingdom of Italy. On their side of this new border, associations like Lampertico's Società Generale were severely restricted; on the other, Italian, side they were actively promoted. In this context, the study of associations seemed anything but academic; to learn and write about these institutions meant, among other things, preparing for the day *after* the Veneto was liberated, when men familiar with the workings of liberal society and government would be needed.[10]

For decades prior to 1861, Italians had used the ostensibly apolitical pursuits of science and erudition to give public expression to liberal and nationalist views. The much-celebrated congresses of Italian scientists, discussed in the previous chapter, are simply one of countless examples of this practice. Nevertheless, there is something extraordinary about the convergence of young Venetian liberals during the early 1860s on the topic of association. In 1859, Emilio Morpurgo completed his university thesis *The Proletariat and Mutual-Aid Societies*, and followed that up in

1863 with a related study entitled *Of Certain Questions Regarding Charity*. Also in 1863, Luigi Luzzatti defended and published his university thesis *The Circulation of Credit and Popular Banks*, and Paolo Lioy published the speech he gave at the awards ceremony for workers attending the Olympic Academy's free night schools in Vicenza. Early the following year in Venice, Alberto Errera gave his first public speech on the subject of "popular credit" at the Venetian Institute of Science, Letters and the Arts, and began working with Luigi Luzzatti to get a mutual aid society started in their native city. Back in Padua, in the summer of 1864, Antonio Tolomei began the first of many articles for the local newspaper, *Il Comune*, with a discussion of the need for savings banks and other popular associations in the countryside.[11] And in hundreds of letters that criss-crossed the region (and beyond), these same men kept track of each other's efforts, exchanging publications, documents, questions, and opinions. Lampertico, who not only wrote about mutual aid societies but ran one in Vicenza, was bombarded with letters. Morpurgo and Luzzatti begged him for "all those positive data" and documents that might help them build their own institutions.[12]

At the centre of this personal and epistolary network was the University of Padua. Practically every prominent figure in Venetian social, cultural, economic, and political life after 1866 had been, at one time or another, either a student or a professor at the university: the future prime minister from Venice, Luzzatti; the renowned poet and priest from Vicenza, Giacomo Zanella; the industrialist from Padua, Vincenzo Stefano Breda; the specialist in statistics from Villafranca, Messedaglia; the landowner from Treviso, Antonio Caccianiga. At a time when restrictions in print culture and travel made it difficult to establish regional ties, the University of Padua literally brought together students from every province in the Veneto and, beyond, from what would become known after unification as the "unredeemed" borderlands of Istria and Trent.[13] Just as important, thanks in large part to the mediation of respected professors like Zanella and Messedaglia, students from different cities who did not attend the university at the same time made the effort to get in touch with one another. That is how Emilio Morpurgo (a graduate in 1859), Luigi Luzzatti (a graduate in 1863), and Fedele Lampertico (a graduate in 1855) became friends.[14]

Long before the cohort of Lampertico, Morpurgo, Luzzatti, and friends came along, the University of Padua held a political place of first importance both in the concerned eyes of Austrian authorities and in the hearts and minds of Venetian liberals. Professors figured prominently among the founders and members of Padua's two most important associations during the Risorgimento, the Reading Room (f. 1830) and the Society for the Encouragement of Agriculture (f. 1842), and were also patrons of the city's main social centre, the Caffè Pedrocchi.[15] Several major clashes with Austrian authorities, including the one that triggered the Revolution of 1848 in Padua, not only involved students and professors, but began outside the main university building, the Palazzo del Bò. This fact was not lost on the Austrian government, which closed the University of Padua for two years after 1848 and removed several professors from their posts. Even in the best of times, Austrian authorities carefully reviewed course curricula and monitored what professors said inside and outside the classroom. In times of unrest, which included the final years of Austrian rule in the Veneto, the policing of university life became more extensive and draconian.[16] Writing about his time at the University of Padua during the early 1860s, Luzzatti recalled taking long walks with his mentor, Angelo Messedaglia, beyond the city gates. There, far from the Palazzo del Bò, they could discuss whatever they wanted without looking over their shoulders.[17]

What did Luzzatti and Messedaglia talk about during their long walks together? Was it the latest report from one of the "secret committees" working to prepare the liberation of the Veneto? Or plans for a new demonstration at the university? Not exactly, judging from the account Luzzatti provided in a long letter to Fedele Lampertico in the summer of 1862. "I talked about economics with him, and about science," Luzzatti began his letter, and one by one he described the topics they covered in conversation: Messedaglia's book on population ("he asked me frankly what my opinion of it was, and I frankly gave it to him"), agrarian credit and savings banks, English laws and liberties, and recent philological studies on Arianism.[18] Lampertico had finished his studies at the University of Padua before Messedaglia arrived in 1858, and was eager to know what the distinguished professor had to say to his favourite student, not to mention what kind of person he was. Unable to meet in person, or to see each other with any regularity, Venetians young and old depended on letters and third parties to make connections. This helps explain the peculiar, forced intimacy of many letters from the period: new friends often felt the need to describe themselves to each other with varying degrees of awkwardness and candour, and to overcome rumours, suspicions, and misunderstandings, sometimes with melodramatic statements of apology or self-justification. Thus, in his first letters to Luzzatti, written in the summer of 1863, Emilio Morpurgo states that "Yes, I believe that I am worthy of your friendship"; tentatively asks permission to share ideas and comments; expresses his disappointment with the formal tone Luzzatti used in a recent letter; admits to feeling depressed about the deterioration of his relationship with a mutual friend, Antonio Tolomei; asks Luzzatti to help him make the acquaintance of "Mr. Lampertico"; and conveys that he was hurt to learn so late (later than Tolomei, for example) that Luzzatti's wife was dangerously ill.[19]

It also helps explain why the study of associations was so exciting. Whether it was Angelo Messedaglia's view on savings banks or Fedele Lampertico's private collection of documents on mutual aid societies, the exchange and circulation of information before 1866 seemed to require concerted action. The main purpose of Morpurgo's first letter to Luzzatti in June 1863 was to ask a very specific favour: he and Messedaglia hoped that Luzzatti might be able to get his hands on statutes and statistical information pertaining to the Venetian Savings Bank, in particular regarding the effects that reforms may have had on the movement of capital deposits. To obtain this information, Luzzatti had to ask at least two friends in Venice for assistance. By the end of the month, we find a grateful Morpurgo passing on a new message from Messedaglia to Luzzatti: Fedele Lampertico is currently studying political economy manuals. Thus, a new sequence of letters and favours began.[20] To say, simply, that many Venetian liberals attended the University of Padua, or that Angelo Messedaglia was Luzzatti's professor and mentor, is to tell only a small part of the story. As an expert in statistics at a time when the collection and publication of statistical information was restricted, Messedaglia understood better than most just how difficult the study of mutual aid societies or savings banks was likely to be in the Veneto. Regular attendance of university classes and long walks with professors were fine, but extra-curricular and extra-local activities were indispensable. Even when school was not in session, the University of Padua was a sort of regional headquarters for Venetian liberalism, and Messedaglia was one of its commanders in chief.

For a dramatic rendering of the search for statistical information, consider Enrico Castelnuovo's response to the news of Alberto Errera's arrest in 1864. Accused of writing *La Vénétie en 1864*, an anti-Austrian pamphlet published in Paris, the twenty-two-year-old Errera was arrested in Venice and sentenced to six years in prison. In a letter to Fedele Lampertico, Errera's friend Castelnuovo explained that, at the time of his arrest, Errera had been working on a statistical study of the Veneto. Thus, in one terrible stroke Venetians lost both a patriot and a patriotic project, for, by gathering information on "those factories [*stabilimenti*], industries, and institutions which still honor our provinces," Castelnuovo wrote, Errera was helping to overcome a "general and deplorable ... ignorance of our own affairs." One of the success stories to be featured in Errera's study was Alessandro Rossi's woolworks in Schio, a small town in the province of Vicenza. Castelnuovo wanted to know: could Lampertico help him complete this one part of Errera's project by procuring information on Rossi's firm, "a sort of historical description of the firm, of its foundation, of its shop, of the workers employed there, of salaries, of mechanical methods, etc."? Lampertico had to inform Castelnuovo that Rossi's wool factories were already the subject of several published works, including a pair of articles that Lampertico himself had written for the Vicenza newspaper *Il Berico* in 1858–59. Embarrassed, Castelnuovo nevertheless recruited Lampertico's help, and a year later published a long article on the Rossi firm in the Venetian newspaper *L'Amico del Popolo*.[21] After all, his own ignorance was more proof of that "general and deplorable" communication gap that Errera had hoped to bridge. As if to confirm Castelnuovo's dramatic version of events, following his release from prison in 1866 Errera picked up where he had left off, publishing a string of historical and statistical studies of Venetian industry and associational life.[22]

Gathering information was not an inherently conspiratorial activity. The church collected statistics, as the era's remarkably detailed and comprehensive pastoral visitation records demonstrate.[23] Austrians collected statistics, too. The month before Castelnuovo wrote with news of Alberto Errera's unfinished study, Fedele Lampertico received a similar but less patriotic request for help from Casimiro Bosio, an administrator and newspaper director in Verona with close ties to the Imperial court in Vienna but also an impressive record of public works projects and publications. The leaders of the Agrarian Society in Vienna, to which, Bosio wrote, he belonged "by chance," had informed Bosio that the government was sending a certain Baron Babo to the Veneto to prepare a statistical study of wine production in the region, and had asked Bosio to put Babo in touch with the leading Venetian vineyard owners and vinegrowing specialists. Bosio had already turned to the Agrarian Academy and Chamber of Commerce in his own city of Verona, and to a leading professor of agriculture at the University of Padua, Antonio Keller. As "a large landowner, the President of the Olympic Academy, and a lover and scholar of statistical works," Bosio wrote, Lampertico seemed like the right man to approach in Vicenza. Baron Babo was a Prussian working for the Austrian government, not a Venetian working on behalf of a victim of Austrian oppression, but the procedural logic of Castelnuovo's and Bosio's requests was identical: in order to study conditions on an extra-local scale, one had to gain access to unfamiliar people, lands, factories, and institutions, and the only way to accomplish this was to enlist the help of influential, well-connected men – "local notables" – like Lampertico.

By the time this exchange of letters took place, in 1864, Venetian proponents of statistical and associational studies had not one but two governments in mind: the Austrian and the Italian. With the creation of a unified Italian kingdom in 1861 came the institution of a centralized statistical office (within the Ministry of Agriculture, Industry and Commerce), the first national census, and a series of other statistical projects aimed at locating, mapping, tabulating, and representing the new nation's population, resources, and institutions. Despite a limited budget, between 1861 and 1869 the government Directorate of Statistics sponsored sixty volumes' worth of investigations of commerce and industry, population, schools, charities, banks, mutual aid societies, and more. Statistical periodicals reprinted and publicized these findings, and conducted studies of their own.[24] For Venetian liberals, reading these reports must have been bittersweet. Stung by the Austrian government's rejection of their proposal to create a new mutual aid society in Venice, Luigi Luzzatti, Alberto Errera, and Enrico Castelnuovo could read that 209 new mutual aid societies had formed in Italy between 1860 and 1862. Nevertheless, they could take comfort in one fact: the urgency and excitement (and challenges) associated with investigating local social and economic conditions were something they *already* shared with the free citizens of Italy. After 1861, it became easier than ever to view the compilation of Venetian statistics as an act of preparation: not a cause for celebration, exactly – not yet – but not an isolated, academic exercise in fact-finding either. Soon enough, young men like Lampertico understood, it would be a representative of the liberal Italian government who wanted to learn about Venetian vine-growing, wool production, and savings deposits.

History Lessons

The *Annuario scientifico ed industriale* (Milan, 1865–69) was one of the many new yearbooks to publicize the Italian Directorate of Statistics' first statistical studies, and otherwise to chart the progress that Italian citizens and institutions had been making since unification. The first volume included a thirty-five-page chapter entitled "Institutions, Congresses, Exhibitions, [and] Competitions," which began with a brief historical profile of the Istituto Lombardo. In two pages, the editors of the yearbook traced the Milanese academy's development, from its first incarnation as the Austrian-sponsored Patriotic Society (f. 1776), through the "disturbances of the end of the century" and the series of changes (in name and structure) that followed under Napoleon, to a period of precipitous decline during the Restoration, limited revival in 1838, increased restriction after 1848, and, finally, "things having changed again in 1859" (!), reform and a new statute approved by the king of Italy in 1864. The six other "institutions" profiled by the yearbook did not include historical summaries. The Italian Agrarian Association, we learn, began as Piedmont's (and Cavour's) Agricultural Association in 1842, but the real story of this segment was the proliferation of new agricultural associations (*comizi agrari*) in a number of Italian provinces. Likewise, the program of free evening lectures in Turin, the Society for the Promotion of Agricultural Exhibitions, the Agricultural Society of Lombardy, the Alpine Club, and the Commercial Industrial Society of Turin were all featured because they were new. An occasional historical reference turns up in the following sections on "congresses" and "exhibitions," which reported, for example, on major centenary celebrations of Galileo and Dante, but here, too, the emphasis was on "firsts" (as in the First Congress of Italian Naturalists, held in Biella in 1864) – that is, on the present and the future, not the past. This was, after all, a yearbook: the point was to register the many things that were new in Italy's first years as a nation.[25]

Nevertheless, the historical profile of the Istituto Lombardo reminds us that institutions could tell stories. During the Risorgimento, these stories tended to be fairly general accounts of European progress and Italian backwardness. Newspapers featured several variations on this theme: the appearance of a new institution elsewhere in Europe provoked stark tales of Italian inertia or conservatism; the revival of activity within various Italian academies elicited praise but also critical questions about the archaic nature of these institutions; and, most common of all, the successful formation of a new institution in Italy inspired a brief historical survey of the institution's origins and development, which almost invariably paid tribute to English and French primacy before going on to chart Italy's modest but promising gains. Even long articles like Giovanni Tomasoni's three-part, thirty-four-page examination of savings banks, which appeared in Padua's *Giornale Euganeo* in 1845, provided little in the way of historical narration, other than some very general thoughts on "civilization," "progress," and "modern times," and instead featured pages of detailed statistical information. In this respect, pre-unification newspapers conveyed the same message as the first post-unification "yearbooks": Italy needed to *overcome* its recent history of institutional underdevelopment, and catch up with the rest of Europe.

In countless other ways, of course, historical consciousness had permeated the Italian Risorgimento. Giuseppe Verdi famously avoided censorship of his operas by staging *medieval* Italian struggles against foreign oppressors. The residents of Italian cities were prohibited from honouring recent or living "patriots," so they proposed erecting monuments to Dante, Columbus, Palladio, and Marco Polo instead. Scholars of Italian art and literature routinely employed the nationalist concept of "rebirth" (*risorgimento*) in their publications. But what role did institutions play in these symbolic and narrative representations of Italian patriotism and resurgence? Where might a reformed prison or a new agricultural association possibly fit in this swirl of epic tales?

These questions were answered by the Venetian generation of 1860. Fedele Lampertico, Luigi Luzzatti, Paolo Lioy, and Emilio Morpurgo, among others, spoke and wrote about institutions in a new way. Like many of the liberal writers and reformers of the 1840s, they drew statistical comparisons and offered general statements of encouragement and concern regarding the "spirit of association" in Italy. But they did something else, too: they produced elaborate histories of institutions, both by developing detailed historical profiles of specific institutions and by connecting the development of "modern" (liberal) institutions to the most dramatic events in European history. They told the members of mutual aid societies and popular banks the familiar story of recent progress, but they also talked about the strengths and weaknesses of medieval guilds and pawnshops, and about the meaning of 1789 and 1848.

Giacomo Zanella's speech to the members of Vicenza's Società Generale, in May 1862, began with a brief discussion of the benefits and costs of the French Revolution. On the one hand, the events of 1789 had been a necessary remedy to the ills of the old regime – to centuries of hoarded wealth, narrow privilege, and legal bondage. On the other hand, there was no denying that with these positive changes came unnecessary destruction and loss: religious orders dedicated to education and poor relief were destroyed; churches (including the newly restored Church of San Faustino in Vicenza, home to the Società Generale) were turned into barracks and warehouses; confraternities and guilds were abolished.

Revolutionaries eliminated guilds in order to obtain the worthy objective of free labour, but at what cost?

> Today the artisan is released from every tie and on his own; but without a store of knowledge [*cognizioni*] that would put him on guard against the splendid but disastrous doctrines of audacious innovators ... [B]ecause he possesses a generous heart and a robust arm, the artisan runs the risk of being caught up in the whirlwind of unjust dissatisfactions and excessive desires that torments the present generations.

The remainder of Zanella's speech fleshed out this story of imperfect progress, recounting the history of labour from the use of slavery in ancient Rome, through the period of craft guilds, to the modern era of free labour. In this grand historical scheme, the Società Generale represented the best of two institutional worlds: on the one hand, the freedom and independence of modern welfare institutions; on the other hand, the lost but now resurgent ties of brotherhood and religion characteristic of the guilds.[26]

Two years later, in a speech inaugurating the Popular Bank of Asola, a small town in Lombardy, Luigi Luzzatti provided a more unequivocally enthusiastic lesson in historical progress. He began by pointing out how often in recent European history it had been small towns like Asola, rather than large cities, which had taken the lead in creating new institutions. More than just a curious geographical fact or accident, the greatness of small towns was the stuff of legends, the urban analogue of that "obscure and solitary man who becomes the hero of the centuries." In fact, Luzzatti went on to explain, each century has had its own distinctive task or mission: the sixteenth century's "lot" was the Reformation, the seventeenth century "needed" to consolidate the changes and freedoms won in England and Holland, the eighteenth century "closed with the French Revolution, and eclipsed the past with its light." And the nineteenth century? Only five years had passed since Lombardy's successful war of independence against the Austrians, but Luzzatti refused to equate the greatness of his own century either with the "triumph of nationality" (a byproduct of political liberty, and thus of the French Revolution) or with war:

> Oh! No; war is understood to be immoral, today it is considered only a necessary means toward the end of a durable peace, reestablishing the equilibrium of peoples on the bases of liberty and brotherhood; today heroes

themselves deplore war! ... The task of the XIXth century is to destroy pauperism and for this reason it will be the most memorable century in history!

Luzzatti might have ended his history lesson there, and turned to the popular banks' specific welfare provisions; after all, it had been only sixteen years since Hermann Schulze-Delitzsch had created the first bank of this kind in Prussia. Instead, Luzzatti told his audience about the long and unfinished battle against ignorance begun by Galileo, Newton, and Voltaire; about "our fathers of '89," who reduced the "old edifice of the middle ages" to ruins; and about the proponents of the three main nineteenth-century "systems" for ending pauperism: the "reactionaries," the "socialists," and the "liberal economists." Finally, after a lengthy description of the superior third system, that of the "young school" of liberal economists, Luzzatti entered into a detailed discussion of the popular banks themselves, including the recent history of their emergence in Germany.[27] Given that Asola was only the third city in Italy to create a popular bank, it is not surprising that Luzzatti took the opportunity to make this inaugural event seem historic. What is interesting is his concern to make it *historical*, to place it in a longer historical narrative of struggle and triumph.

As Zanella's and Luzzatti's speeches attest, the institutional histories Venetians recounted could be surprisingly different. Which institutions were progressive and which were antiquated? What impact (positive or negative) did the French Revolution or the revolutions of 1848 have on various institutions? Did the advent of "modern" institutions imply a decline in the role of the church or religion in public life? On the whole, the Venetian clergy took a defiant stance: the French Revolution had been a disaster and the campaign against religious corporations was offensive.[28] Nevertheless, an influential group of reformers earned the label "liberal Catholic" by submitting even the most radical religious ideas (freedom of conscience, the popular election of priests, the termination of the church's temporal power) to serious reflection and debate.[29] Venetian liberals sometimes disagreed with each other on key issues, as Lampertico and Luzzatti clearly did on religion; more often, however, they produced slightly different visions of history because they could; that is, they took advantage of the considerable freedom historical narration allowed to suit very specific circumstances and needs: to project ideological views, yes, but also to reflect subtle differences in local political culture. In short, what counted as progressive, modern, or heroic was variable; the determination to "make" history – that is, to infuse their own associational activities with a sense of historical purpose – was the only constant.

In Vicenza, Fedele Lampertico and Paolo Lioy organized their histories of the Risorgimento around two very different institutions, the Olympic Academy and the Società Generale. Everyone in the region recognized the novelty and importance of Vicenza's mutual aid society of artisans, but how exactly was the city's exclusive, three-hundred-year-old academy a centre of progressive or heroic action? By the middle of the nineteenth century, academies had more detractors than admirers in Italy. In the 1840s, newspapers frequently employed a bemused or sardonic tone when reporting on academies; that certain academies managed to do more than sponsor ponderous speeches on arcane topics or throw gala parties for the local nobility was noteworthy, but it did not change the fact that academies represented an old, and perhaps outdated, model of sociability – more old-regime officer corps than revolutionary militia. In letters to Lampertico and other friends, Luzzatti railed against academies, which he likened to "pontificates" of "scientific feudalism," places of intellectual boredom and "nonsense."[30] Lampertico and Lioy's response to such criticism was to call the Olympic Academy a "hardly academic academy," a purveyor of useful, not arcane, knowledge and a truly public institution, where noblemen rubbed shoulders with artisans.[31]

Lampertico did not believe that the Olympic Academy had to reject its past in order to become modern. On the contrary, he pointed out that the men who revived the Olympic Academy in the 1840s were actually resuming the useful work begun by local elites back in the 1760s. Vicenza's Agrarian Academy (f. 1768) had promoted improvements in crop cultivation, created a model garden (which Arthur Young admired during a visit in 1787), and held regular meetings. Artisans had not been invited to these gatherings, but noblemen, bourgeois, and clergy all took part. "In the middle of the old regime," Lampertico wrote, "privileges and class distinctions disappeared almost without anyone noticing." If Vicenza had a great revolution, it was not the "consternation" of 1789 but rather the local revolution of 1848, which brought local noblemen, bourgeois, priests, and the people together on the field of battle.[32]

Unlike his mentor and compatriot Giacomo Zanella, Lampertico did not extend his appreciation of the old regime so far as to mourn the disappearance of guilds. In a paper on mutual aid societies that he presented in 1865 to the members of an academy in Venice, Lampertico acknowledged the connection between the "old arts and crafts guilds" and mutual aid societies, adding, "one can never be displeased that the new societies have traditions [memorie di casa]." But he also recognized the novelty of the mutual aid society: "for new times new forms," he wrote,

"and mutual aid societies as they are at present have their own characteristics." In England, he noted, the "love of genealogy" led the founders
of associations to give their new creations ancient or medieval names like
the Society of Druids or the Knight's Templar. Far from recommending
this practice, Lampertico advised paying attention to the "more recent
history" of mutual aid societies in Italy, for example, the studies presented in the 1840s at the congresses of Italian scientists and in the pages
of newspapers like the *Rivista Europea*. In contrast to his speeches and
writings on the Olympic Academy, the only history of mutual aid societies Lampertico seemed to care about was modern history.[33]

What exactly did Lampertico mean by "new times" and "new forms"
of association? Clearly, he did not equate "new" with "secular." Religion, he wrote, should not be used to oblige or exclude potential members of a mutual aid society, but nor should it be shunned altogether.
From its foundation in 1858 until 1911, Lampertico's own Società
Generale in Vicenza plainly identified itself, in Article 1 of its statute, as
a "Christian brotherhood," and maintained the tradition of holding annual patron saint's day celebrations in a restored church, complete with
"sacred speeches" by members of the local clergy.[34] Nor did he mean to
equate "new" with "democratic." Both in his general writings on mutual aid societies and over the course of his thirty-year tenure as president of Vicenza's Società Generale, Lampertico consistently defended
the practice of dividing members into two categories, "honorary" and
"ordinary," and of using the wealth (and wisdom) of the former to
support the welfare of the latter. Such assistance, he argued, was not
"alms" (*limosina*) but a modern form of "charity" (*carità*) informed
by "science." In short, new times demanded that two very established
local groups – the clergy and the aristocracy – continue to play leading
roles in public life.

Elsewhere in the Veneto, liberals of Lampertico's generation drew a
sharper, more dramatic line between the old and the new. Luigi Luzzatti
was one of several Venetians to use the metaphor of ruins when speaking
of medieval institutions; to question the place of religion in associational
life; to refer to the French Revolution as a positive turning point in European history; and to promise the advent of democracy and equality in
workers' associations. Never mind that the church's vast network of institutions for the poor and needy continued to shape public life (and defy
major government reform efforts) long after unification. It is substitution, not continuity, that informs most Venetian histories of institutional
change. The era of confraternities and guilds was over, the workers who

joined a mutual aid society or popular bank no longer needed to go to hospitals or pawnshops for assistance.[35]

The novelty of large, general mutual aid societies – as opposed to trade organizations (of just carpenters, say, or hatters) – made it easier for men like Lampertico and Luzzatti to find common ground. The Società Generale might meet in a church and celebrate Saint Joseph, but it brought together most of Vicenza's artisans into one, efficiently run association. Lampertico founded the Società Generale just ten years after the first general association of artisans in Italy appeared in the Piedmontese town of Pinerolo; after unification, scores of organizers and workers in cities throughout Italy followed suit, creating general mutual aid societies in Florence and Naples (1860), Perugia (1861), Taranto and Macerata (1862), Modena (1863), Fermo (1864), and many more cities and towns, large and small. Some of these associations were run by Mazzinian democrats, others by moderate liberals, and others still by a mix of the two groups. But they all tended to equate the concentration of workers in larger, united organizations with meaningful progress and change.

Making the case for novelty was easy enough. The challenge lay in giving stories of institutional change the narrative depth and excitement associated with historical writing. A striking example of how Venetian liberals met this challenge is Luzzatti's writings and speeches on popular banks. Luzzatti first began to promote these banks in Italy in 1863, only fifteen years after Hermann Schulze-Delitzsch created the first one of its kind in Prussia. A certain amount of drama derived naturally from the opposition Luzzatti and his "German" banks received, above all from Vincenzo Boldrini and Gian Giacomo Alvisi, the main proponents of other banks. Why, Boldrini asked, should Italy look to feudal, reactionary Prussia for institutional models? Why not adopt instead the type of credit associations emerging in France, a nation much closer to Italy in terms of political culture and historical development? Luzzatti answered these questions with a lesson in comparative history, centred around the European revolutions of 1848.

In essence, it was a tale of two countries, France and Germany, and of two very different institutional "daughters of revolution," Pierre-Joseph Proudhon's Banque du Peuple and Schulze-Delitzsch's Volksbanken: the one a failure characteristic of the larger shortcomings of utopian socialism, the other a liberal success made even greater by the fact that it came in the face of socialist and government opposition in Germany. Whereas the "splendid promises" made by French socialists in 1848 quickly (and inexorably) ended in disappointment, the "effective remedies" developed by Schulze-Delitzsch triumphed. Placing himself at the head of "a small formation of liberals," Schulze-Delitzsch went from town to town in Prussia, tirelessly promoting the idea of popular credit. Mocked, opposed, and ignored along the way, his popular banks thrived and spread, first in Germany – "in Protestant and Catholic towns, in the noisiest industrial centers as in the remotest and poorest locales" – and then in France, England, Holland, "even distant Russia and Egypt." In the history of European liberalism, Luzzatti suggested, 1848 *was* a major turning point: thanks to the leadership of "heroes" like Schulze-Delitzsch, a new generation of liberals found inspiration in the conflicts and defeats of 1848. Both the dangerous failures of the French socialists and the unexpected success of courageous men like Schulze-Delitzsch sent a clear message: in order to win the battle against pauperism, liberals needed to take immediate action. In Luzzatti's mind, this meant creating new institutions.[36]

Social Battles

It is interesting to consider Luzzatti's call to action, and his vocabulary of heroism more generally, in light of the standard view of liberal retrenchment and compromise following the revolutions of 1848–49. To the extent that we associate "action" with developments in Italy during the 1850s, it is the failed campaign of insurrection waged by Mazzini's Action Party that comes to mind. The triumph of moderate Cavourian liberalism, we usually read, was not the result of dramatic public action, but of strategic political and diplomatic alliances worked out behind the scenes. The term "revolution" itself lost favour among moderate liberals, tainted not just by the unsuccessful outcome of events in 1848–49, but also by the spectre of violent class warfare. And a significant number of disillusioned republicans and democrats converted to the practical, if somewhat disagreeable, idea that the primary political objective of Italian unification could only be achieved under the leadership of moderate and monarchical Piedmont. Suffice it to say that Luzzatti's account of an inspired and proactive – indeed, breathless – liberal response to the *social* lessons of defeat in 1848–49 has not made it into many history books.

New cultural histories of "invented traditions," "realms of memory," and even of the myth of the Risorgimento have also failed, by and large, to make room for heroic bankers and academicians. Kings and battles, national flags and celebrations, Verdi and Dante were all undeniably central to the construction of Italian national identity before and after

unification. But they also tend to obscure the variety of mythologies surrounding Italy's rebirth. Consider the tributes given to a pair of Piedmontese officials in Bologna in the early 1860s, as recounted by Steven
Hughes in his study *Crime, Disorder and the Risorgimento*. The two
men, Pietro Magenta and Felice Pinna, who both began their appointments in Bologna in October 1861, were credited with exposing a sinis-
ter Bolognese "association of criminals" that dated back to the time of
the revolution of 1848–49. When Magenta died in a carriage accident in
1863, Bologna's town council voted to build a monument to this man
who, they wrote, "in a short period of time revitalized public administration and resurrected that security of property and people that for so
long we had lamented as lost." Magenta's tombstone in Bologna's cem-
etery put it more bluntly: he had "rendered the city safe from swarms of
scoundrels." As for Pinna, he received a commemorative album thanking
him for "dispersing the many criminals" who had "infested" the city.[37] I
suspect that this is just the tip of the iceberg, that if we look for unconventional heroes and myths of the Risorgimento we will find them by
the dozens. Furthermore, I would be surprised if a significant number of
these forgotten claims on local and national memory did not share a concern with institutions.[38]

Claims of any kind are rarely innocent of power, and this is certainly
true of the institutional narratives we have been examining. By celebrating the revitalization of the Olympic Academy in Vicenza or the spread
of popular banks in Europe, Fedele Lampertico and Luigi Luzzatti were
also demonstrating their own fitness to join Liberal Italy's emerging ruling elite. However, this does not fully explain their commitment to making claims that were *historical* and *heroic*. Writing in the early 1860s,
when Italian independence had already been achieved and the rulers of
Italy were busy extending and consolidating the new nation's institutions
of government, Venetian liberals could have praised and promoted associations in much simpler – more sober and journalistic – terms. While ac-
knowledging the need still to liberate Venice and Rome, they could have
drawn attention to the equally urgent task of governing and reforming
the Italy that already existed. In the new age of prosaic state-building,
the political future of civic leaders like Lampertico and Luzzatti seemed
secure.

And yet these authors of statistical studies and institutional histories
wanted something more: namely, to place themselves within the heroic
tradition of the Risorgimento. As might be expected, when the Veneto
was liberated in the summer of 1866 there was a rush to determine

(and debate) who the leading patriots in the region had been. Had Lampertico and Luzzatti begun constructing their accounts of the Olympic Academy and the popular banks at this time – at the eleventh hour, so to speak – we could simply chalk their dramatic claims up to political opportunism. But in fact they did not wait until 1866 to make institution-building seem heroic. To read their private as well as public writings, the years 1862, 1863, 1864, and 1865 were also a time of bold, historic action.

"Bold" is not a word one naturally arrives at to describe Fedele Lampertico, but there is no mistaking the excitement he felt on the occasion of the first awards ceremony for Vicenza's night school students, in 1862. In a letter he wrote shortly after the event to Luzzatti, Lampertico conveyed not only the emotions stirred by Paolo Lioy's speech that evening, but the delight that came from transgressing the sacred space of the Olympic Academy's historic Palladian theatre:

The Olympic Theater, reserved at one time to sumptuous displays, was opened Sunday to honor the commoners [*popolani*] who have attended the school of reading, writing, and accounting. Woe to us if the ghosts of the old academicians had been reawakened at this point.[39]

Prior educational initiatives in the Veneto had never culminated in an *event* of this type, and more than Lioy's words it was the act of gathering together "the various orders of citizens" that thrilled liberals elsewhere in the region. In a series of letters to Lampertico, even Giacomo Zanella found himself excitedly charting the ripple effect that "opening the banquet of science to the children of the people" was having in Padua and Venice. "God and the fatherland," Zanella wrote Lampertico, "will reward you for this."[40]

In exile after 1863, Luzzatti found himself at the centre of one inspiring event after another, an experience made even more exciting by the fact that he had to compete (with Vincenzo Boldrini, among others) for the public's support. By the spring of 1865, in letters to his friend Antonio Tolomei in Padua, Luzzatti seemed, like the Prussian Schulze-Delitzsch before him, breathless.

21 March. Now for four days I have to leave Milan to open banks in Cremona, Castiglione, Bergamo; it is an immense effort this, which I took upon myself! At the beginning of May in Turin we have the congress of Italian popular banks; and you can imagine how hard those days are going to be

for me. Boldrini will return to propose his theories and I will have to be in the breach again to defend [the principle of] mutuality.

28 March. Everywhere the doctrinaires have been defeated in the breach; everywhere one returns to meditate on this simple, but always forgotten truth: that revolutions are not made by four fat bourgeois, but by all people. Communism is a lie, but the doctrine of the fat bourgeois is an even worse lie. – Now that things are going well some people accuse me of being in a hurry ... as if one could ever do what is good in too much of a hurry!

19 April. I am writing to you from Asola, where I have spent the Easter holidays, rekindling in these nearby lands the faith in cooperative associations. In this manner I, too, celebrated Easter! Everywhere I received delighted welcomes and my word was accepted with much favor. In Castiglione dello Stiviere, not the least of the Lombard hamlets for its spirit of brotherhood and solidarity, after my speech the commoners [*popolani*] rushed to sign up and in this way the bank was constituted in an instant. Tomorrow I'll go to Cremona for the same reason.[41]

The heroic nature of the movement to create civil institutions in Italy during the early 1860s is a theme to which Luzzatti returns, again and again, in his memoirs. Of his first tour of Lombardy, in the fall of 1864 – "the most pure and beautiful days of my life" – Luzzatti writes, "every speech was an act, every act translated into an institution useful to the fatherland [*patria*]." Elsewhere, he refers to the local notables who assisted him in the foundation of Italy's first popular banks as "the forgotten names of heroic soldiers" in the "civil battles" of the period before unification; and to the "Garibaldian audacity" with which he and these other men founded popular institutions. "All of us," Luzzatti writes, "in the ardor of our patriotism, felt the duty of achieving, with the economic redemption of the workers, the political redemption of the fatherland."[42] Luzzatti composed his memoirs in the 1920s, long after the "pure and beautiful days" of the early 1860s had passed and gone. Looking back, Luzzatti took every opportunity to put a heroic, or at least patriotic, spin on his activities during the last phase of the Venetian Risorgimento. To do so meant redefining the Risorgimento in terms of social or civil, as opposed to military, battles. After all, the heroes and veterans of Italy's wars of independence had never suffered from neglect. Could the same be said of a figure such as Tiziano Zalli, who worked with Luzzatti to create Italy's first popular bank in Lodi? Zalli, Luzzatti wrote in his memoirs, belonged to those modest and strong ensigns of democracy and of the public good who returned from battle, tranquil heroes, with the conscience of a duty accomplished, to work in the fields, in industries; a strange contrast with the throngs of clamorous apostles and rewarded martyrs, swarming, all the more as we moved away from the mystical origins of our Risorgimento, before reaching the renewed heroisms of the latest war of redemption [i.e., World War I]. His advice, neglected and precious, contributed to improving many institutions and laws of a social nature and, without being a [parliamentary] deputy, he performed the duties of a provident legislator.[43]

Writing in the 1920s, with the memory of the First World War and the fascist cult of the war veteran fresh in his mind, Luzzatti was no doubt too inclined to find "heroes," "soldiers," and "veterans" in the remote pages of his own, civilian history. Nevertheless, it is important to keep in mind that he began his effort to redefine the Risorgimento long before he wrote his memoirs. In 1884, while monuments to Victor Emmanuel II (d. 1878) and Giuseppe Garibaldi (d. 1882) were springing up all over Italy, Luzzatti paid public tribute to a different kind of hero in his eulogy for the parliamentary deputy and minister Quintino Sella:

One person sacrificed himself on the gallows, some other gave his life in order to restore, with [sound] finances, the honor of the nation; and in different ways all of them died piously.[44]

Twelve years earlier, for the Italian translation of a book on popular banking by Hermann Schulze-Delitzsch, Luzzatti had gone so far as to compare this Prussian magistrate to a conquering Roman hero:

[In his book on popular banks] Schulze describes his world, narrates what he did, and just as Caesar recounted his battles in the pages of the Gallic war, so the illustrious German registers in this book the history of his social battles, which did not cost humanity a sole drop of blood.[45]

In fact, as we have seen, Luzzatti's heroic view of institution-building dates back to his earliest years as a public figure, that is, to the period of his own "social battles" in Lombardy before 1866. And he was not alone.

Back in Padua, in the pages of the local newspaper, *Il Comune*, Antonio Tolomei echoed his friend Luzzatti's call to action. Where should one begin to address the problem of illiteracy in Italy, Tolomei asked his readers in January 1866. "Good God!," he responded, "from all sides," and with no delay.[46] By the spring of 1866, the thoughts of every Venetian turned to the region's impending war with Austria. "I set down to write about popular libraries," Tolomei wrote in May 1866, "and after the first period the pen stumbles, thoughts go off in a gallop, and I find my mind full of artillery noise, and wartime fanfares, much more than of limpid readings for the worker." But the subtext of Tolomei's remark was clear: as soon as the Austrians were defeated, attention would return to popular libraries, mutual aid societies, savings banks, and cooperatives, a group of institutions that already in 1864 Tolomei was calling the "new means" to Italy's Risorgimento.[47]

Fedele Lampertico's delight in 1862 at seeing commoners inside Vicenza's Olympic Theater, and thereby rankling the ghosts of the city's three-hundred-year-old academy, has led the historian Emilio Franzina to make an arresting observation: "I may be mistaken," Franzina writes, "but I almost detect the sound of a 'Jacobin' use of the Olympic Theater, in the move by which Lioy, Lampertico and the other notables [*maggiorenti*] opened the rooms of this aristocratic Palladian creation, in order to confirm ... the moderate revolution under whose banners all citizens, without distinction, would come together ... [yet] whose direction would be solidly in the hands of a wealthy and educated few."[48] Was there really anything revolutionary, let alone "Jacobin," about moderate liberals in Vicenza, or any other Venetian city during the Risorgimento? In so many respects, these men appear to be the very antithesis of a Danton or Robespierre: Lampertico struggled to *increase* the presence of the Catholic religion in public life; Morpurgo, among others, *opposed* the principle of political centralization advanced after 1861 by the new Italian government; and several of them, Luzzatti included, believed that the political club was the very *worst* kind of association. When the Veneto was liberated, moreover, few of them insisted on placing "new men" in public office, or otherwise punishing persons who either had been sympathetic to the Austrian government or had benefited in some way from Austrian policies and appointments. What kind of Jacobin credentials are these?[49]

And yet a range of different sources from this era suggest that Franzina is not mistaken. Lioy, Lampertico, Luzzatti, Morpurgo, and Tolomei did not dwell on putting new men in power, but they did speak of building a new society. In the 1830s and 1840s, liberal proponents of new associations had talked a great deal about the need for "encouragement" and "improvement"; by the 1860s, Venetian liberals were using a more ambitious and dynamic set of terms: they promised "regeneration," "redemption," even "revolution." The conjuncture of two institutional "battles" in the early 1860s encouraged Venetians to employ this rhetoric of daring novelty. In the Veneto, the ongoing struggle with Austrian authorities and restrictions transformed countless moderate, liberal initiatives into exciting "firsts": the first gathering of artisans and aristocrats in Vicenza's Olympic Theater, the first attempt at getting a modern mutual aid society of workers started in Venice, the first complete record of industrial statistics in the region, the first public lecture on the importance of savings banks. At the same time, in the Italian Kingdom, the difficult process of discovering and governing a historically divided society appeared to confirm what Venetian liberals had already begun to believe: namely, that the key to Italy's future lay in the creation and consolidation of a wide range of new civic institutions. As far as young Venetians like Fedele Lampertico and Luigi Luzzatti were concerned, there was nothing modest or prosaic about this task; on the contrary, it was urgent, dramatic, patriotic, even legendary.

3

A New Public

Throughout the summer and fall of 1866, countless journalists, political hopefuls, and leading citizens proclaimed the beginning of a new era of freedom and progress in the Veneto. Again and again, they contrasted life as it had been under the Austrians with the life of liberty promised by the Italian state. In September, the industrialist Alessandro Rossi told an assembly of notables and officials from the province of Vicenza: "we have just emerged from a tomb of silence, when the best minds of the country covered their faces, and in many inertia and apathy were adopted out of desperation, and in everyone a rage against foreign oppression burned."[1] A month later, a spokesman for the Popular Circle of Padua, the first political association to form in the city after unification, assured those who were "new to liberty" that it was now possible to participate sincerely in public life.[2] Observers celebrated the proliferation of newspapers and associations, the advent of free elections, even the act of meeting and speaking freely in public. In early October a newspaper in Vicenza noted that an evening lecture on Italian history at the city's Olympic Theater constituted "a new custom for us, so unfamiliar with public life."[3]

What did it mean to say that public life was new and unfamiliar? Leaving aside the world of markets, fairs, festivals, taverns and churches, to name just a few traditional sites of public encounter, something resembling what Jurgen Habermas termed the "bourgeois public sphere" had begun to take shape in the Veneto, as elsewhere in Italy, well before unification.[4] As we saw in the previous two chapters, during the Risorgimento most Venetian cities had at least a handful of associations: a cultural academy, a social club, a reading room, and perhaps three or four other associations as well. Moreover, in a variety of settings – in associations, in the pages of newspapers and periodicals, and at events like the annual congresses of Italian scientists – a critical "public opinion" gathered enough strength to fuel the fires of revolution in 1848 and, later, to convince statesmen throughout Europe that Tuscans, Sicilians, Venetians, and Romans wanted to be part of a united Italy. Nevertheless, there were definite limits to' this public sphere. In the Lombard-Veneto kingdom, the Austrian government subjected associations and newspapers to tight controls. For years on end, residents of provincial cities like Padua and Vicenza could only turn for information to the official newspaper of the Austrian government, the *Gazzetta privilegiata di Venezia*; and the few independent, liberal newspapers that formed generally led short and precarious lives. Generally speaking, during the Risorgimento the word "public" signified, first and foremost, the legal and institutional authority of the Austrian government and, second, the spaces and locations within a city where the arm of this official authority had the greatest difficulty reaching or maintaining control, such as cafes, theatres, piazzas, and streets: zones of discreet sociability and political rebellion, but not of freedom – in short, a kind of negative public sphere. Filling this void became the self-styled heroic mission of a cohort of young Venetian liberals during the final years of Austrian rule.

Although at times between 1814 and 1866 the Austrian government had eased some of its restrictions on public life, the situation *did* change radically in 1866. To the handful of associations and the even smaller number of newspapers that carried over from the period of Austrian rule, dozens were added in the first few years after unification: political associations, popular libraries, horse-racing clubs, consumer cooperatives, veterans' associations, and societies for the production of wine, the collection of fertilizer, and the cultivation of silkworms. Countless Venetian writers and commentators equated unification with the triumph of liberty and progress and, not coincidentally, also with the start of a long-awaited age of association.

If there was plenty of cause for celebration in the summer and fall of 1866, however, there was also reason for concern. Many of the journalists and politicians who decried the tyranny of Austrian rule also noted the potentially damaging effects of this experience on the population. After years of silence, inertia, apathy, and isolation, how well could Venetians possibly understand the rules of citizenship and public life? The Popular Circle of Padua speculated that citizens would be uncertain about how to vote. Other commentators were more pointed. In Vicenza, a newspaper writer made it clear that the bad habits acquired under the Austrians – the "idle cafe gossip," "personal denigrations," "family battles," and "petty debates" – had not simply gone away with the enemy. Another spoke in even darker, more anxious terms about the challenges that lay ahead. It was necessary, he wrote,

> to restore strength to this society, to redeem it from the poverty, the vices, the prejudices, the errors which in long years of servitude may have infested it.

This meant understanding that "a bad tree cannot bear good fruit":

> that where there is ignorance, poverty, deficiency, moral disenchantment, and civil neglect, to look for strength, prosperity [and] progress is to ask for bitter disappointment.[5]

But perhaps the most suggestive of these statements was also the simplest: in 1866, Venetians were "unfamiliar with public life." Whatever progress had been made during the Risorgimento to build new public *institutions*, Venetians still lacked the public *habits* of free speech and enterprise. Would Venetians prove to be just as civic as Tocqueville's Americans, immune to the pressures of family and state, committed to the idea of a free and independent public sphere? This crucial question, and the profound doubt that inspired it, appeared to weigh heavily on the minds of the Veneto's first generation of post-unification leaders. These men did not expect a liberal public culture to form, miraculously, as soon as the Austrians departed. Rather, they assumed that this new and unfamiliar culture would need to be introduced, promoted, organized, and displayed. The local and national elections held in the fall of 1866 helped determine who, exactly, would take the lead in fashioning a new public culture in the Veneto: moderate liberals – a group that included older, aristocratic landowners like Count Andrea Cittadella Vigodarzere of Padua as well as the young proponents of new associations featured in the previous chapter – triumphed in these first elections and went on to dominate political life in the Veneto for the next thirty years. As we shall see, however, rival groups of progressive liberals promoted similar ideals of public life. In short, it is possible to speak in general terms of a distinctly liberal conception of public culture and cultural transformation in Venice.

How did Venetian liberals envision this process of cultural transformation? The answer to this question is surprising, both in light of an older set of assumptions derived from liberal political theory, and in light of

more recent scholarship on the cult of nationalism in Italy.[6] First, Venetian liberals were not simply slow but positively reluctant to draw a sharp
line between private and public interests. In their minds, the private possessions and personal authority of local notables were not something to
be excluded or erased from public life, like an embarrassing vestige of
feudal lordship, but rather should be regarded as positive, even exemplary resources that made the creation of a new public culture possible
in an impoverished land. Second, Venetian liberals demonstrated little
faith in the voluntary process of civic action admired by Tocqueville and
many other nineteenth-century liberals. They developed a remarkably
strict and procedural model of associational life, at the centre of which
stood not the free, voluntary, and individual act of joining (or leaving)
an association, but the orderly associational meeting, an event defined
by a series of detailed statutory rules and regulations, yet also capable of
providing a lively, ritualized show of liberal governance, of wise leaders
observing the "order of the day" and receiving, in turn, the assembled
members' support and respect. Third, before the late 1870s and early
1880s, Venetian liberals showed relatively little interest in promoting an
explicitly nationalist public culture. Newspapers practically ignored national holidays while celebrating a series of other, more sober events: a
scientific meeting, a funeral, a local agricultural exhibition. In the first
decade after unification, making liberals was simply more important than
making Italians.

Elitism – a term often used to describe nineteenth-century Italy's political culture – does not sufficiently explain this curious mixture of anxi-
eties, precautions, and enthusiasms. While it is true that Italian liberals
showed little tolerance for large, impromptu demonstrations in streets
and squares, in other contexts they actively encouraged participation in
public events. Indeed, what seem like peculiar features of Venice's public culture – the centrality of private resources and personal status, the
attention to authority and procedure – were viewed by the founders of
museums and associations and the organizers of exhibitions as positive,
enabling conditions: they served to widen, not narrow, the social bases
of public life, by providing even the most uneducated or inexperienced
groups – artisans, peasants, even women – with a clear model of orderly
and productive public behaviour. Rules of inclusion, of course, also function as rules of exclusion. In practice, codes of "reasonable" public behaviour are not universal and self-evident but authoritative, and thus
subject to more or less subtle forms of discrimination, not to mention
condescension. Far from from being a measure of Italian exceptionalism,

however, such attention by propertied, educated men to the construction of new relations of authority was the very definition of nineteenth-century European liberalism – liberalism understood, as Colin Gordon (following Michel Foucault) writes, "not simply as a doctrine, or set of doctrines, of political and economic theory, but as a style of thinking quintessentially concerned with the art of governing."[7]

Exemplary Ownership

Although it may be no more than a shadow of its former self, the bourgeois public sphere of eighteenth- and nineteenth-century Europe is still with us today.[8] Indeed, many of the institutions and spaces that continue to shape our understanding of public culture – museums, libraries, gardens, parks, and zoos – first became public during the years 1750–1850. A handful of public museums existed in sixteenth- and seventeenth-century Italy, it is true, but they were exceptional. Far more common were the private art galleries or "cabinets of curiosities" to which only a fortunate and well-connected group of royal patrons, noblemen, and scholars had access. By the middle of the nineteenth century, the reverse was true. France's first public museum, the Luxembourg Gallery, was created in 1750. Three years later, the British Museum was opened. And between the 1770s and the 1830s, these large, national institutions were joined by dozens of smaller, provincial museums. At about the same time, animals and books also began to make their way into the public domain, as zoological gardens replaced the private menageries of kings and princes and public libraries grew in size and number. Everywhere in Europe, the goal of making culture public resulted in the transformation of existing institutions, buildings, and spaces and the creation of new ones.[9]

Among the new institutions was the association. Eighteenth-century assembly rooms and race meetings, for example, emerged out of the need for larger or more suitable spaces than most private houses could provide for public entertainment. In the one case, the goal was to construct a building or rooms where local elites could gather for plays, concerts, or lectures. In the other case, it was to prepare the grounds and stands needed for horse races, a task made increasingly difficult by the changes in land use associated with the enclosure movement.[10] As important as associations were to the growth of public entertainment, their impact was even greater in the field of education and print culture. The reading rooms that spread throughout much of Europe in the late eighteenth and early nineteenth centuries made large collections of books and periodicals available to their members for an annual fee. Although the first reading rooms in Italy resembled little more than extensions – literally, warehouses – of a few print shops and bookstores, in effect they functioned as an early form of public library. By the early nineteenth century, they were among the most important cultural institutions in Italy.[11] Agrarian associations and "encouragement societies," meanwhile, formed collections of their own, consisting of the latest agricultural tools and machines, and loaned them out on a rotating basis to local landowners. In these, as in so many other nineteenth-century associations, the principal goal was the "diffusion" of knowledge.

The expansive goals and effects of these new public institutions make it easy to ignore a basic fact: well into the nineteenth century, public culture in Europe continued to revolve around the private possessions and personal authority of a small social and cultural elite. Art lovers and amateur scientists routinely found what they were looking for in private homes and gardens rather than public museums. Patrons of the arts, sciences, and civic life continued to make their presence felt within public institutions, not simply as faceless benefactors but as prominent, exemplary men and women. Celebrating specific individuals in this way would seem to contradict the egalitarian ideal of association. After all, it is one thing to encounter a donor's name under a painting or inside a book jacket, quite another to find associations disposed to pay personal tributes. Was it not true that the association – the word itself – promised to fuse private individuals into a collective public body? Too often, in fact, this unitary and fraternal image of associational life has led historians to ignore the role that individual leaders and patrons play within associations, and thus also to ignore the variety of ways in which leadership could be expressed, including surprisingly ostentatious shows of wealth and privilege, as well as bold calls to social and cultural action.

Let us begin with possessions, and the private sources of public culture, as they appear in city guidebooks published during the Risorgimento. Among the interesting features of these volumes is the large amount of space dedicated to the collections of art, literature, historical documents, and artefacts found in the private homes of Padua's elite families. For example, the section on private homes in Giannantonio Moschini's *Guide to the city of Padua for the friend of the arts*, published in 1817, occupies twenty-two of the seventy-eight pages reserved for the city's "profane" places of interest.[12] In it we learn that the De Lazara family "has a large room filled with various paintings," including works by Padovanino and Tintoretto, as well as a group of interesting sculptures and an impressive library of art books. Also, the residence of the "very courteous lawyer" Antonio Piazza had an important collection of books and manuscripts relating to the history of Padua, while the home of the noble Da Rio family featured a gallery of paintings, a library, a collection of fossils, and a cabinet of items illustrating the lithology of the nearby Euganean hills.

Twenty-five years later, a new guide to Padua included chapters on the countryside surrounding the city, giving the authors an opportunity to describe the villas and gardens belonging to the area's leading aristocratic families. Count Andrea Cittadella Vigodarzere, author of the 1842 guide's section on the Euganean hills outside of Padua, invited the reader "to climb the gently sloping hill" and visit "the hospitable abode of the counts Papafava de' Carraresi." And Giovanni Cittadella, in turn, described the "pleasures" of Andrea Cittadella Vigodarzere's villa and garden at Saonara.[13] The same is true of an exhibition catalogue published in Vicenza in 1855. A chapter on gardens by the noted local writer Jacopo Cabianca amounts to a lively tour of the privately owned palaces, villas, greenhouses, gardens, and grottoes scattered throughout the province.[14]

There are a number of possible explanations for this apparent confusion of private with public resources. First, it is a reflection of the fact that Padua, like so many other provincial cities in Europe at the time, did not have many public museums. The city's historic university possessed an impressive library and a museum of natural history, the first of its kind in the region when it was installed in 1734. Otherwise, Padua had no public museums or galleries to speak of. In fact, most of the places defined as public and profane in 1817 by Moschini were *exterior* surfaces rather than *interior* spaces: old or new buildings with interesting facades, a half-dozen piazzas, the old gates to the city.[15] Second, it was a convention of the time to open impressive private art galleries, libraries, and gardens to the public, at least on certain days of the week. In Padua, the Piazza and Treves de' Bonfili families effectively turned the property surrounding their homes into two of the city's largest public gardens. In return, grateful visitors recognized the owners' generosity and hospitality.[16] Third, Moschini no doubt assumed that his readers were members of that elite group of men and women who could afford to travel and "befriend" the arts, and thus might very well be capable of directly contacting and visiting the owners of Padua's most interesting private collections. Moschini did not explain how to go about making such arrangements, but he routinely invited the reader to "visit" and "see" the cultural riches found inside the city's most elegant and comfortable homes.[17]

Another explanation for the inclusion of private possessions in a public guidebook, however, has less to do with the limits of provincial Italy's public culture, and more to do with an assumption most Italian liberals of the time had regarding how best to *extend* that culture. They regarded men like Antonio Piazza and Girolamo Da Rio not as privileged and elitist owners of objects but as active and illustrious collectors, whose efforts benefited the wider public in a number of ways: by enhancing a city's cultural and scientific reputation; by preserving and organizing resources that might otherwise have deteriorated or disappeared; and, perhaps most important of all, by providing an example for others to follow. Surprisingly, this model of exemplary ownership – and, more generally, that of a fluid exchange between private and public culture – carried over into Italian associational life, too.

Associations generally did not benefit from the kind of large donations that filled public libraries and museums. Some did not bother with collections at all. Others sought only those objects whose novelty, utility, or size set them apart from the materials found in most private collections: a steam-powered threshing machine, for example, or the latest political newspaper from Paris. Nevertheless, the public culture of association emerged out of the same cultural and physical environment that produced the public museum and library, namely, the world of private homes and possessions, hospitality and display. Threshing machines, no less than Tintorettos or first-edition Dantes, belonged to individuals before they made their way into institutions, were symbols of scientific or cultural progress but also of personal wealth and status, and inspired associations to pay frequent tribute to the notables who acquired them and shared them with others.

The leaders of agrarian associations made a point of praising the estates of individual landowners in terms remarkably similar to those used in guidebooks to describe private museums, libraries, and gardens. Antonio Keller, a member of the Society for the Encouragement of Agriculture in Padua (f. 1846) and, later, president of the local Agrarian Association (f. 1869), reviewed the accomplishments of a select group of landowners in countless publications. To the members of Padua's academy of arts and sciences, he praised three individuals' efforts at land reclamation; to the Agrarian Association, he described the work done by three others to create and care for vineyards; and to the readers of the local periodical, *Il Raccoglitore*, he reported on a number of landowners' admirable projects, which ranged from the creation of a model farm to the acquisition of farm machinery. As was true of the art and book collectors found in city guidebooks, the landowners mentioned by Keller typically came from the wealthiest and most influential families in the region: the Treves family in Padua, the Papadopoli family in Venice, the Fogazzaro family in Vicenza. Agrarian associations and periodicals also addressed the needs of small landowners and peasants, but they took for granted that stories about elite members' machinery purchases and "continuous study and travels" would inspire everyone. When they reported on group excursions to the most impressive estates in the area, they noted the "vastness" and "comfort" of the surroundings; on a more regular basis, they announced certain members' generous offers to hold courses – for example, on silkworm or wine cultivation – in their own houses and villas.[18]

Associations in nineteenth-century Italy often met in private rather than public spaces. Comfortable, spacious rooms were hard to come by in most cities. Rather than constantly (and often vainly) appealing to the city government for permission to use a certain building, or waiting to purchase just the right property, associations made do. Between 1846 and 1875, the Society for the Encouragement of Agriculture in Padua changed locations no fewer than ten times and often turned to other institutions, including the city's university and reading room, for a place to meet. In Vicenza, several different associations pooled their resources to create a single reading room. Over time, and especially after unification, associations began to occupy more impressive public and civic spaces. In Vicenza, the Olympic Theater was the location of choice. There, against Palladio's famous *trompe l'oeil* background of a city in ancient Greece, different associations held meetings, lectures, and concerts. In Padua, a number of historic and centrally located municipal buildings vied with theatres as meeting places. On occasion, too, associations put their own stamp on civic architecture, as when the Popular Bank of Vicenza purchased the sixteenth-century Palazzo Thiene (another design of Palladio's), and proceeded to hire a painter to add a frieze and three frescoes depicting the history of labour, commerce, and scientific progress. Nevertheless, far more common were those associations that went on holding meetings in members' private homes.[19]

Nor was the use associations made of private space simply functional. Often, it reflected that celebration of elite hospitality which was a recurring theme in guidebooks. No association showed a greater appreciation for individual acts of hospitality than the Vicenza branch of the Italian Alpine Club, a national organization of hiking enthusiasts. The attractions of this club were many: the beauty of the Alps, of course, and the benefits of physical exercise, but also the chance to study geology, botany, and metereology far from the academic classroom, and to meet up with the members of clubs from neighbouring provinces, which for *alpinisti* in Vicenza included the politically charged ("unredeemed") borderland of Trent.[20] But a standard feature of the excursions taken by the club in Vicenza were visits to private villas en route to and from the mountains. On one trip in 1877, a group of ten *alpinisti*, including the brothers Guido and Giovanni Piovene, set out for the Beric and Euganean hills between Vicenza and Padua. Not very far along the way, the group stopped at the Piovene family villa in Brendola. Only four people continued on from there, with stops at the villas of two other notables and a tour of Giuseppe Nardi's apiary. A year later, without Guido or Giovanni in attendance, a group of eight stopped in Brendola again, where the heads of the Piovene household, the countess Adele Sartori Piovene and Count Felice Piovene (a member of the club) greeted them, with music provided by a group under Felice's direction.[21] In between social events of this kind, the members not only climbed mountains but collected minerals, fossils, and flowers, continuing the work, the club's newsletter stated, of the many "distinguished geologists, botanists, and entomologists in the region," who created "stupendous collections, herbariums, works of every kind, true monuments ... erected to themselves."[22]

Moving Objects

The vast majority of associations, however, considered it part of their purpose to transcend the limits of private culture. The fossils and flowers collected by alpine club members ended up in public museums as well as private homes. Agrarian associations not only gave members access to new tools and expensive machines, they made a point of bringing this technology directly to landowners and farmers, for example by organizing on-site experiments and demonstrations in the countryside. In fact, in a number of different ways, associations could claim to surpass the modern, enlightened purpose of other public institutions. Once a public museum or library was created – once enough individual acts of donation and transfer were arranged and a suitable building was acquired – its public role tended to become fixed. Visiting hours might be publicized, citizens and tourists might be encouraged to visit, exhibits and collections might change or grow, but for the most part the public mission of a museum or library was already completed when it opened its doors. By comparison, associations often had the opportunity to develop a more

dynamic public identity. Alpine club newsletters told of members ven-
turing out and up to the original, living source of Europe's natural history museums, where they did not simply *acquire* a valuable collection
of minerals, but found and removed the rocks themselves. Agrarian associations prided themselves on the fact that their collections of machines
and books did not sit idly on display, but rather toured the province and
thus promised to effect real change. And the association-based organizers of public book readings and circulating libraries made very similar
claims. Ultimately, these associational activists encountered many of the
same problems facing the founders of civic museums, including a lack of
space, resources, and community involvement. Nevertheless, for most of
the nineteenth century, Italian liberals identified the association and not
the museum as the institution best suited to popularize scientific and cultural knowledge.

We should be careful not to overstate the novelty or dynamism of associations. Before there were hiking clubs or natural history societies,
there were distinguished individuals who hiked mountains and created
their own collections of fossils. The long history of collecting is filled with
remarkable stories of the journeys – through space and time – made by
valuable objects. How did a fossil make it from one of the world's highest mountain peaks to a Venetian gentleman's villa? How did a painting commissioned four hundred years ago by a Florentine prince end up
in the Louvre museum in Paris, France? The answer to such questions,
more often than not, is by indirect means. We know, for example, that
sixteenth-century princes commissioned other men to bring exotic plants
and animals back from the Americas, and that art collectors today need
only write very large checks to acquire paintings by Rembrandt or Pi-
casso. During the nineteenth century, however, a more direct and active
practice of collecting was in vogue, one that joined the privileged experience of travel and study to the emerging, middle-class ideal of "do-it-
yourself." Thus, guidebooks and exhibition catalogues inform us that
Nicolo Da Rio created his own impressive collection of minerals by ex-
ploring the Euganean hills outside of Padua, and that Alberto Parolini
travelled much farther, from Bassano to "Mount Ida in Asia Minor," to
get the seeds of a new species of pine tree for his garden. Back home, we
are told, he took a different kind of action, using mines to blast his way
into a spectacular grotto on his property.[23]

Therefore, the main advantage associations had over individuals was
not their capacity to find or acquire objects. Rather, it was their ability to share those collected objects with others, either by placing them

in a conveniently located repository – for example, in a city centre as opposed to a remote country villa – or by deliberately promoting their circulation. The objects Italian liberals most wanted to distribute were books and tools. Throughout the Risorgimento, the challenge of getting books into the hands of as many people as possible inspired a variety of solutions, from the publication of cheap, pocket-sized editions to organized giveaways of readings deemed beneficial to the local population. But the involvement of associations in this task increased dramatically in the 1860s, inspired in part by the sense of civic freedom and action that accompaned unification, and in part by the efforts of European reformers like Jean Macé, who set out to create a new network of town libraries aimed at the working classes. The first of these "popular libraries" in Italy was instituted in 1860, in the Tuscan town of Prato, and by 1874 there were 520 of them scattered throughout the peninsula. Before the spread of these new institutions, the vast majority of public libraries in Italy had served one or another elite group of scholars: seminarians, university students and professors, amateur enthusiasts. In 1846, the priest and seminary teacher Pietro Mugna contributed a brief article on libraries to Padua's liberal periodical, *Il Giornale Euganeo*. Rhetorically asking "What is a library?," Mugna offered the famed early-nineteenth-century German librarian (and monk) Martin Schrettinger's answer: "it is a considerable collection of books, whose organization allows the scholar to make use of everything the library contains without losing time." For Mugna, what distinguished libraries from "comfortable and pleasurable" reading societies was not their promise of greater public access, but their seriousness.[24]

Popular libraries departed significantly from this scholarly model. Unlike most civic libraries, whose primary function was to preserve archival materials of historical interest, popular libraries featured contemporary books and loaned them out to interested readers. Unlike most university and seminary libraries, which were large and grandly situated, popular libraries tended to have modest accommodations and amenities. In a sizeable provincial capital like Padua, a popular library might possess one or two thousand volumes and a comfortable reading room, but many in smaller towns had one or two hundred volumes and no headquarters at all. Elementary schools hosted most of the popular libraries in the Terra di Lavoro region (between Naples and Rome), a reflection of the central role municipal governments played in getting libraries established there. In many cities throughout Italy, mutual aid societies often took the lead. In Perugia, the Mutual Aid Society of Artists and Workers created

a library that became an important cultural centre. In Bologna a number
of mutual aid societies pooled their resources to create a library with over
five thousand volumes.[25]

Many libraries, however, were the work of ad hoc associations of citizens, which helps explain the variety and the simplicity of these institutions. Both of these features come across clearly in a general manual
on popular libraries that the moderate liberal from Vicenza Paolo Lioy
published in 1870. In a few pages of text (followed by a long list of recommended book titles), Lioy tries to convince potential organizers that
these institutions need very little in the way of standards and regulations.
If money is short, it is enough to collect one hundred or so books and use
whatever furniture is on hand to shelve them. Who donates the books is
not important – it could be one generous resident, the town government,
or several residents grouped together in an association. Nor is it worth
worrying too much about the books disappearing.[26]

Flexible rules and structures allowed library promoters to improvise,
for example by organizing public readings of books or delivering books
to hospitals, prisons, and remote villages. Alberto Errera proudly recalled
the involvement of the Popular Library of Venice in both of these activities. Errera helped arrange a public reading in Venice that, he later wrote,
attracted "workers, still ragged and worn out from work, some of them
with the tools of their trade; children, young, old, all awaiting the reading, with untiring attention." The audience appears to have responded
most enthusiastically to a reading from Manzoni's novel *I Promessi
sposi*, but Errera also found time to discuss more contemporary and scientific topics, among them the inspiring lives and careers of industrialists
like the British engineer George Stephenson. Not knowing what to expect
of the event clearly added a measure of excitement for Errera, who could
barely disguise his wonder that the workers who attended made "astute
observations" and "posed questions and doubts (for example, regarding
steam-powered machines)" in an orderly fashion. Likewise, the Venice
library's circulation beyond the city proper and into "places among the
most resistant to civilization" – namely, the province's rural districts –
gave Errera another chance to sound a note of proud transgression. "If
the books return crumpled [by the peasants] to the Library," he noted,
"at least it shows that they were not left to lie on some village teacher's
dusty shelves." In Errera's mind, the stakes of such initiatives were very
high: after all, the goal was not simply to expose new groups of people
to knowledge or culture, but rather to "shake even the crudest plebeians
out of their lethargy."[27]

It was popular libraries, not museums, that inspired Italian liberals to make their most explicit appeals for cultural reform. When the mayor of Padua, Antonio Tolomei, gave a speech to (re)inaugurate the city's Civic Museum in 1880, he said next to nothing about the general public and its access to cultural resources. Instead, he described and praised the museum's "rich" collections, one by one – the picture gallery, the library, the archive, and so on – and confirmed that these contents were "dear and familiar" not to just anyone, but rather to scholars conducting "patient, disinterested, and cheerful research"; and not to merely curious scholars, but to those scholars who are able to remove themselves from the everyday world of competition and envy in their search for truth. Thirteen years earlier, before he was mayor, Tolomei had given the members of Padua's Popular Library a much different speech, both in tone and content. He told the quiet but revolutionary story of the journey books were now taking from the private homes of the elite to public libraries and, from there – specifically, from popular libraries – to the lowliest worker's "hovel." Cultural limits and how to transcend them were the dominant themes throughout. Thus, the largesse of the wealthy citizen who opened his private library to friends and scholars, and his park and gardens to everyone, was admirable, but it was not enough; public libraries helped but "were still a privilege," in that they were aimed at advanced scholars and only existed in larger cities; and, so, was the man who did not enjoy any special fortune – "who sweated, who cried, who trembled at times before the threat of imminent poverty" – condemned to never experience the joys of reading Homer, Dante, Machiavelli, and Galileo?[28] This is the rhetoric we expect to hear from the great proponents of public culture in nineteenth-century Europe. And Errera outdid Tolomei:

> When the books which lie in a wretched state of gentlemanly display, in elegant little boxes, standing in beautiful rows like those soldiers which decadent peoples send into the field to make a show of their brilliant uniforms, leave their elegant store-rooms, to run, hand to hand, from the lady to the milliner, to the poor female prisoner; when the thousand volumes which, amidst the dust and mold of the shelves, comfort the eyes of academics who may never have placed a hand on them, circulate among people who are alive and longing for culture, from the gentleman to the daylaborer, to the convict, will we not have gained a great deal?[29]

Rhetoric aside, the leaders of popular libraries paid unusual attention to the practical, physical limits that determined the true extent of an ordinary man or woman's access to culture. Errera liked to offer his audiences the generic images of peasants descending from the hills to ask for books, and of library custodians having to guard the doors as throngs of workers pressed to get inside; however, he also addressed the specific issue of library hours, in particular the need to offer workers libraries that were open in the evenings and on weekends. The same concern for detail turns up in his praise for a popular school in Venice, whose directors carefully chose *where* in the city to set up the school: not close to a large piazza or in a wealthy neighbourhood, but right outside the shops and factories.[30] More ambitious, but no less practical, was the strategy of using various workers' associations as distribution points for books. As a promoter of popular libraries in Siena put it in 1867, the ties between multiple popular associations – libraries, schools, mutual aid societies, savings banks, and the like – made it easier to make a difference in the life of someone who "too often is left alone and defenceless in the fight between good and evil." As a connected group, associations had the ability to function like a circuit, something no civic museum or library could do.[31]

Italian liberals also spoke in dramatic and practical terms of the spread of new agricultural technology, and once again they turned to associations to accomplish what individuals could not easily do. Sharing machines, as opposed to books, presented unique challenges. As a rule, public demonstrations of large agricultural machines depended on the generosity of wealthy landowners; indeed, the presence of "very refined ladies" at some of these events suggests that the arrival of, say, a state-of-the-art plough could become the basis for an elite social gathering.[32] Proponents of reform assumed that leading landowners were the key to effecting change, and that the mass of peasants was stubbornly opposed to the use of new machines. As the president of the Agrarian Association of Vicenza put it in 1868, "the example, which is everything in agriculture, has to be provided by the richest and most intelligent people." Nevertheless, agricultural associations also took steps to bridge the technological divide between the landowning elite and the peasants. Vicenza's association paid an itinerant teacher to travel throughout the province, providing peasants with practical lessons, pamphlets, and the chance to discuss the latest inventions. It also formed a "museum" of new agricultural tools and machines – ploughs, shears, continuous-action bellows for spreading fertilizer, machines for cracking grain, and so on – and demonstrated their use in a series of public experiments. Two ploughs in the collection, the association's annual *Bulletin* reported, "made a tour almost of our entire District and inspired a real competition among land-owners who asked for one or the other in order to try them out."[33]

Where progress was slow, reformers did not hesitate to expose the limits of elite patronage and the need for action on a larger scale. Thus, the leaders of the Agricultural Association of Thiene, a small town in the province of Vicenza, delivered a series of dispirited reports on local conditions to the membership. In this district, vice-president Giovanni Carraro told members in 1868, "no one understands what an Agricultural Association is." The advantages of new machines and more efficient cultivation were only understood by a "few intelligent owners," and even their successes were modest. The only hope was that the government, by passing compulsory education laws, would help reduce the crippling ignorance of the population. Carraro's speech a year later was more upbeat, but he lamented the failure of both private citizens and town governments to support the association. Echoing Carraro, the president, Nicolo Cibele, noted that the "largesse" and the "philanthropic intentions of a few individuals" were not enough to fund the association's many activities; and he registered his hope that the government would help by arranging to make municipal subsidies of the association mandatory.[34] In a city the size of Venice, Padua, or Vicenza, circulating libraries and museums could appear to complement a set of other, private collections and civic institutions. But in countless smaller towns they seemed like unprecedented agents of change.

It is surprising to learn that associations played such a leading role in cultural reform, in part because they were limited, members-only organizations. Public gardens, libraries, and museums were designed to accommodate a general public: a collective, anonymous, and indeterminate body of visitors. By contrast, the members of associations constituted a number of more or less specific and restricted publics, consisting of landowners or war veterans or hiking enthusiasts, of men or women (but rarely both), of only those men who could afford the membership fees, and so on. How could a great cultural transformation take place in such a fragmented and exclusive setting? Venetian liberals acknowledged the dangers of social division and isolation. Nevertheless, they had little faith in general publics of any kind. They were certain that they needed to teach ordinary citizens how to act in public, and that associations were perfectly suited to this task. For assemblies did not simply happen, they were convened; and in the same manner limits were set, rules were applied, and order was maintained. By and large, the individuals who determined when and how often meetings occurred, as well as the many other rules that governed an association's operations, were members of a city's political elite: men like Luigi Luzzatti and Emilio Morpurgo in Padua, Fedele Lampertico and Paolo Lioy in Vicenza. The example they wished to set derived not from the ownership of particular objects but from a capacity to organize other men. The resource they most wanted to share and display was leadership.

Public Order

After unification, the formation of an association involved a fairly standard sequence of events. Following whatever behind-the-scenes efforts were necessary to gather a nucleus of supporters, the leaders of the initiative to form a new association would make a public announcement of the projected institution in newspapers and on wall posters, generally in the form of an appeal to all who might be interested in participating. This was followed shortly by a public meeting, at which potential members could sign up, or at least hear more about the initiative. At this or a subsequent meeting, interested members would elect one or more commissions responsible for the preparation of an official "statute and regulation" or a report on the association's goals and needs. After a short time during which the growing list of subscribers would be published at intervals in the local newspapers – the prestige of a first set of notable participants being an incentive for others to join – a final, constituitive meeting would be held to announce the association's formation, approve the reports and proposals of the commissions, and elect the new association's leadership and administration.[35]

The same attention to procedure characterized associations after they were formed. As might be expected, statutory rules and regulations determined the processes by which individuals were admitted to (and expelled from) associations, meetings were called, elections were conducted, leaders and administrators interacted with the membership, and associations dissolved. What is more surprising is how public and publicized these rules were. Announcements of upcoming meetings – on wall posters and in newspapers – were not general and exuberant, they were precise and rule bound: they listed, in numerical order, the specific items of business that would be addressed at the gathering. Daily newspaper accounts of completed meetings were equally restrained and formulaic, emphasizing how smoothly meetings went and rarely reporting conflicts or debates. Print culture helped Venetian liberals convey a powerful, twofold message: first, by announcing meetings on a regular basis, it offered proof

that the liberal leaders of associations respected Italy's new political culture of accountability and openness (*pubblicità*); second, by affirming
the successful outcome of one meeting after another, it suggested that the
ordinary members of associations fully shared their leaders' appreciation
for order.

As we saw in the previous two chapters, the leading liberal proponents of associations in the Veneto paid close attention to statutory
rules and regulations for a variety of reasons: to satisfy the legal requirements of the Austrian government; to help define an association's
social composition (above all, through specific rules of admission); to
ensure that newer forms of welfare association – for example, mutual
aid societies and popular banks – did not get into financial trouble;
and, last but not least, to discuss the pros and cons of different types
of existing Italian and European associations, at a time when the opportunity to form new associations of their own was limited. As far as
Luigi Luzzatti, Fedele Lampertico, Emilio Morpurgo, and friends were
concerned, a good statute was critical to the long-term success of each
and every association, but especially in the case of large welfare associations. Not only were the operations of a mutual aid society or popular
bank highly technical, but their memberships were "popular," which
is to say, they consisted of artisans and farmers as well as shopkeepers, professionals, and large landowners. The moderate liberal founders
and leaders of these new associations firmly believed that the popular
classes, in particular, needed the kind of clear guidelines and binding
rules that a formal statute provided; that is, they needed to learn the
importance of order in associational life.[36]

Order was especially valued at meetings. For the vast majority of associations, including agrarian associations, reading rooms, mutual aid
societies, veterans' associations, cultural academies, social clubs, and political associations, the rules regarding meetings were practically identical. Associations had one or two general meetings each year, which
invariably centred on the following events: a statement by the president
about the state of the association, its accomplishments in the past year,
and its plans for the year to come; a report by a group of two or more appointed auditors on the association's finances, followed by a vote ratify-
ing the budget for the coming year; and the election of some or all of the
association's leaders and administrators. All other general meetings were,
by definition, "extraordinary," and could only be called by the leadership
or by a quorum of members, usually no fewer than ten to a dozen. All
topics of discussion and deliberation had to be decided upon before the

meeting, and were arranged to form a precise agenda, or "order of the day" (*ordine del giorno*). Further rules defined proper conduct at meetings, from the president's powers of intervention and mediation to the protocol of speaking and voting in an orderly fashion.

Parliamentary forms and procedures helped make the associational meeting an exclusively male ritual. Although relatively few in number, associations of women did form in nineteenth-century Italy, as elsewhere in Europe. But their meetings were rarely announced, let alone reported on, by newspapers. Within mixed-sex associations, women were often prohibited from attending meetings, or at least from speaking or voting at them. For example, in Perugia's Mutual Aid Society of Artists and Workers (f. 1861), women initially had to send a male family member (father, husband, or brother) to represent them at meetings; a few years later, a new statute granted them permission to attend meetings but not to participate in them.[37]

The meeting's agenda was usually included in the formal announcement (*avviso*) that indicated, at least a week in advance, when and where the meeting would take place. Before 1866, meeting announcements were sent individually to members' homes, or posted inside the rooms or buildings occupied by an association. The only non-members informed were representatives of the Austrian government, who reserved the right to attend and supervise all meetings. After unification, though, most associations adopted new forms of publicity. Article 3 of the *Regolamento* of Padua's Society of Volunteer Veterans (from the wars of) 1848–49, an association formed in 1868, read:

> The order of the day of the convocations, ordinary as well as extraordinary, decided in advance by the Council [*Consiglio di Direzione*], must be made known to the members by means of a printed announcement to be posted in the city's most frequented locales. The said announcement will also be inserted in the city's newspapers.[38]

Some associations continued to send *avvisi* directly to members' homes; but, of these, most specified that some other, public form of announcement was also necessary.[39]

The consistency of associational procedures regarding meetings enabled newspapers to cover these events in a highly standardized way, which involved announcing meetings several days in advance, and then providing accounts of the meetings shortly after they took place. The announcements were invariably brief, but the follow-up reports could occupy as much as a column or more of a newspaper page, and this at a time when most Italian newspapers were only four pages long, with the fourth page typically consisting solely of advertisements and legal notices. Furthermore, although the typical association might only hold a general meeting once or twice a year, two or three dozen different associations existed at any given time in provincial cities the size of Padua or Vicenza. Factor in the frequent occurrence of extraordinary meetings, and the decision by many newspapers to announce some meetings multiple times, and it becomes easy to imagine how large and continuous the presence of associational news really was in provincial newspapers. In fact, it is possible to argue that, taken together, the regular flow of associational announcements and reports that appeared in newspapers constituted something like a public, everyday language of associational life.

The formal announcements that appeared in newspapers tended to replicate the procedural language of associational statutes.

> Società del Casino [Social Club] – On Sunday 10 December 1876 at 1 p.m. in the rooms of the Casino the General Meeting foreseen by the Statute will take place, at which the following topics will be treated:
>
> 1. Reading of the report by the Leadership on the state of the Club.
> 2. Examination of the Estimated budget for the year 1877 and deliberation on the same.
> 3. Nomination of two Auditors [Revisori ai Conti].
> 4. Replacement of four Members of the Council, who will be chosen by lot, and who may be re-elected, and substitution of a fifth [Member] who did not accept the position.
>
> If, for the lack of a legal number [of members in attendance] a second convocation should be necessary, this will take place on the evening of the following Tuesday, December 12 at 8, and the relevant announcement will be publicized in the rooms of the Casino, and inserted in the Newspapers of the City.[40]

Newspaper accounts of meetings, too, confirmed the importance of order and leadership. Take, for example, the coverage of a meeting of the Popular Bank of Padua provided by *Il Giornale di Padova* in February 1868. The long article followed the "order of the day" to the letter

– "The meeting opened with a reading of the minutes from the last meeting"; "The President then read his report"; etc. – and documented the
gathered members' approval "without objections" of each item. The only
significant editorial content consisted of occasional words of praise for
the leaders' rhetorical skills ("the clarity and serenity of the exposition,"
"the elegant severity of the form," "that polished style," etc.) and regret
that space did not allow for a longer report.[41]

Usually, newspaper writers adopted a more efficient and impersonal
tone. "The motion was approved with only slight modifications ...,"
"[the meeting] then proceeded to discuss the Statute ...," "the following people were then elected to the leadership ...," were the shorthand
phrases employed.[42] In effect, the only members of an association who
were not given this passive, collective, and approving voice were the leaders, whose speeches continued to occupy a prominent place in newspaper
accounts. Occasionally, journalists made a point of noting that the membership's silence at meetings was real, even suggesting that it reflected a
general agreement with the ideas put forward by an association's leaders.
Rare indeed were the moments like the following, from an 1868 meeting
of Padua's Mutual Aid Society of Artisans, Merchants and Professionals,
when a leader exhorted members to express themselves:

> Pronounce your opinion, then, rising up freely from your seats, and raising
> your hand as a sign of approval, pronounce your opinion on the question I
> put to you: Are you satisfied that the new leadership, which you are about
> to nominate, will assume the honorable task of fusing into ours all the other
> [mutual aid] societies of Padua in one family ...? (*Very lively and general
> signs of approval – out of everyone's mouth a* Yes *sounds!*)
>
> Yes, worker friends, I await from you this full, public and solemn vote
> [*suffragio*].[43]

And yet, even here, silent and generic approval is encouraged: a raised
hand counts as a form of communication, the word "Yes" stands in for
fully articulated opinions.

The exceptions to this rule stand out dramatically: the appearance in
the pages of *Il Corriere di Vicenza*, in the early 1870s, of a series of reports on the meetings of the city's Popular Bank, which made specific
mention of various members' "interventions" and "objections"; a similar
development within the Popular Bank in Padua several years later, which
received extensive coverage not only in the city's newspapers but in the
pages of the bank's published annual reports; the detailed and highly

critical accounts that appeared in the radical-democratic newspaper
L'Amico del Popolo, in the early 1880s, of the meetings held by Vicenza's elite-led mutual aid society of artisans.[44] Exposure of this kind generally reflected moments of crisis or change for specific associations, not to
mention conflict between rival political groups. Not surprisingly, in the
weeks prior to local or national elections, the newspapers representing
opposing parties often printed polemical accounts of the meetings held
by each side's political associations. Thus, shortly before the political
elections of November 1876, the newspaper of the progressive liberals in
Padua, *Il Bacchiglione*, recounted that only forty people showed up for a
meeting of the moderate liberal Constitutional Association, and boasted
a week later that the room reserved for the meeting of the Progressive Association "was too small to hold the numerous people present."[45]

As the voice of the minority party in Vicenza and Padua, not simply in
municipal and parliamentary politics but also in most local associations,
progressive liberal newspapers were more likely to print in full the verbal
exchanges and debates that took place at meetings. Nevertheless, they
were also just as likely to emphasize the orderly, procedural nature of
most associational meetings; and, when covering associations that progressive liberals founded or dominated, just as likely to report the membership's unanimous approval of the leaders' words and actions. Thus,
Il Bacchiglione's coverage of the Progressive Association's large meeting in the fall of 1876 was entirely consistent with the rhetoric found
in so many other newspapers, and applied to so many other forms of
association:

> The distinguished lawyer Danieli, member of the [electoral committee],
> read a beautiful report, interrupted many times by roaring applause, which
> we will publish in tonight's edition. The committee proposed the following
> candidates:
> [... names follow]
> The Progressive Association, without any discussion, welcomed the pro-
> posal of its Committee among the most lively acclamations ...[46]

Although there is no point in citing example after example of newspaper reports and their subtle variations on the theme of the calm,
orderly meeting, it is important to emphasize how consistent and widespread this rhetoric was. At the heart of this language was a terse, almost coded replication of associational procedures and protocol: on the
one hand, a reminder to members of what to expect at a meeting and

an account to the wider, reading public of the event itself; on the other hand, a ritualized presentation of rules and regulations, order and authority, and their *observance* in practice. It made for dull journalism and, no doubt, dull meetings as well: the order of the day, the unanimous approval of deliberations, the re-election of an association's leaders. But as many theorists of power have pointed out, the fact that these practices were repetitive, mundane, or taken for granted, does not make them any less important.[47] Moreover, through newspapers, periodicals, wall posters, and a series of other special publications, this power was not only practiced but displayed. Large or small, eventful or dull, the associational meeting always presented the leaders of an association with the opportunity to demonstrate – in public – their leadership and authority; it was an arena of power but also a visible lesson in the responsible exercise of power. And in these sober terms it was a powerfully affirmative ritual.

The link between publicity and power is crucial to an understanding of the difference between associational life before and after unification. Although by the 1840s the benefits of association were already at the centre of public discussion, the tangible signs of a new and vibrant "age of association" were scattered. The various governments on the peninsula might not be able to stop the circulation of ideas regarding associational life, but they could and did limit the transformation of those ideas into actual organizations. Furthermore, they placed limits on the articulation of associations with the public at large. The paucity of newspapers in general, and the exercise of censorship in particular, ensured that news regarding associational activities would not reach a wider public. At the same time, governments restricted the use of city buildings and squares as ceremonial spaces. In short, there existed a "public opinion" but not a public culture of association.[48]

Few groups understood the importance of this change better than the Catholic clergy and laity. At each stage in the process of Italian unification, from the events of 1859–60 to the occupation of Rome a decade later, relations between liberals and Catholics appeared to worsen. Catholics were alarmed at the speed with which godless liberals had "invaded and corrupted" every region of public life, from the press, universities, and schools to theatres, courts, and the legislature.[49] For their part, liberals accused Catholics of trying to subvert the new state. Local Catholic groups were slow in forming associations and newspapers of their own after unification. At a council for Venetian clergymen in 1859, one speaker announced that it was time "to combat the enemies with their weapons and on their terrain, opposing their words and press and associations, with Catholic words, press and associations."[50] At first, Catholics took the defensive position of protecting local men and women against the corrupting effects of anticlerical propaganda.[51]

More proactive Catholic groups often struggled to establish a positive public identity. A good example is Vicenza's Catholic Youth Circle, which formed in 1869, following the example of lay activists in the cities of Viterbo and Bologna. Although the goal of the national organization was to "train all individuals ... to have a frank and courageous spirit in professing publicly the Catholic religion," the five young men who started the circle in Vicenza were so concerned that their "meagre number of members" would make them look bad that they opted to meet away from the city centre, in an old hilltop convent. A local democratic newspaper got wind of this and took the occasion to "unmask" the group for all to see, in a fine piece of journalistic anticlericalism:

> Why do they hide among the shadows and not dare to show their face? Why do they run to their agreed meeting place with their heads down, suspicious and in silence, almost [as if] pursued by the executioner? ... We have seen them run one by one into well-known houses, we have seen them suspicious, wary like the Christians of the catacombs, the Jews of the Middle Ages ... [But] we are warning them that if this indecent and disloyal war which they wage does not end, we will unmask their hidden meetings, we will announce the names of the zealots who attend them, so that at least our friends, friends of liberty and the light can protect themselves ... against the cholera and the plague.[52]

Catholic journalism lagged even farther behind. In Padua, a string of largely ineffectual Catholic weeklies came and went; one of them, *La Specola,* did well enough to stay in print from 1882 to 1894, but it struggled constantly to find subscribers. Vicenza's two main Catholic periodicals, *Il Foglietto Religioso* (1870–82) and *Il Berico* (1876–1915), were more successful, but it is significant that no Catholic daily existed until *Il Berico* became one in 1886. (Padua's Catholics had to wait until 1897 for their first daily, *L'Ancora.*) Thus, although the statutes and regulations adopted by Catholic associations had much in common with their counterparts in liberal associations, they could not be publicized to the same extent.[53] Unable to take full advantage of print culture, Catholic activists focused on the more direct and confrontational tactic of physically appearing in public: in Good Friday processions, on pilgrimages to nearby or distant shrines, at papal jubilees and a wide range of local religious celebrations.

Italian liberals, too, participated in rituals more spectacular than the associational meeting. Unification inspired a series of memorable public affirmations of Italy's constitutional monarchy: plebiscites were held in every region to ratify the decision to join the Italian nation; the new king, Victor Emmanuel II, made triumphant visits to the leading cities of each annexed territory; and citizens tore down the insignia and other symbols of the defeated regimes.[54] Late to join Italy, the Veneto was not deprived of its chance to mark the transition from Austrian to Italian rule. In the years to come, too, Venetians celebrated Constitution Day every June, waved flags, wrote flattering histories of the Savoy dynasty, erected monuments to Victor Emmanuel after his death in 1878, and participated enthusiastically in national exhibitions. Nevertheless, Venetian liberals remained profoundly ambivalent about public celebrations, even nationalist ones, and they demonstrated much greater enthusiasm for other public ceremonies that more closely approximated the order and sobriety of the associational meeting.

In many respects, the Italian war of independence of 1866 was a failure and a disappointment, a fact that complicated the politics of national celebration and commemoration in the Veneto. Resounding defeats on land and sea and a humiliating peace settlement cast a shadow over Venetian liberation, making the fall of 1866 a time of celebration but also of sombre and angry reflection. In the Veneto, returning émigrés, soldiers, and conspirators took aim at residents who had been sympathetic to the Austrian government, or who benefited in some way from Austrian policies and appointments. The provisional royal commissar in Padua, Gioacchino Pepoli, dismissed sixteen professors from the city's university on these grounds; throughout the region, debates erupted around the "patriotism" or "Austrianism" of various individuals, especially the candidates for the first round of local and parliamentary elections. Another inviting target was the church, which had been defended by the Austrian Empire in times of revolutionary upheaval, and favoured within the Lombard-Veneto Kingdom. The Italian government supported this antagonism by renewing its warnings against clerical interference in elections (especially the plebiscite to annex the Veneto to the Italian Kingdom), and by voting, in early 1867, to sell at auction the church lands seized by the state. As the first anniversary of liberation approached, campaigns to change the names of streets and squares in Venetian cities developed a strong anticlerical edge, and attacks on church buildings were reported.[55]

Proponents of a radical break with the past put Venetian elites on the defensive. After all, a significant number of Venetian notables had spent the final years of the Risorgimento not in exile, on the battlefield, or at the head of secret committees of anti-Austrian resistance, but rather in the thick of local political and social life, as the leaders of government-approved associations and local governing bodies of one kind or another. In a variety of public settings, leading moderate liberals warned against either defining patriotism too narrowly or dwelling on specific individuals' past relationships to the Austrian government. Privately, they noted the population's failure to heed this advice. Thus, in September of 1866, Luigi Luzzatti wrote a letter to Giacomo Zanella describing the tense political atmosphere in Venice and Padua, to which Zanella replied:

> Here too things are going from bad to worse; ... everyone seems to be afflicted with vertigo; *the friends of liberty circle*; *the moderates' circle*; *the democrats' circle*; *the friends of the people circle*; grand meetings; grand chatter; grand shouts of "viva Garibaldi"; and then everyone slips away with their heads dazed but barren of any good ideas ... [L]et's hope that, once the ardor of the moment has ceased, the population will turn their attention to more mature considerations.[56]

The message was clear: political passions – including passion for the nation ("viva Garibaldi") – were dangerous and disruptive; the sooner the excitement surrounding liberation came to an end, the better.

This background helps explain the moderate *Giornale di Padova*'s wary coverage, in July 1867, of the one-year anniversary of the city's liberation from Austrian rule. "Padua, patriotic city *per eccellenza*," the paper stated, "does not need incitements [*eccitamenti*] in order to celebrate this most propitious anniversary." Individuals attending the popular demonstration needed only to remember the importance of the day and leave everything else to the "distinguished citizens" on the organizing committee. Furthermore, people were reminded not to take the whole day off from work or school, but to put their flags out in the morning, break a little early from work in the afternoon and go to the city's main piazza for music, a promenade, illuminations, and songs.

> But let us await the instructions of the good patriots who are promoting the organization of the celebration.[57]

So many of the elements of the organizational order found in associational meetings are repeated here: the prominence of elite leaders, the desire to organize the event in advance, the attempt to define (and limit) the time and space in which the event will occur. Missing, however, is the confidence that this anniversary celebration would, in fact, go according to plan.

Fears and suspicions of public disorder were built into the Italian constitution, which guaranteed the right to associate in "closed" spaces (such as associational meeting halls) but not "in public spaces or spaces open to the public." Italian liberals repeatedly emphasized the dangers of the piazza and its political predators, the demagogues and agitators who attempted to manipulate the ignorant masses.[58] Often, when public demonstrations occurred, moderate liberal journalists went out of their way to make them appear illegitimate, refusing to recognize the participation of upstanding citizens (including, in Padua, university students, a group often in the thick of demonstrations), reducing the sociology of the participants to entirely marginal groups of "street urchins" and "idlers," drawing attention to acts of senseless vandalism, and so on.[59] In reality, most demonstrations followed very precise and predictable paths: beginning in a large public square or at the headquarters of the group leading the protest; proceeding along the city's main streets to a meaningful point of protest, usually not a government building but rather the residence of a local authority (mayor, prefect, MP); and ending in a round of noise-making (whistles, shouts, songs, etc.) followed by some kind of formal political statement, such as a speech by a local opposition leader or the presentation of a written petition. Such events were certainly noisier and more confrontational than associational meetings, but they were hardly chaotic.

Nevertheless, large public gatherings were inherently more difficult to control than associational meetings. A case in point is the funeral in Padua in March 1870 of Count Andrea Cittadella Vigodarzere (1805–70), one of the most controversial figures of the post-unification period, thanks to his close relationship with the Austrian government during the Risorgimento. His election to Parliament in 1866 from the electoral district of Cittadella (in the province of Padua) appalled the city's most embattled patriots.[60] There are few signs of controversy or ill will in the *Giornale di Padova*'s account of Cittadella Vigodarzere's funeral. "In this solemn demonstration of affection," it reported, "citizens of every order, of every age, of every sex were represented, and without distinction of ideas; almost as if to pay their respects to a union of spirits which in vain is sought elsewhere." To highlight the event's ritual order, the same observer noted that "the people crowded along the streets" and "the women [watched] from windows," anonymously making room for the procession of authorities, delegations, and "leading families."[61] But a collection of documents relating to the funeral offers a different view, both of the political mood surrounding the event and of the forms of participation it inspired. In the days leading up to the funeral, at least a dozen people, including several self-described "commoners" (*popolani*), composed and posted – on city walls and doors – their own poems, epitaphs, and statements in honour of the deceased. Some of the dedications came from family, friends, and dependents; others were anonymous. Many of them reflected not a harmonious union of spirits but deep and lasting feelings of resentment. An anonymous epitaph included the following angry repudiation of Cittadella Vigodarzere's opponents:

> Opposed by some ambitious nonentities, who first tried to court him, and did not care to know his virtues, or who became annoyed by so much brilliance, ... [Cittadella Vigodarzere] left the city bitter, establishing his dwelling in the capital of the Kingdom [Florence], where everyone's love and regret followed.*[62]

Not only were the tensions associated with Risorgimento patriotism still alive four years after the liberation of the Veneto, they were capable of spilling over the boundaries of orderly participation in public life.[63]

Six months after Cittadella Vigodarzere's funeral, people thronged the streets and squares of Padua again, this time to celebrate the news that Italian troops had captured Rome. As the historic date of 20 September 1870 approached, leading Venetian moderates braced themselves for the unruly, albeit patriotic, festivities that were about to occur. Emilio Morpurgo wrote to Alberto Cavalletto in Florence of the atmosphere of uncertainty and nervousness in Padua; afterwards, another friend of Cavalletto's fulfilled his request for more information regarding the reports of disorder and vandalism in Padua that had begun to reach the capitol.[64] In Vicenza, Mariano Fogazzaro expressed to Fedele Lampertico his disgust at the local celebrations: "All of the cheers, the flag waving, the light shows, the childishness of the Italian cities, including the bell-ringing in Vicenza, make me blush with shame."[65] No doubt many moderates feared that this particular event would mobilize Garibaldian democrats and anticlericals, who had led the push to capture Rome throughout the

1860s. But it is also possible to detect a more general attitude in these exchanges: noisy public celebrations were an unwelcome, if unavoidable, part of the new nation's political culture.

Soon enough, city governments throughout the Veneto made the adjustment to a more uniform and established calendar of patriotic events. Originally a cause for concern, the 20th of September eventually became one of two official national holidays, and thus subject to the organizational ideals of local governments and civic leaders. Also part of liberal Italy's fixed patriotic calendar was Constitution Day (*Festa dello Statuto*) in June, which commemorated King Charles Albert of Sardinia's initial approval, in 1848, of what later became the Italian constitution, plus one or two dates of local significance, which in the Veneto typically referred to important events from the revolutions of 1848–49.

It is not difficult to find evidence of enthusiasm for these annual celebrations. Not surprisingly, men who fought in Italy's wars of independence, marching under the banner of veterans' associations, could be counted on to participate. But other groups also got involved: agrarian associations occasionally highlighted successful celebrations in year-end reports; popular banks arranged to have event organizers award small savings accounts to night school students; and mutual aid societies had local newspapers print announcements reminding members "to turn out in large numbers," as one of these items read, and show their "love of liberty and Italy."[66] Nevertheless, such evidence is surprisingly thin and fragmentary. Venetian newspapers barely covered annual patriotic celebrations at all. They did not announce the specific agendas and precautions that organizing committees worked to establish ahead of time, nor did they offer detailed descriptions of the events after they happened. It is largely thanks to associational periodicals, annual reports, and special issues that we know anything about the speeches and ceremonies at the heart of most patriotic celebrations.[67]

The lack of publicity, if not enthusiasm, for annual patriotic festivals stands in sharp contrast to the excitement generated by a series of other public events, including royal visits, scientific congresses, and economic exhibitions. The presence of distinguished visitors often made these events memorable, and allowed for public demonstrations of elite hospitality, much as the culture of collection and association did. When Vicenza hosted the Third Meeting of the Italian Society of Natural Sciences in 1868, the *Giornale della Provincia di Vicenza* provided extensive coverage not just of the scientists' scholarly discussions of bees, lichens, fossils, and limestones, but also of the many banquets they attended, and of the excursions they took – in a line of twenty carriages – from Vicenza to the villas of Count Andrea Piovene in Lonedo and the Pasini family in Arcugnano. As we might expect, it was reported that the distinguished visitors to these private estates marvelled at the owners' gardens, paintings, greenhouses, and museums. More surprising is the newspaper's decision to print a complete list of the meeting's participants, which indicated not only where but with whom each person was staying.[68]

But the event that came closest to realizing Italian liberals' new public ideals was the economic exhibition. At this event one can see – on display – the three aspects of Italy's emerging public culture discussed in this chapter: the personal possessions of local elites, the mobilizing ambitions of associations, and the virtues of orderly assembly. Exhibitions advertised the intellectual and material achievements of local elites; gave organizers the opportunity to demonstrate the importance of discipline and authority to the success of any public endeavour; turned productivity, rather than political passion, into a cause for local and national celebration; and, most extraordinary of all, mobilized a general public without appearing to sacrifice the central liberal principles of enlightened tutelage, procedural order, and publicity.

Understandably, Italian historians of exhibitions have tended to focus on the largest and most spectacular exhibitions of the nineteenth century: on the one hand, the great international exhibitions that, during the second half of the century, took place every six or seven years in a major European capital (usually London or Paris); on the other hand, the national Italian exhibitions of 1861 (in Florence), 1881 (in Milan), and 1884 (in Turin).[69] To appreciate the importance of exhibitions within the context of local public culture, however, it is necessary to examine the smaller but more frequent exhibitions organized at the local, provincial, and regional levels. In the Veneto, these smaller exhibitions followed in quick succession after unification. There was an agricultural-industrial exhibition in Verona in 1868; an exhibition of agriculture, industry, and the arts in Padua in 1869; and a regional Venetian exhibition in Vicenza in 1871. And by the time the last of these events took place, plans were already underway to hold the next regional exhibition in Treviso the following year.[70] Participation in the great international exhibitions might inspire politicians or manufacturers to publish their impressions in leading newspapers and periodicals, but it was the seemingly endless string of local exhibitions that filled the pages of provincial newspapers and led to the publication of special-issue periodicals and commemorative albums.

The formal, organizational similarities between exhibitions and associational meetings are striking. In both cases, an elite group of organizers worked hard to define and structure the events in advance. Thus, the executive committees responsible for preparing exhibitions drafted official regulations; set up offices; printed admission forms, registers, and protocols; and determined the range as well as the order of the materials on exhibit. They determined the general systems of classification but also issued countless specific instructions to exhibitors regarding the safe transport of spirits and oils, the timely arrival of fresh vegetables, the proper handling of live animals, and so on.[71] Once they opened, exhibitions ran for weeks or months and allowed visitors a freedom of movement and speech that was clearly missing from associational meetings. Nevertheless, exhibitions were also relatively quiet and authoritative events, free of confrontation or debate, culminating in the selection (sometimes election, by secret ballot) of award-winning exhibits by designated juries of experts.

There were also ideological similarities. Even more than the associational meeting, the exhibition was touted as a productive rather than a festive public event. Large national and international exhibitions offered visitors an increasingly varied and spectacular set of diversions: food and drink, concerts and dances, circuses, magic lantern shows, fireworks displays, and amusement rides of all sorts. But most of these amenities and amusements were absent from local exhibitions, at least during the first decade or two after unification. Proponents of local exhibitions took pride in this fact. As one writer from Vicenza put it in 1871, at Europe's great exhibitions "the curious and the tourists" outnumbered "the men who were drawn by the need to see and to learn."[72] The opening and closing ceremonies of the regional exhibition held that year in Vicenza were devoid of entertainment: much like an associational meeting, they consisted of a few speeches by local notables, nothing more.

Exhibition periodicals and albums reinforced the seriousness of the events by focusing on exhibitors rather than visitors, exhibits rather than diversions. This was even true of illustrated publications, which featured dozens of small drawings of works of art, design, and industry – paintings, jewellery, carriage axles, threshing machines, mobile water pumps (an early firetruck), and so on – but precious few of visitors and even fewer of exhibition-sponsored leisure or entertainment. By contrast, the illustrated periodical covering the national exhibition in Milan in 1881 is filled with scenes of bourgeois sociability, of ladies and gentlemen strolling through various exhibition rooms, of parents and children, of bourgeois women watching working women ply their trade. And although there are no colourful accounts of the rough or respectable behaviour of workers at the exhibition, there are general discussions of exhibitions' moralizing influence, and specific articles about organized "worker visits." The organizers of the local exhibitions held a decade earlier in the Veneto had a different concern: not the conduct of a large and potentially unruly general public of visitors, but the response of local farmers, manufacturers, and artists. The editors of an album on Padua's exhibition in 1869 noted with regret that the exhibition's president, Antonio Keller, delivered his inaugural address to "a restricted public," but they had far more critical words for exhibitors. When they declared that "everything that limits the participation of the public seems to us unjustified and damaging," it was exhibitors, above all, they had in mind. Or, rather, missing exhibitors, unresponsive and irresponsible would-be exhibitors who, "allowed to participate, did not rush to avail themselves of this right." Agriculture was not adequately represented, and respected local makers of carriages, windows, bells, and compasses did not show up at all. Why was that? "Why did a single town with one and a half thousand souls send over fifty exhibitors, while entire districts only came up with 3 or 4?"[73]

These critical remarks are interesting for a number of reasons. First, the forceful demand for public participation in exhibitions differs significantly from the general pattern of cultural change in Italy at this time. It is rare indeed to find the leaders of civic museums and libraries, or the organizers of patriotic celebrations, drawing attention to the damaging effects of "everything that limits the participation of the public." Second, we need to consider the significance of the the local public's failure to participate in exhibitions. Why did producers from certain towns in the province of Padua stay away from the exhibition of 1869? Italian exhibition documents are filled with questions of this sort, and so, interestingly enough, are associational documents. If a group of enlightened citizens in Venice created a popular library and sponsored public readings there, who would come? If the Agrarian Association of Thiene demonstrated the greater efficiency of a new plough to a group of local farmers, how many of them would end up changing the way they tilled their lands?

These were not rhetorical questions. They expressed real gaps in knowledge and communication, and often real doubts about the prospects of overcoming them any time soon. By mid-century, most Venetian liberals were convinced that associations were the best way to effect social and cultural change; however, the tension between their confidence in associational solutions and their lingering questions and doubts never went away. If associations failed to mobilize society's best and brightest, its successful and skilled producers, could they really provide the basis for a new, more inclusive public culture in Italy? Could they involve, let alone transform, society's popular classes any more than a private library or civic museum?

4

Popular Capitalism

The true focus of associational life in united Italy was economic modernization. A concern for greater productivity led many liberals to turn away from traditional forms of religious charity, craft organization, and elite sociability, and towards associations that promised to increase the wealth, education, and welfare of a broader cross section of society. Venetian liberals were especially convinced that new forms of "popular association" – mutual aid societies, cooperatives, credit unions, libraries, and schools – were the key to addressing the daunting socio-economic problems of poverty and illiteracy. In a yearbook documenting the proliferation of popular associations in the Veneto soon after unification, Alberto Errera boasted that the familiar image of the ragged poor was giving way to a new and inspiring scene, that of "the beggar who becomes an artisan, an industrialist, a capitalist!" This great transformation, Errera conceded, was slow to get underway in the region's rural districts; nevertheless, the progress evident in dozens of Venetian towns suggested that there were effectively no limits to the socio-economic miracles associations were capable of achieving.[1]

Not everyone believed in the economic power of association. Among the sceptics was one of the Veneto's – and, for a time, Italy's – leading industrialists, Alessandro Rossi. As the owner of a large and modern complex of wool-producing factories in and around Schio, in the province of Vicenza, Rossi felt certain that men like Errera were putting the cart before the horse when they forecast the success of workers' associations even in "cities of ours which are devoid of industry," in "places where a proper working class does not exist." In established centres of industry, workers could found their own welfare, saving, and cooperative institutions, ideally with the support of their employers but certainly without recourse to "outside" help; in short, the network of popular associations touted by Errera and others should "come on its own." As it was, Italy had too many "apostles of saving" and too few "creators of salaries and founders of industries."[2]

Without a doubt, one of the self-styled apostles of saving Rossi had in mind was his fellow Venetian, Luigi Luzzatti, who by 1867 was Italy's leading promoter of credit unions. Luzzatti was only in his early twenties in 1863, the year he left the Veneto and began promoting what he called "popular banks" in a string of towns throughout Lombardy, but he quickly established himself as a leading authority on a wide range of economic and social issues. In Italy's leading liberal newspapers and periodicals, he offered his views not just of credit unions and other, related forms of popular association, but of the wider causes of poverty and the dangers of large joint-stock companies. Rossi's irritation both with Luzzatti's (journalistic) medium and his (small is beautiful) message was destined to grow and intensify in the years to come; by the mid-1870s, the two men were engaged in a memorably angry dispute over whether factory laws were needed in Italy to protect women and children.

Rather than waiting for the workers at his wool factories to create their own institutions, Rossi took the step of promoting a range of institutions for them: a mutual aid society, infant nursery school, theatre, gymnastics facilities, music and drama schools, bathing and laundry centres, dowry funds, a cooperative food store, an orphanage, and low-income housing. By the late 1870s, Schio was the most impressive factory town in all of Italy.[3] There was no mistaking, however, that this was Rossi's creation; it did not "come on its own." For all their differences, therefore, Rossi and the leading proponents of popular association shared at least two important assumptions about the economic modernization of Italy: first, that the social and economic conditions of Italy at the time of unification were such that modernization was bound to require the strong leadership of men like themselves, above all because in many towns the foundations of industrial capitalism had to be created from scratch; second, that the human dimension of this change – the reform of Italy's working classes – demanded the introduction of not just one or two but a series of new institutions: modern factories and banks, of course, but also mutual aid societies, schools, libraries, theatres, cooperatives, and more.

Scholars eager to identify a specific ideology of Italian industrialization have tended to ignore this institutional common ground. Half a century ago, when large-scale factory production and decisive "take-offs" to sustained economic growth defined European industrialization, Italian historians were most impressed by Rossi's technologically sophisticated and politically forceful vision. In the past two decades, a revised appreciation of small enterprise has led to much greater interest in Luzzatti's cooperative model. And if Italy's current economic woes last or worsen – in particular, if the much-admired "industrial districts" of central and northeastern Italy (the so-called Third Italy) do not adapt well to the new global economy – we can almost certainly expect yet another revision. To strike a helpful balance, we might follow Vera Zamagni's suggestion, "that there was no one single ideology of industrialization which had the upper hand over others; but rather that Italy, a nation of many different cities and different types of agriculture, is also a nation of many different ideologies – and not only of industrialization – which sometimes converge, whilst sometimes they conflict with one another, producing an inextricable tangle of ideas and policies." Solidaristic populism, technocratic modernism, and nationalism, to name just three important ideological strands, competed for public attention and political resources in late-nineteenth-century Italy.[4]

Well below the national level, in fact – within one region, province, or economic district – it is possible to see the interplay of these multiple economic ideologies; just as important, it is possible to gauge the impact of practical experience on ideology. After all, the immediate post-unification period was a time of uncertain transition, of new opportunities, challenges, investigations, and reforms. Rhetorical indulgences aside, men like Errera and Luzzatti did not expect new workers' associations to thrive, more or less automatically, in every town. They encountered opposition, entertained doubts, conducted investigations, and made what they believed were necessary adjustments. In a more focused and controlled setting, Rossi faced similar challenges, as he struggled to justify his workers' apparent inability to secure their own welfare. Could enlightened factory owners or association leaders build communities of producers, investors, workers, and consumers? Could they transform thousands of workers and peasants into modern economic agents? These questions did not simply divide Italy's captain of industry from its apostle of saving, they tested the ability of Italian liberals to broaden the bases of industrial capitalism in Italy.

Buried Treasure

After unification, it was not uncommon for the local press to track and support the progress made by new business ventures. Newspapers encouraged citizens to attend promotional meetings and published complete lists of companies' first shareholders.[5] By highlighting the constitutional, procedural similarities between associations and businesses – after all, both aspired to bring people and capital together, voluntarily – newspapers made it appear that businesses, no less than associations, were civic entities. By producing long lists of shareholders, they helped determine the true extent of the population's material resources. How many citizens had money tucked away under a mattress or in a savings bank? What would it take to entice them to invest their money in new business ventures? Could this broadening of economic life extend far enough to make the popular classes active participants in the Italian economy? As we shall see, Venetian liberals offered different – even conflicting – answers to these questions.

In nineteenth-century Italy, the linguistic distinction between association and business enterprise was not as clear as it is today. During the first two-thirds of the century, especially, the most common Italian words for association – *associazione* and *società* – were widely used to refer to businesses. Members of a *società del teatro*, for example, could be any of the following: the owners of a theatre business; investors in the purchase, construction, or renovation of a theatre building; subscribers to a season of theatrical performances; or a troupe of actors and singers. Likewise, the members of an *associazione enologica* could easily be amateur wine enthusiasts or professional wine producers and merchants. Over the course of the nineteenth century, more precise legal terms emerged to distinguish joint-stock companies (*società anonime*) and limited partnership companies (*società in accomandita*) from ordinary associations. But as late as the 1880s, city directories and guidebooks continued to mix the two together. Among the "miscellaneous associations" (*società diverse*) listed in the 1878 and 1884 editions of a combination yearbook and guide to Padua, somewhere between the city's drama and social clubs and the associations dedicated to horseracing, beekeeping, stenography, and cremation, one finds Vincenzo Stefano Breda's Società Veneta construction company, which was not just the largest industrial firm in Padua at the time, but one of the largest in all of Italy.[6]

Terms aside, many Italian liberals consciously emphasized the civic benefits attached to business ventures. In 1846, after the Austrian government authorized the creation of a new ironworks company in Padua, a local newspaper, *Il Caffè Pedrocchi*, praised the initiative and encouraged readers to support it. The newspaper's pitch centred on a predictable theme, Italy's need to compete with the industrial powers of Europe by employing new technology and forming business associations. The high price of five hundred Austrian lire per share, not to mention the

promise of annual dividends, made this a very particular kind of association. But this is not how it comes across in *Il Caffè Pedrocchi*, which
grouped the ironworks together with two other new groups in Padua
– the Society for the Promotion of Gardening and the Society for the
Encouragement of Agriculture – before exulting, "may the spirit of consociation spread, burn, grow, intertwine and prosper variously in every
part of Italy." Conversely, when the ironworks company struggled to attract enough investors to get started, *Il Caffè Pedrocchi* questioned the
courage, intelligence, and patriotism of the initiative's "adversaries." And
it questioned their capacity for civic action: in Padua, *Il Caffè Pedrocchi*
complained, people "always have a thousand reasons not to do anything,
none for doing something."[7]

Entrepreneurs had the frustrating sense that the capital they sought
existed yet remained out of reach. The Austrians could be blamed up to
a point: Venetians were naturally going to think twice about investing in
a business if that meant exposing their wealth to the prying eyes of tax
officials. In 1855, the promoters of an economic exhibition in Vicenza
acknowledged this problem, but refused to accept the way citizens had
responded to it, which was to allow themselves to become fatally "discouraged," "inert," and divided. For, as one observer noted, the only answer to "the rising taxes and the misfortunes that still plague us" was to
bring together "persons of all classes" – "the rich man" as well as "the
man of moderate wealth" – in economic associations. In some industries,
unity was going to be hard to achieve: producers were "scattered" and
associations were "almost unknown." In fact, the main purpose of the
exhibition in 1855 was "to get to know the true state" of Vicenza's economic conditions and resources, and to allow local industrialists "to get
to know each other."[8] If this gap in communication and knowledge existed among the area's producers, what were the chances of involving a
broad range of citizens in new enterprises?

The long and frustrating search for a business community helps explain why, soon after unification, newspapers began printing the names
of investors in local businesses. What exactly was new about this practice? As we have seen, the public promotion of new businesses in newspapers dated back to the 1840s at least. Older still was the tradition of
using subscription lists to raise funds and show the extent of public support for a worthy cause. There are many references to subscriptions, but
no lists of names, in Padua's two main newspapers during the 1840s, *Il
Giornale Euganeo* and *Il Caffè Pedrocchi*. Beyond its obvious functional
value as a method of fundraising, the subscription provided nationalists

with a subtle tool of political expression, as when the subjects of one "Italian" state raised money to help flood victims or build a monument in another.[9] Two important changes in this practice, however, followed unification: first, the number of subscription lists increased dramatically, in part because *popular* involvement required lists printed in a dozen or more instalments, containing hundreds of names; second, lists of share-holders began to occupy as much space as lists of charitable donors.

Not surprisingly, the biggest lists of all in the immediate post-unification period were patriotic in nature: collections for the families of soldiers injured in Italy's wars of independence, for the construction of monu-ments to Risorgimento heroes, and the like. Rivalling them in size, how-ever, were lists of the men (and some women) who joined consumer cooperatives and credit unions. Whereas the cost of one share in many joint-stock companies could be prohibitive, the ten or twenty lire it took to buy a share in one of Italy's new "popular associations" was within the reach of most artisans and small landowners. At least, that is what the promoters of these institutions said, and what the display of com-plete lists of shareholders was meant to prove. The names of wealthy and influential citizens (and the number of shares they purchased) rou-tinely appeared at the top of published lists; however, in cooperatives and credit unions these notable names were interspersed with those of perfectly ordinary citizens – persons of all classes uniting to form eco-nomic associations.

No Venetian, and perhaps no Italian, worked harder to prove that the social foundations of Italian capitalism could be broadened than Luigi Luzzatti. In countless publications and speeches, Luzzatti emphasized that the cost of a share in one of his popular banks (a form of credit union, or savings and loan association) was low enough that any worker could afford to buy one. Beyond that, he suggested that these "humblest" of bank members could also become eligible to take out loans, if neces-sary by pooling their resources to provide collateral. In the meantime, every member was also a shareholder, which meant the receipt of a divi-dend at the end of each year. If members were unfamiliar with any or all of these operations – with shares, collateral, dividends, and so on – that was not a problem either, for regular meetings gave the members an op-portunity to learn about the operations first-hand.[10]

In reality, most of Italy's first popular banks were hard pressed to live up to Luzzatti's populist rhetoric. They grew rapidly in part because the early promise of high annual dividends inspired wealthy citizens not only to join but to purchase multiple shares. As a result, loan committees had the low-risk option of extending credit to wealthy and established clients. Bank leaders and administrators reviewed all of these facts and figures with the shareholders at annual meetings, which, however, rarely attracted more than a fraction of the banks' thousands of members. In short, in terms of both operations and membership size, most of Italy's new popular banks quickly began to seem less like popular associations and more like, well, banks. Luzzatti refused to portray them this way, however. One sign of his commitment to the banks' popular and associational image was the publication, four times during the 1870s, of a complete list of the members of the Popular Bank in Padua, Luzzatti's main political base. Unlike most of the lists of shareholders that had been appearing regularly in Venetian newspapers after 1866, this one did not draw attention to the bank's most notable members, or indicate how many shares each member owned. Instead, it gave the appearance of a true democracy of shareholders by listing, in alphabetical order, each member's name, occupation, and place of residence. Thus, Luzzatti himself appeared on page 12 of the list of 786 members in 1869, sandwiched between a windowmaker named Andrea Luca and a student named Luigi Luzzatto, all three of them residing in Padua. Including each member's place of residence was an especially nice touch, for, by demonstrating that the vast majority of shareholders were from the city and province of Padua, it subtly confirmed the bank's identity as a civic association. This was no ordinary bank, the lists said: it was created by local citizens in response to local needs; its shareholders knew one another (or at least knew one another's names); its meetings could realistically attract large numbers of interested members.[11]

Luzzatti was not the only Italian liberal to promote the ideals of popular association and economic democracy. His closest friends and political allies echoed his claims about the transformation of workers into capitalists, and disputed the charge that popular banks actually served the interests of bourgeois clients; moreover, beyond his immediate circle of influence, there was no shortage of admirers of Luzzatti's favourite protagonist, the small shareholder. Writers and politicians celebrated the appearance of this new economic citizen in a free and united Italy, and defended his right to an equal voice in the affairs of large banks and corporations.[12] Civic leaders, meanwhile, applauded local entrepreneurs when they set low share prices for new business ventures. When, for example, shortly after unification, the backers of a struggling wine production company in Padua turned to the local Agrarian Association for help, they were asked to demonstrate their commitment to some "principle" other than profit. Could they claim, for example, to have any sort of educational mission, as the Agrarian Association did? A spokesman for the wine producers replied by offering to clarify their educational purpose in the company's statute, and by noting that their willingness to sell shares at a modest price belied a focus on mere profit. The president of the Agrarian Association, in turn, expressed his support of the fledgling company, "since it aims at education and the formation of capital with small shares."[13]

All of this attention to the small shareholder was bound to rub large industrialists like Alessandro Rossi the wrong way. Rossi's father, Francesco, rose to prominence in the wool industry with the help of a small number of partners, not hundreds of shareholders. The first Rossi Woolworks company began in 1809, shortly after a failed revolt against the region's French rulers prompted two of Schio's leading wool producers, Luigi and Sebastiano Bologna, to seek a new partner to shield their company from political retribution. Francesco Rossi reorganized the firm in 1818, with a new principal partner, Eleonoro Pasini, and a working capital of 100,000 lire. Following in his father's footsteps, Alessandro expanded the company's operations to the point where, by the early 1870s, he decided to convert the family firm into a corporation, the Società Anonima Lanificio Rossi. At this point he, too, had shareholders to consider, but only sixty-six of them, wealthy owners of 120,000 shares worth fifteen million lire.[14]

As early as 1866, Rossi began publicly challenging the idea that associations of small shareholders were the key to Italy's economic future. At the end of a celebratory profile of the new Nodari paper factory in Lugo Vicentino, Rossi questioned the popular view "that the spirit of association is the sole panacea for our ills," and suggested that Italy's greater untapped resource was "the spirit of enterprise" possessed by a limited number of resourceful individuals. Were large subscriptions needed to get new businesses up and running in Italy? Rossi's answer was "no," and to make his point he quoted from Samuel Smiles's international bestseller, *Self-Help*, which featured the exemplary achievements of a few dozen European industrialists. The Nodari brothers' great contribution to the town of Lugo was not to go to the main square and call forth the town's citizen-shareholders. Rather, it was to bring modern, industrial "civilization" to a "poor village" and bread to the tables of 120 families.[15]

A wider scepticism about the power of economic association can be registered in the newspaper that reprinted Rossi's essay on the Nodari factory. *L'Esposizione regionale veneta* (1871–72) was created to cover the first major economic exhibition to be held in Vicenza since 1855. Unlike the promotional documents and catalogue that the 1855 exhibition inspired, *L'Esposizione regionale veneta* only occasionally mentioned associations and instead focused on the uplifting stories of specific entrepreneurs. Moreover, the editors of the newspaper openly expressed their doubts about what associations could contribute to the economy. In the course of a discussion of Alberto Errera's prize-winning study of Venetian economic history, which ended, characteristically, with praise for the region's new popular associations, the editors of *L'Esposizione regionale veneta* offered these thoughts:

> The association is not yet applicable with great advantage to the present industrial and intellectual conditions in the Veneto, [and] as long as the educated and hard-working man is an exception [here], individual initiative will obtain much more satisfying results than those which would come from the union of inept and discordant elements.[16]

It was foolish to go looking for hundreds of investors in Italian towns, not just because many of these towns were poor but also because most of the towns' residents lacked a basic education, let alone an understanding of modern capitalism.

The leading proponents of association shared the sceptics' belief that popular education and popular participation in the economy were inextricably linked. After all, one of the purposes of providing detailed newspaper coverage of businesses soon after unification had been to reveal how companies formed, and to demonstrate that this process closely resembled the many other new but simple acts of civic participation occurring in united Italy: just come to the meeting, hear the plan, and join. Likewise, the annual meetings of mutual aid societies and popular banks became occasions for presenting educational speeches and didactic budget reports to workers and peasants. The leaders of these associations did more than support a generic program of popular education, they acted on a belief that ordinary Italians were fully capable of learning the ins and outs of modern capitalism.

Lessons in Political Economy

Between 1862 and 1866, no fewer than four future members of Parliament from the Veneto – Fedele Lampertico, Paolo Lioy, Luigi Luzzatti, and Emilio Morpurgo – shared the experience of teaching free night school classes to local artisans. Under the auspices of prestigious institutions like the Olympic Academy in Vicenza and the Society for the Encouragement of Agriculture, Commerce and Industry in Padua, these young members of the region's educated elite taught subjects ranging from basic lessons in reading and writing to advanced courses in economics. In Vicenza, Lampertico gave classes on "the abc's and little more," as he put it in a letter to Luzzatti, but also a three-year course on political economy that included lectures on the division of labour, patent law, and the Bank of London; Luzzatti, first in Venice and then in Milan, recounted the recent history of insurance companies, consumer and producer cooperatives, mutual aid societies, and credit unions. Their courses were sophisticated enough to attract some distinguished guests – including the famed economist Carlo Cattaneo, to one of Luzzatti's classes in Milan – but it was the prospect of educating "the people" that gave them the greatest thrills.[17]

The involvement of prominent men and elite associations in the cause of popular education did not begin in the 1860s. Padua's Society for the Encouragement of Agriculture, Commerce and Industry (f. 1842) used competitions and prizes to increase awareness of new farming techniques and published a popular almanac and periodical. Its leaders, in turn, had followed in the footsteps of such well-known advocates of popular schooling as the Milanese Count Federico Confalonieri and the Tuscan intellectual Pietro Vieusseux. What was novel in the 1860s, therefore, was not the goal of teaching the masses but, rather, the goal of teaching *political economy* to the masses. Mid-century popular almanacs and periodicals had not done this; they had provided very practical information about crop cultivation and local markets, and didactic tales of a very basic sort, such as a fictional conversation between two artisans who discover the evils of the tavern and the virtues of saving. Likewise, the schools Cosimo Ridolfi and Vieusseux had created a decade earlier in Tuscany taught arithmetic to boys and sewing to girls, but not economics, and they focused the energies of teachers and students on the enforcement of disciplinary rules and regulations.[18] By contrast, Lampertico and Luzzatti were eager to expand the curriculum of popular education to include the ideas of Frederic Bastiat and John Stuart Mill and the practices of workers' associations in Rochdale (England) and Mulhouse (France). As Luzzatti proudly recalled in his memoirs, this break with tradition won the praise of noted periodicals like the *Annali universali di statistica*, which had this to say about Luzzatti's lectures in Milan:

It was the first time that the working people of Milan heard a course in popular economy, heard the words of a science which until now has only resonated in the privileged halls of the Universities and within the confines of Parliament. It is difficult to believe how much attention there was in the crowded audience, which listened to the teachings of political economy and saw explained, one by one, the most intimate phenomena of the science of riches.[19]

Venetian liberals continued to teach adult workers after 1866, and they continued to do so in associations: by sponsoring public readings at popular libraries, holding free courses in beekeeping and winemaking at the homes of agricultural association members, and organizing night schools for mutual aid society members. In addition, the leaders of mutual aid societies and popular banks routinely told members that these associations themselves were schools of welfare, or "providence" (*previdenza*), which taught everyday lessons in saving, credit, budgeting, and accounting. Over time, as leaders found that they were not reaching as many workers and peasants as they had hoped, they either tempered their rhetorical promises of institutional transformation or sought entirely new ways of involving the popular classes in economic life.

If this chapter in the history of Italian education is unfamiliar, it is probably because the pupils in question were adults. Most historical accounts of primary education in post-unification Italy focus not on the programs associations arranged for adults but on government-sponsored elementary schools for children. The reasons for this focus are many and compelling. Schools were the first line of offence in the battle to lower the nation's alarming illiteracy rates, in the debates over lay versus religious education, and in the campaign to strengthen national identity by promoting (and inventing) a shared Italian language, culture, and history. Nevertheless, in the immediate post-unification period, concerns about the countless men and women who had already missed their chance to attend school kept the question of adult education very much alive. The chapter on "primary education" in Emilio Morpurgo's *Saggi statistici ed economici sul Veneto* (1868), for example, contains a lengthy analysis of elementary schooling in the region, but it begins and ends with the spectre of ignorant adults endangering Italy's social and political order, and it includes a twelve-page appendix on "schools for adults in 1866–1867." Statistically, too, as this and other studies revealed, adult students and schools made up a surprisingly large percentage of the total figures on schooling, both in the Veneto and in the nation as a whole.[20]

On the topic of adult school curricula, Morpurgo advised teachers to proceed carefully and to adopt practical books like those which helped workers perfect their crafts. He also complained, however, about the lack of "good popular books" for adults, in particular "books which might sensibly guide the people through the labyrinth of those social questions to which they often turn their minds and which they rarely know how to resolve in the best possible way." He noted that books that might "clarify economic problems for the people," even humble pamphlets with titles like *Catechism of Political Economy*, simply did not exist in Italy.[21] Other Venetian liberals agreed. In 1863, Luigi Luzzatti wrote, "In the future plan for the education of the working classes, let us not forget the principles of political economy." "Why," he asked, "should the people who work from morning until night go through life unaware of the laws of labor?" Alberto Errera also recommended "introducing the study of liberal doctrines and political economy" to the people. Understanding Italian unification ("the Italian revolution") meant studying not simply Cavour the statesman but Cavour the economist. "Our young commoners will gain little from our political order, if no one will reveal to them the mechanism of the social world, the laws of wealth, the principles that govern commerce and industry, and the whole harmonious weave of phemenona that constitute the science [of economics]." More than just bread, he argued, what the "multitudes" need is the "science of bread."[22]

As the co-founder of a popular library in Venice, Errera had the chance personally to oversee the readings made available to workers. He was one of the volunteers who read books aloud at the library, and thus was able to direct audiences to books that described the latest industrial inventions, told the stories of self-made men like the British railroad engineer George Stephenson, and explained the impact that the opening of the Suez Canal was going to have on international commerce. Others, like the superintendent of schools in Vicenza, Paolo Lioy, published lists of recommended titles for popular libraries, including books on political economy, economic exhibitions, and workers' associations and self-help. What visitors to the libraries actually read is another matter. Errera's own recollection of the public reading he gave in Venice suggests that the audience was most eager to hear and discuss selections from Alessandro Manzoni's novel *I Promessi sposi*, not Errera's account (no doubt via Samuel Smiles) of Stephenson's life. And the statistics he collected on the most requested books at popular libraries in the Veneto indicate that readers gravitated towards "light reading," "moral tales," and histories of Italy.[23]

Another way to bring good books to the attention of readers was to write them yourself. Several Venetians tried their hands at writing inspirational self-help books for workers. Paolo Lioy specialized in works of popular science, from *Life of the Universe* (1859) to his many later books on mountains and mountain-climbing; in between, however, he published the speeches he delivered to Vicenza's night school students (1863–64) and the self-help book *Slow and Steady Wins the Race* (1871). Carlo Leoni published his *Book for Workers* (1866) in three parts: first, a biography of Benjamin Franklin, "the greatest worker in the world"; second, a discussion of major vices and virtues (opposing hypocrisy and superstition, drink, foul language, lotteries, and tobacco to religion, honesty, goodness, character, savings banks, and reading and writing); third, a collection of Venetian proverbs, which the author deliberately left in the regional dialect, or, as he put it, "the language you speak." Aside from the brief reference to savings banks, and some introductory words of praise for the Veneto's leading manufacturers (beginning with Alessandro Rossi), Leoni's *Book for Workers* contained little in the way of modern economic principles.[24]

But the most extraordinary pages of self-help literature to come out of the Veneto were Alessandro Rossi's anonymous contributions to Cesare Cantù's *Portafoglio d'un operaio* (*A Worker's Wallet*) (1871). *Portafoglio* is the invented autobiography of Savino Sabini, a Neapolitan labourer whose family fortunes and work experiences take him on an enlightening tour of industrial Italy, from the silk-producing towns of Lombardy to the sulphur mines of Sicily. Through his own hard work, clean living, honest dealings, and the goodwill of a few employers, Savino rises from poverty to become the manager of a large factory. Many of Savino's life lessons reflected Cantù's longstanding conservatism, in particular his promotion of Catholicism and what he considered the values of rural, agricultural society. Benevolent priests help out Savino on numerous occasions, providing advice, work, knowledge, and friendship. Some are traditional but most are modern. While working as a railway accountant, Savino gets to know a parish priest by the name of don Benigno. Small-town curates insisted that the railway, classic symbol of modernity, was leading people to drink and dissolution, but don Benigno is free of such reactionary superstitions. He talks to the railway workers, who come to love him. He offers to write letters home for them, and when local mine workers suffer injuries he treats them with modern, effective medicine.[25]

Thanks in part to Rossi's input, however, Cantù gave modern industry a central and positive place in *Portafoglio*. Thus, Savino encounters a few unethical factory owners but more who are fair and honest; he marvels at the invention of railroads and textile machines; he even goes to Paris to attend the 1867 world exhibition, an event that inspired the real Alessandro Rossi to write a study of the wool industry. Cantù's debt to Rossi was especially evident in the central section of the book, which began with a long conversation between Savino, two other workers, a military captain, and a local justice official, on the topics of work, production, property, equality, wealth and poverty, salaries, factory laws, and strikes. At times, when either the captain or the official spoke, the conversation turned into a crash course in political economy, as in this excerpt:

> Capital, therefore, is the part of production which is not consumed, and which gets converted into new production. Agricultural tools and provisions, manufacturing machines are capital. Those canals which our old folks used for navigation and irrigation are capital. The operations that you do around your shop, the wells you dug out at your lodging, the water which you drew at your mill, the mine that you opened, are capital. Capital, therefore, is an accumulation of labor; and so it is only right that it gets remunerated, and that each person can dispose of it as he sees fit.[26]

This was a something more than the standard message about the benefits of hard work and the dangers of drink.

But we should not limit our understanding of popular education to the classroom and the printed word. As the leaders of cooperatives, mutual aid societies, and popular banks, Venetian liberals had the opportunity to teach important principles of political economy directly to those members who attended annual meetings and celebrations. What better way to convey the importance of saving than to point out, each year, the number of mutual aid society members who received sick pay (and thus avoided ruin) because they regularly paid their dues, or the number of workers in popular banks who earned the trust of administrators and received loans. Rather than telling the personal and individual success stories of specific members, however, the speakers at associational meetings routinely emphasized the moralizing and improving effects of the associations themselves. These were tales of self-help once removed, of workers helping themselves by joining modern, provident institutions.

Workers' institutions do not play a very big role in Samuel Smiles's *Self-Help*. The idea for the book, Smiles explained in his introduction to the first edition, came about when he was "requested to deliver an address before the members of some evening classes" in Leeds, which is to say, in precisely the type of associational forum that engaged Venetian liberals in the 1860s. Smiles was careful to note, however, that it was not he but the young workingmen of Leeds who "resolved to meet in the winter evenings, for the purpose of improving themselves"; Smiles's role, he claimed, was limited to "a few words of encouragement, honestly and sincerely uttered." In the book's first chapter, Smiles made his position even clearer:

> Whatever is done *for* men or classes, to a certain extent takes away the stimulus and necessity of doing for themselves; and where men are subjected to over-guidance and over-government, the inevitable tendency is to render them comparatively helpless.
>
> Even the best institutions can give a man no active help. Perhaps the most they can do is, to leave him free to develop himself and improve his individual condition. But in all times men have been prone to believe that their happiness and well-being were to be secured by means of institutions rather than by their own conduct.[27]

A similar message comes across in Cantù's (and Rossi's) *Portafoglio d'un operaio*. The turning point in Savino Savini's career, we learn, came when he got a chance to work for the benevolent wool manufacturer Edoardo Pensabene, a thinly disguised stand-in for Alessandro Rossi himself. Pensabene paid his workers well enough that they could eventually afford to buy their own homes and educate their children. He taught them the importance of saving, not by directing them to join banks but by pointing out how easy it was to "render themselves independent by reducing their needs and desires": by buying the cheaper suit, smoking one less cigar per day, no longer wasting money at the tavern, and resisting the fashion of attending parties and contributing to public subscriptions. Later in the story, the real Alessandro Rossi visits Pensabene and explains to the workers the advantages of various associations, before adding: "But so many drawbacks!" The banks and cooperatives, it turns out, demanded that members already have some capital and expertise, and thus were "a good investment for some, not a remedy for everybody"; and workers' associations risked luring workers into the communist First International and otherwise encouraging them to subvert the social order. The morning after Rossi's speech, we read, Savini heard a local resident offer the following opinion:

> People say great things about them, but those associations are a complement, not a supplement, of the taverns. I have two sons ages 18 and 20.

They enrolled in the workers' association immediately after it threw that big inaugural party, and with these scoundrels they have started to haunt the tavern.

Significantly, too, when Rossi broke down the annual living expenses he thought a worker should have – 75 lire for rent, 642 lire for food, 100 lire for clothes, and so on – he did not factor in any associational dues.[28]
Nevertheless, as Adrianna Chemello has pointed out, institutions occupy an unusually large place in nineteenth-century Italy's self-help literature. In the 1860s, Francesco Viganò published a series of books that identified the worker's greatest opportunity or fortune – his "true California," as one title put it – in mutual aid societies, cooperatives, and lending banks. In *Il Libro dell'operaio* (1866), Cesare Revel explained that mutual aid societies "*render* the worker moral and independent" and ensure that "the sentiment of individual responsability spreads widely among the poor classes." And Enrico Fano singled out mutual aid societies as the institutions best suited to help the worker "raise himself up, morally and economically," if only he could be made aware of their great benefits.[29]
Luigi Luzzatti did not write any self-help books, but the countless speeches he delivered to night school students and the members of popular banks and mutual aid societies are filled with comparable stories of personal change taking place within associations. His message often seemed like the familiar one of individual initiative: the poor man who works hard and saves money will go far in life. Just as, in *Portafoglio d'un operaio*, the humble labourer Savino Sabini rose to the position of factory manager, so the commoner who joined a popular bank was destined to become a "worker-banker." Yet Luzzatti made it clear that this personal transformation was due in large part to the bank itself. On his own, a worker was unlikely to fend off poverty, let alone obtain credit, but as soon as he joined a popular bank he became part-owner of an institution with considerable capital, and thus possessed a much greater incentive to save than he could possibly have had before.[30] On occasion, Luzzatti explicitly doubted whether the Italian people would ever learn the importance of saving without such institutional help. If all we do is "theoretically preach the love of saving," he wrote in 1871, "it is likely that the people [*i volghi*] will continue to waste their savings." What was needed was direct, institutional action: "When we demonstrate the advantage of depositing those savings with interest in a provident institution, then the overriding idea of profit will lead them to develop a

propensity to save."[31] Some workers, Luzzatti argued, had such a poor understanding of saving that they first needed to join a mutual aid society, and there learn the importance of putting aside a small portion of their pay before they would be ready to enjoy the benefits of credit in a popular bank. To emphasize this notion of a graduated institutional education, Luzzatti likened Italy's cluster of new popular associations to a school system, in which mutual aid societies functioned as "primary schools of providence," which prepared workers for the popular banks' more advanced lessons in credit. [32]

A corollary of this faith in the transformative power of institutions was the firm belief that not all institutions were alike. Popular banks, mutual aid societies, and cooperatives – the new popular associations of the mid-nineteenth century – promised to do more than provide temporary assistance, as countless charities had done for centuries. Rather, they taught people to secure their own futures by saving and investing money. Again and again, Venetian liberals promoted both the idea of welfare (*previdenza*) and the institutions that embodied it. Some of them drew a sharp, historical and categorical, distinction between welfare institutions (*istituzioni di previdenza*) and charitable institutions (*istituzioni di beneficenza*), while others maintained that the practices of charity and welfare could be combined in "provident charities" and "modern philanthropy." But everyone agreed that a process of institutional modernization was necessary, that this meant the replacement of at least some inferior institutions with newer and better ones, and that the principle governing the identification of good and bad institutions was fundamentally economic in nature.[33]

But institutions – preferably associations: and none were better than mutual aid societies and popular banks – were indispensable. Without them, Italy's popular classes were unlikely to learn how to save, or to stay out of taverns. The importance of institutional education and self-help is captured beautifully in an illustration that appeared in a Turinese newspaper in 1878: the "angel" of mutual aid leads a respectable-looking man away from a hellish pub (den of crime, poverty, and socialism) and into a savings bank.[34] Liberal elites were more likely to present themselves as expert "doctors" of mutual aid rather than as angels. They were eager to demonstrate that only they – and not, for example, democratic and socialist champions of greater worker autonomy – possessed the knowledge of modern economic and administrative science that was necessary to create sound, durable workers' associations. Thanks to their study of economic history, for example, they understood why single-trade associations were inefficient; thanks to their knowledge of accounting and administration, they could handle the challenges of scale and complexity that new, general associations of workers entailed.

Most Venetian liberals stressed the importance of modern economic and administrative principles, but few were as inclined as Luigi Luzzatti to proclaim that institutions could turn workers into capitalists. In Vicenza, Paolo Lioy and Giacomo Zanella waxed poetically to workers not about investments and dividends, but about the honesty of sweat and calluses and the beauty of smoke-darkened faces, and they warned artisans not to equate progress with the abandonment of their noble trades. The priest Zanella praised both the modern principles of free labour and self-help and the conservative effects of religion, which protected artisans against "the splendid but disastrous doctrines of audacious innovators" and brought comfort to workers whose lives are "always hard and scarcely enviable." To a group of design school students in Padua, in 1863, he praised savings banks, mutual aid societies, and credit unions and wished that these "magnificent institutions ... might spread to every town, like schools of civilization and good behavior"; however, he also openly doubted whether the people were ready to absorb the lessons these institutions taught, and advised against schools "that teach things which are of no use to [the people] in their state and which stir up inexpiable wants."[35]

Many new popular associations struggled to get off the ground and to stay solvent over time. In elite-led mutual aid societies, the contributions of honorary members and wealthy benefactors helped offset losses and build up reserve funds, but also risked undercutting every principle of self-help, whether institutional or individual. This was an especially noticeable and controversial feature of the General Mutual Aid Society of Vicentine Artisans, which in 1867 began to create a sizeable pension fund largely thanks to the extraordinary gifts of a few individuals. Thus, although the association's stated purpose was to create a brotherhood of artisans who helped each other out "according to their means," in practice its leaders seemed to be teaching artisans that the future growth of the association depended heavily on charitable donations.[36] Under Emilio Morpurgo's leadership, the Mutual Aid Society of Artisans, Merchants and Professionals in Padua was much more committed to balancing regular membership dues against sickness and pension payments. But this put Morpurgo in a different kind of awkward position: having to discover, during his yearly statistical reviews, that rising sick pay claims and declining membership figures threatened the very survival of the association; and having to confess this disappointing news to the members.[37]

Outside of major cities, the challenges were much greater. On 11 October 1874, Luigi Luzzatti attended a banquet held in his honour by the members of the Popular Bank of Asolo, a small town in the province of Treviso. The bank had only been in existence for a year, and Luzzatti was eager to see how it was progressing, so that morning he stopped by the bank's office and reviewed its records. Having noticed that the bank's level of deposits was low, he determined that most of the deposits had been made by residents of Asolo proper, few by residents of the small towns in the surrounding area. Luzzatti told the banqueters all of this, and then made a suggestion: put the bank – the point of deposit – closer to where these people work and live. Why?

> A peasant from Borso or Crespano [two towns near Asolo], who works hard all day, has too long a road to reach Asolo and deposit his few hard-earned savings. Such long roads are full of seductions, especially on weekend days.

In part, Luzzatti conceived of the problem in the familiar terms of moral weakness, which routinely led the peasant (and the "modern artisan") to waste his savings on "a few glasses of wine" and to "rely on charity" when he became too sick or old to work. In part, however, Luzzatti saw the problem in far more specific and contingent terms: there were certain "supreme hours" when the peasant or artisan "wavered" between doing the right thing by putting his savings in a bank and doing the wrong thing by squandering them. Giving him "easy and wise" speeches about the importance of saving was not the answer; it was necessary to capture his impulse to save "the moment it is born" and lock it up, by collecting deposits right where he lived – in towns throughout the district – and then discouraging him from making withdrawals by requiring him to take the long road to the main bank office in Asolo to do so.[38]

A year later, on the floor of Parliament, Luzzatti restated the problem and supported another solution: follow England's lead and set up state-sponsored postal savings banks in small towns throughout Italy. Statistics, he confessed, had revealed that "the veins of popular saving had barely been tapped, the mine is deep, mysteriously deep, and it descends far down into the bowels of the earth." Creating new savings banks in urban centres was not going to change anything; no, savings banks had to become "omnipresent," and the best way to do this was to place one inside every little town's post office, and thus make it as much a part of the local fabric of life as the elementary school and the church. If this

meant enlisting the help of the state, so be it. Faced with a "vast and obscure" society, Italian liberals needed to put aside their doctrinaire, Pan-
glossian books on free-market economics and take whatever action was
necessary.[39]

The remarks Venetian liberals began to make in the 1870s seemed to
mark the limits of popular association. Plans to teach workers advanced
concepts in political economy faded as doubts grew about their capacity
simply to set aside a small portion of their earnings. And so did much of
the bold talk about social mobility and change, as the workers in mutual
aid societies appeared to become more, not less, dependent on others for
help, and the workers that popular banks promised to transform into
capitalists failed to join at all. What did it say that, in 1875, the region's
leading proponent of popular association was still looking for buried
treasure, and yet no longer convinced that associations could bring that
treasure to the surface? That is, unless the state joined the effort, too.

Interventions

Luigi Luzzatti understood that many Italian liberals viewed the words
"state intervention" with great suspicion and alarm. In his speech to Parliament on postal savings banks, he made it clear that he only favoured
certain, absolutely necessary forms of intervention, such as making elementary schooling mandatory (against the wishes of the "greedy father"
who wants to keep his son in a state of ignorance), investigating the
working conditions of children in factories and mines, and assisting in
the difficult task of promoting popular saving. The model he claimed to
admire most was not Bismarck's Germany but Britain, the land of Adam
Smith and of strong traditions of local self-government but also of Europe's first modern factory laws.[40] In keeping with Tocqueville's discussion of associations in *Democracy in America*, Luzzatti, along with most
other Venetian liberals, reserved his strongest praise for local associations and institutions (libraries, schools, banks, etc.) that were created
by private citizens, not government bodies. Nevertheless, Luzzatti is not
remembered for such classic liberal views; rather, he is remembered as the
controversial advocate of state interventionism, as one of the leaders of
a "Lombard-Veneto school" of economists and politicians who clashed
dramatically with their laissez-faire opponents.

One reason why so many people remember this aspect of Luzzatti's career is that it culminated in a pair of very public and personal disputes.
The first one began in 1874 and pitted Luzzatti against Italy's leading

advocate of laissez-faire economics, Francesco Ferrara. Although it was a fairly theoretical debate, it drew wider attention because it coincided with two politically charged events: the formation in Italy of rival associations of political economic thought (Ferrara's Adam Smith Society and Luzzatti's Association for the Progress of Economic Science), and the parliamentary split within Italy's governing party of moderate liberals over the issue of state intervention in the economy. By the time the moderate liberals lost control of the government in 1876, the back-and-forth between Luzzatti and Ferrara had already begun to die down.[41] The second fight overlapped with the first, in that it centred on one of the examples of positive state intervention used by Luzzatti in his debate with Ferrara: Italy's need for a factory law on child and female labour. This time it was Alessandro Rossi – an industrialist, not an intellectual, and a fellow Venetian – who clashed with Luzzatti. On several occasions in the 1860s, as we have seen, Rossi had publicly questioned Luzzatti's ideas regarding the economic benefits of popular association and the virtues of small shareholders. But he was positively enraged by Luzzatti's push for factory legislation. Like Ferrara, Rossi exchanged barbs with Luzzatti in the pages of Italy's leading newspapers and periodicals. He went further, however, and turned the critical spotlight on Luzzatti by writing a series of long essays about the limitations (and inflated reputation) of Luzzatti's popular banks.

This institutional coda to Rossi and Luzzatti's exchange is important, because it reminds us that their battle, at least, was not over rival economic doctrines (laissez-faire versus state interventionism) so much as it was over different approaches to economic modernization. Rossi and Luzzatti were both, in their own ways, interventionists: they viewed Italian society as backward and therefore in urgent need of reform; and they focused on the problem of improving the moral and economic conditions of workers. They disagreed about how best to accomplish these necessary changes and, in particular, about the roles different institutions might play in the reform process. Nevertheless, they both promoted the creation of new institutional landscapes – of connected factories, schools, libraries, banks, theatres, and stores – for a new generation of Italian workers.

How did Luigi Luzzatti and several other prominent Venetians become Italy's leading advocates of state interventionism? In part, the answer is political. Soon after the Veneto was annexed to the Italian Kingdom, Luzzatti, Lampertico, and Morpurgo, among others, quickly found themselves on various government committees to investigate social and economic conditions and propose reforms, regarding everything from monetary policy and railroad construction to the state of the nation's industries; remarkably, Luzzatti was still in his twenties when, in 1869, he was named secretary general of the Ministry of Agriculture, Industry and Commerce by the prime minister, Marco Minghetti. But there is also a deeper, cultural and intellectual answer, which derives from the group's shared experience as students of political economy and statistics at the University of Padua. The professor they all looked up to, Angelo Messedaglia, followed in an Italian (and Austrian) tradition of statistical thinking that viewed the state as an instrument for the improvement of society. More important, Messedaglia's embrace of the Belgian mathematician Adolphe Quetelet's positivist search for social "laws" did much to inspire the wave of state-sponsored inquiries into social and economic conditions that immediately followed unification. The inductive method of scientific experiment and observation, Messedaglia and his disciples argued, should apply to the study of society just as it applies to the study of physics or astronomy, and the discovery of new social "facts" should naturally inspire new approaches to government.[42] In addition, they believed that a proper understanding of historical change made the need for state intervention abundantly clear. As Fedele Lampertico put it in the introduction to his massive, five-volume *Economy of Peoples and States*, those contemporaries who invoked the name of Adam Smith to oppose giving "ever new functions [*mansioni*]" to the state were taking Smith out of context and ignoring the spirit of his teachings. For whereas "the most urgent need in the time of Adam Smith was to knock down the many privileges and obstacles which still interfered with human liberty," almost a century later those monopolies and barriers were gone, and sovereign governments representing "everyone's interests" saw opening up before them "a new field of action." The point was not to replace the doctrine of laissez-faire with a new doctrine of state intervention, but to explore the positive role of the state with an open mind.[43]

It is no doubt significant that Alessandro Rossi was not part of this intellectual circle. Rather than attend the University of Padua like most of the leading Venetian liberals of his day, Rossi spent his young adulthood learning the family wool business, first on the floor of his father's factory in Schio and then on a tour of wool factories throughout Europe. This is not to say, however, that Rossi was uneducated or anti-intellectual. As a young man, he received a classical education at Vicenza's seminary; befriended a number of university students; sought out the works of Vico, Locke, Voltaire, and the Physiocrats at the private library of a friendly priest; left notes in the margins of books by Adam Smith, Jeremy Bentham, and John Stuart Mill; and took an interest in Saint-Simonian ideas during his visit to Paris. Nevertheless, in his writings as an adult, Rossi frequently took aim at those theoretical men of science who "never set foot in a shop" and yet had the nerve to claim to know what was best for industrialists and workers.[44]

Theories aside, Rossi believed that greater positive steps needed to be taken to help Italy's working classes. One of his earliest biographers, Ferruccia Cappi Bentivegna, recounts an event that made a big impression on young Alessandro when he was working in his father's factory. "One Monday morning" – the year is not given – an altercation on the factory floor resulted in the stabbing of an overseer by a worker. Although Rossi witnessed the scene, we are told, he did not punish the worker; on the contrary, he represented him in court, vouching for his good work record and attributing his crime to the fatigue brought on by a day off spent getting drunk, which is to say, to weakness of character and ignorance. To the workers, magistrates, and "rich bourgeois and industrialists" assembled in the courtroom, Cappi Bentivegna writes, "Alessandro Rossi spoke new, unexpected, passionate and just words":

> Our workers are too abandoned to themselves, to their poverty and ignorance. That is why you accuse them of being full of vices, that is why one of them resorted to killing. It is we, the owners, who are responsible for their moral life; we have to educate and change their life, make of it a civil life of men and of workers. I don't ask for clemency for an assassin; I don't ask for pity for a reject; I ask for justice for a worker; and which of us is truly responsible, think about it.[45]

Nor did Rossi oppose the state's efforts to protect industry. While the Veneto was under Austrian rule, he was an advocate of free trade. But after unification, the new competition Venetian industries faced in Italy and abroad led him to embrace protectionism. Before long he became Italy's most vocal and consistent proponent of economic nationalism and a powerful lobbyist for the protectionist commercial treaties of 1878 and 1887. Rossi's main points were that the successful development of Italian industry could not be taken for granted, especially in the face of competition from Europe's great powers; and that, in a late-industrializing nation like Italy, the state needed to offer industrialists positive assistance. Conversely, Rossi argued, the state had no business hindering Italian industry with restrictive factory laws.

The story of Rossi and Luzzatti's public battles has been told many times, but it is worth remembering that they went beyond the immediate issue of factory laws and became an equally heated exchange over the virtues of popular association, which is another way of saying that the dispute quickly became personal. On several occasions, Rossi laced his arguments with disparaging remarks about Italy's Jews, saying, for example, that they were too loyal to their race to be good patriots and that they promoted banking at the expense of Italy's truly productive, industrial interests. On the specific issue of factory laws, in an essay published in January 1876 in *Nuova Antologia*, Rossi found a way to mention that Jews did not observe Sunday as a day of rest. Understandably, Luzzatti took offence. In a letter to Fedele Lampertico, Luzzatti threatened to travel to Rossi's town of Schio and speak about the need for factory laws directly to his workers. At the top of his letter to Lampertico, Luzzatti scribbled, "Let Rossi know that if he runs into me on the way, it's better that he not greet me because I would spit in his face, his allusion to my religion is an infamy, but I will say how the Jesuits helped him create his factory." Although Luzzatti ultimately refrained from going to Schio, the feud put Lampertico in the awkward position of mediator, not only between Luzzatti and Rossi, but between the various political groups that formed around or against Rossi in the province of Vicenza. Lampertico warned Luzzatti against going to Schio to retaliate, adding that "you would have found your most faithful friends blocking the road; first you would have had to trample me, before you could do something so damaging to the country, which would have discredited you forever." As for the offence to Luzzatti's religion, if it were true – Lampertico claimed not to see it – it was certainly not a good idea to reveal it to the public.[46]

In this context, it is hard not to see as personal, too, Rossi's subsequent campaign to reveal the limitations of Luzzatti's popular banks to the public, this time in a much longer, serialized essay that appeared in four issues of *Nuova Antologia* between December 1878 and August 1879. Technically, Rossi's essay, entitled "On Popular Credit," was a comparative analysis of popular credit institutions throughout Europe. But the unmistakeable objects of Rossi's criticism were the popular banks in Italy and their tireless promoter, Luigi Luzzatti. Rossi's point was simple enough: despite all of Luzzatti's noble ideals and eloquent speeches, his "so-called popular banks" were in fact hardly different from any other credit institutions in Italy. The social composition of their membership (prevalently large merchants, industrialists, and landowners), the average number of shares owned by each member (high), and especially the banks' operations – savings deposits and loans but also investments and dividend payments, each clearly reflecting the interests of a business elite – all brought the banks' popular title into question. Unlike the German banks from which Luzzatti first drew inspiration, the Italian banks counted few peasants or workers among their clients. In short, they were "formed by the commercial bourgeoisie for the most part with the capital of wealthy, speculative people, charmed into wanting to appear or be called at least sisters of the German popular banks." It was not the Italian banks' financial success that irked Rossi, but rather their claims to be in any way special.[47]

Rossi was not the first person to question whether Luzzatti's banks were really popular. In Vicenza, critics of the local popular bank could hardly fail to notice the institution's rapid expansion beyond the dimensions of a humble credit union. From the time the bank was created in the fall of 1866 to 1873, as membership grew from 120 to almost 3,000, the weight of wealthy shareholders within the bank increased dramatically: the average number of shares each member owned rose from a modest two in the first two years to eight in 1870 and then ten in 1873. And these changes reflected a whole series of statutory modifications that allowed the bank to respond to the investment boom of the early 1870s. But Rossi's polemical essay focused public attention on the issue. Shortly after the first installment appeared in *Nuova Antologia*, at the annual meeting of the Popular Bank of Vicenza the president, Emanuele Lodi, offered the assembled shareholders a few general, statistical examples confirming the bank's "*popolarità*," and administrators appealed to all "commoner shareholders" in the hope that these "sons of the workshop, of industry, and of small commerce might persuade themselves of the holy idea that is saving." A few months later, the membership nominated a commission to reform the bank's statute.[48]

Luzzatti immediately set to work refuting Rossi, both in the periodical press and at countless popular bank meetings, including a rousing one in Padua in February 1879. Several speakers at this event, including the local bank's president, Maso Trieste, prepared the floor for Luzzatti, whose long speech (as reported in the bank's annual report) was punctuated by the familiar, parliamentary sounds of "*benissimo*," "laughter" – at Rossi's expense – and, above all, "applause." Trieste, Luzzatti, and the other speakers' comments had at least some of the detail and bite of Rossi's criticisms, and together formed a revealing assessment of the bank's evolution. Furthermore, unlike the reports coming out of Vicenza, the publications of the popular bank in Padua after 1878 offered a series of statistical tables, organized around a social categorization of the bank's membership, which itself represented a first meaningful attempt to define the bank's popular basis. By revealing the large presence of merchants, industrialists, and landowners among the bank's clients, these publications confirmed Rossi's portrayal of the popular bank as a predominantly middle-class institution. Luzzatti tried to obscure this fact by defining small merchants, industrialists, and farmers – and civil servants, too – as "popular," and thus adding their numbers to the modest ones of artisan and peasant members. For the first time, however, Luzzatti also began drawing consistent distinctions between those portions of Padua's working classes (for example, independent artisans) who could realistically hope to join a popular bank and those (for example, day labourers) whose modest savings limited them to joining a mutual aid society.[49]

Luzzatti also had the opportunity to defend and redefine his banks at the meetings, or "congresses," of the Association of Italian Popular Banks, an organization that he spearheaded in 1876 and presided over for decades. At the first congress, which was held in Milan in April 1877, Luzzatti gave the umpteenth version of the great transformation speech he had been delivering since 1863, which praised popular banks for offering credit "to small merchants and farmers, to workers and peasants" and for "alleviat[ing] poverty by educating the poor." At the second congress, held in Padua in December 1878, Luzzatti spoke of the banks' association of "that part of the wealthy and ruling classes which ... did not fear the emancipation of the multitudes," before adding:

> aware of the the immensity of the misfortunes and needs which afflict the less wealthy classes, [we do not] have the audacity to administer with popular credit a sort of panacea which is able to cure all ills. We only represent a small fragment in this work of reparation which the nineteenth century must accomplish to destroy or weaken the plague of the proletariat.

Nor, Luzzatti, went on, were all of the provident institutions put together – the popular banks, mutual aid societies, food cooperatives, employers' profit-sharing arrangements, and low-income housing projects – ever going to remove the pain and envy felt by the disinherited. By the third congress, held two years later in Bologna, Luzzatti was positively defensive, saying "it is not true that we promised *all of the poor* the use of capital; the only ones who will have it are *those deserving poor* who earned it with acts of assiduous providence." It was only within the larger complex of cooperative institutions that one could find "every gradation of poverty" represented.[50]

Luzzatti was not about to concede that his banks belonged outside the circle of popular associations that he, Lampertico, Morpurgo, Errera, and others had been promoting for two decades. But his acknowledgment that popular banks lacked a broad, working-class base clearly posed a problem. Luzzatti's solution was to establish new and closer ties between popular banks and those associations that did have predominantly working-class memberships. Hence the recurring theme in his speeches from the late 1870s of the popular banks' place within a much larger and rapidly expanding cooperative movement, and the frequent references to banks that assisted mutual aid societies and cooperatives in one way or another. Central to this strategy was the development of a new "honour loan" program that required the formal collaboration of popular banks and mutual aid societies. The idea was to offer small loans at low interest to individuals who, Luzzatti explained, were too poor to join a popular bank but enjoyed good standing within a mutual aid society. For the program to work, mutual aid societies had to perform the crucial task of overseeing both ends of the lending process: they had to elect their own representatives to honour loan boards, which, in turn, determined which worker-members should get loans; and then they were responsible for ensuring that the recipients repaid the loans on time. The only active part popular banks played in this new program was to put forward the loan money. The loan recipients were not popular bank members, they were members of mutual aid societies. Why shift attention and resources to mutual aid societies in this way? Because, Luzzatti confessed in 1878, mutual aid societies were in a better position than his banks to "judge the needs and means of workers."[51]

At issue here was not simply the mutual aid society's greater number and concentration of workers, but its superior capacity, as a social and fraternal organization, to stay in direct contact with workers. For years, as we have seen, Luzzatti had done everything in his power to demonstrate that popular banks, too, performed the ideal functions of an association: they published membership lists, held regular and well-publicized meetings, let members elect the banks' leaders and administrators, and so on. By the late 1870s, however, he seemed increasingly willing to emphasize the banks' role as financial service providers, especially in larger cities. Small-town banks – especially those just beginning to dot the south – continued to inspire Luzzatti to compare bank members to intimate friends and neighbours, but not the banks in Milan or Padua or

Bologna. Where bank memberships numbered in the thousands, the goal was no longer for bank members to stay in close touch with one another, but rather for the banks themselves to stay in close touch with mutual aid societies, where the fraternal ideals of association lived on. In short, Luzzatti appeared to be conceding that his banks were neither very popular nor very associational, except by proxy.[52]

Politically, it was bold of Luzzatti to put his faith in the bonds between popular banks and mutual aid societies. During the first decade after unification, the moderate liberal leaders of mutual aid societies in Padua and Vicenza were unusually successful at fending off opponents and rivals, but this began to change in the late 1870s. In particular, the proliferation of trade organizations (of shoemakers, printers, etc.) inevitably drew members and resources away from the general associations that Lampertico and Morpurgo had led for years. Thus, when the Popular Bank of Padua began to administer honour loans, that meant not simply working with Morpurgo's Mutual Aid Society of Artisans, Merchants and Professionals but with about ten other trade associations as well. In other Italian cities, especially large cities like Milan and politically divided cities like Bologna, the relationships between popular banks and workers' associations were bound to be more complicated. Some banks rejected scores of honour loan requests, others were slow to embrace the practice of granting loans to non-members. Luzzatti could not count on building quick or easy bridges with a range of different groups.[53]

Venetian liberals had always stressed the importance of not one or two popular associations, but an entire, connected series of them. Back in the 1860s, when Luigi Luzzatti promoted Italy's first popular banks and Alberto Errera prepared his yearbooks of popular institutions, the series consisted of five types of association: popular libraries, night schools, popular banks, cooperatives, and mutual aid societies. If we follow Luzzatti's endless string of publications and speeches over time, however, we can see the series change and grow. Gymnastics facilities make the list in a speech to a small Venetian popular bank in 1876, low-income housing societies at the second popular bank congress in 1878, producer cooperatives and cooperatives for the acquisition of raw materials at the third congress in 1880. In an essay on a glassworkers' cooperative in Altare (Liguria), published in 1881, Luzzatti marvelled at the network of civic initiatives that sprang out from this one small association: an old-age insurance group, a mutual aid society, a design school, music programs, historic preservation, and public health. And then there were the new institutions and programs administered by the state and by individual employers: postal savings banks, public school giveaways of bank books to children, national retirement and disability funds, profit-sharing arrangements, and so on. The result is a much denser, more complex institutional landscape than the one Luzzatti and many other Venetian liberals had promoted back in the 1860s. At the same time, new civic outlets allowed Luzzatti and other popular bank leaders to keep alive the heroic rhetoric of socio-economic modernization. If it was no longer convincing to speak of turning workers into capitalists, it was possible to claim a new "economic and moral" victory: the transformation – via savings, that is, "capitalized labour" – of workers into homeowners. And with these new outlets came scores of new banks, especially in southern Italy.[54]

More and more, as it grew in scope, Luzzatti's vision of a fully institutionalized society came to resemble the remarkable factory town Alessandro Rossi had been busy creating in Schio. Here, too, a handful of initiatives in the 1860s – a mutual aid society, infant nursery school, night school, and theatre – had evolved into a comprehensive network of institutions and amenities, which included a maternity ward, a reading room and library, choral and band programs, a fencing and gymnastics school, food cooperatives, public baths, and a vast new housing project, complete with public washing and ice facilities, a fountain, and houses for workers. Rossi took enormous pride in his creation, pointing out, for example, that his housing for workers consisted of attractive, individual buildings located in Schio proper, unlike the cramped and isolated apartment complexes under construction on the outskirts of Milan; and noting, above all, that he had found a way to improve the lives of his workers without any help from the state.

Like Luzzatti, however, Rossi also felt the need to justify the institutional choices he was making. In 1879, he published a study entitled *Worker Question and Social Question*, which amounted to a defensive, 191-page answer to the question, Why didn't Rossi allow his workers a share of his company's profits? As usual, Rossi skilfully explained the technical and managerial reasons why profit-sharing did not work in a large enterprise like his; unlike a small cooperative of fishermen, who sensibly agreed to divide their catch, a large industrial firm brought together owners, managers, and workers whose financial and intellectual contributions were so different that a clear and fair division of the profits was next to impossible to determine. As a result, he created a system of indirect participation in the company's profits: each year, Rossi directed that 5 per cent of the firm's profits go to the institutions and facilities he had created over the years for his workers. Technical arrangements aside, however, Rossi felt compelled to explain why paternalism of this sort was needed in order to "educate and raise the moral conscience of workers":

> The worker in his current state is unable to reach this goal by himself, and in those places where experiments have been done to leave him on his own with respect to the attainment of his moral and material progress, we have seen instead of his economic and moral emancipation, his subjection to the swarm of vices and passions that come from libertinage.
>
> [...]
>
> ... I do not intend to slander our workers, in whom I recognize many virtues which English and German workers still lack; but the worker's *Self-help* is not enough unless it is joined to that of the ruling classes.[55]

At about the same time that Luzzatti began suggesting workers and peasants might need to be compelled to deposit their meagre savings in a bank, Rossi was creating and funding institutions that were designed to shape every stage and dimension of his factory workers' lives. By reviving his warning against leaving workers on their own, which he had first made to a crowded courtroom back in the 1840s, Rossi appeared to join Luzzatti in offering workers a qualified, refracted message of self-help. To the extent that these evolving messages and strategies pointed to the limits, if not the outright failures, of popular association, Rossi could feel vindicated. But the larger question facing him and Luzzatti – and liberals throughout nineteenth-century Europe – was less comforting and not easily dismissed: when exactly would workers be ready to participate directly and spontaneously in the modern arenas of business, civic association, social reform, and parliamentary government?

5

Notable Politics

In December 1866, Fedele Lampertico, Vicenza's most prominent liberal politician, was elected to Italy's Chamber of Deputies. The following summer, over four hundred people in Vicenza signed a petition, posted throughout the city, protesting Lampertico's vote in Parliament against the state's sale of church property. Before he came up for election again in 1870, Lampertico announced his retirement from the Chamber, citing "family reasons," at the age of thirty-six; he was quickly nominated to the Senate, a position he held until his death in 1906. Nor was he the only important political figure in the Veneto to prefer a permanent, unelected position in the Senate to the vicissitudes of life as a representative in the Chamber of Deputies. Alessandro Rossi, another target of Vicenza's petitioners, quickly followed Lampertico into the Senate, as did Giulio Camuzzoni, one of Verona's leading politicians.[1] Countless others professed their distaste for electoral programs and speeches, for campaign visits, even for political associations. Italian liberals viewed political associations with suspicion, and openly encouraged citizens to direct their energy towards other, "civil" associations instead, in particular the economic and educational associations discussed in the previous chapter. Lacking strong public support, political associations became the least durable and visible associations in Italy. They routinely formed for the purpose of an important election and then disappeared a year or two later, and they rarely inspired their leaders to publish annual reports or membership lists.

But this is only half of the story. Fedele Lampertico continued to run for elected positions in local government, where no senatorial option existed: he was a member of Vicenza's city council from 1851 to 1905, retiring for health reasons just a year before his death; and a member of the provincial council, which did not exist before unification, from 1867 to 1905. More striking, he also continued to run for election in the Società Generale, the large workers' association that he helped found in 1858. For twenty-five years, without interruption, Lampertico chose to serve as the elected president of this association, many of whose members did not have the right to vote in parliamentary or municipal elections. The same was true of Emilio Morpurgo, a leader of Padua's largest mutual aid society for almost twenty years; Luigi Luzzatti, vice-president of the Popular Bank of Padua from its foundation in 1866 until 1882; and dozens of other local notables, albeit for more modest positions or periods of time. Not only did these men accept that elections regularly occurred within all associations, they ensured it by including election rules in the formal statutes that governed associations, and in addition often made a point of promoting and defending association members' constitutional right to vote.

There are a number of explanations for Italian liberals' apparently contradictory attitudes regarding elections. Lampertico, Luzzatti, and Morpurgo were not simply among the better known members of Vicenza's and Padua's mutual aid societies and popular banks; they were the founders of these associations. Along with the prestige that more or less naturally comes with being a founder, these men could also claim to know better than anyone else how to govern what were often large and complex institutions. In addition, it was easy to focus on ostensibly cut-and-dry matters of technical expertise within a mutual aid society or credit union, because these associations had relatively limited, well-defined objectives: mutual aid societies provided health insurance, credit unions gave out loans, and so on. If the founders of such organizations were careful, and they almost always were, little room would exist for political divisions and disagreements, even though it was plain that one political group – the moderate liberals – dominated associational life. At election time, the incumbent leaders of mutual aid societies did not present programs, they simply gave reassuring reports on the association's progress (its membership figures, finances, etc.) and awaited an approving vote. While such ritual demonstrations of competence and affirmation unfolded, the members in attendance were essentially free to speak their minds, but rarely did. In short, rather than simply viewing associational life as a refuge from the strife of politics, Venetian liberals saw it as an alternative, governmental ideal of politics: where voters were not volatile but quiet and respectful; where meetings and elections were predictable, orderly events; and, above all, where it was possible to promote change without conceding power.

Reality differed from the model. Although the moderate liberal leaders of associations hardly seemed to notice, a fundamental tension existed between their presumptions of authority and their promotion of a series of essentially free and public practices – of voting, meeting, discussion, and the like – that made challenges to that authority not only possible but likely. And this tension grew over time, especially within larger associations, as the number of elected representatives increased to keep pace with changing administrative needs, making the election of leaders and administrators who were not moderate liberals almost a necessity. Men such as Fedele Lampertico and Luigi Luzzatti might claim that political conflict had no place within mutual aid societies and popular banks, but they could hardly stop the emergence of new, "minority" leaders and groups when up to forty or fifty elected positions needed to be filled. How prepared were Lampertico and Luzzatti to accept genuine conflict or opposition within the associations they founded and led? And what do their actions tell us about the political culture that Italian liberals promoted after unification?

Ever since Max Weber drew attention to the lasting political importance of social prestige, historians have tended to emphasize the curious informality of nineteenth-century liberal politics. Power belonged to notables, that is, to men whose considerable wealth and education made them respected in their communities long before they ran for elections, and gave them the ample time and resources needed to maintain a high profile in community life: they were literally free to join clubs and attend social events, to sit on town committees and boards, to perform countless favours for friends and acquaintances. In much of this literature, the notable appears to be an inherently fragile and transitional figure. The loosely organized and deferential environment in which he thrived, we are made to understand, could not survive the many transformations that define nineteenth-century European history: rapid urbanization, the creation of a national communications network, the formation of popular political movements and organized parties, and the expansion of the bureaucratic state. Even the creative, late-nineteenth-century tactic of "inventing traditions" to appeal to the masses comes across as an act of desperation, a show of smoke and mirrors to delay the inevitable decline of liberalism as a political force.[2]

In recent years, Italian historians have provided a somewhat different portrait of the notable, one that recognizes the increasing complexity of the networks he commanded, and challenges the notion that personal and informal political practices were a fatal anachronism.[3] Still unclear,

however, is the notable's response to the range of public and formal practices of assembly, discussion, and voting that are an equally characteristic feature of nineteenth-century history. What happened when a notable
left the intimate confines of his private study or a bank's boardroom, and
entered a public meeting hall to address the members of an association?
How important was social prestige in this setting?

A Distaste for Politics

In Italy, a Liberal Party was not officially constituted until 1921, one year
before the fascist "march on Rome." By that time several other parties
had already formed, and something resembling an organized party system of government had begun to take shape. A few parties, most notably
the Radical and Republican parties, dated back to the first decade of the
twentieth century; one – the Italian Socialist Party – was established as
early as 1892. But if some of these first attempts at party formation were
led by groups that might be defined as left liberal, nevertheless the main
body of the liberal ruling classes in Italy remained outside of parties altogether before the First World War. Governments were made and broken
(and remade) by loosely defined parliamentary factions that tended to
form around specific political leaders – Marco Minghetti, Giuseppe Za-
nardelli, Giovanni Giolitti, and so on – rather than around specific party
platforms. Outside of Parliament, these formations had a very imperfect
relation to the multiple structures and ideological positions of local political life; being "Giolittian" in Padua could mean something different
from being "Giolittian" in Florence, Milan, or even Vicenza. All in all, it
was an institutional arrangement that Italian liberals seemed to be comfortable with, at least until the early twentieth century. To the extent that
they proved willing to organize public opinion and mobilize political support, they did so through clubs, circles, and associations that possessed
few or none of the institutional characteristics of the modern political
party. They were relatively small, rarely surpassing five or six hundred
members; they were not very durable, although frequent name changes
often belied considerable continuity; they possessed a bare minimum of
internal hierarchies and regulations; and, with a few exceptions, they
were decidedly local in scope.[4]

It is not enough, however, to say that Italian liberals preferred local associations to national parties, because they showed little enthusiasm for
either. Many Venetian liberals expressed doubts and concerns about political associations right off the bat. "Woe to the party that believes it can

realize its program simply with political associations," warned a writer for *Il Corriere di Vicenza* in August 1866:

> This is the illusion which has made us witness in Italy to so many circles, assemblies, and *clubs* that lead a useless if not harmful existence, increasing partisan anger, fomenting personal disagreements, wearing themselves out with declamations, and dying for the most part from exhaustion, not leaving behind any trace other than rabid, small, and intolerant factions [*consorterie*].
>
> [...]
>
> Our hopes and attention must be directed towards economic, industrial, agricultural and scientific associations; in a word, toward *civil* associations much more than toward *political* associations. These are the ones that constitute the true glory of modern society.[5]

Unfamiliarity with the institutions and practices of political organization no doubt heightened Venetians' sense of excitement, as well as alarm, as the first political associations in the region formed and met. In the years prior to unification, men such as Paolo Lioy, Fedele Lampertico, and Luigi Luzzatti had worked feverishly to learn as much as possible about the new workers' ("popular") associations of the time: mutual aid societies, cooperatives, circulating libraries, and so on. They read books on these associations, studied model statutes and regulations, and formed opinions of their own, all the while exchanging this information with their friends, asking advice or arguing small points of detail.[6] The same was not true of political institutions, however. The restrictions set by the Austrian government on the discussion of political topics were particularly strict; certainly, the impossibility of legally or publicly forming a political association must have diminished Venetians' intellectual enthusiasm for the subject. The political clubs existing elsewhere in Europe remained a source of "great confusion," as Lampertico put it in a letter to Luzzatti in 1862; on the whole, "permanent political clubs" seemed unnecessary and dangerous.[7]

In their own way, Lampertico's remarks were prophetic. Political associations in Padua and Vicenza after unification were highly impermanent institutions. In between spurts of activity, they led a phantom existence as little more than ad hoc electoral committees, surfacing two or three weeks before an election and disappearing just as quickly when it was over. Thus, none of the political associations that formed in 1866–67 in Padua (the Popular Circle and the Electoral Association) and Vicenza (the Liberal Society, the Friends of Liberty Association, the Popular Democratic Circle, and the Patriotic Association) still existed in 1870. Of course, there were also plenty of non-political associations that struggled to maintain a stable existence. Nevertheless, in most provincial centres the size of Padua or Vicenza, a dozen or so leading associations led a stable and active existence, and political associations were rarely among them.

Political associations were also the least public of all associations. In the first place, their public presence was generally limited to electoral campaigns. Few political associations, for example, held an annual meeting, which for the vast majority of other associations was a standard event, an occasion not just for the members to gather together but also for the leadership to provide a show of accountability, by reviewing the accomplishments of the previous year, detailing the state of the budget, and discussing plans for the future. It was not even routine for a political association to publicize or distribute a formal statute and regulation, or in any other way to indicate the responsibilities of the association to its members and the public at large. Furthermore, political associations kept a conspicuously low profile in the civic life of most cities. Occasionally they organized special meetings and delegations for patriotic celebrations, funerals, and other civic events, but relative to other associations – veterans' groups, for example, or mutual aid societies – their participation in these events was limited.

Electoral campaigns, it is true, generally followed a standard order of events: the convocation of a public meeting to nominate an electoral committee; the preparation by the electoral committee of a list of candidates for election: the presentation of this list at a subsequent meeting, to be discussed and approved by a vote of the membership; the dissemination of this list to the public (generally through the periodical press). When a political association failed to follow these procedures, whether by maintaining some kind of secrecy about its activities or by delaying preparation of a list of candidates, the local press was usually quick to offer its criticism. In this respect, the press served as a kind of watchdog organization. In addition, however, newspapers often performed the role of political associations by presenting their own lists of candidates.[8] Thus, during the periods when political associations either did not exist at all, or did not participate in electoral campaigns – in the early 1870s, for example, in Padua and Vicenza – newspapers frequently served as informal sites of political organization and debate.[9] Nevertheless, on these occasions the local press did no more than political associations to mobilize the electorate. Electoral meetings might begin with a discussion of the lists prepared ahead of time by a city's leading newspapers. Or there might not be an electoral meeting at all, the publication of a list by each newspaper being sufficient.[10]

Major political events did inspire Italian liberals to go beyond the limits of local association. The so-called parliamentary revolution of 1876, which brought the liberal left to power for the first time since unification, inspired politicians on each side of the Chamber of Deputies to organize political associations at the national level for the first time. And the greater threat of republican and socialist gains, magnified by Italy's first electoral reform and a deepening economic crisis, prompted similar action in the 1880s. Nevertheless, the results of these concerted efforts were relatively meagre: networks of affiliated associations collapsed a few years after they formed, clear party identities and rivalries succumbed to the centrist politics of *trasformismo*, of broad coalition-building among all supporters of Italy's constitutional monarchy.[11]

It was not simply political associations but the entire political process that lost the enthusiastic support of leading Venetian liberals in the years following unification. Everything from political programs to meetings and petitions increasingly seemed like forms of political obligation, not opportunity. Rare indeed was the case of Vincenzo Stefano Breda, MP from Padua's second district from 1866 to 1879, who every year presented a report of his activities and views to his electors in the form of a published pamphlet.[12] It was far more common for candidates to excuse themselves from presenting a formal program, or better yet to have themselves excused by influential friends and supporters. The candidate who rushed onto the scene with a political program in his hand was someone to worry about, and call to order. This was evident when the moderate liberal Emilio Broglio ran for election to Parliament in March 1871, in the provincial district of Thiene, north of Vicenza. Broglio's record was impressive. He had participated in the 1848 revolution in Milan, serving as secretary of the provisional government. In the same year, he was elected to be a parliamentary deputy in the Kingdom of Piedmont-Sardinia. By the time he ran for election in Thiene, he had already held several important government positions: minister of public works; minister of public instruction; minister of agriculture, industry, and commerce; and vice-president of the Chamber of Deputies. And yet, as the election of 1871 approached, Fedele Lampertico expressed his concern about Broglio to Paolo Lioy,

I too am beginning now to see hope for Broglio. But for goodness sake, tell him ..., if he is going to draw up programs, not to upset the situation. On the other hand ..., can political programs really be necessary to a man whose whole life is a program? Tell him, tell him these things directly and in my name if you like.[13]

The phrase "his whole life is a program" appears again and again during Italian election campaigns, in the speeches and newspaper articles promoting individual candidates from just about every point on the political spectrum, including radical democrats and Catholics. More often than not, that "whole life" referred to the candidates' patriotic actions during the Risorgimento, as participants in the revolutionary governments of 1848–49, for example, or as members of Garibaldi's volunteer armies.

Of course, getting elected (and especially re-elected) required something more than a glorious past. As countless letters to and from Fedele Lampertico attest, elections were generally decided by local notables, those large landowners and multiple officeholders who appeared to protect and assist local citizens – often directly, in the form of personal favours – and, in turn, demanded their political support. After winning the election in Thiene in 1871, Emilio Broglio recognized, in a letter to Lampertico, that his victory had little to do with his or his opponent's views on specific political questions, and much to do with the efforts of local men like the abbot and university professor Giambattista Pertile, whom Broglio had never met, but who "exercised his natural and legitimate influence with his townsfolk, thanks to your intervention, to promote my election." One group of promoters winning out over another: this was how elections worked, Broglio recognized, in Britain as well as in Italy, at least outside of large cities, where popular demagogues held sway; moreover, Broglio added, this was how it should work.[14] Lampertico clearly agreed with Broglio about the insignificance of political programs. He must also have appreciated Broglio's reluctance to schedule a formal "visit to the electors" of Thiene, upon the request of one of his local promoters, just two months after his election victory. A "friendly party among friends" is one thing, Broglio wrote to Lampertico, a visit marked by "protests and counter-demonstrations" is another.[15]

Emilio Broglio was one of several prominent liberals elected to Parliament in the Veneto who chose to run in small, rural districts, far from the cities where they lived or exercised the greatest influence. Alberto

Cavalletto, the leader of the clandestine movement to liberate the Veneto from Austrian rule, was actually defeated in the first parliamentary election held in Padua in the fall of 1866. So it was understandable that he went on to run for election elsewhere, in the districts of St Vito and Pordenone in the province of Udine. More surprising was Luigi Luzzatti's decision to bypass both Padua, where he was a university professor and a central figure in associational life, and his hometown of Venice for the remote district of Oderzo in the province of Treviso. The defeat of Cavalletto in Padua seemed to offer a singular lesson for the region's other nationally recognized political figures: it was better not to expose one's political fortune to the caprices of a relatively large voting public, which, even under the restrictive electoral laws in effect before 1882, could easily number in the thousands in a medium-sized city like Padua. In small provincial localities, it was possible to build and maintain a loyal political following; in these districts, the risks presented by an unfriendly or unpredictable public could be safely reduced through the efforts of a dozen or so provincial notables. When Luigi Luzzatti was re-elected to Parliament in the district of Oderzo in 1880, the results from the district's three voting centres were as follows: Motta: 166 voters, 162 for Luzzatti; Oderzo: 285 voters, 274 for Luzzatti; S. Biagio: 79 voters, 79 for Luzzatti. Thirty years and one electoral reform later, in the election of 1909, the total number of voters in the Oderzo district had increased fourfold (from 530 to 2,294), but Luzzatti continued to win by carrying a string of small towns, with an average of 143 voters per town.[16]

Regardless of their choice of electoral districts, parliamentary deputies routinely entertained fantasies of retiring from politics. Luzzatti's statement to Quintino Sella in September of 1876 was typical:

> [The other day] I thought of my wife who is still sick, and of my children who need me, and I decided in my mind to liquidate my most urgent political affairs and then leave politics forever and return to my studies.[17]

Before finally retiring in 1879, Emilio Morpurgo confessed to his wife that for years he "had had all that he could take," and that he dreamed of "hopping on a train" that would take him back to Padua and his position there as a university professor.[18] A recurring theme in these threats, idle or not, was the contrast between the public world of politics and the private pleasures offered by family life and scholarship. Even the decision to begin a political career drew upon this theme; thus, in his electoral letter of the fall of 1866, Paolo Lioy stated his willingness to "bid farewell to the holy peace of private life (blessed oasis of existence)."[19] When an MP actually followed through on his threat to leave the world of politics, the most frequent explanation he offered the public was, quite simply, "family reasons."[20]

Associational Elections

Family life was not the only blessed oasis from which elites viewed the turbulent world of politics. Associational life, too, in its civic and non-political forms, provided a model of tranquility and goodwill. On occasion, Venetian liberals made the apoliticism of associational life an explicit goal. At an early meeting of the Popular Bank of Milan, in 1865, Luzzatti warned a crowd of some 350 people to stay clear of politics. "Let the popular bank be like the sanctuaries of the middle ages," he said, "almost a city of refuge against the clash of political passions."[21] But the same men also invested associational life with political meaning. Popular banks and mutual aid societies made a point of participating in national Constitution Day celebrations; hiking club members offered patriotic toasts to Italy's "unredeemed lands" across the Alps; agricultural associations and chambers of commerce debated how to get out the vote for their own elections. Countless other associations emulated the Constitution by drafting formal statutes and regulations, and they emulated Parliament by establishing procedures and protocols for members' behaviour at meetings. Thus, associations that were technically non-political in nature routinely adopted the language, forms, and practices of liberal government.

Evidence of an apolitical ideal certainly exists. In the early 1860s, the issue of whether or not workers' associations should occupy themselves with politics was the subject of heated debate in Italy. The first congresses of workers' associations held after Italian unification had exposed the contrast between a moderate Piedmontese tradition of apoliticism and the more radical positions held by several other regional groups, including Genoese and Milanese contingents of democrats. At the Milan Congress in September 1860, a proposal that mutual aid societies demand a reform of the Italian electoral franchise (in favour of universal suffrage) met with strong disapproval from the moderates, and a formal split was narrowly averted. A year later, at the congress in Florence, the compromise reached in Milan fell apart: before a resolution supporting the discussion of politics in workers' institutions could be put to a vote, the Piedmontese delegation walked out in protest. In the years that followed, this division only deepened, and moderate attendance at the congresses of workers' associations dropped; at the Congress of Parma, in October 1863, only sixty workers' societies were represented, less than half the number represented at Florence in 1861 and only one-eighth of the total number of associations then in existence in Italy.

Nevertheless, by 1866, when the Veneto was liberated, the controversy had already begun to die down. The Eleventh Congress of Workers Associations, held in Naples in October 1864, was the last one for seven years, and thus a leading forum for discussion of the "political question" within workers' associations ceased to exist. At about the same time, the attention of the Italian labour movement began to shift from the political ideals of Mazzinian republicanism to the social and economic demands of international socialism, and the revolutionary deeds of anarchism. In 1871, the issue was still hot enough to involve Fedele Lampertico in the moderates' boycott of the Twelfth Congress of Workers Associations, and their organization of a counter-congress the following year. As president of Vicenza's largest mutual aid society of artisans, the Società Generale, Lampertico defended the moderates' position, saying, "our association cannot fail to applaud the principle manifested in the [protest] circular of 21 October that provident associations must absolutely keep themselves outside of political discussions."[22] But how typical was such an open declaration of apoliticism? Giacomo Zanella, no great admirer of politics, rarely mentioned the topic in the many speeches he gave to the artisans in Lampertico's Società Generale. And the same was true of Luzzatti, Morpurgo, and most of the other moderate liberal leaders of Venetian associations. In addition, we need to weigh this relative silence on the matter against the same leaders' often vocal and active promotion of associational elections.

Take, for example, the efforts made to increase participation in the annual elections held by agricultural associations and chambers of commerce. These two organizations were unusual in that they were affiliated with the state, and thus their elections were supervised by the Ministry of Agriculture, Industry and Commerce (MAIC). Voter turnout at agricultural association and chamber of commerce elections was often remarkably low. For example, in the first few years of the Agrarian Association of Vicenza's existence (1869–72), an average of only nineteen out of over two hundred members attended the meetings at which elections occurred.[23] The numbers for Padua's chamber of commerce during the same years were only marginally better: an average of two hundred out of 1,174 members came out to vote, in this case not at the end of regular meetings but at organized commercial elections, complete with official lists of eligible voters and designated polling centres.[24] MAIC encouraged local chambers to address "this sad and damaging state of affairs." In response, chambers considered a variety of reform proposals, including holding commercial elections in the summer instead of the winter, or at the same time and location as administrative elections, and increasing the number of electoral districts and voting centres.[25]

Furthermore, chambers of commerce elections frequently drew the attention and involvement of a wider political public, so often, in fact, that these ostensibly non-political events became an established part of the Italian political calendar. Each year, in late November or December, local newspapers announced the approach of the area's commercial elections, often presenting a recommended list of candidates or reproducing one or more of the anonymous lists that were circulating in the city. Instead of "several electors," the anonymous tag familiar from political election campaigns, the commercial lists were signed "several merchants." Annual popular bank elections also drew the attention of local newspapers, and occasionally inspired pre-election meetings, the circulation of lists (recommended by "several shareholders"), and high turnouts of members.[26] Even the relatively narrow elections of artisanal "trade heads" (*capi d'arte*) in general mutual aid societies could become public affairs, as rival workers' groups put up wall posters with the names of the men they would like to see representing their town's butchers, printers, stonecutters, stovemakers, porters, and so on.

At times, even political associations figured in local efforts to mobilize these ostensibly non-political electorates of merchants, landowners, artisans, and shareholders. Discouraged by the low turnout at the commercial elections of 1872, for example, the *Corriere di Vicenza* lamented the fact that the city of Vicenza seemed incapable of forming "a liberal *club* where one can meet and discuss the serious issues which pertain to local and state government [*amministrazione*]."[27] The Popular Bank of Vicenza's elections in 1880 inspired *Il Giornale della Provincia di Vicenza* to register a similar complaint. A "large, preparatory meeting," it noted, would have helped bank members narrow down a list of suitable candidates; instead, only one "very small" meeting was held, leaving small groups of shareholders free to devise their own lists. *Il Giornale della Provincia di Vicenza* presented a list of its own, and was pleased to report, after the first round of elections was over, that twelve of the fifteen men elected had been on its list. Nevertheless, it could not approve the other figures that emerged from the election: of the city's four thousand or so shareholders (over six thousand in the province), only one hundred turned out to vote, and they voted for no fewer than forty candidates.[28]

Beyond simply following associational elections, liberals also defended members' voting rights, including those of bank and business shareholders. Businesses did not observe uniform rules of meeting and voting; some gave multiple votes to large shareholders, others restricted the vote to the owners of a set number of shares. Many commentators, however, upheld the liberal-democratic principle of "one share, one vote" and criticized the businesses that violated it. In 1869, for example, the official periodical of Vicenza's Agrarian Association reported that a large new enterprise called the Agricultural Bank (with headquarters in Milan) only allowed the owners of twenty or more shares to vote at meetings. There are banks, it stated, that are based on "mighty capital" and "illustrious names," and then there are banks that have "a local colour and a democratic constitution." The agricultural bank in question would suffer from having board directors who were not in touch with ordinary landowners; Italy would benefit from having credit institutions with "less aristocratic forms."[29] Other champions of shareholders' rights addressed the question of where meetings and elections took place, again making a link between locality and democracy. Luigi Luzzatti drew attention to the practical problem created by large, centralized banks and businesses, whose scattered shareholders often had to travel great distances in order to attend meetings.[30] On occasion, Luzzatti – the same Luzzatti who had told popular bank members in Milan to avoid political passions – could sound more like a democrat of the left than a moderate liberal of the right. "The word of the common man [*popolano*]," he wrote in 1871, "is worth as much as the word of the rich man" in popular banks: "The common man ... is encouraged to participate at meetings, to speak his mind freely, and is capable of holding an office, and of taking part in the administration of an institution which is essentially his own."[31] Moderates outside of the Veneto made similar comments.[32]

It is worth noting that Luzzatti made this statement in the early 1870s, that is, after most moderate liberals had ceased to show much enthusiasm for mobilizing voters for political elections (local or national), but before they faced a political challenge of the sort that might explain a strategic use of populist rhetoric, such as the moderate liberals' parliamentary defeat in 1876 or the expansion of the suffrage in 1882. Nor did their statements consist simply of abstract or vague references to members' "rights." Rather, they addressed precisely the kind of practical, procedural limits to participation – the number and location of polling places, the silencing effects of intimidation at ostensibly open meetings, and the like – that political associations in this period rarely acknowledged, let alone discussed. Moreover, at least some of the would-be voters and speakers defended by Luzzatti and others were, in fact, commoners who did not possess the right to vote in Italy's political elections. Few prominent Venetian liberals championed these "lower classes" of associational voters with as much regularity or enthusiasm as Luzzatti, but, as the leaders of workers' associations in their home towns, fewer still could afford to ignore them. After all, Luzzatti, Lampertico, Morpurgo, and friends were the *elected* leaders of workers' associations. Again and again, these men who expressed their distaste for parliamentary politics put themselves up for re-election in local mutual aid societies and popular banks, with hundreds if not thousands of eligible voters. Why?

Administrative Democracy

It is not enough to point out that attendance at the meetings where elections occurred was, in fact, often very low, for an unhappy group of fifty or seventy-five members at such meetings could have unseated the existing leadership – or simply made the experience of running for re-election unpleasant – just as easily as a group numbering in the hundreds. Yet this rarely happened. On the contrary, there was something automatic about the re-election of men such as Fedele Lampertico and Emilio Morpurgo, presidents for many years of the largest mutual aid societies of artisans in Vicenza and Padua, respectively. Several factors help explain this extraordinary combination of electoral success and tranquility. First, considerable prestige was naturally attached to the men who founded associations, a group that did not simply include leading Venetian liberals but was dominated by them: Lampertico in Vicenza, Morpurgo in Padua, Luzzatti in Padua and Venice, and so on. Second, the expertise of these individuals in associational law, administration, and finance made them seem indispensable to members with far less experience or education. Finally, the formal statutes and regulations that determined how most associations were run favoured the type of orderly and respectful conduct at meetings that tended to affirm rather than challenge existing leaders' authority, and thus also to increase the likelihood of successful re-elections.

Venetian liberals' pretensions to leadership and expertise went largely unchallenged for the first decade after unification; however, by the late 1870s, the liberal ideal of quiet meetings ending in the uncontested re-election of leaders and administrators came under attack. Democratic and socialist organizers began pressing workers to assert their autonomy from local elites, either by forming new associations of their own or by reforming existing associations. If workers were not able to act alone, they could at least demand that associations eliminate the distinction between honorary and ordinary members, or try to gain greater representation on boards of directors. In moderate liberal strongholds like Padua and Vicenza, opposition groups were especially tempted to challenge the dominance over local workers' associations of men like Fedele Lampertico and Luigi Luzzatti. Venetian moderates continued to win parliamentary and municipal elections after 1876, the year when national power shifted to the left, but they could not prevent rivals establishing a stronger presence within the more open, quasi-parliamentary realm of associational life.

The problem was not simply political, a matter of disgruntled opposition groups setting their sights on these institutional strongholds of moderate liberalism. It was also administrative, a matter of increasing the number of elected positions within associations to keep pace with expanding operations. As we saw in the previous chapter, the leading proponents of workers' associations in the Veneto deliberately made the case that associations, too, benefited from economies of scale; that it was financially beneficial for a city to have one large ("general") mutual aid society of artisans rather than twenty smaller, craft-based societies. Conveniently, with larger memberships and budgets came an apparently greater need for expert leaders like themselves, who, for example, knew how to set the rates of sickness and pension payments in accordance not only with the income from weekly membership dues, but also with calculable rates of sickness, injury, and mortality among different groups of workers. Less convenient, however, was the need for larger and larger bodies of administrators. As the number of elected positions in mutual aid societies and popular banks went from one to several dozen, it became more and more likely that the moderate liberal notables who founded and ran these associations would have to share power with other groups. How Luigi Luzzatti and Fedele Lampertico responded to this change tells us a lot about the politics of associational life.

The Popular Bank was the largest association in Padua, with almost eight hundred members in 1869 and almost four thousand members a decade later. Just as important, in accordance with its remarkable size and resources, it was the association with the greatest number of elected leaders and administrators. In the bank's first decade of existence, the vast majority of leaders and administrators were moderate liberals. For example, no fewer than twenty-one of the twenty-eight men who made up the bank's administration in 1878 had been among the first members of the moderate Constitutional Association two years earlier.[33] By this time, however, all popular banks in Italy had begun to face new scrutiny, as critics of the institutions questioned whether the banks were, in fact, benefiting the popular classes.[34] Not coincidentally, attendance at the annual meetings of Padua's Popular Bank shot up in the late 1870s, and the meetings became occasions for vocal debates and disagreements. When, for example, in 1879 some of the bank's moderate leaders proposed that bank administrators be forbidden to borrow funds themselves, a group of members, including Michelangelo Fanoli, Angelo Wolff, Alessandro Marin, and Carlo Tivaroni, all of them important members of the city's progressive and democratic opposition parties, took the floor to reject the leaders' proposal as "antidemocratic," as tantamount to "placing the Popular bank in the hands of large property and large capitalists, who more rarely are in need of assistance."[35]

A longer and more heated exchange took place two years later, over the question of how best to supervise the bank's expanding loan operations. At issue was the relationship between the institution's predominantly elite board of directors and its larger but subordinate loan committee. On all decisions concerning loans, the former had final and executive authority, but the latter, a rotating group of between fifteen and twenty-four members, performed the more basic and time-consuming task of reviewing all prospective bank clients. As the bank's operations grew, so did the team of loan committee members and supervisors, and with it the opportunity for both non-moderate and non-elite members of the bank to increase their representation among the bank's administrators. Inevitably, the question arose: should the board of directors step in and establish greater control over the loan review process, either directly or through a permanent (non-rotating) supervisory loan commission? It is not clear how or when the leaders of Padua's Popular Bank planned to present the idea for such a change to the membership, because the first mention of it came not from the leadership but from two members, Angelo Wolff and Alessandro Marin. In an unusually dramatic confrontation at the bank's annual meeting in 1881, Wolff and Marin questioned the bank's president, Maso Trieste, on the constitutionality of creating a new loan commission without first consulting the membership. Clearly on the defensive, Trieste accused Marin of making an interpellation, a familiar parliamentary tactic that forced leaders to account for their actions and often to ask the assembly for a vote of confidence, the outcome of which generally determined whether the existing leadership had the support necessary to stay in power without resorting to new elections. By keeping his focus on proper, constitutional procedure, Marin calmly demonstrated his non-partisan loyalty to the greater good of the bank, without letting Trieste off the hook.[36] Rather than appearing to fight against the moderate-led Popular Bank, he and a group of other critical members appeared to be fighting for a particular vision of the bank: as constitutional but also democratic, which is to say, inclusive enough to entrust new men with the day-to-day affairs of the bank.

Parliamentary tactics at popular bank meetings went hand in hand with behind-the-scenes negotiations before elections. By the early 1880s, local progressives and democrats had successfully occupied six positions on the Popular Bank of Padua's board of directors; moreover, the anticipated resignation of the president Maso Trieste in the summer of 1883 made further changes seem likely. The bank's vice-president and unofficial leader, Luigi Luzzatti. consulted with the minority leader, Carlo Tivaroni. Their negotiations are recorded in a remarkable letter that Tivaroni sent to Luzzatti:

> Naturally we will ask for the reconfirmation of the six [board members]. We have been made to understand that if we were to give up the re-election of one of these, to be chosen by the majority, they would accord us the right to eliminate one of theirs, chosen by us.
>
> ... Of our six, (we can speak directly) only two are likely to be chosen for exclusion: Alessio or Poggiana.
>
> We cannot and must not abandon either the one or the other ...
>
> Therefore, if in the interest of the institution and in order to satisfy the *amor proprio* of the majority, it is necessary to sacrifice one of our own – *we will not refuse* – but we want to decide – that is, we will indicate today whom we are disposed to leave out: in order to prove that we are sincerely disposed towards an honest transaction.[37]

What makes the letter remarkable is its explicitly political content; as the historian Angelo Ventura has pointed out, only in the last paragraph of the letter does it become clear that Tivaroni is speaking about the Popular Bank, and not municipal politics.[38]

Was Luzzatti offended by this intrusion of party politics into his beloved bank? Hardly. Having already been stung by critics who exposed the paucity of working-class members (and especially loan recipients) in popular banks, by the late 1870s Luzzatti was eager to demonstrate that these banks were not simply bourgeois institutions, let alone blunt instruments of moderate liberal hegemony. The banks' increasingly technical operations made it highly unlikely that significant numbers of *popolani* were ever going to sit on the banks' elected boards and committees, next to the landowning notables, the professors, lawyers, and accountants. Nevertheless, within the limits of administrative competence, Luzzatti actively wanted to attract a diverse group of leaders and administrators. Echoing Luzzatti's thoughts, his close friend (and the mayor of Padua) Antonio Tolomei wrote in a letter to Luzzatti, in the fall of 1883, that the goal was for the Popular Bank of Padua to "welcome ... all the active forces in the country."[39] This last phrase unmistakeably invoked the national political strategy of *trasformismo*, of overcoming the division between Italy's two main groups of liberals – the moderate right and progressive left – by forming governments with the participation and support of both. On the face of it, the application of such a strategy to popular banks seems odd. The Popular Bank of Padua was not Parliament, not even the city council. In order to prosper and grow, a popular bank did not need to include "every active force in the country," least of all on its board of directors. And yet, in Luzzatti's mind, popular banks were – or could be – representative bodies in their own right. If the time had arrived in Italy for greater democracy, and for the transcendance of old political divisions, civic associations too must join the effort.[40]

While negotiating the transformation of Padua's popular bank, Luzzatti remained in close contact with Fedele Lampertico, his friend and political ally in Vicenza. As the undisputed leader of Vicenza's moderate liberals, and a central figure in local associational life, Lampertico found himself in a situation very similar to the one faced by Luzzatti in Padua. In particular, as president of the Società Generale of artisans, Lampertico also had to answer members' demands for greater participation and power. The difference, however, between Lampertico's and Luzzatti's responses to this challenge could not have been greater. Far from promoting the democratization of the Società Generale, Lampertico personally intervened to prevent its occurrence. In the process, he displayed an authoritarian disregard even for the constitutional rights of assembly, speech, and election that governed the association.

It was artisans, not local political leaders, who pressed for change in Vicenza. Like most of the workers' mutual aid societies created by moderate liberals in Italy, the Società Generale had two distinct categories of

members: honorary members, who, according to the association's founding statute, were "those who help [*beneficare*] the Society with donations
or with some distinct service"; and ordinary members, namely, artisans
who made weekly payments in exchange for subsidies in times of sickness
or injury. From the outset, fearing that ordinary members might abuse the
system by pretending to be sick, the society's leaders – all of them honorary
members – arranged to send representatives of the association directly to
members' homes to verify each sickness claim. Usually one or two artisan
delegates, or "trade heads" (*capi d'arte*), would accompany a doctor to the
sick member's home, "comforting him with [their] presence and affectionate words" while also "making observations on the progress of the illness
and on the real state of the sick member."[41] In effect, with the necessary
supervision, the general membership would police itself. The trade heads
also helped recruit new members and collect dues, assisted at administrative meetings, and gave formal representation to the general membership,
whose needs and opinions they communicated to the leadership. For close
to thirty years, the size and configuration of the Società Generale's leadership remained unchanged, consisting of one president, two vice-presidents,
a secretary, a treasurer, and four counsellors. But the number of elected
trade heads increased along with the size of the membership, until, by the
early 1880s, there were over fifty. To the extent that the Società Generale's
small corps of leaders had any regular contact with the general membership, it was through an expanding roster of delegates.[42]

The mediating function of the trade heads was apparently not sufficient to bridge the divide between the Società Generale's nine leaders and
its one thousand or more ordinary members. Already in 1879, there were
signs here and there of members' frustration with the association. One
member, Giobatta Perobelli, speaking on behalf of several others, sent a
five-page letter to the leadership on the subject of the society's general
assemblies. Perobelli expressed his concern over the lack of discussion:

> [A]mong the ordinary members there are many who abstain from speak-
> ing at meetings because they do not feel capable of developing their ideas in
> clear terms, others because they are not endowed with readiness of mind,
> others because they become overwhelmed by fear, and others so as not to be
> silenced for their improper language, and of these, believe me Mr. President,
> there are many, more than others believe.

Unlike most associational statutes, the one prepared for the Società
Generale in 1858 did not require that leaders publicize the agenda of

upcoming meetings. If members knew ahead of time what the issues to be discussed at a meeting were, Perobelli noted, they would have time to work out their ideas and write speeches.[43]

Three years and numerous letters of protest later, frustrated members identified an even greater problem: the Società Generale's failure as a social institution. In 1882, a group of Società Generale members formed a new organization, called the Workers' Circle, which aimed not to replace the Società Generale but to provide its members with a new outlet. In a letter sent to all members of the Società Generale in July 1882, one of the Workers' Circle's founders explained:

> In fact, we belong to a mutual aid society of artisans but we do not have the fortune of being able to mutually express our frank opinions, our needs; ... because we cannot meet together more than two times per year, and as a result are lacking the reciprocal acquaintance, that intimacy and trust which is so necessary among individual members.
>
> Here then, instituting this Workers' Circle, will remove so serious a drawback, it being [our] first goal, that of meeting as often as possible, daily even, all it takes is to want it and, thus gathered, conscientiously to examine all of the questions to be resolved; taking care more and more to fight for all of our rights as workers and citizens.[44]

The moderate liberals' decades-old turn away from sociability, as a primary goal of associational life, was beginning to catch up with them.

Letters of protest were sometimes met with counter-protests aimed at discrediting the opposition.[45] Meanwhile, criticism of the leadership intensified. Take, for example, the series of letters written by an anonymous member of the Società Generale – "a worker" – and addressed to Fedele Lampertico. The letters take aim at the moderate liberal and Catholic leaders who imposed a religious stamp on the association (in the form of masses, donations to churches, patron saint celebrations, etc.), and who further insulted and demoralized the members by presenting them as the fortunate recipients of their superiors' pious acts of charity. Once again, the true focus was the Società Generale's internal relations of authority and, specifically, the pretensions of the leadership and the subservience of the membership:

> Why does our association have to become like lambs in the service of one or a few notables [benemeriti], instead of offering them a most respectful bow and telling them clearly and roundly what a worker might do?[46]

The anonymous "worker" assigned much of the blame for this state of affairs to Fedele Lampertico. In one particularly biting passage, he comes close to discrediting Lampertico's entire twenty-five-year tenure as the Società Generale's president.

> He [Lampertico] spoke often of cooperation, of workers' credit unions, of so many other provisions to the advantage of workers suggested by economic science, and then? ...
>
>   Now if he could only tell us the truth, he is afraid, because his cowardly heart prefers a churchyard or a sheepfold, to a meeting in which people [*la gente*] might speak or discuss freely their opinions.[47]

The same author warned against politicizing the Società Generale and criticized fellow members, including several *capi d'arte*, for failing to respect the need for order and decorum at the society's meetings. By reducing meetings to shouting matches, the "worker" insisted, these members ended up working together with Lampertico and the other leaders of the Società Generale to make meaningful debate impossible. "When a worker ... demands an explanation of a fact or a number," he writes, "the President nods his head, dawdles with pencil in hand," says a few "evasive words" and then "turns to whisper a few more words in the ear of his co-president." When the worker asks to speak again, others start hissing and shouting until "the Leadership raises its omnipotent hands" to order silence. It was as if Lampertico "found joy in his heart to see the opposition *suffocated*." And, sadly, the strategy worked, because "whoever speaks in public and, like us workers, is not very used to doing so, and expects to provoke shouts, will not risk saying another word again."[48]

Despite the occasional flirtation with proto-socialist ideas and rhetoric – "workers, always workers, everything for workers"[49] – what is most remarkable about these letters is not their radicalism but their orthodox liberalism. Religious tolerance, the preference for mutual aid over charity, the importance of orderly public meetings and discussions, even an aversion to party politics, these were the main themes that the "worker" presented to Lampertico in his letters. They were also the principal themes of liberal associational life after unification.

How did Lampertico respond? We know that he and the other eight leaders of the Società Generale, as a group, stretched their statutory powers to invalidate (in 1880) and suspend (in 1882) trade head elections. They also denied several requests from the membership for a greater role in the reform of the Società Generale, requests by trade heads to have input in pension decisions, as well as a request by a group of seventeen members for a special meeting ("so that everyone can freely express their own good ideas about the future development of the Society").[50] It is not always possible to know what position Lampertico himself took in these decisions. But a pair of letters sent by Lampertico to Luigi Luzzatti in the fall of 1882 makes his personal views very clear. In the first letter, Lampertico described the difficulties confronting the Società Generale:

> for some time now various members, rather a few, have continued to demonstrate their insolence in the newspapers, to insult both us and the Society with letters, to raise questions at every possible moment.

These were actions, Lampertico assured Luzzatti, for which the members in question could be punished in a court of law. But Lampertico preferred to resolve the problem inside the association. The society's official statute recognized the possibility of arbitration for "questions" arising between its leaders and members. But this was not what Lampertico had in mind:

> Here, however, we are not talking about true questions, but about the future direction of the Society, of actions by the Leadership which cannot be made into material for arbitration.

Indeed, Lampertico had to confess that the association's statute, unreformed since 1858, was now quite useless:

> I have not sent you the Statute because it says nothing. That is, it says nothing to me: perhaps it will say something to you.
>
> ...
>
> In fact, we are in the process of reforming it, but the reform itself cannot be considered as long as those few [members] are there to make everything difficult.

With or without the statute, Lampertico's sole concern was the elimination of the Società Generale's "insolent" members.

> Is it possible without breaking the law, is it possible in such a way that a jury of any kind from within the mutual aid society might say we were right, to exclude them? How?[51]

In his second letter, dated 8 October, Lampertico made his disregard for liberal procedure even clearer. For the purposes of eliminating "a few" of the Società Generale's members, Lampertico was prepared to ignore the association's statute. He was also eager to avoid resolving the issue before a general meeting of the membership. "A large meeting," he explained to Luzzatti, "can always expose you to surprises."[52]

Although, for the moment, Lampertico did not succeed in eliminating any members from the Società Generale, he did manage to remove at least one opponent, Giovanni Panozzo, from the roster of trade heads. More important, by the time new *capi d'arte* elections were held, in February 1883, a calmer mood prevailed in the association. Attendance at the elections was low, itself perhaps a statement of protest, but there were no angry letters, no insults, no questions raised. Six months later, the controversial task of reforming the mutual aid society's statute culminated in a decisive victory for Lampertico and the other leaders of the association. Despite the opposition of a vocal group of trade heads, their reform proposals carried the day with 183 out of 240 votes.[53] The calm did not last long. The leadership was forced to revise the group's statute again in 1886, prompting another wave of acrimonious debate. As for Lampertico, he remained president of the Società Generale until 1888, when he resigned after yet another successful re-election; a year later he was elected honorary president of the association. At no time during this most tumultuous period in the Società Generale's history did Lampertico appear to lose the formal support of most members. As the most powerful man in Vicenza, Lampertico was a patron that any association could ill afford to lose.[54]

Nevertheless, the continuities exhibited by the Società Generale cannot obscure the striking failure of Lampertico to respect the basic tenets of liberal government within associational life. First, by refusing meetings, discounting election results, and ignoring statutory rules of conduct, he discredited the ideal of civic participation within formal, procedural limits. Second, by reacting so strongly both to the profusion of critical letters and newspaper articles and to the threat of an unruly or simply unpredictable public meeting, he threatened to cut the Società Generale off from a wider public audience and culture, much as political associations did. Third, by refusing to accept the critical opinions of the society's general membership, by refusing its input on matters affecting the future of the association, he sacrificed the goal that he and so many other leading Venetian liberals had set out to achieve: to involve the popular classes in associational life.

The situation Lampertico found himself in, along with Luzzatti and other associational leaders in the same period, also reveals something very important about the politics of associational life after unification. The leaders of mutual aid societies and popular banks oversaw the creation of popular associational constituencies at a time when a relatively small percentage of Italians possessed the right to vote in municipal or parliamentary elections. They may even be said to have encouraged popular interest in politics, insofar as they provided, within ostensibly non-political associations, a template for participation and power-sharing. By the 1880s, opposition groups in Padua and Vicenza, both inside and outside of associations, were growing in number and strength. At the same time, moderate liberals had their own reasons to fear that their days as leaders were numbered.

6

The Death of a Generation

On the 10th of June 1897, a fight broke out in the city of Vicenza. In fact, it was not one but several fights, and although the main conflict started in the centre of the city, it extended along the processional route to Mount Berico, a religious shrine and historic battlefield north of the city. At issue was the manner in which the city would celebrate the anniversary of its battle against the Austrians at Mount Berico, in June 1848. Would there be just one religious ceremony and procession to the holy shrine in the morning, as Count Roberto Zileri Del Verme, the head of Vicenza's first-ever Catholic government, proposed? Or would there also be a "patriotic" procession to the scene of battle in the evening, as a range of liberal, radical, and socialist groups insisted? The previous year, the same issue had resulted in an altercation, when a veteran interrupted the ceremony at the shrine by tearing the city's official flag out of the hands of the government-appointed flagbearer and crying, "This flag must never enter a church." A struggle ensued as the mayor himself tried to take back the flag, before policemen stepped in and arrested the veteran. But this incident paled in comparison to what happened in 1897.

A Catholic journalist named Adriano Navarotto recounted the sequence of events years later, in a colourful memoir about Vicenza. "As soon as the City flag appeared" outside of the local government's offices, he wrote, "there broke out a storm of whistles and applause, of cheers and boos, of insults, clapping and curses [loud] enough to cover the clang of the municipal brass bands." By the time the procession towards Mount Berico got under way, the streets were practically impassable. Once again, "bellicose groups" tried to prevent authorities from bringing the city flag inside the church atop Mount Berico, only this time what ensued was not simply a scuffle but a brawl. And the violence spilled back into the city centre that evening, as protesters besieged Zileri Del Verme's home, demanding that the mayor remove the Italian flag from his balcony and then smashing several windows. Almerico Da Schio, a local notable who witnessed the events, commented, in a letter published several weeks later in a Venetian newspaper, "we all agree that the demonstration of X June went beyond the limits of a civilized people."[1]

Italy's most intense era of violent political confrontations had not yet begun; the street battles between nationalists and socialists that preceded the First World War were years away, the fascists' campaign of brutality and destruction even more distant. Broken windows and brawls were still uncommon enough to seem barbaric. Perhaps that is why Adriano Navarotto did not take the events of June 1897 seriously. In his account, they are little more than moments of excitement in the history of a sleepy, provincial town. In fact, he noted, in the years prior to the conflict Vicenza's celebrations of patriotic events had been lackluster at best. On more than one occasion, liberal city council members and veterans' association leaders had suggested not bothering to hold them at all. From this perspective, the confrontation atop Mount Berico begins to look like the last, desperate gasp of Vicenza's Risorgimento liberals, who rose from their torpor for the sole purpose of driving the city's Catholic government from office.

Seen from a different perspective, however, the same events allow us to identify a series of interesting changes in Italy's political environment. Trivial or not, it would be difficult to imagine this kind of conflict occurring in Vicenza thirty years earlier. Not only were the Catholics out of power in 1867, they also occupied a relatively marginal place in the city's public sphere. Vicenza's ruling moderates did everything in their power to avoid large or unruly public demonstrations, even if it meant restricting the size and number of patriotic celebrations. By comparison, the last two decades of the nineteenth century were a period rich in public ceremony. Apathy and attrition within Vicenza's veterans' associations may have begun to take their toll on the city's celebration of the 10th of June in the years prior to 1897, but in general the end of the Risorgimento – symbolized most powerfully by the deaths of King Victor Emmanuel II in 1878 and Giuseppe Garibaldi in 1882 – had the effect of generating a new and more elaborate culture of public commemoration. With the prospect of political as well as generational decline staring them in the face, Italy's liberal political leaders descended on the public sphere with new determination, erecting monuments, sponsoring pilgrimages to patriotic sites, writing histories of the Risorgimento, and in countless other ways developing what one Italian historian has called a "patriotic pedagogy."[2]

Along with this culture of commemoration came a new attention to political iconography. Symbols such as flags became a fundamental part of any group's quest for political legitimacy. After all, public visibility was not something to be taken for granted in cities like Vicenza and Padua, where one group had dominated local public and political life for years. Thus, left liberals and Catholics, the first groups to challenge moderate liberal hegemony in the Veneto after unification, made a point of being seen and heard in public: at patriotic celebrations, funerals, royal visits, public meetings, and demonstrations. As leaders of their own new associations, they promoted large public gatherings, mobilized workers and women, and claimed to represent "the nation" and "the people."

A focus on nationalism has led many scholars to exaggerate and simplify the late-nineteenth-century crisis of European liberalism. In George L. Mosse's *The Nationalization of the Masses*, elitist liberals squander the grass-roots energy that made German unification possible; whereas in Hobsbawm and Ranger's *The Invention of Tradition*, conservative ruling elites belatedly discover the political value of pageantry. In both studies, however, it is implied that liberals lacked the conviction to defend what they really believed in: constitutional government and material progress. More recent scholarship on "realms of memory" and the mass appeal of Risorgimento nationalism have not challenged this view. A local history of civil society offers a different perspective on the crisis of Italian liberalism. Venetian liberals were generally elitist and reluctant to embrace the politics of spectacle, but they also made a concerted effort to defend the institutions and principles they valued most. They commemorated not just the King and Garibaldi but local notables; they used colour, symbolism, and ceremony not just to "make Italians" but also to reaffirm the importance of local associations.

Challenge

The parliamentary elections of 1876 resulted in a lopsided victory for the liberal left at the national level, but not in the Veneto. Moderates in Padua and Vicenza retained control of most parliamentary seats and still dominated local government. Nevertheless, the national shift from right to left had a profound impact on associational life. In the summer and fall of 1876, leading Venetian progressives and democrats either created anew or revived a series of new associations, including associations of veterans, sharpshooters, and gymnasts. Significantly, all three of these associations employed the rhetoric of nationalism, either by paying tribute to the soldiers who fought in Italy's wars of independence or by ensuring that the next generation of men to go to battle would be trained and fit for duty. Nationalism acquired new significance for local men of the left – and, as we shall see, for women, too – in 1876.[3]

The leaders of Vicenza's new veterans', sharpshooting, and gymnastics associations understood well the advantages of having their own groups, as opposed to simply belonging to ones founded by moderates. As we saw in the previous chapter, one way in which progressives and democrats could challenge the moderates' monopoly of local power was by establishing a larger and more vocal presence within key moderate-led associations such as Padua's Popular Bank and Vicenza's General Mutual Aid Society of Vicentine Artisans. But the creation of new associations allowed progressives and democrats to do much more. First, it demonstrated their capacity to organize and command the loyalty of a large number of people, itself a challenge to the moderates' appearance of local dominance. Second, it gave them a chance to appear in public not simply as a vocal minority or opposition movement, but as leaders in their own right. Newspapers covered the new associations' meetings and featured the speeches of leading progressives and democrats. These same men now began to appear in an official capacity, as the leaders of new associations, at a variety of public events: at patriotic celebrations, funerals, royal visitations, and inaugurations of public works. And they were often joined by delegations of members carrying the new associations' distinctive flags and banners. At political demonstrations they were joined by much larger numbers of citizens, either to protest the actions of moderate city officials or to rally support for the governments of the left in Rome. Moderate newspapers suddenly found it difficult to dismiss these rallies as the work of a few dozen idlers and malcontents. Local progressives and democrats literally occupied the political space that opened up for them in 1876.

Being seen also meant being heard, which for Venetian progressives and democrats meant the opportunity to claim some of the national authority that the Italian left as a whole had acquired in 1876. Thus, in October 1876, the interim president of Vicenza's Society of Veterans, Giovanni Fabrello, told the assembled members that it was up to them to keep patriotic sentiment alive, because "the sacred memories of the sacrifices and virtues of the Italians seemed ... condemned to oblivion."[4] Leading left politicians in Padua used their Society of Veterans to rally support for Agostino Depretis's program of reforms, asking members in early 1877 to vote for the abolition of the grist tax (*macinato*) and the death penalty.[5] In November 1878, the leaders of various progressive and democratic associations in Padua expressed their support for Depretis's successor, Benedetto Cairoli, in far more dramatic fashion.

The occasion was the anarchist Giovanni Passanante's attempted assassination of King Umberto I in Naples. Passanante drew a dagger but missed his target and instead wounded Cairoli, who courageously stepped in front of the king. Throughout Italy, news of the incident triggered a massive show of support for the king, but a more politically divided show of appreciation and concern for Cairoli. In Padua, progressives and democrats responded by organizing a "popular meeting" in honour of the king and Cairoli at the Garibaldi Theater. Carlo Tivaroni, a spokesman for the Democratic Association, told the crowd: "Long live the loyal king who accepted the abolition of the *macinato*, long live the loyal king who accepts the widening of the vote, long live the king who does not fear the people." Michelangelo Fanoli, a representative of the Society of Veterans, declared that "when Cairoli put himself between the assassin and the King, it was the people who saved, in the king, the popular monarchy."[6] For local opposition groups in search of a wider public identity and following, this was a rare opportunity to speak on behalf of the monarchy, the nation, and the people.

In Vicenza, the close ties between local moderates and Catholics presented a unique challenge as well as an inviting target. Inspired by the anticlericalism of the Depretis and Cairoli governments in Rome, progressives and democrats in Vicenza questioned municipal expenditures on church repairs and votive candles, advocated civil weddings and funerals, and accused the "clerico-moderate establishment [*consorteria*]" of undermining the annual commemoration of Italy's occupation of Rome on 20 September 1870.[7] Annual Constitution Day celebrations in June were also subject to dispute because they coincided with a local holiday of greater meaning to Vicenza's Catholics: the anniversary of the June 1848 battle against the Austrians at Mount Berico, a strategic overlook outside of the city but also the site of a convent. Moderate chroniclers of the revolution of 1848 often noted the participation of priests in this battle and thus the historic solidarity of patriotic liberals and Catholics. The moderates who founded the city's first veterans' association in 1867 called themselves the Volunteers of 1848, whereas the association founded a decade later by progressives and democrats assumed the more inclusive title of the Veterans of Patriotic Wars.[8]

The anticlericalism of the left, in turn, prompted Catholics to take action. No longer content to join veterans atop Mount Berico on the 10th of June, Vicenza's Catholics began organizing their own processions to the holy site; moreover, they scheduled these and other events to coincide and compete with patriotic celebrations. Thus, in 1877 Catholics in Vicenza held a papal jubilee a week before the annual Constitution Day celebration, and a week later organized a pilgrimage to Mount Berico. On a much larger and more dramatic scale, the fifth regional pilgrimage of Venetian Catholics was planned for Mount Berico in early September 1881, shortly before the 20th of September holiday. The Catholic newspaper in Vicenza beckoned its readers: "To [Mount] Berico! To [Mount] Berico!" By the end of the decade, September events had become a local Catholic tradition: all but one of the annual "federal festivals" organized by Vicenza's diocesan committee between 1889 and 1898 took place between 9 and 28 September.[9] Catholics, too, were determined to be seen and heard.

By organizing large public demonstrations, Catholics and the left went beyond the ideal limits that moderate liberals had assigned to the public sphere immediately after unification. And moderate liberals occasionally let their frustration and concern show. *Il Giornale di Padova* saw no reason why the "popular meeting" of December 1878 was necessary when a public demonstration in support of the king and Cairoli had already taken place two weeks earlier; moreover, it questioned the political legitimacy of the meeting by noting that more than half of the people in attendance were students and therefore (according to the legal age requirement) non-electors. *Il Giornale della Provincia di Vicenza* reacted more strongly to the Catholic newspaper *Il Berico*'s appeal to women for help during the administrative election campaign of 1881. A year later, the conflicts surrounding Vicenza's response to the death of Giuseppe Garibaldi brought the new forms and dimensions of public politics into clear view.

Bernardo Baldisserotto, the editor of the radical-democratic newspaper *L'Amico del Popolo*, helped set the confrontational tone in Vicenza by delivering a fiercely anticlerical eulogy of Garibaldi at a public ceremony. There as a delegate of the Democratic "Liberty and Brotherhood" Society, the lone political association representing the left in Vicenza at the time, Baldisserotto called on citizens to show "that – no – Vicenza is not the city of [the Virgin] Mary, but the city of the 10th of June! That – no – it is not the city of privilege, but the Vicenza of the people! That – no – it is not the city of obscurantism, but the foremost sentinel of progress!"[10] A few days later, when Vicenza's moderate mayor, Count Guardino Colleoni, proposed that the city contribute to the project to build a national Garibaldi monument in Rome, but refrain from erecting a monument in Vicenza, local progressives, democrats, and radicals quickly acted to rally public support for a local monument. They appealed to individuals and municipal governments throughout the province for donations and, for months after Garibaldi's death, *L'Amico del Popolo* printed running lists of contributors and stories of the battles taking place within town councils as far away as Bolzano, in the Austrian-controlled province of Trent.[11] The "Liberty and Brotherhood" Society also opened a "popular subscription of 20 *centesimi*," breaking with the tradition of general public subscriptions, which often listed the names of wealthy and powerful contributors first, followed – in the same inclusive and "classless" list – by ordinary donors of much smaller amounts.[12]

It was not the mobilization of "the people," however, that generated the most controversy in Vicenza during the summer of 1882, but the mobilization of women. Among the many public responses in Vicenza to Garibaldi's death was a "letter-circular," prepared by four women, which called upon the "Women of Vicenza" to help assemble a crown of flowers to be placed on Garibaldi's tomb.[13] The participation of women in civic or patriotic initiatives was nothing new. In fact, four years earlier the leaders of Vicenza's all-male sharpshooting association had issued a circular appealing to "all the courteous ladies of Vicenza" to donate objects that could serve as prizes for an upcoming shooting competition. The circular from 1878 began with the dramatic proclamation, "Honorable lady!," praised women for their love of the city and their "powerful stimulus to human virtues," and ended by listing the names of the first women to come forward with donations.[14] But the 1882 circular was different. First, it was prepared by women, not men. Second, it was addressed not to an implicitly elite group of "ladies," but to all women. Third, it was far more assertive, both in content and tone. "We Italian Women," it began, "while the men of Italy, upset and reverent, pay tribute to the memory of Giuseppe Garibaldi with dreams of supreme sadness and the highest veneration, do we not want to join in this immense mourning? Do we not want to throw flowers on his tomb?" Although gathering flowers and attending funerals hardly constituted radical new forms of women's action, the rhetorical force of the circular, its many injunctions and proclamations ("rush with all of Italy to his funeral," "Vicentine Women!," etc.), made it read like countless other political manifestos from the period – manifestos, that is, prepared by and for male citizens, legitimate participants in the world of politics.[15]

The Catholic newspaper *Il Berico* expressed its disapproval by disclosing the names of the women who signed the circular, and then rallying its own group of women supporters, including none other than the mayor's wife, the countess Carolina Colleoni. Throughout the month of August and into September, new installments of the two rival lists of women – for Garibaldi on the one hand, for *Il Berico* on the other – continued to appear in the city's newspapers.[16] Then tragedy struck – floods devastated the Veneto in the second half of September – and suddenly the lists of women who defended *Il Berico* against the excesses of the democratic left gave way to lists of citizens providing assistance to flood victims. Throughout the city and the province of Vicenza, from every point on the local political spectrum, relief efforts multiplied. After a summer of mobilization, it all looked very familiar, except now the public donations and organizing committees converged around a common cause. Women continued to play a highly visible role in the mobilization effort, but now they were directing their energies towards a far less controversial goal. Nevertheless, it is interesting to note the speed with which the local Catholic movement created a "committee of women" for flood relief. Was this committee the reflection of women's traditional involvement in philanthropic work, or a continuation of the very unconventional mobilization that followed the death of Garibaldi? Significantly, the floods also inspired "popular subscriptions" on behalf of the victims, such as the one presented in late October by a group of bakers and goldsmiths, their names and contributions appearing in the pages of the radical-democratic newspaper *L'Amico del Popolo*. The controversy surrounding the monument to Garibaldi died down, but the competition for the city's new political public appeared only to grow.[17]

Response

Moderate liberals in Vicenza and Padua did not simply react defensively to the political moves of local progressives and democrats; they actively engaged in the new politics of commemoration and mobilization. The focus of their efforts was the monarchy. Following King Victor Emmanuel II's death in January 1878, a moderate-led committee in Vicenza worked quickly to erect a monument two years later. Padua's monument went up in 1882, and that same year moderate liberals in the city named their newest political association, the Popular Savoy Association, after the royal family.[18] In 1883, to mark the fifth anniversary of the king's death, the moderate municipal government in Padua inaugurated a new Victor Emmanuel II orphanage, and began preparing for an extraordinary, sixth-anniversary pilgrimage to Victor Emmanuel II's tomb at the Pantheon in Rome. For three days in January 1884, approximately sixty-eight thousand people from all over Italy, most of them part of organized groups, visited the tomb. Provincial delegations brought albums containing signatures from people (including women and illiterates) who could not make the pilgrimage, and presented them to King Umberto I. What began as an anniversary celebration ended as an exhibition: over a 209-day period, as many as five hundred groups of workers took advantage of reduced train fares and free admission to visit the king's tomb. King Umberto and Queen Margherita entered the exhibit thirty-three times, and the king bolstered his reputation as the "Father of the People" by dropping by, unexpectedly and without a retinue, to greet the workers whose job it was to dismantle the exhibit after it closed.[19]

Moderates in Padua promoted a public cult of the monarchy in the pages of the Savoy Association's official periodical, *La Libertà*, which ran from 1886 to 1890. Several issues featured abstracts taken from recent publications on various aspects of the royal dynasty's history from the sixteenth to the nineteenth centuries; included, of course, were tales from the field of battle during Italy's wars of independence, but also accounts of seventeenth-century sonnets attesting to the House of Savoy's early feelings of national sentiment, and of popular songs inspired by the eighteenth-century Savoy princess Carolina.[20] Naturally, special attention was paid to Victor Emmanuel II. One article, entitled "The Warrior King," related a series of anecdotes from the Battle of Custoza in 1848, comparing the king at one moment to a lion, "hurling himself" to face the Austrian army, at another to "a turbine" atop his Arabian horse. The reader was also assured that newly discovered documents "from the secret State archives" dispelled any doubts regarding "the immense, preponderant part" Victor Emmanuel played in the unification of Italy.[21] Another issue featured a local veteran's public commemoration of the king in 1887, on the ninth anniversary of his death, in which the following tribute was paid to his civil as well as military achievements:

[He] wanted to fortify the Monarchy with the suffrage of the citizens [*regnicoli*], and conquered the most splendid of crowns, that of the affection of his people.[22]

More than any other political symbol, the king inspired moderate liberals to do what only the left had appeared capable of doing several years earlier: invoke "the people" as their allies. Indeed, there is evidence of a real desire on the part of some moderate liberals to promote the notion of a popular monarchy, which went beyond unique events like the national pilgrimage to Victor Emmanuel II's tomb or the inauguration of local monuments. Naming an orphanage after the deceased king – and reminding the orphans to honour "the name of the Immortal One" – was one way to extend as well as perpetuate the cult of the monarchy.[23] Another was to encourage citizens to leave crowns at the base of local monuments to the king, as both veterans' associations and the municipal government in Padua did.[24]

Umberto I bolstered the Crown's popularity in the 1880s by assisting the victims of a string of disasters, beginning with the floods that devastated the Veneto in 1882. Several newspapers, including the Catholic *Osservatore Romano*, emphasized the king's determination to visit the poorest of the stricken areas. When an earthquake hit the resort town of Casamicciola on the island of Ischia in 1883, Umberto reportedly risked danger in his effort to "see everything," and insisted on continuing the rescue effort against the orders of the minister of public works. A year later, he showed his courage and commitment again by visiting Naples only a week after an outbreak of cholera struck the city.[25] Plaques commemorating Umberto's actions joined the increasingly crowded field of monuments to his father and to Garibaldi.[26]

Moderates also made a political statement by belatedly promoting a commemorative cult of Camillo Benso di Cavour, who died in 1861. On Constitution Day in 1886, Luigi Luzzatti delivered a rousing tribute to Cavour before a large crowd at Padua's Garibaldi Theater, the site of the left's rally for Cairoli and Umberto in 1878. Luzzatti began his speech by stating that "the cult of Cavour grows stronger every day," but he also recognized the competition Cavour faced from "pretenders" who confused "temporary national enthusiasms" with greatness. Although Luzzatti did his best to portray Cavour as a popular political leader, it appears that the cult of Cavour was in fact weak. In Padua, the moderate liberal press celebrated the inauguration of a monument to Cavour in 1888, but it struggled to make the commemoration of Cavour an annual event. More successful was the effort simply to place Cavour alongside Victor Emmanuel II and Garibaldi in lapidary or statuary arrangements – notably, in the grand hall that marked the entrance to the Risorgimento exhibition of 1884 in Turin – and of course also in increasingly harmonious historical accounts of Italian unification. At commemorative gatherings as in

Parliament, the politics of *trasformismo* brought the Cavourian right and the Garibaldian left together in the name of national unity.

Undeterred by the political radicalism that defined Garibaldi's final years, Venetian moderates commemorated the legendary hero's death in generically inclusive and unifying terms. In Padua, Domenico Coletti declared that "with Garibaldi the epic period of our *risorgimento* comes to a close," and Antonio Tolomei identified Garibaldi with an entire generation of Italian men who knew how to create "true and lasting freedom."[27] Moderates in Vicenza were initially less enthusiastic, but by the time the contested project to erect a monument to Garibaldi in the city was finally realized, in 1887, they too had lent their names and literary talents to an album commemorating the event. In smaller Venetian towns, the same unifying effect was achieved at a much lower cost by erecting plaques to both Garibaldi and King Victor Emmanuel II, often on the same day and in the same building. In fact, outside of the region's dozen or so largest cities, the inauguration of monuments to these two figures continued throughout the 1880s, forcing more than one patriotic association in Padua to acknowledge the strain of attending so many events.[28]

The commemorative culture of the 1880s centred on Victor Emmanuel II and Garibaldi, but it also addressed a variety of other subjects. A four-year run of *La Libertà* (1886–90) yields the following list: the revolutions of 1848–49 (including famous revolutionaries such as Daniele Manin, but also a comprehensive album of the dead and wounded from the province of Padua); recently deceased members of "the Thousand" (the volunteer army that invaded Sicily with Garibaldi in 1860); heroes of anticlericalism such as Paolo Sarpi; the Italian "victims" of the Battle of Dogali in Ethiopia; the martyr-figure of Italian irredentism, Guglielmo Oberdan; Italian participants in the Crimean War; former prime ministers such as Giovanni Lanza, Marco Minghetti, and Bettino Cairoli; and local notables such as the epigraphist and art historian Carlo Leoni and the associational leader and member of Parliament Emilio Morpurgo. In the pages of this provincial periodical, commemorations of Victor Emmanuel II and Garibaldi were outnumbered by commemorations of other institutions, people, and events.

Associations were in the thick of this commemorative frenzy. While veterans' associations and brass bands were sometimes overwhelmed by the growing demand for their presence at ceremonial events, other associations sought to increase their participation in such events. For example, political associations and mutual aid societies began to show a new interest in the commemoration of deceased members. Throughout

Europe, funeral benefits of one kind or another were among the most common features of associations. Whether it was an elite social club or a workers' mutual aid society, participation in the funerals of fellow members attested to the group's fraternal bonds. Workers' associations also helped pay for funerals and otherwise looked after members' widowed spouses and children. But funeral benefits were not common features of many Venetian associations until the 1880s. This is especially true of the associations founded by the region's political leaders, including the large mutual aid societies created by Fedele Lampertico in Vicenza and Emilio Morpurgo in Padua. The statutes governing Morpurgo's group, for example, limited the commemoration of fellow members to a roll-call of the deceased at each annual meeting.[29]

It is hard to say whether this anomalous disregard of funeral services was the conscious decision of men who thought sociable rituals played too big a part in associational life, and hoped to teach workers the importance of fiscal restraint. What is clear is that the ritual commemoration of the dead became a more important part of Venetian associational life in the 1880s. It is telling that the first statute drawn up for the Popular Savoy Association, which Morpurgo helped found in 1882, included a large section on "funerary honours"; and that the leaders of the group spent the better part of a year revising these articles, prompting detailed discussions of the optimum number of members needed at each funeral, of the best means of getting word of a member's death out to the association as a whole, and of the special funerary honours leaders and committee members might enjoy. The Savoy Association's official organ, *La Libertà*, solicited and published obituaries of recently deceased members, including a good number of veterans of the revolutions of 1848–49 and Italy's wars of independence, but also some notably ordinary men. In *La Libertà*'s provincial news, we learn that the elite-led Workers' Society of Monselice acted to introduce funeral services for the first time in 1886, twenty years after the association was founded, while the Workers' Society of Montagnana engaged in a lively debate over whether or not to acquire a hearse, in keeping, as one advocate put it, with the evolution of funerary practices in nearby towns.[30]

Closely related to the new interest in funeral ceremonies was a passion for flags. Flagbearers – their number, election, and actions – figured centrally in the Popular Savoy Association's discussion of funeral rituals. And the pages of *La Libertà* are filled with news about the flags belonging to various associations. The ceremonies to inaugurate associational flags were major events, especially in small towns, where the festivities included speeches, banquets, concerts, dances, fireworks, and raffles.[31] With or without a flag, associations also began celebrating the anniversaries of their foundation: first anniversaries, tenth anniversaries, twentieth anniversaries, even a twenty-second anniversary.[32] Emilio Morpurgo did not live to see the twenty-fifth anniversary celebration of Padua's Mutual Aid Society of Artisans, Merchants and Professionals in 1889, but he would have approved of its relatively restrained and serious program, which featured speeches in the morning by two of the group's leaders and two local officials and a performance of the royal march by the municipal band; a late afternoon banquet for members willing to pay five and a half lire; and a vocal and instrumental concert the following evening at the Verdi Theater, benefiting the association's pension fund and a local gymnastics society's program for children with rickets.[33]

Morpurgo might not have approved of his old association's decision to commission a bust in his honour, or to ceremonially lay a crown upon his grave five years after his death. Before he died, he had left in writing the following request: "I wish that my corpse be placed in the ground without the slightest pomp. And I formally express this wish, thinking that my role as [parliamentary] deputy could provoke some type of honour."[34] In an age of escalating pomp and almost constant commemoration, Morpurgo's wish stands out. But it also reflects a real tension, felt not only by Morpurgo but by most moderate liberals of his generation, between the mid-century notable's traditional deflection of public scrutiny and the late-century demand for ritual and symbolic display. Associations experienced this tension, too, for their identities were often bound up with those of their founders. For moderates, in particular, who dominated local politics and associational life after unification, the commemorations of the 1880s were not only bittersweet but positively troubling.

Crisis

Death was especially cruel to moderate liberals in Padua. In March 1881, shortly after he became mayor, Antonio Tolomei announced the death of two local notables, Sebastiano Giustiniani and Ferdinando Coletti, to the city council. "It is not death," he said, "but extermination which has entered here among us to thin the ranks of our best men."[35] Others at Coletti's funeral expressed the same sentiment. After all, it had been less than a year since Coletti himself had commemorated the death of Francesco Marzolo, a veteran of the battles of Solferino and San Martino and rector of the University of Padua, and only a few months since the death of Giusto Bellavitis, the celebrated mathematician and former rector of the university. In an epigraph prepared after Coletti's death, the director of the moderate *Giornale di Padova*, Cesare Sorgato, wrote:

AND YOU LEAVE DEAR SOULS
ONE BY ONE TACITURN AND PENSIVE
YOU LEAVE – AND WHO REMAINS?[36]

In fact, the "extermination" continued well into the 1880s, claiming the lives of several prominent politicians, including Emilio Morpurgo but also Francesco Piccoli, Padua's mayor from 1871 to 1881 and its principal representative in Parliament from unification until his death in 1883 at the age of forty-eight. Piccoli's death, the result of injuries sustained during a carriage accident, came as a shock to everyone. At Piccoli's funeral, after once again presenting the roll call of recent losses – "Oh Pietro Selvatico! Oh Giacobbe Trieste! Oh Francesco Marzolo! Oh Giusto Bellavitis! Oh Ferdinando Coletti, where are you?" – Antonio Tolomei wondered aloud not only who but *what* was left now of the Fatherland:

Oh truly, if *Patria* for us means that land which contains all of what our soul most jealously adores, my perturbed thoughts in this instant become uncertain, and in a vision of blessed ghosts rising up from that casket I ask myself if by now my *Patria* is not found more beyond the grave than here with us.[37]

On the heels of the loss of two of the nation's greatest heroes, Padua appeared to be approaching a historic generational abyss.

In truth, late unification ensured that at least one generation of participants in the Venetian Risorgimento would survive into the early twentieth century. By the 1880s, veterans of the Venetian revolutions of 1848–49 were approaching old age, but plenty of men and women who lived through the final years of Austrian rule in the Veneto were still in their forties. The latter group included several of the region's most powerful moderate liberals – Luigi Luzzatti, Fedele Lampertico, Paolo Lioy, and Tolomei himself – and would have included Emilio Morpurgo and Francesco Piccoli had fate been less cruel. Vicenza, for example, lost a handful of influential notables during the 1880s, but none as great as Lampertico, who lived until 1906, or Paolo Lioy, who lived until 1911. Nevertheless, during the 1880s moderate liberals in both cities repeatedly intimated that a generational shift – and worse: a generational crisis – had begun. At the funeral in 1885 of Francesco Molon, a veteran of Vicenza's revolution of 1848 and the wars of 1866, Paolo Lioy joined countless others in mourning the disappearance of an entire generation of great men, and the end of a poetic era. But there was also a note of dismay in his eulogy that was lacking in most commemorations of the king or Garibaldi. "Slowly," Lioy told the crowd, "inexorably, something great appears to be sinking."[38]

It was the demise of local men and institutions, far more than the deaths of the king and Garibaldi, that allowed Venetian moderates to defend their own achievements as political and associational leaders in the region. If this claim seems new or surprising, it is largely due to the fact that when historians focus on national symbols, rituals, monuments, and memory – as they have done in recent years with great intensity – they tend to disregard much of the evidence that points in other directions: to aristocratic family ties and relationships between classes; to church and parish; to land and the environment; to people and places in other countries; to the region; but above all to local communities – the city, the town, the village. Moreover, the evidence of local symbols, rituals, monuments, and memory is far more scattered – and, thus, easier to miss or disregard – than the evidence of nationalism.[39] Nevertheless, for every statue or commemoration that aimed to shape citizens' relationship to the nation, first and foremost, there were many more – one, two, three dozen? – that directed citizens' attention to local relationships, institutions, and events. This was as true of the monuments erected to local figures of national renown, such as Francesco Piccoli or the poet Giacomo Zanella, as it was of the eulogies and obituaries granted to lesser notables.

Residents of Padua did not have to wait long to celebrate the memory of Francesco Piccoli; on the second anniversary of his death, the city erected a monument to him, a bronze bust set atop a marble column. In 1882, the city inaugurated busts of Ferdinando Coletti and Francesco Marzolo; in 1887, a bust of the late senator Giovanni Cittadella; and in 1891, a bust of Piccoli's successor as mayor, Antonio Tolomei. Together with the monuments erected in the same years to King Victor Emmanuel II (1882), Garibaldi (1886), and Cavour (1888), this cluster of honours represented a significant departure from the commemorative silence of the immediate post-unification period: between 1866 and 1882 there were only two noteworthy constructions in the city of Padua, a monument dedicated to Petrarch on the fifth centenary of his death in 1874, and a bust of Andrea Cittadella Vigodarzere in 1876.[40] And the same basic pattern appears to hold for other Venetian cities as well. Thus, in Vicenza, the monument erected at Mount Berico in 1870 to "the men who died for Italian independence" was followed by the monuments to

Victor Emmanuel II in 1880, Garibaldi in 1887, Giacomo Zanella (the priest and poet) in 1893, and Cavour in 1897.[41]

Less visible to the public eye, plaques and institutions also paid tribute to local notables as well as national heroes. In 1884, the Venetian marine hospice, a charitable organization formed in 1868 to bring children with scrofula and other diseases to the Adriatic ocean for curative salt-water baths, honoured one of its founders, Ferdinando Coletti, with a commemorative plaque. The Popular Bank of Vicenza erected plaques to its first two presidents alongside one to King Victor Emmanuel II. The Vicentine novelist Antonio Fogazzaro helped honour his father, Mariano, by naming an infant nursery after him.

Men of more limited fame were usually commemorated not in stone or bronze but in print. Take, for example, the collection of short obituaries that the Trevisan moderate Antonio Caccianiga included in his book *Feste e funerali*, published in 1889. Part memoir, part local history, Caccianiga's 423-page volume pays tribute to eighty-nine of Treviso's "illustrious men" (and two women) who died between 1866 and 1888. The honorees include leading politicians – members of Parliament, mayors, city and provincial council members – and prominent figures from the Risorgimento, but also a humbler group of citizens from Treviso and surrounding towns: doctors who risked their lives by treating victims of cholera, modest librarians and museum directors, a photographer who died tragically young, a bell manufacturer who carried on his family's trade, a poet who was born to a poor family, and a lawyer whose selfless public service led him to die penniless. As Caccianiga noted in a preface to the obituaries,

> The memory of illustrious men is conserved by history, but many worthy men in the more modest spheres of life are forgotten as soon as they enter the darkness of the tomb.
>
> Death notices are published, with vain titles, with bombastic and generic phrases, which attribute to the deceased the most common virtues, and then it is all finished.
>
> Instead a few biographical notices, simple and sincere, done with brief pen strokes, like a sketch of a portrait, conserve the true moral physiognomy of the deceased, and put together, they present a true portrait of society, and of a town in a given epoch.[42]

There is at least one Venetian precedent for Caccianiga's collection of obituaries: the Vicentine abbot Gaetano Sorgato's *Memorie funebri*, published in five volumes between 1856 and 1864. Unlike *Feste e funerali*, of which Caccianiga was the sole author, each volume of *Memorie funebri* is a compendium of funereal writings, with different authors and in various forms, including everything from formal public eulogies to random gravestone inscriptions. Predictably, Sorgato's collection is also more traditional than Caccianiga's: more aristocratic and religious, more likely to include inscriptions written in Latin or posted on church doors, more attentive to family lineage and acts of charity. But for its time it was surprisingly inclusive, largely thanks to the editorial practice of reproducing epigraphs penned by family members or spotted at churches and in cemeteries by passersby. Towards the end of the final volume, one contributor explicitly defended the publication of obituaries honouring a wider range of individuals (beyond "those few" who enjoy considerable fame), and concluded by saying that a collection of good obituaries – written with sincerity, simplicity, and good taste by people who really knew the deceased – "would be like a course in popular psychology, like a gallery of moral portraits," a source of great delight and instruction for many readers.[43] Sorgato's collection, however, reflects the late Risorgimento's buoyant optimism rather than a concern with generational decline.

Far more common than these collections were commemorative publications dedicated to specific individuals. These publications typically took the form of small pamphlets, which reproduced just one family member's or friend's dedication in prose or verse. As such, along with writings inspired by announcements of births and nuptials, they adhered to a predominantly aristocratic tradition whereby family rites of passage became public events. By contrast, the type of publication that began to proliferate in the 1880s was a large commemorative album, typically containing newspaper reports of the person's death and funeral throughout the country, telegrams of condolence from important friends and political figures, poems and epigraphs written for the occasion, and a portrait of the deceased. Ferdinando Coletti, Francesco Piccoli, and Emilio Morpurgo were all honoured in this way before their busts were unveiled, as were men who did not inspire any busts or statues, such as the Paduan notable Ferdinando Cavalli and the Vicentine notables Francesco Molon and Mariano Fogazzaro.[44]

In monuments and commemorative albums, moderate liberals struggled to find the right balance between their traditional embrace of sobriety and restraint and the new imperatives of public tribute and display. Their ambivalence informs the statues they commissioned for local notables, which stand on pedestals several feet above the streets and squares they occupy, yet depict men in frumpy suits, standing still, unaccompanied by

lions, crowns, or swords. Most of these figures stand erect and have looks
of authority, if not pride, on their faces. Some, however, are remarkably
– even excruciatingly – humble in appearance: the figure of Fedele Lampertico, the most powerful man in Vicenza for half a century, painfully
stoops; the statue of Giacomo Zanella looks tired and lonely. In a speech
inaugurating the monument to Zanella, Antonio Fogazzaro remarked,
"this marble adds nothing to His glory," and a short time later he wrote
that it suited "the old marble priest" to be "left alone to think, with a
book in his hand, in a deserted piazza." More than just rhetorical statements about Zanella's quiet virtues, Fogazzaro's words remind us of the
contradiction at the heart of these modest monuments. It is relatively
easy to interpret the monuments to Victor Emmanuel II and Garibaldi,
because they rarely stray from the themes of royal grandeur and heroic
action. But what were the same period's monuments to local notables trying to say? That these men were great precisely because they did not want
the monument before your eyes? That no hyperbole – no mythic details
or dynamic poses – was necessary for such men, yet monuments were?
The whole range of monuments to local notables – statues but also busts,
plaques, and even commemorative albums, which were often attractive
but rarely ornate – brings to mind the phrase that supporters of notable
politicians used at election time to deflect public demands for campaign
speeches and publications: "the man himself is a program." The commemorative culture of the 1880s allowed moderate liberals to perpetuate their traditional claim to unspoken and unquestioned authority, but
in an increasingly crowded and contested public arena this message often
sounded defensive, melancholy, and unconvincing.

   Again and again during the 1880s and 1890s, Venetian moderates
expressed their qualms with public display and political mobilization
in commemorative speeches and writings. They reminded mourners
that Francesco Molon and Mariano Fogazzaro did not seek popularity, that Francesco Piccoli avoided the din of the crowd and the piazza,
that Giovanni Battista Maluta and Antonio Pazienti showed no interest
in special honours. In *Feste e funerali*, Antonio Caccianiga repeatedly
painted a moving picture of citizens of every social class spontaneously
showing their love and respect for the worthy men of Treviso, with no regard for cold or pompous ceremony. The moderate *Provincia di Vicenza*
newspaper noted that Vicenza's municipal brass band would not play at
Mariano Fogazzaro's funeral, by express wish of the deceased. Reporting
on the inauguration of a plaque in honour of Ferdinando Coletti at the
Venetian marine hospice, the *Osservatore Veneto* observed that Coletti's

modesty – "Ferdinando Coletti did not need this stone" – extended to the hospice, which managed to be one of Italy's most beneficial institutions "without the pomp of democratic robes or humanitarian bombast."[45]

Bitterness and pessimism crept into Venetian moderates' commemorations of local notables and institutions. For the leaders of many associations in the 1880s and 1890s, annual meetings triggered painful discussions of generational decline. Naturally, veterans' associations were especially vulnerable to the ravages of time. In his 1884 report on the Society of Volunteers of 1848 in Vicenza, Antonio Negrin Caregaro refered to the membership as an "already exiguous bunch." Although the association continued to sign up new members, it lost existing members at an even faster rate; in 1887, its total membership was down to 120.[46] The same trend was clearly at work within the Society of Volunteer Veterans of 1848–49 in Padua. In 1893, it still had 295 members, but this was down from a peak of more than one thousand members twenty years earlier. A profound sense of mortality pervaded the speech that E.N. Legnazzi delivered at the Association's twenty-fifth anniversary celebration in 1893. Although the organization still had over 25,000 lire in capital, the needs of its aging and increasingly infirm members were growing with each passing day. More to the point, before long – exactly twelve years, according to Legnazzi's calculations – the number of surviving members would be too small to maintain the association at all. "Our Association," Legnazzi explained, "is condemned to a very brief life."

True to the spirit of its moderate liberal founders, the Society of Volunteer Veterans of 1848–49 in Padua celebrated its twenty-fifth anniversary not with a pilgrimage or banquet – judged to be "a waste of money, which should only be spent for the benefit of sick or needy Members" – but with a sober and constructive act: the publication of a commemorative album, which included a history of the association and a set of related documents (membership lists, statutes, and financial records). Legnazzi's speech at the event, however, was profoundly sad and critical. He expressed his hope that the commemorative album might allow surviving members to "refresh the sacred memories of the past, resting there a tired mind and a soul perturbed by the melancholy and often discouraging realities of life." And he expressed his fear that the younger people attending the event found his speech pitiful or boring, condemning not just the veterans but their memories to a short life, as "honest remains of a strong generation in decline, ... honest and poor remains, left by so many ruins, which do not agree with the empty theatricalities of our present day."[47]

Even in associations that confronted the basic problems of survival and renewal without much trouble, such as the Olympic Academy in Vicenza, the passing of members during the late nineteenth century invariably inspired mourners to speak of some greater institutional loss. At a meeting in January 1892, the academy's president, Antonio Fogazzaro, ended his commemoration of the eight members who had died the previous year with a hopeful statement, calling upon "the generation that rises" to bring new life to the institution. He began the speech, however, by discussing the increasingly isolated position of academies throughout Italy. Whereas at one time academies were "instruments of civil progress," now they were busy performing the conservative task of honouring bygone virtues along with the men who upheld them.[48] Venetian moderates often found it difficult to distinguish between personal and institutional losses. Who would fill the void left by a figure like Emilio Morpurgo in Padua's Mutual Aid Society of Artisans, Merchants and Professionals? After all, as the associational leaders of Morpurgo's generation had always been eager to point out, the era of the Risorgimento featured "civil" as well as military heroes; their deaths, too, constituted great losses for the Fatherland.

Although less dramatically than veterans' groups, mutual aid societies, too, had to confront the problem of aging (and ailing) memberships. At the 1880 annual meeting of Padua's Mutual Aid Society of Artisans, Merchants and Professionals, Emilio Morpurgo expressed his concern over the steady increase in disability payments since 1875, and recommended that the association begin to recruit new members from among the city's "youthful forces." In fact, over the course of the 1880s, the membership grew significantly, from just over seven hundred in 1880 to just under one thousand at the end of the decade. Nevertheless, during that period, one after another of the moderate liberal leaders of the association passed away, including, in one ten-month period between 1884 and 1885, all three of the association's presidents in the post-unification era: Giovanni Battista Maluta, Morpurgo, and Luigi Camerini. At the same time, the composition of the membership continued to be a source of concern. On the one hand, those people who joined the association in the first few years after unification – the financially troublesome "aging members" – continued to make up a large percentage of the overall membership; on the other hand, the association's growing contingent of members from the suburbs of the city included many workers whose professions appeared to present unusually great health risks.[49]

In an official capacity, as mayor of Padua, the moderate liberal Antonio Tolomei oversaw the expansion of the city's roster of mutual aid societies.

In May 1883, he spoke at the inauguration of the Society of Carpenters. A year later, in a week's time he attended three more inaugural ceremonies: one for the newly created Society of Porters, and two others marking the introduction not of new institutions but of new institutional symbols, namely the banners representing the twenty-five-year-old Society of Stonecutters and the more recently founded Society of Butchers. In all of Tolomei's speeches, there are expressions of congratulations, praise, and best wishes for the future, but also of concern. And behind the concern lies a thinly veiled suspicion, shared by many moderate liberals at the time, that the proliferation of independent workers' associations went hand in hand with a deterioration of social and political relations in Italy. There is a hint of resignation in Tolomei's first words to the Society of Butchers: "And the flags of the people continue to march past."

More striking, though, are Tolomei's efforts to recast the celebration of the various associations' individual identities into a common mould. To do so, he appealed not to the artisans' shared appreciation of local ruling elites as wise leaders and administrators, nor to the lessons and principles of modern capitalism, but rather to a far more unlikely and, by most accounts, retrograde source: the medieval guilds. Tolomei did not fail to mention that "science and civilization today give more effective and complete form and discipline" to mutual aid societies. But he praised the guilds of centuries past for their strong and unifying sense of community, reflected in the inclusion in each guild's flag of its native city's coat of arms. The unifying community of the modern age was not the commune but the nation: "Italy, sceptred, honest and powerful in the shadow of the cross of Savoy." Nevertheless, Padua's tradesmen were right to celebrate the "return" of their flags and the revival of old but noble sentiments. Having read the original statutes of several medieval guilds, Tolomei confessed to being "seduced by the charm of these visions of other times."[50]

Flags, in Tolomei's string of speeches, were not *new* symbols of political independence or institutional fragmentation, they were *old* symbols of civic unity and tranquility. No doubt, Tolomei's "visions of other times" included a period of much more recent vintage than the Middle Ages: namely, the 1860s, a time when public life was shaped by associations rather than symbolic politics; when associations themselves were a source of unity rather than division; and, above all, when moderate liberal elites like Tolomei could claim to speak on behalf of the people as well as the *Patria*.

7

Unknown Territory

In 1878, the moderate liberal newspaper *Il Giornale di Padova* sponsored the publication of *L'Osservatore Euganeo*, a combination yearbook and directory. A practical guide to the institutions and services available to residents of the city and province of Padua, it listed the names and addresses of the area's professional groups (lawyers, doctors, engineers, etc.), merchants, and artisans; and the schedules of court hearings, postal and telegraph offices, public transportation, fairs, and markets. Also included was information regarding the city's many institutions and associations: charities, mutual aid societies, theatre groups, social clubs, and commercial institutions. For almost all of these organizations, some basic information was provided: the names of leaders and administrators, the number of members, the size of the budget, and, in a dozen or so cases, a brief historical profile of the organization. More than just a guidebook, the *Osservatore Euganeo* was a "civic" (self-)portrait, a vision of Padua not so much as a layered creation of history – Roman, medieval, Venetian, Italian – but rather as the site of liberal institutions and government.[1]

To be specific, it was a *moderate* liberal portrait, the particular vision of writers and publishers working for the *Giornale di Padova*. A show of political and journalistic arrogance? Yes. But then, at the start of the year 1878, moderate liberals still dominated political and public life in Padua. The left liberal opposition's power – among other things, as the leaders of associations – was just beginning to grow; its first successful efforts at joining the board of directors of the Popular Bank, holding a minority position within local government, and mobilizing workers still lay ahead. Local Catholic groups had barely begun to construct an associational network of their own.

Another pair of yearbooks, entitled *L'Osservatore Veneto*, appeared in Padua in the early 1880s, under the auspices of the city's new moderate liberal newspaper, *L'Euganeo*.[2] In some respects, these volumes were more ambitious than the ones published five years earlier. True to their title, the scope of their contents extended beyond the city and province of Padua to the region as a whole. The first volume, for example, contained a long account of the damage caused throughout the Veneto by the great floods of 1882, as well as a profile of the leading industries in Venice; both volumes featured articles with a regional focus on railroad construction and alpine hiking. The second volume also included a guide to Padua proper (for "the professional, merchant, business man, student, etc., etc."), complete with a list of associations, only this time without the detailed information or narrative descriptions provided by its predecessor, the *Osservatore Euganeo*. In fact, no other guides quite like the *Osservatore Euganeo* were ever published again in Padua. A *Guida pratica della città di Padova* appeared in 1895, but it, too, contained only names and addresses.[3] Even more indicative of the future of guidebook literature was Ottone Brentari's *Guida di Padova* (1891), a tourist guide organized around the complementary concepts of itinerary and neighbourhood, its roster of associations lost in a crowd of other "general information" – below hotels, restaurants, public coaches, banks, newstands, and photographers – and set apart from the main text.[4]

By the 1890s, the authors of city guides had good editorial reasons for eliminating detailed profiles of associations. For, between the appearance of the *Osservatore Euganeo* in 1878 and the *Guida pratica di Padova* in 1895, the dimensions of associational life in Padua had changed dramatically. Whereas the earlier guide's list of "various associations" numbered eleven, the same category in the *Guida pratica* yielded a total of forty-one. Charitable institutions rose from thirteen to thirty-nine and mutual aid societies from sixteen to twenty-eight.[5] Telling, too, was the *Guida pratica*'s introduction of a separate list of Catholic associations, which numbered twelve. There was now a Catholic reading room, a Catholic bank, even a Catholic association of university students. Had the guide appeared a year earlier, before Francesco Crispi ordered the repression of "subversive associations" throughout Italy, it might have provided a list of socialist organizations, too. Regardless, the pattern was clear: as associational life in Padua grew, its identification with the city's moderate liberal ruling elite appeared to weaken. Portraits of the city as the coherent sum total of its civic institutions no longer seemed feasible; self-portraits were out of the question.

Neither Brentari's *Guida di Padova* nor the *Guida pratica della città di Padova* looked beyond the city limits to the surrounding province; however, on the face of it, conditions there did not give liberals much to cheer about. The *Osservatore Veneto* of 1883 put the best light possible on the previous "year in agriculture"; prior to the floods that devastated the region in the fall, it reported, things had been looking up. Or had they? The same year, Emilio Morpurgo's parliamentary report on agricultural conditions in the Veneto appeared, detailing the grave state of rural housing, health, and nutrition, not to mention working conditions, pay, and credit.[6] Although some landowners objected to Morpurgo's critical assessment of rural labour relations, few denied that the international depression in agricultural prices had produced an agrarian crisis in Italy. And conditions were destined to get worse before they improved. Peasant unrest in the Polesine region of the Po Valley in 1884 set off the first in a series of alarms for ruling elites, as did the spread of Catholic and socialist associations in the countryside and the rapid increase in peasant emigration to the Americas.[7]

The *Osservatore Veneto* of 1884 reveals a very different provincial landscape. In a section entitled "Notes and Memoirs from the Provinces (1883)," the guide presented a chronicle of the year's events in the many small towns that dotted the map of the Veneto. Some of these events take us back to the previous chapter's discussion of death and commemoration; thus, we read that plaques to King Victor Emmanuel II and Giuseppe Garibaldi were erected in the towns of Piove, Brugine, Bovolenta, Monselice, Montagnana, and Cittadella, all in the province of Padua. Other events, however, invoke the progressive, expansive mood that had prevailed in Padua during its early years of associational growth. In Este, a new workers' mutual aid society was inaugurated to great fanfare; in Montagnana, an infant nursery school; in Merlara and Urbino, "agricultural workers' associations"; and in a dozen towns throughout the province, soup kitchens for the poor.[8] Space permitting, for each of these towns the editors of the *Osservatore Veneto* could have provided the kind of detailed, institutional profiles that had once been possible for the city of Padua. One workers' association, a pair of cultural societies, an infant nursery school, a handful of charitable institutions – this was still the basic pattern of social organization in Italy's vast landscape of small, provincial towns.

Were these small-town celebrations the last gasp of Venetian liberalism, or the start of a new lease on life? It is difficult to say, because the story of socialist and Catholic expansion during the 1880s and 1890s

has obscured our view of liberal associations.[9] How did liberals respond
to the proliferation of rival networks of association? To new public demands for improvements in housing, health, and employment? To the
trend towards national, mass-membership and special-interest organizations? Venetian liberals did not find easy answers to these questions, either in the city or in the countryside, but they did come up with several
strategies for extending and prolonging their power.

The Limits of Liberal Association

During the 1860s and 1870s, Italian liberals worked hard to construct
urban associational networks capable of meeting of the needs of the popular classes. Mutual aid societies and popular banks, in particular, served
as organizational (and financial) centres of an expanding set of civic initiatives, from the opening of public libraries, night schools, and cooperative stores to the construction of low-income housing and the relief of
flood victims. The accumulating crises of the 1880s, however, led many
people to question the effectiveness of associational approaches to public assistance and reform. Worsening economic conditions put greater
pressure on the leaders of associations. In Padua, several associations
joined the effort to construct low-income housing. A Hygiene Association, founded in 1879 by the noted clinician Achille De Giovanni, led the
effort to construct public dormitories. And the Society of Veterans (Società dei Reduci) used a portion of its budget surplus to create a foundation
for the construction of worker housing. Nevertheless, in five years, the
Society of Veterans managed to fund only the construction of one building, equipped with four rooms and a small garden, which it was hoped
would be rented by a "Veteran, member [and] worker, preferably with
children, for the price of 180 lire per year."[10]

The outbreak of cholera in the Veneto in 1884–86 further exposed the
limits of associational solutions to such large-scale problems. In Padua
and Vicenza, ad hoc groups of volunteers went door to door to assist the
sick, and reported their findings to municipal health and charity commissions. The Catholic Workers' Association in Vicenza (f. 1883) won
wide praise – and a thousand-lire award from the government – for
its efforts. In Padua, the Popular Savoy Association's neighbourhood-
based district committees drew attention to the need for cleaner water,
better housing, and more efficient quarantine hospitals. After the fact,
members of several suburban districts expressed their frustration with
the municipal government's response to the crisis. Representatives from

the Bassanello district compiled a long list of complaints and demands: for more and better public lighting, a "more active and effective" police presence, greater regulation of porters and brokers, the relocation or replacement of a questionable water fountain, and removal of watermelons (and their merchants) from the area. The president of the Volta Barozzo district called for a connecting road and several wells, and left little doubt that the only way to get this done was through greater government spending. "Poor people," he said, "cannot undertake such an expense." And neither could the Popular Savoy Association.[11]

Pressure for greater government action also mounted in the many small towns surrounding Padua and Vicenza, but there it did not reflect a loss of faith in the virtues of association. In 1887, the Prefect of Vicenza proposed supporting the efforts made by "small and poor towns, some with fewer than 1,000 inhabitants" to build public schools, roads, fountains, and baths. A little government support would go a long way: for the poor residents of towns in the foothills of the Alps, a few thousand lire would help speed up construction of a mountain pass, which in turn would facilitate the local trade in wood and charcoal; a few hundred lire would help producers of wood toys and the members of a dairy cooperative to modernize their industries.[12] Some officials worried that the use of public works projects to appease the unemployed might actually encourage worker unrest; why not let workers' mutual aid societies perform their intended function of providing self-reliant, dues-paying members with assistance in times of need?[13] After all, the dramatic increase in the number of mutual aid societies and cooperatives in Italy during the 1880s was due in large part to the proliferation of these associations in small towns.

Significantly, in 1887 city district reports vanished from the pages of *La Libertà*, the organ of Padua's Savoy Association, and were replaced by reports from "all of the workers associations in the province."[14] With few exceptions, the first organizations to send meeting reports to *La Libertà* were old and new associations from Padua proper; however, it was not long before associations from towns outside of Padua began responding to the call. Thus, the first issue of *La Libertà* in 1888 featured reports from eight associations in Padua and four from the towns of Loreggia, Montemerlo, Castelbaldo, and Campo San Martino. In addition, there were short notices on recently founded associations in Cervarese Santa Croce, Piove, Brugine, Codevigo, San Pietro in Gu, and Trebaseleghe. Over the next few issues, the list of towns with new associations grew: Abano, Montagnana, Este, Cittadella, Monselice, Bovolenta, Villa del Conte, Merlara, and Battaglia. Not surprisingly, the accounts of provincial associational life began to fill each issue of *La Libertà*, occupying three or four times the amount of space needed to cover the Savoy Association's news. By and large, the provincial reports that appeared in *La Libertà* derived from two types of association: the mutual aid society and the credit cooperative, or rural bank.[15] Not all of the mutual aid societies under review were new; some, like the Workers' Society of Cittadella and the Workers' Society of Montagnana, made news by celebrating anniversaries of twenty or more years. But many of them, especially those from the area's smaller towns, wrote to *La Libertà* to announce their foundation, or else to report the progress they had made in their first few years of existence. All of the rural banks were of recent vintage. The first one in Italy was founded in 1883 in Loreggia, a small town in the northern part of Padua province; five years later, there were thirty-six in all of Italy, twenty-seven of them in the Veneto and seven in the province of Padua alone, not surprising given that the person who first introduced these institutions to Italy, Leone Wollemborg, was himself a native of Padua.[16]

In the 1890s, Catholic activists began forming rural banks with remarkable speed. In 1891, the first Catholic rural bank was created in Gambarare, in the diocese of Venice. Five years later, there were 378 in all of Italy; then, between 1896 and 1897, their number practically doubled to 691. More impressive still was the fact that this explosion of institutions was largely concentrated in a few regions of northern Italy. Thus, no fewer than 336 (89 per cent) of the 378 banks counted in 1896 were located in the three regions of the Veneto (203), Lombardy (81), and Piedmont (52); and the figures for 1897 were not very different (409, 108, and 78, respectively, for the three regions, adding up to 595, or 86 per cent of the national total). Incredibly, the Venetian dioceses of Treviso, Verona, Padua, and Vicenza, as a group, had as many banks (281) in 1897 as all of the other dioceses in Italy put together.[17]

In the same period, Catholic workers' associations increased in number from 284 in 1891 to 784 in 1897, again with the greatest gains occurring in northern Italy.[18] In his study of the Catholic movement in Vicenza, Ermenegildo Reato recounts the history of the first Catholic workers' associations in the province, beginning with the association founded in Schio in 1881. "Immediately after the Catholic Union of Schio," he writes, "not far from that city, were born the Catholic Workers' Associations of Torrebelvicino and Magrè, S. Vito di Leguzzano, Santorso, Malo, Marano and Pievebelvicino." In 1883–84, new associations formed in Creazzo, Arzignano, Vicenza, and Barbarano. And there were many more to come – about twenty between 1884 and 1891 – most of them forming in small towns; moreover, by October 1888 a Federation of Catholic Workers' Associations had been created, with a monthly periodical, *The Catholic Worker*, and a series of annual "federal" meetings and celebrations in the works.[19]

It was not just the number or geographical scope of Catholic associations that concerned many liberals, but the strength of the Catholic movement's organizational structure. For, in most areas, the spread of Catholic associations was preceded by the formation of a network of parish- and diocese-based "committees," answering to the centralized organization of the Catholic laity known as the Opera dei Congressi.[20] In a report on "the moral and economic conditions of the Province" of Vicenza, prepared in 1890, the Prefect of Vicenza noted that the Opera dei Congressi "could be cause for serious concern in the event of grave political disturbances, because, apart from any consideration of fanatacism, said association can have at its disposal a not insignificant number of members and count with certainty on the concurrence of the Catholic workers' associations, which would certainly not delay in responding to its call." By comparison, Vicenza's various liberal, republican, and socialist groups did not appear very strong. Concluding a review of the area's "political parties," the Prefect noted that the "clerical party ... has an organization and a discipline which it would be uesless to hope for in any other group."[21]

In fact, a closer look at the records of Catholic associations reveals that their founders struggled with a set of growing pains not dissimilar to the ones liberals experienced a decade or two earlier. It took Vicenza's Catholic Youth Circle a dozen years to secure a suitable meeting place. The leaders of circles in smaller towns found themselves short of funds (to get a circulating library up and going, for example), personnel, and, most troubling of all, of general public recognition and support. In towns where it proved impossible to form viable youth circles, activists had to settle for becoming corresponding members of the circle in Vicenza. Parish committees were hastily improvised and then faded from view. In 1887, the president of Vicenza's Diocesan Committee, Giovanni Bertolini, lamented that the rural population "did not yet understand" what the words "Catholic movement" truly meant. When the Diocesan Committee sent a circular requesting statistical information out to the 119 parish committees in the diocese, only 41 responded; the information it gathered suggested that about half of the existing parish committees, "if they are not completely dead, exist only in name," and that a quarter of them showed only minimal signs of life.[22]

Nor were liberals completely lacking in organization or discipline. In Vicenza and elsewhere, the agrarian crisis prompted the formation of several new associations, including the Agrarian Defense League, a group formed in Turin in 1885 by the industrialist Alessandro Rossi, among others, with an explicitly political purpose: to pressure the Italian government to enact a protectionist tariff reform. Generally speaking, too, the agrarian crisis marked the beginning of a trend towards the consolidation of institutional power, at least at the provincial level, which ultimately resulted in the creation, alongside the increasingly ineffectual *comizi agrari*, of a new group of agricultural associations, the *sindacati agricoli* (agricultural unions).[23] In addition, there were large "federal" organizations like Luzzatti's Association of Italian Popular Banks and Wollemborg's Federation of Rural Banks, which held congresses and published periodicals, much like their counterparts in the Catholic movement. But was there any liberal equivalent of the parish committees, groups that attested to the "capillary" form of the church's power in Italian society? The Prefect of Vicenza did not seem to think so, and most historians are inclined to agree. But then again, historians have tended to rely heavily upon the prefect's point of view for an answer to this question; after all, it is to the provincial *archivio di stato*, with its boxes of prefectoral records – letters, reports, profiles, and questionnaires – that scholars turn in order to measure the liberal state's reach into local society. Not surprisingly, given the content of reports like the one prepared by the Prefect of Vicenza in 1890, what many historians find is an overbearing but ineffectual state and a divided, unmotivated ruling class.

To a surprising extent, the province remained an institutional terra incognita after unification. During the Risorgimento, a surge of interest in geography and statistics inspired the preparation of some unusually comprehensive studies; nevertheless, most guidebooks from the period speak briefly and generically of the "environs" or "territory" surrounding Italy's major cities. Bishops' pastoral visitations yielded unusually detailed information about even the smallest communities in a given diocese, but it was hardly feasible to investigate what often amounted to several hundred parishes with any regularity.[24] To gather accurate and up-to-date information on a wider array of environmental, economic, and civil conditions was even more difficult. Take, for example, the ambitious but unrealized program for a "monograph" of the province of Vicenza devised in 1868 by the leaders of the city's Industrial and Professional Institute. As planned, the study would have contained twenty-one chapters, some with six or seven sections and as many authors. The chapter on "moral" conditions alone aimed to generate a provincial survey of theatres, cafes, inns, taverns, lotteries, pawnshops, vagabonds, begging, prostitution, theft, fighting, homicide, and more.[25] Source problems aside, scholars' fascination with Italian urban (*campanilismo*) and regional identity has led them to underestimate, if not ignore, the importance of the province.[26]

The partial and fragmented record of provincial power helps explain why we rarely get a clear *and* comprehensive view of liberal associational networks. Focused studies like the Ministry of Agriculture, Industry and Commerce's regular surveys of mutual aid societies, and the congressional reports of Luzzatti's Association of Italian Popular Banks and Wollemborg's Federation of Rural Banks, provide helpful estimates of the total number and geographic distribution of specific associations, but they offer few hints regarding the exercise of power within a given territory (city, province, region). At the other end of the spectrum lie unusual resources like Sebastiano Rumor's *Bibliografia storica della città e provincia di Vicenza*, a large (if selective) inventory of local publications and documents. Nevertheless, even if one were to track down several dozen of the associational publications listed in these volumes, it would be difficult to determine what connections, if any, were shared by the associations in question. In this respect, the periodical *La Libertà* is a particularly interesting and valuable source. For while it aspired to be the organ of a wide range of "welfare institutions," it also maintained a relatively precise, territorial focus on the province of Padua.

Civic Miniatures

True to the spirit of the liberal public sphere, *La Libertà* organized its profiles of provincial associations around the meeting report, or *verbale*. Thus, we learn that the annual general assembly of the Mutual Aid Society of Loreggia was "very orderly and well-attended"; that, following a review of the institution's finances, "the Assembly approved the budget with manifest satisfaction"; and that the association's internal elections resulted in the re-election of its president, Leone Wollemborg, "by acclamation." Minutes from a meeting of the Rural Bank of Montemerlo indicate that, after the fifty-five members in attendance unanimously approved the budget, they also approved the president's motion to send a letter of thanks to Leone Wollemborg, the bank's honorary president, "for such a beautiful and useful institution." Similarly, the syndics of the Rural Bank of Abano, in their annual report to the membership, attributed the

institution's progress – in only eight months of existence – to the "scrupu-
lous diligence and loving prudence of the Administration."[27]

As fairly recent additions to the ranks of Italy's "welfare institutions,"
the area's rural banks contributed some of the most enthusiastic and
long-winded meeting reports to *La Libertà*. Several provided detailed information on the number, type, and terms of the loans that had been
issued during the past year, with due emphasis on the modesty of the
banks' clientele. The author of a special review of "rural banks in the
province of Padua" noted, for example, that the very first bank, in Loreggia, was created by thirty-two members, "almost all of them peasants ... except for three: Dr. Wollemborg, the municipal secretary and the
municipal doctor, who were invested, respectively, with the positions of
president, accountant, and head-syndic." In Wollemborg's own words,
the second bank in the province (and third overall in Italy), in the town
of Trebaseleghe, "formed and is governed by sole virtue of the people – a
municipal scribe, an elementary school teacher and a priest make up the
leaders [*le forze dirigenti*]."[28] In another contribution to *La Libertà*, entitled, "Where rural banks should be founded and who should take part
in them," Wollemborg wrote:

> As long as it is possible to find [in a given town or village] only two men, re-
> spectable in terms of the seriousness of their character, animated by a sense
> of the public good, not without a modest education, willing to assume the
> essential offices in a rural bank of president and accountant (treasurer), one
> can certainly think of founding [a bank].[29]

In fact, the leadership of the Padua's rural banks was not always so
modest. The names of more than a few notables pop up in the *verbali* that
rural banks in the province submitted to *La Libertà*. Thus, the president
of the Rural Bank of Montemerlo was Francesco Papafava dei Carraresi,
member of one of Padua's oldest noble families and co-founder with Wollemborg of the Federation of Rural Banks; and among the founders and
leaders of the bank in Abano was Leone Wollemborg's brother, Maurizio,
and two fairly active members of the Comizio Agrario di Padova, still
the province's leading agrarian association.[30] More often than not, too,
it was the mayor rather than the town scribe or doctor who provided
a fledgling bank with the necessary "seriousness of character." In this
respect, the following short news item from the February–March 1889
issue of *La Libertà* is telling:

Rural bank of Rovolon. By invitation of the mayor of the town, cav. O. Regensburger, on November 18 Dr. Wollemborg came to this town ... to give a lecture on the institution of a rural bank. In the municipal meeting room, in front of a crowded and intelligent audience, including the mayor, the archpriest and the principal residents of the place, as well as Count F. Papafava dei Carraresi and the administrators of the nearby bank of Montemerlo, the founder of the rural banks widely exposed the concept and the organism of the desired association. Then a committee was formed of 15 members ..., among them the mayor, the archpriest Menegotto Don Domenico, Mr. Fasolo, and other landowners.

On this occasion, there was no mention of peasants.[31]

The place of notables among the leaders of provincial mutual aid societies was even more prominent. Among the first elected leaders of the Agricultural Workers' Society in Abano (founded in April 1889) were Count Antonio Cittadella Vigodarzere (the association's president), and two of the Wollemborg brothers, Maurizio and Leone (vice-president and counsellor, respectively). In S. Pietro in Gu, the creation of a new mutual aid society of artisans, day labourers, and tenant farmers was the "laudable initiative" of two other notables, Emilio Rizzetto and Eleonoro Negri. On more than one occasion, *La Libertà* printed a mutual aid society's appeal to local elites for financial support; moreover, several meeting reports attested to the material as well as symbolic importance of donations.[32]

If the use of meeting reports to represent associations was in keeping with liberal definitions of the public sphere, the positive attention *La Libertà* paid to associational celebrations was not. Between the last issue of 1888 and the first issue of 1890, the periodical covered "workers' celebrations" in Battaglia, Montagnana, S. Angelo di Piove, Cervarese S. Croce, Monselice, Cittadella, Bovolenta, and Padua. Some of them marked special occasions, such as the twentieth anniversary of the Workers' Society of Cittadella, but others originated as requests from the membership; some were given the sober title "festivals of work," but most went by the more festive one of "workers' banquets."

Celebrations of this kind were certainly not new. A large *festa del lavoro* was held in Padua in 1869; in Vicenza, the Società Generale held annual patron saint's day celebrations. But the frequency with which celebrations began to occur in the 1880s, and the attention that liberal elites began paying to them, both in the press and in associations, were unprecedented.

After all, an event like Padua's "festival of work" in 1869 had been treated by its organizers as something *other* or *more* than a celebration. As a rule, liberals viewed associational celebrations as frivolous in at least two respects: on the one hand, they represented the waste of an association's valuable resources; on the other hand, they distracted members from the productive goals of moral and material improvement. It was certainly uncommon in the 1860s, or even the 1870s, for a mutual aid society to decide, as the Association of Artisans, Workers and Small Merchants of Cervarese S. Croce did, at a meeting in February 1889, "to hold a celebration every year in order to maintain among the members that spirit of brotherhood which is necessary for the long life of certain institutions," or to organize a spectacular bicycle race in the association's name, as the Workers' Society of Montagnana proposed in July of 1888.[33]

What explains this wave of celebrations? On the one hand, it is possible to view them in terms of the wider symbolic politics discussed in the previous chapter. Some celebrations, that is, appeared to be a show of unity and strength on the part of the area's liberal ruling elites. More than one event was held on Constitution Day, and incorporated visits to local monuments to King Victor Emmanuel II and Giuseppe Garibaldi. The *festa del lavoro* in Battaglia attracted delegations from sixteen "sister associations" throughout the province, as well as three parliamentary representatives. The flags of the participating associations adorned the banquet hall. After lunch and the obligatory sequence of toasts, "all of the Authorities and honorable [parliamentary] deputies went into town, fraternizing with the workers and buying tickets for the charity raffle on behalf of the [town's] infant nursery schools."[34]

Still, there was little political content or edge in *La Libertà*'s reporting of this or most other celebrations. On the contrary, the emphasis was clearly on the events' prevailing atmosphere of social harmony and solidarity.

> Montagnana 1 November [1887]
> ... It was beautiful the other day to see 224 regular and honorary members of our Workers' Society come together at a banquet. We did not have anything to celebrate, but ended up celebrating once again the pact of brotherhood between the various social classes. There in the room of the Infant Nursery School where the children of the rich and the poor are taught and educated, it was beautiful and useful to see the hand that pays shake the hand that works, a token of harmony that will never be forgotten.

Of course, to praise class harmony was to make a political statement; moreover, it was directed at an increasingly broad yet precise target: the radicals, republicans and, above all, socialists who tried to persuade workers to distrust and reject the "hand that pays." Happily, though, as far as *La Libertà*'s correspondent was concerned, the source of the problem was far removed from Montagnana. "It is a fact," the above account of the town's banquet began, "that certain manifestations of brotherhood and of well-understood democracy are only possible among us, in this dear town, which does not let itself be swept away by those fatal winds which, [while] appearing to enliven, [in fact] corrode every freedom and all prosperity."[35]

In fact, the politics of associational life in small towns were not so simple. Workers sought to maintain control over their own associations, for example by insisting that wealthy patrons not vote at meetings or hold office.[36] Nevertheless, a small community's limited human and material resources often led to the creation of one general workers' association, rather than multiple trade-specific groups, and this outcome strongly favoured the inclusion, if not the leadership, of local elites. It is telling that these general mutual aid societies frequently became pivotal civic centres, performing a variety of charitable functions and sponsoring the creation of affiliated welfare organizations.[37] Liberals of the 1880s and 1890s could not hope to dominate such networks as they had a generation earlier; after all, Catholics and socialists were busy creating not simply rival associations but rival networks of welfare assistance. Nevertheless, for a time liberals could appreciate the contrast between contested cities like Padua and Milan and those many small towns where workers continued to appreciate the assistance provided by elites, and where power still rested clearly with the mayor and a dozen or so notables.

Territory

The political importance of small, provincial towns in the 1880s and 1890s was more than symbolic. Liberal newspapers covering the political elections of the 1890s are filled with items like the following, from *Il Comune* in Padua:

> An imposing assembly of electors from Isola della Scala, with a broad representation of all the Towns in the district, unanimously and enthusiastically proclaimed the candidacy of cav. Emanuele Romanin-Jacur.

Today at 10 in the Room of the Vittoria Hotel, the Electoral-political committee of the district of Este-Monselice met so as to proceed to the proclamation of a candidate.

All the Towns of the two Districts were represented by 3 or more members.[38]

The thirty-member electoral committee of Abano, whose names appeared below a manifesto in support of Luigi Luzzatti, represented twenty towns in the district, many of which had figured prominently in *La Libertà*'s review of "welfare institutions," including Abano, Bovolenta, Battaglia, and Cervarese S. Croce; not surprisingly, among the committee members were several people who had been leaders of workers' associations or rural banks in the area.[39]

Provincial towns were also the site of countless campaign speeches and banquets. Candidates carried out electoral tours of their districts, stopping at several towns along the way to give speeches. Newspapers did their best to keep track of their preferred candidates' activities. "Electoral speeches are the order of the day," *Il Comune* noted in the fall of 1892, "and, even if we wanted to, it would be impossible to occupy ourselves with all of them. In our province alone, six were delivered [yesterday], four of them by candidates who are our friends, and two by a candidate who is our adversary." It proceeded to report on the speeches given by one of its "friends," Alessandro Casalini, in a pair of small towns in the recently created Vigonza district. In the town of Curtarolo, at the home of a local notable,

> there convened ... a truly select company of electors, among which we noted senator [Vincenzo Stefano] Breda, Mr. Eugenio Busetto, Mr. Pini mayor of Campodarsego and Mr. Garola mayor of Limena, our eminent Dr. Scalco, Mr. Piacentini and other distinguished persons, whom it would take too long to specify.

At Casalini's second stop, Ponte di Brenta, *Il Comune* estimated that over two hundred people turned out. After noting the presence of "large Delegations of various Towns in the District," the newspaper went on to identify fifteen attending notables by name, adding that there were "many others whose names we do not know," not to mention the "many, many villagers" who came from the surrounding area.[40] Here, too, on the campaign trail, a familiar pattern emerged: several mayors, an important national figure or two, anywhere from a handful to fifteen or twenty notables, and then the rest, the "many others," the appreciative townsfolk.[41]

Newspapers in Vicenza during this period followed the same pattern. *La Provincia di Vicenza*'s report on the banquet held in Orgiano for Giovanni Mazzoni, the moderate liberal candidate in the district of Lonigo and a native of Orgiano, left no doubt as to the existence of formal, hierarchical distinctions among those in attendance.

> The table in the shape of a horseshoe was prepared in the Town Meeting Room [*Sala Municipale*]. Around the table sat seventy people who had come together from all parts of the District of Lonigo to give proof of their friendship and respect to the former [parliamentary] deputy and then to hear him speak.
>
> There were among them the heads and representatives of fourteen Towns out of the twenty which make up the District; influential and devoted electors.
>
> At the center of the table Mazzoni sat between two friendly gentlemen: Paolo Dalla Pozza Mayor of Orgiano and Luigi Chiericati Mayor of Campiglia.
>
> ... Once the happy and expansive meal was finished, the room was cleared to make space, and the public was admitted.
>
> In an instant [the room] filled with electors, who were crammed in tight.[42]

Campaign stops in provincial towns did not begin in the 1890s. The campaigns that preceded the political elections of November 1876, for example, were characterized by a relatively high level of mobilization. Newspapers reported on meetings and banquets throughout the province, and duly noted the presence of mayors and local notables at each event. Nevertheless, the real novelty of the 1876 campaign was not the individual candidates' territorial ambitions, but rather the organizational structure provided by a new group of political associations. Thus, in its account of one candidate's visit in 1876 to the district centre of Thiene, the moderate liberal *Giornale della Provincia di Vicenza* noted the presence there of the vice-president of the Constitutional Association of Vicenza, and explained that the president of the Constitutional Association could not attend because he was assisting at the speech that Marco Minghetti (one of Italy's leading moderate politicians) was presenting in the nearby district of Legnago, in the province of Verona.[43]

The electoral reform of 1882 inspired greater attention to provincial constituencies. In addition to tripling the electorate, this reform introduced a new system of voting in Italy. Before 1882, Italian voters elected members of Parliament on a one-member, one-district (or single constituency) basis; that is, each voter selected only one candidate to represent the district in which he was registered. With the reform, voters elected MPs according to a list-voting system (*scrutinio di lista*). First, all electoral districts were increased in size, thereby reducing the total number of districts in Italy from 508 to 135; second, each voter was asked to select not one but several candidates to represent the much larger district to which he now belonged. Thus, for the elections of November 1882, the province of Padua's six electoral districts were reduced to two. In 1892, after just three national election cycles under the new list-voting system, Italy's voting system reverted back to the single-member constituency.[44]

The *scrutinio di lista* system encouraged candidates to view the electorate in broader, territorial terms. A candidate for the reformed district of Vicenza in 1882 had to win the support of electors in a considerable number of towns, including the district centers of Barbarano, Lonigo, Valdagno, and Thiene. Towards this end, establishing and maintaining local contacts became increasingly important; the support of mayors and town officials was essential. In 1890, Giovanni Mazzoni began his electoral speech in Barbarano with a poetic tribute to the land as well as the people of the surrounding Riviera del Brenta:

> I salute your hills for its festive grape-harvests, populated with houses and olive groves; I salute this genial land, crouched like an eagle at the foot of his cliffs, which the rain bathes and the wind lashes, land which with the remains of its castle reminds me of centuries of fierce battles, eras of vexations and sorrows, and with the kindness of its inhabitants shows me the path travelled by civilization.[45]

The campaign trail continued to include provincial towns like Barbarano in 1892, when Italy's voting system reverted back to the single-member constituency. In the political elections of 1892 and 1895, liberal elites in Padua and Vicenza demonstrated their appreciation of the provincial *comune*, not simply as a unit of political territory, but also as a site where campaign visits and speeches could be turned into public celebrations. Even newspaper accounts inspired by the meetings and banquets of rival candidates, for example, seem to confirm the importance of appearances during these campaigns. While promoting the candidacy of Guardino Colleoni in the district of Thiene-Asiago in 1895, *La Provincia di Vicenza* made a point of recording how poorly Colleoni's opponent,

Attilio Brunialti, was received in various towns, and how unimportant were the people who greeted him. When asked to play at a meeting of Brunialti supporters in the small town of Grumolo, the town band of Thiene refused; that, the newspaper added, was just one indication of Brunialti's unpopularity in the district centre.[46]

At the opposite end of the spectrum was the reception that awaited Lelio Bonin in Marostica in 1892, again, according to *La Provincia di Vicenza*. "I will only write a few lines," the paper's correspondent from Marostica began, "because it is absolutely impossible for me to give you in such restricted time any kind of report which might give the faintest idea of today's celebration: I say celebration because I would not know how, with another name, to signify better the greetings given by our town to Count Bonin." With an enthusiasm reminiscent of the accounts of "workers' celebrations" which appeared in *La Libertà* in the late 1880s, the correspondent described the day's events, from Bonin's speech and the banquet that followed, to the procession of the town's band "through the streets, where Count Bonin was also given a very hearty welcome."[47]

It was one thing to celebrate labour and a local workers' association in this manner, another to celebrate politics and politicians. The streets, at any rate, were not usually invested with positive political meaning in the liberal press. But these were the streets of a provincial town, where a small group of notables could still claim to be the principal electors in the district; where elites continued to play an active part in workers' associations; and, above all, where it was still possible to choreograph an affirmative, public display of liberal power. Nevertheless, it is also important to recognize what was new about Italian electoral politics in the late nineteenth century. Not every liberal notable was pleased, for example, with the increase in territorial scope that appeared to characterize election campaigns in the 1890s. Bonin himself was surprised to find that an opponent in Marostica had been conducting "almost an electoral tour" of the district, as he put it in a letter to Fedele Lampertico.[48] Luigi Luzzatti felt pressured to give speeches and attend banquets in small towns within the electoral district of Abano.[49] For his run in the Oderzo district of Treviso in 1909, Luzzatti agreed to attend a ceremony inaugurating a bust to one of Oderzo's notables; meet with the district's mayors, communal secretaries, workers' associations, agrarian associations, and electors; and conduct a two-day tour of the district. Four years later, running again in Oderzo in Italy's first elections since the adoption of universal male suffrage, Luzzatti added to his list of institutional allies the presidents of the area's popular banks and low-income housing associations.[50]

The Luzzatti archive in Venice offers a stunning, panoramic view of a major liberal politician's ties with dozens of government ministries and agencies, hundreds of personal friends and allies, and thousands of associations from every part of Italy. As the president of the Association of Italian Popular Banks, Luzzatti corresponded with the leaders of several hundred local banks, and prepared for a string of regional and national "congresses." Whereas in 1867 there were only twenty popular banks concentrated in northern Italy, by 1887 there were over six hundred banks throughout Italy. And most, if not all, of these banks had ties with many of the country's five thousand mutual aid societies and one thousand cooperatives, not to mention with local night schools, library associations, charitable organizations, housing initiatives, agrarian associations, and savings banks. As the honorary president of countless workers' associations, Luzzatti attended inaugural and anniversary celebrations all over the country. Last but not least, as a powerful government minister and the author of important labour and welfare legislation, Luzzatti received a steady stream of personal requests for favours, large and small, regarding associations: from people in search of jobs at popular banks, public works contracts for cooperatives, information on the national pension plan, government approval of changes to statutes, prizes for sports clubs and veterans' groups, honorary titles for the proponents of new housing associations. In all of these capacities, Luzzatti bore witness to three important, interrelated changes taking place between 1880 and 1914: a second wave of liberal associationism, above all in small cities and towns; liberals' first significant steps towards regional and national organization; and the state's growing involvement in the affairs of Italy's expanding network of workers' associations.

Together, these changes call into question a number of the standard criticisms of Italy's liberal ruling elites. Historians frequently emphasize the fragmentation of the Italian bourgeoisie and the isolation of politicians from the concerns of ordinary people; they speak of a widening gap between the state and civil society or between "legal" and "real" Italy. But the rapidly changing profile of associational life in the late nineteenth and early twentieth centuries suggests that the ties between the state and local elites and the organized working class were becoming greater, not weaker.[51] The law passed in 1889 that made it easier for cooperatives to win bids on public works contracts immediately altered the relationship between local producers and elites; and the creation of a national pension fund in 1898 had a similarly dramatic effect on mutual aid societies, prompting them to reconsider the often thorny relationship between workers' self-help and wealthy citizens' patronage. The proliferation of associations in small towns gave liberal paternalism a new lease on life, but it also reflected liberals' engagement with the challenge posed by Catholic and socialist organizers.

One could argue that the second wave of liberal associationism came too late, that by the 1880s the legitimacy of Italy's liberal ruling elite was too badly damaged to be repaired. As the nineteenth century came to a close, Italy was still a poor and diseased land of desperate emigrants, malnourished children, unsanitary cities, and malarial marshlands. The ruling liberals' failure to modernize Italy was most apparent at the national level. Parliament held up the passage of badly needed legislation for years, and turned a blind eye to inept or corrupt local authorities.[52] At the local level, however, Italian liberals made a more concerted effort to reform society, above all by creating a range associations aimed at improving the lives of the popular classes. This was certainly true of Venetian liberals. Their approach to the social and economic problems of the day was paternalist, but not doctrinaire: over time, as they experienced failure and encountered resistance, they learned to lay the groundwork for a more cooperative and contractual and less hierarchical relationship with the popular classes. The combination of stasis in Rome and lingering paternalism in the localities proved to be too great a liability. Rival centres of loyalty grew stronger, political opponents multiplied, the demands of total war upset the delicate balance between state and civil society, and the postwar cycle of political conflict and violence shattered the liberals' confidence.

Conclusion

This book began as a doctoral dissertation, which I defended at the University of Michigan in the spring of 1996. The speaker at the university's winter commencement that year was Supreme Court justice Sandra Day O'Connor. With a few friends, I listened as the first woman on America's highest court recounted the story of her remarkable life. Ten or fifteen minutes into the speech, Justice O'Connor turned her attention to the history of associational life and made a special point of mentioning the important new research on associations in modern Italy. My friends' jaws dropped: was it possible that Sandra Day O'Connor had read my dissertation in advance and incorporated its findings into her commencement speech? No. She was referring to Robert Putnam's recently published book, *Making Democracy Work: Civic Traditions in Modern Italy*. Then as now, Putnam was best known for his essay on the decline of civic life in America, "Bowling Alone." In fact, *Making Democracy Work* and "Bowling Alone" both attempt to show that democracies thrive where citizens are "actively involved in all sorts of local associations," a point that Alexis de Tocqueville had made over a century and a half earlier in *Democracy in America*.[1]

Making Democracy Work is a study in regional variation, contrasting the high levels of civic engagement and effective governance in northern Italy with low levels in the south. It is also a historical study in that Putnam traces Italy's variable civic habits or "traditions" all the way back to the twelfth century, when a string of northern towns became self-governing republican communes while the autocratic rulers of southern Italy strengthened their feudal power. But Justice O'Connor did not address these fine points of Italian history and geography in her speech. She focused on a broader, simpler, and more upbeat summary of Putnam's

findings: the idea that individuals, acting on their own and working together, can form a civil society that is independent of the state. This is an
old idea, older than Adam Smith's *Wealth of Nations* and Alexis de Tocqueville's *Democracy in America*, but it experienced a powerful revival
in the 1990s, the decade of post-communism in Eastern Europe, welfare
reform in the United States, and proliferating NGOs (non-governmental organizations) throughout the world. It is also an idea that has informed most histories of associational life in modern Europe, including
this one. However, what I found in my research challenges both Justice
O'Connor's general faith in the power of "joiners" and Robert Putnam's
more specific conclusions about Italian regional and civic history.

Throughout nineteenth-century Italy, in the north as well as the south,
the most passionate advocates of associational life doubted that ordinary Italians could form a modern, progressive civil society on their own.
They read Tocqueville's *Democracy in America* and recognized the virtues of voluntary association and self-help; however, they also took to
heart Tocqueville's point that some people – in particular, the remarkable
Americans – were more inclined to form associations than others. They
believed that the average Italian was too isolated, poor, and ignorant – in
a word, too backward – to organize and improve himself.

Such doubts greatly influenced the moderate liberals who dominated
associational life and politics in the Veneto after unification, men like
Luigi Luzzatti, Fedele Lampertico, Emilio Morpurgo, and Paolo Lioy.
This cluster of mutual friends and political allies studied the various
workers' associations proliferating in Europe and America, and made
it their mission to introduce the best types to their hometowns. They assumed that the vast majority of their fellow citizens were unfamiliar with
the basic practices of association: with how to get associations started,
balance budgets, organize meetings, and hold elections. To create a successful workers' association, they believed, it was not enough to call a
meeting and let the self-activating mechanism of voluntary association
run its course. So they prepared statutes in advance, promoted workers'
associations in the press, mobilized the support of local elites, and calcu-
lated the best means of convincing commoners to join. In short, they took
nothing for granted. To write the history of associations in nineteenth-
century Italy, then, we need to shift our attention from generalized bodies
of joiners to the specific relations of power existing within associations.

We also need to pay closer attention to the pivotal event of nineteenth-
century Italian history: unification. Putnam sees Italy's regionally variant
civic traditions as deeply historical and continuous. Thus, he argues that

the most important new forms of association of the nineteenth century, workers' mutual aid societies and cooperatives, harked back to the medieval communes and thrived where these self-governing republics were most durable, in north-central Italy. In Putnam's sweeping medieval-to-modern narrative, unification receives little attention; it appears to have had practically no effect on Italy's civic culture. Putnam implies that the fault for this anticlimax lies with the moderate liberals who guided the unification process, for they favoured the vertical ties of political patronage over the horizontal ties of association. He is more impressed by what occurred a decade or two after unification, when socialists and Catholics – the true heirs of Italy's solidary tradition, in Putnam's view – began creating their own, more extensive networks of workers' associations.[2]

But the leading advocates of association in nineteenth-century Italy were in fact liberals, not socialists or Catholics, and they did not look to the distant past for inspiration. Cultural nationalists in Italy might invoke the greatness of ancient or papal Rome, they might erect statues of Dante and write operas about medieval uprisings. Social and economic reformers, however, took a different view. For them, historical continuity was not a blessing but a curse, for it signified the backwardness of Italy – north, centre, and south – in relation to other European nations. What inspired them most was the recent past of French and British history, the modernizing legacy of the French and industrial revolutions. The formula was simple: archaic institutions and beliefs stood in the way of progress, modern associations and ideas made progress possible. Restrictive guilds and usurious pawnshops had to be replaced by large mutual aid societies and profit-sharing credit unions; the idle recipients of charity had to learn the modern values of industry, saving, and personal independence. What Italy needed most was not a revival of ancient traditions but a break with the past.

Historians of Italian nationalism emphasize a more disheartening break: the shift from the "poetry" of the Risorgimento to the "prose" of the post-unification period. By this account, the epic revolutions and battles of the years 1815–60 cast a shadow over the calculating and unimaginative rulers of united Italy. Government leaders squandered the ordinary citizen's goodwill and members of Parliament allowed local interests to shape policy. It was only a matter of time before a new generation of poets called for a return to the high ideals of the Risorgimento.[3] But this stark contrast between poetic national feeling and prosaic liberal government can be misleading. Venetian liberals deliberately blurred the line between the two by casting the seemingly prosaic task of institution-building in heroic terms. As the founders of new forms of "popular association," which had been limited if not prohibited by the Austrian government before 1866, they drew upon what Alberto Banti calls the "deep images" of Risorgimento nationalism: they spoke of oppressors and martyrs, crusades and battles.[4] At the same time, they gave the Risorgimento a more contemporary and politically moderate meaning, as an ongoing quest to reform Italian society. Over time it became less expedient to promise a radical break with the past, more convincing to speak of a gradually expanding network of modernizing institutions. By the 1880s, when the founders of the region's first popular associations began to die off and Catholic and socialist opposition intensified, Venetian liberals began to sound downright pessimistic. Nevertheless, the belated proliferation of associations in small, provincial towns prompted a new round of momentous – historic yet modern – speeches and celebrations.

The argument for a modern, institutional *risorgimento* began with a critique of recreation. Under the Austrians, the skeletal associational life of most Venetian cities revolved around exclusive social clubs, where local nobles and wealthy bourgeois conversed, played games, and hosted balls, leaving ordinary citizens to gather in streets and squares, cafes and taverns. In light of numerous developments – the proliferation of enterprising associations in Britain and the United States, the condescension of foreign rulers and tourists, the persistence of widespread poverty and illiteracy – such idle pleasures began to seem retrograde. After unification, elite social clubs and working-class taverns continued to thrive, Masonic lodges proliferated, and a variety of new recreational groups appeared: hiking clubs, town bands, sharpshooting societies, and many more.[5] Nevertheless, Venetian liberals worked hard to establish a new, more productive and sober model of association and public life. They made the spread of economic and educational associations for workers a priority, and within these associations they preached fiscal austerity.

More remarkably, for a time they showed an almost total disregard for the traditional virtues of sociability. They aspired to create large associations with hundreds if not thousands of members, dimensions that discouraged talk of familial or fraternal ties. One or two annual meetings was the norm, and these were highly uneventful affairs, featuring parliamentary rules of order, dry business reports, a bare minimum of discussion, and the members' rote approval of their leaders' actions. Newspapers reinforced this ritual display of procedural order by routinely providing terse accounts of associational meetings, and by favourably comparing these calm assemblies with a variety of unruly or simply unpredictable public demonstrations.

Unification provided a political and ideological framework for the ruling liberals' new conception of associational life. On the one hand, the cult of patriotic action encouraged even moderate liberals to exaggerate the daring novelty of their efforts to promote new forms of popular association. On the other hand, the fragile process of unification presented local elites with the urgent task of creating a new civil order. The limited resources of the debt-ridden state and the apparent backwardness of society combined to make associational life a crucial site of liberal reform. No doubt late unification gave Venetian liberals a sharper view of Italy's problems and of the role associations might play in addressing them. But although the aims and outcomes of associational activity varied from one region to the next – indeed, as this study shows, from one town to the next – everywhere in Italy the leaders of new associations confronted the challenge of modernization. They gathered statistical information, created modest collections of books and tools, organized exhibitions and adult education programs, and set up cooperative stores and banks. They also assembled citizens (not just voters but producers, professionals, merchants, artisans, landowners, and peasants), and propagated the ideals of constitutional law and order, parliamentary government, secular education, and economic progress.

For united Italy's first generation of ruling elites, the primary goal was not to keep the state in check or to defend the autonomy of civil society; rather, it was to assist the state in identifying and organizing a civil society.[6] The forceful leadership implicit in this view – and what lay behind it: the concerns, uncertainties, and doubts about Italy's future – should not surprise us. By the mid-1990s, when Robert Putnam published "Bowling Alone" and Sandra Day O'Connor spoke at my commencement, scholars and policymakers had already begun to voice doubts about the formation of civil society in many areas of the world. Books chronicling the "emergence" or "revival" of civil society in western Europe and the United States continued to appear, but now alongside a growing number of more troubled titles, which teach us that the transition to democracy can be "uncertain" and that civil societies can be hidden, weak, or nonexistent.[7] More recent studies have tended to go further, highlighting the need to "build" democracy and civil society and to "craft" community.[8] The space for Tocquevillian tales of deep-rooted civic habits and spontaneous grass-roots action has been shrinking; at the centre of today's global literature on democratization are leaders, organizers, patrons, and donors. Slowly but surely, historians have begun to view associational life "from above" as well as "from below."[9]

The concerns and activism of Venetian liberals should, however, surprise students of modern Italian history. Historians have done such a good job of documenting northern Italians' negative stereotyping of the south, it is easy to forget that northerners found plenty of evidence of "backwardness" much closer to home. The leaders of popular associations in Padua and Vicenza did not put much faith in local workers' capacity for self-help; rather, they took it upon themselves to teach artisans and peasants how to save money, read books, balance budgets, and much more. When workers came to meetings, leaders expressed surprise; when they failed to turn up (or pay their dues, or follow advice), leaders got discouraged. Politically ambitious proponents of association exaggerated the challenges they faced, to inspire audiences but also to make their own ambitions and accomplishments seem greater, more dramatic. At the same time, their concerns were real and they never completely went away. Today, Padua and Vicenza are among the wealthiest cities in Italy, and the Veneto is considered one of Italy's most prosperous and productive regions. But this is a relatively recent development. At the turn of the twentieth century, the Veneto was still a poor region with a limited number of modern industries.[10]

A traditional focus on parliamentary politics and state-sponsored reform has obscured the actions of local elites, in the arena of municipal politics but especially in the wider contexts of associational life and public culture. The conventional high-political view of Liberal Italy seems clear and discouraging: a narrow suffrage gave united Italy's first generation of parliamentary elites little incentive to concern themselves with the general populations' needs and woes, or to engage the masses in the creation of a broadly liberal or democratic political culture; left to their own devices, they practised the arts of unprincipled compromise and clientelism. Insularity bred corruption and stasis: Italian liberals failed to reduce the gap between rulers and ruled, state and society, "legal" Italy and "real" Italy. As this book demonstrates, the view from Padua and Vicenza is different: immediately after unification, leading Venetian liberals acted to reduce the gap between rulers and ruled in a variety of ways, above all through the creation of popular associations: mutual aid societies, credit unions, consumer cooperatives, libraries, and night schools. Within these associations, leaders deliberately promoted a liberal-democratic culture of public assembly, constitutional law, open discussion, and free election.

The results of these efforts were mixed. Popular associations proliferated but failed to produce the dramatic social change their founders had promised. Associational leaders' fundamental paternalism – their assumption that they needed to teach ordinary citizens how to associate responsibly – exposed the limits of their openness to democratic governance. However, it also inspired them to take action in the first place, to effect a cautious yet profound transformation of local economic, social, and cultural life. Venetian liberals' commitment to association-based reform did not extend to political life: they showed little enthusiasm for political associations and even less tolerance for organized opposition and conflict, within or between associations. Nevertheless, Venetian liberals could not insulate themselves, or associational life, from political challenges. In fact, so many of the standard critiques of Italian liberals – for example, that they did not extend their reach into the countryside or recognize the importance of national organization – fail to apply convincingly to the history of associations.

The temptation to project a twentieth-century "crisis of liberalism" back onto the whole post-unification period is great. But to see how the strengths and weaknesses of liberal associations might relate to the rise of fascism, one would need to conduct an intensive study of associational life in the years immediately preceding and following the First World War. In this study, one can see the outlines of a crisis as early as the 1880s, when several of the Veneto's leading liberals let their distaste for political pluralism show. But one can also point to evidence of liberalism's lasting strength, as associational networks extended out to provincial localities and up to an emerging welfare state. To see the strengths of Italian liberalism, it is helpful to view the immediate post-unification period on its own terms, as a time of uncertain yet momentous change.

Notes

Introduction

1 I will use the term *liberal*, here and throughout the book, to describe both of Italy's main ruling groups after unification: the moderate liberals of the so-called Historic Right, who dominated parliamentary politics and government from 1861 to 1876, and the progressive liberals of the Historic Left, who led the government after 1876, thanks in large part to a strategy of alliance-building with their moderate rivals. Understandably, parliamentary politics and government have shaped historians' (generally negative) assessments of Italian liberalism; however, it is crucial to examine what liberalism meant at the local level, as a political force but also as a more widely diffused ideology, taking concrete form in a range of organizations and institutions: associations, museums, libraries, banks, factories, charitable organizations, and welfare institutions.

2 Silvana Patriarca, *Numbers and Nationhood: Writing Statistics in Nineteenth-Century Italy* (Cambridge: Cambridge University Press, 1996), pp. 176–209.

3 An English translation of Villari's article appears in the compendium of documents edited by Denis Mack Smith, *The Making of Italy 1796–1870* (New York: Walker, 1968), pp. 392–6. A prior war of "internal conquest," the Italian government's violent struggle to pacify much of southern Italy, had occupied most of the Italian army's men and resources from 1861 straight through to 1866.

4 Luigi Luzzatti, Memorie *autobiografiche e carteggi*, vol. 1 (Bologna: Zanichelli, 1931), pp. 208–9; Alberto Errera, *La Biblioteca popolare della provincia di Venezia e le letture in commune. Relazione dei promotori e parole*

d'inaugurazione del prof. Busoni, del dott. Alberto Errera e dei sigg. Senatore Torelli prefetto e G. B. Giustinian sindaco di Venezia (Venice: Antonelli, 1867), pp. 25–8. All translations are my own unless otherwise indicated.

5 Alexis de Tocqueville, *Democracy in America*, trans. George Lawrence, ed. J.P. Mayer (New York: Harper Collins, 1988), p. 513; Robert D. Putnam, *Making Democracy Work: Civic Traditions in Modern Italy* (Princeton: Princeton University Press, 1993); Jürgen Habermas, *The Structural Transformation of the Public Sphere: An Inquiry into a Category of Bourgeois Society*, trans. Thomas Burger (Cambridge, MA: MIT Press, 1989). An important critical and contextual study of liberalism is Thomas C. Holt, *The Problem of Freedom: Race, Labor, and Politics in Jamaica and Britain, 1832–1938* (Baltimore: Johns Hopkins University Press, 1992). Studies linking the spread of associations in Europe and the United States to the emergence of civil society and the rise of the middle class are too numerous to list here, but important examples include: Mary P. Ryan, *Cradle of the Middle Class: The Family in Oneida County, New York, 1790–1865* (Cambridge: Cambridge University Press, 1981); R.J. Morris, *Class, Sect and Party: The Making of the British Middle Class, Leeds 1820–1850* (Manchester: Manchester University Press, 1990); Carol E. Harrison, *The Bourgeois Citizen in Nineteenth-Century France: Gender, Sociability, and the Uses of Emulation* (Oxford: Oxford University Press, 1999); Stefan-Ludwig Hoffmann, *The Politics of Sociability: Freemasonry and German Civil Society, 1840–1918* (Ann Arbor: University of Michigan Press, 2007); and Joseph Bradley, *Voluntary Associations in Tsarist Russia: Science, Patriotism, and Civil Society* (Cambridge, MA: Harvard University Press, 2009).

6 On associations as microcosms of constitutional government, see Margaret C. Jacob, *Living the Enlightenment: Freemasonry and Politics in Eighteenth-Century Europe* (New York: Oxford University Press, 1991).

7 R.J. Morris, "Clubs, Societies and Associations," in *The Cambridge Social History of Britain 1750–1950*, vol. 3, *Social Agencies and Institutions*, ed. F.M.L. Thompson (New York: Cambridge University Press, 1990), pp. 395–443. On the lasting importance and appeal of voluntarism in Britain, see Brian Harrison, *Peaceable Kingdom: Stability and Change in Modern Britain* (New York: Oxford University Press, 1982), and M.J.D. Roberts, *Making English Morals: Voluntary Association and Moral Reform in England, 1787–1886* (Cambridge: Cambridge University Press, 2004). Martin Weiner puts the revival of interest in voluntarism in context in "The Unloved State: Twentieth-Century Politics in the Writing of Nineteenth-Century History," *Journal of British Studies* 33 (July 1994), pp. 283–308.

8 Philip Nord, "Introduction," in *Civil Society before Democracy: Lessons from Nineteenth-Century Europe*, ed. Nancy Bermeo and Philip Nord (Lanham, MD: Rowman & Littlefield, 2000), pp. xx–xxi. Nord's impressive study of France's mid-century transition is *The Republican Moment: Struggles for Democracy in Nineteenth-Century France* (Cambridge, MA: Harvard University Press, 1995). On Austria, see Pieter M. Judson, *Exclusive Revolutionaries: Liberal Politics, Social Experience and National Identity in the Austrian Empire, 1848–1914* (Ann Arbor: University of Michigan Press, 1996). On Russia, see Bradley, "Subjects into Citizens: Societies, Civil Society, and Autocracy in Tsarist Russia," *American Historical Review* 107:4 (2002), pp. 1094–1123.

9 On the impact of late-twentieth-century events, see Nord, "Introduction," p. xiii; Frank Trentmann, "Introduction: Paradoxes of Civil Society," in *Paradoxes of Civil Society: New Perspectives on Modern German and British History*, ed. Frank Trentmann (New York: Berghahn, 2000), p. 5; R.J. Morris, "Introduction: Civil Society, Associations and Urban Places: Class, Nation and Culture in Nineteenth-Century Europe," in *Civil Society, Associations and Urban Places: Class, Nation and Culture in Nineteenth-Century Europe*, ed. Graeme Morton, Boudien de Vries, and R.J. Morris (Aldershot, UK: Ashgate, 2006), p. xv.

10 To appreciate the historiographical tilt towards the years 1750–1850, it is enough to note that several of the leading historians of associational life – including Maurice Agulhon (on France), R.J. Morris (on England), Otto Dann (on Germany), and Marco Meriggi (on Italy) – have focused on this period. On the *fin-dè-siecle* as a time of crisis, see Habermas, *The Structural Transformation of the Public Sphere*; Stephen Yeo, *Religion and Voluntary Organisations in Crisis* (London: Croom Helm, 1976); and Morris, "Clubs, Societies and Associations," pp. 419–30. In German history, an important exception is Rudy Koshar, *Social Life, Local Politics, and Nazism: Marburg, 1880–1935* (Chapel Hill: University of North Carolina Press, 1986). Social scientists' traditional exclusion of political and confessional organizations from their definition of "voluntary association" helps explain why most historians viewed the late nineteenth century, a period of intense socialist and Catholic associational activity, in terms of crisis rather than growth. See *International Encyclopedia of the Social Sciences*, s.v. "voluntary association" (New York: Macmillan, 1968).

11 On the impact of the French Revolution and Napoleon on Italian associational life, see Alberto Mario Banti and Marco Meriggi, "Premessa," in *Quaderni storici* 77 (1991), pp. 357–62; Marco Meriggi, *Milano borghese: Circoli ed élites nell'Ottocento* (Venice: Marsilio, 1992), pp. 3–50. On the

reforming impulse of the 1830s and 1840s, see Meriggi, *Milano borghese*, pp. 87–150.

12 John A. Davis, "Modern Italy: Changing Historical Perspectives since 1945," in *Companion to Historiography*, ed. Michael Bentley (London: Routledge, 1997), pp. 591–619; Lucy Riall, *The Italian Risorgimento: State, Society and National Unification* (London: Routledge, 1994).

13 John A. Davis, "Remapping Italy's Path to the Twentieth Century," *Journal of Modern History* 66 (June 1994), pp. 291–320; Raffaele Romanelli, "Political Debate, Social History, and the Italian Borghesia: Changing Perspectives in Historical Research," *Journal of Modern History* 63 (December 1991), pp. 717–39; Alberto Mario Banti, *Storia della borghesia italiana: L'età liberale (1861–1922)* (Rome: Donzelli, 1996). On the German *Sonderweg* debate, see Geoff Eley and David Blackbourn, *The Peculiarities of German History: Bourgeois Society and Politics in Nineteenth-Century Germany* (Oxford: Oxford University Press, 1984).

14 Daniel Roche, "Sociabilità culturale e politica: Gli anni della pre-Rivoluzione," in *Sociabilità nobiliare, sociabilità borghese*, ed. Maria Malatesta, *Cheiron* 5:9–10 (1988), p. 19; and the comments of Simonetta Soldani in Alberto Mario Banti, Marco Meriggi, Gilles Pécout, and Simonetta Soldani, "Sociabilità e associazionismo in Italia: Anatomia di una categoria debole," *Passato e presente* 10:26 (May–August 1991), p. 23. See also Giuliana Gemelli and Maria Malatesta, *Forme di sociabilità nella storiografia francese contemporanea* (Milan: Feltrinelli, 1982).

15 An example of a social boundaries approach to sociability is Harrison, *The Bourgeois Citizen*.

16 Philippe Boutry, "Società urbana e sociabilità delle élites nella Roma della Restaurazione: Prime considerazioni," in *Sociabilità nobiliare, sociabilità borghese*, ed. Maletesta, pp. 59–85. Simonetta Soldani's detailed examination of the Tuscan town of Prato suggests that a similar range of groups and institutions existed in cities much smaller than Rome. "Vita quotidiana e vita di società in un centro industrioso," in *Storia di Prato*, vol. 3, *Il tempo dell'industria (1815–1953)*, ed. Giorgio Mori (Prato: Comune di Prato, 1988), pp. 663–806.

17 Maurizio Ridolfi, *Il circolo virtuoso: Sociabilità democratica, associazionismo e rappresentanza politica nell'Ottocento* (Florence: Centro editoriale toscano, 1990).

18 Meriggi, *Milano borghese*; Cardoza, "Tra caste e classe. Clubs maschili dell'élite torinese, 1840–1914," *Quaderni storici* 77 (1991), pp. 363–88; Raffaele Romanelli, "Il casino, l'accademia e il circolo. Forme e tendenze dell'associazionismo d'élite nella Firenze dell'Ottocento," in *Fra storia e*

storiografia: Studi in onore di Pasquale Villani, ed. Paolo Macry and Angelo Massafra (Bologna: Il Mulino, 1993), pp. 809–51.

19 Philip Nord helpfully refines the standard general definition of civil society (as occupying a place between the family and the state), noting that "the qualifier 'civil' is meaningful, for it implies activity that is ordered, nonclandestine, and collective" ("Introduction," p. xiv).

20 Meriggi, *Milano borghese*. In *Associazionismo e sociabilità d'élite a Napoli nel XIX secolo* (Naples: Liguori, 1996), Daniela Luigia Caglioti recognizes Meriggi's point, but argues that in Naples unification constituted a more important turning point.

21 Important studies of the politics of public culture in nineteenth-century Italy include Raymond Grew, "The Paradoxes of Nineteenth-Century Italy's Political Culture," in *Revolution and the Meanings of Freedom in the Nineteenth Century*, ed. Isser Woloch (Stanford: Stanford University Press, 1996), pp. 212–45; John A. Davis, *Conflict and Control: Law and Order in Nineteenth-Century Italy* (Atlantic Highlands, NJ: Humanities Press International, 1988); Richard Bach Jensen, *Liberty and Order: The Theory and Practice of Italian Public Security Policy, 1848 to the Crisis of the 1890s* (New York: Garland, 1991); and Ilaria Porciani, *La festa della nazione: Rappresentazione dello stato e spazi sociali nell'Italia unita* (Bologna: Il Mulino, 1997).

22 Simonetta Soldani, "La mappa delle società di mutuo soccorso in Toscana fra l'Unità e la fine del secolo," in *Istituzioni e borghesie locali nell'Italia liberale*, ed. Mariapia Bigaran (Milan: Franco Angeli, 1986), pp. 247–92; Giovanni Gozzini, *Il segreto dell'elemosina: Poveri e carità legale a Firenze 1800–1870* (Florence: Olschki, 1993).

23 See Laura Cerasi, "Identità sociali e spazi delle associazioni. Gli studi sull'Italia liberale," *Memoria e Ricerca* 10 (1997), pp. 123–45.

24 On parliamentary politics, see Dora Marucco, *Mutualismo e sistema politico: Il caso italiano (1862–1904)* (Milan: Franco Angeli, 1981). An example of a local study with broad significance is Arnaldo Cherubini, *Il problema sociale e il mutuo soccorso nella stampa senese (1860–1893)* (Siena: Accademia Senese degli Intronati, 1967). One of many helpful recent studies is Paolo Giovannini, ed., *"Uniti e solidali": L'associazionismo nelle Marche tra Otto e Novecento* (Ancona: Il lavoro, 2002).

25 Alberto Mario Banti, *La nazione del Risorgimento: Parentela, santità e onore alle origini dell'Italia unita* (Turin: Einaudi, 2000); Albert Russell Ascoli and Krystyna von Henneberg, eds., *Making and Remaking Italy: The Cultivation of National Identity around the Risorgimento* (Oxford: Berg, 2001); Alberto Mario Banti and Roberto Bizzocchi, eds., *Le immagini della*

nazione nell'Italia del Risorgimento (Rome: Carocci, 2002); Alberto Mario
Banti and Paul Ginsborg, eds., *Storia d'Italia, Annali*, vol. 22, *Il Risorgimento* (Turin: Einaudi, 2007); Christopher Duggan, *The Force of Destiny: A
History of Italy since 1796* (Boston: Houghton Mifflin, 2008); Emilio Gentile, *La Grande Italia: The Myth of the Nation in the Twentieth Century*,
trans. Suzanne Dingee and Jennifer Pudney (Madison: University of Wisconsin Press, 2009); *Nations and Nationalism* 15:3 (2009), special issue on the
new history of Risorgimento nationalism, ed. Lucy Riall and David Laven;
Silvana Patriarca, *Italian Vices: Nation and Character from the Risorgimento to the Republic* (New York: Cambridge University Press, 2010).

26 Alberto Mario Banti and Paul Ginsborg, "Per una nuova storia del Risorgimento," in Banti and Ginsborg, *Storia d'Italia, Annali*, vol. 22, *Il Risorgimento*, p. xxvii.

27 Simonetta Soldani and Gabriele Turi, "Introduzione," in *Fare gli italiani:
Scuola e cultura nell'Italia contemporanea*, vol. 1, ed. Soldani and Turi
(Bologna: Il Mulino, 1993), pp. 17–19.

28 In recent years, scholars of nineteenth-century Italy have begun to write explicitly international histories of the Risorgimento and Italian nationalism.
See, for example, Maurizio Isabella, *Risorgimento in Exile: Italian Émigrés
and the Liberal International in the Post-Napoleonic Era* (New York: Oxford University Press, 2009); and Mark I. Choate, *Emigrant Nation: The
Making of Italy Abroad* (Cambridge, MA: Harvard University Press, 2008).

29 The comparison between Venice and Milan is especially telling, for both
were capital cities within the Austrian Lombard-Veneto Kingdom from 1815
to 1859. During this period, Milan rose above Venice as a social, cultural,
and economic centre. To cite one example, whereas in the eighteenth century
Venice was arguably the most important publishing centre in all of Italy, by
the middle of the nineteenth century it was greatly overshadowed by Milan.

30 Renato Camurri, ed., *La scienza moderata: Fedele Lampertico e l'Italia
liberale* (Milan: Franco Angeli, 1992).

31 Emilio Franzina, *Il poeta e gli artigiani: Etica del lavoro e mutualismo nel
Veneto di metà '800* (Padua: Poligrafo, 1988). See also Luca Pes, "Sei schede
sulle società di mutuo soccorso a Venice. 1849–1881, *Cheiron* 7:12–13
(June 1991), pp. 115–46.

32 See especially by Renato Camurri, "Il mutualismo e la diffusione dello
'spirito d'associazione' dopo l'Unità," *Venetica*, s. 3, 17:10 (2004): *Spazi
laici: Strutture e reti associative tra Ottocento e Novecento*, ed. Renato Camurri and Marco Fincardi, pp. 23–54; and "La 'seconda società': L'associazionismo borghese nel Lombardo-Veneto (1848–1866)," in

Memorie, rappresentazioni e protagonisti del 1848 italiano, ed. Camurri (Verona: Cierre, 2006), pp. 249–76.

33 For an introduction to the historiography on the "Third Italy," see Marco Bellandi, "'Terza Italia' e 'distretti industriali' dopo la seconda guerra mondiale," in *Storia d'Italia, Annali*, vol. 15, *L'industria*, ed. Franco Amatori, Duccio Bigazzi, Renato Giannetti, and Luciano Segreto (Turin: Einaudi, 1999), pp. 843–91.

34 Piero Bevilacqua, *Breve storia dell'Italia meridionale dall'Ottocento ad oggi* (Rome: Donzelli, 1993); Robert Lumley and Jonathan Morris, *The New History of the Italian South: The Mezzogiorno Revisited* (Exeter, UK: University of Exeter Press, 1997); John Dickie, *Darkest Italy: The Nation and Stereotypes of the Mezzogiorno, 1860–1900* (New York: St. Martin's Press, 1999); Nelson Moe, *The View from Vesuvius: Italian Culture and the Southern Question* (Berkeley: University of California Press, 2002).

35 Gabriele De Rosa, "La società civile veneta dal 1866 all'avvento della sinistra," in De Rosa, *Giuseppe Sacchetti e la pietà veneta* (Rome: Studium, 1968), pp. 173–232. See also Marino Berengo, *L'agricoltura veneta dalla caduta della Repubblica all'Unità* (Milan: Banca Commerciale Italiana, 1963).

36 Silvio Lanaro, ed., *Movimento cattolico e sviluppo capitalistico: Atti del Convegno su movimento cattolico e sviluppo capitalistico nel Veneto* (Padua: Marsilio, 1974); Lanaro, ed., *Le regioni nella storia d'Italia: Il Veneto* (Turin: Einaudi, 1984); Emilio Franzina, *La transizione dolce: Storie del Veneto tra '800 e '900* (Verona: Cierre, 1990). See also Paul Ginsborg, *Daniele Manin and the Venetian Revolution of 1848–49* (New York: Cambridge University Press, 1979); and David Laven, *Venice and Venetia under the Habsburgs, 1815–1835* (New York: Oxford University Press, 2002)

37 Silvio Lanaro, *L'Italia nuova: Identità e sviluppo 1861–1988* (Turin: Einaudi, 1988), pp. 28–9.

1 In Search of Associational Life

1 See, for example, Pietro Selvatico's list of key events in Padua's history in *Guida di Padova e dei principali suoi contorni*, published in Padua in 1869. Between the Austrians' occupation of the Veneto in 1814 and their departure in 1866, only four events make the list: the visit of the Austrian Emperor to Padua in 1815, a destructive hailstorm in 1834, the fourth congress of Italian scientists, and the revolution of 1848. General analyses of the scientific congresses include Giuseppe Carlo Marino, *La formazione dello spirito borghese in Italia* (Florence: La Nuova Italia, 1974); and, more recently,

Maria Pia Casalena, *Per lo stato, per la nazione. I congressi degli scienziati in Francia e in Italia* (Rome: Carocci, 2008). On the Venetian congresses – in 1847, the ninth congress was held in Venice – see Maria Luisa Soppelsa, "Scienze e storia della scienza," in *Storia della cultura veneta*, vol. 6, *Dall'età napoleonica alla prima guerra mondiale,* ed. Girolamo Arnaldi and Gianfranco Folena (Vicenza: Neri Pozza, 1986), pp. 526–35.

2 *Guida di Padova e della sua provincia* (Padua: Seminario, 1842), p. 145.

3 Moschini, *Guida per la città di Padova all'amico delle belle arti* (Venice: Gamba, 1817).

4 *Guida di Padova* (1842), pp. 264–5, 381–2. Technically, according to Austrian law, the city's academy of arts and sciences (described in the guide, pp. 374–5) also qualified as an association. Historical practices of state sponsorship and honorary membership make academies seem categorically different from voluntary associations. However, nineteenth-century Italian academies did perform many of the functions expected of associations: keeping membership lists, holding administrative elections, organizing private and public meetings on a regular basis, and publishing records of their proceedings. Even after unification, writers sometimes refered to academies as associations. See, for example, the profile of Vicenza's Olympic Academy, which appeared in a series of newspaper articles entitled "Intellectual Associations": *Il Berico*, 13 January 1867.

5 Marco Meriggi, *Milano borghese: Circoli ed élites nell'Ottocento* (Venice: Marsilio, 1992); Maurizio Ridolfi, *Il circolo virtuoso: Sociabilità democratica, associazionismo e rappresentanza politica nell'Ottocento* (Florence: Centro editoriale toscano, 1990).

6 David Laven, *Venice and Venetia under the Habsburgs 1815–1835* (Oxford: Oxford University Press, 2002); Marco Meriggi, *Il Regno Lombardo-Veneto* (Turin: UTET, 1987); Giampietro Berti, *Censura e circolazione delle idee nel Veneto della Restaurazione* (Venice: Deputazione, 1989).

7 An 1844 guide to Milan, for example, which was prepared for the sixth Congress of Italian Scientists, listed the city's main cultural and recreational associations. See Marco Meriggi, "Vita di circolo e rappresentanza civica nella Milano liberale," in *Milano fin de siècle e il caso Bagatti-Valsecchi*, ed. Cesare Mozzarelli and Rosanna Pavoni (Milan: Guerini, 1991).

8 Fedele Lampertico and Jacopo Cabianca, *Vicenza e il suo territorio* (Milan: Corona e Caimi, 1859); Fedele Lampertico, *Commemorazione funebre di Valentino Pasini letta nel Teatro Olimpico il 5 maggio 1864* (Vicenza: Paroni, 1864), p. 9; Antonio Ciscato, *Guida di Vicenza* (Vicenza: Paroni, 1870), pp. 14–15.

9 *Regolamento della Società del Casino al Duomo in Vicenza* (Vicenza: Tremeschin, 1834), p. 3. As its name suggests, the club was located in a building across from the city's cathedral (or *duomo*, in Italian).

10 Antonio Ciscato, *Il Vecchio Casino dei Nobili. Per le nobili nozze Arrigoni-Mugani* (Vicenza: Paroni, 1874).

11 Pierfrancesco Morabito, "Divertimento e élites sociali a Bologna nella prima metà dell'Ottocento: La Società del Casino," in Maria Malatesta, ed., *Cheiron* 5:9–10 (1988), pp. 169–91; Anthony Cardoza, *Aristocrats in Bourgeois Italy* (New York: Cambridge University Press, 1998), pp. 155–61; Alberto Mario Banti and Marco Meriggi, "Premessa," *Quaderni storici* 77 (August 1991), p. 358.

12 *Regolamento della Società del Casino al Duomo in Vicenza* (1834); *Statuto della Società dei Nuovi Casinisti al Duomo* (Vicenza: Paroni, 1858); *Statuto della Società del Casino Pedrocchi* (Padua: Prosperini, 1857). The latter two statutes contain identical articles offering a "guarantee of [social] homogeneity," a sign perhaps that this guarantee was demanded by the Austrian government and not the club's members. But it is also significant that this article stayed in the statutes of Vicenza's and Padua's clubs after unification. In Vicenza, see *Statuto della Società del Casino in Vicenza* (Vicenza: Burato, 1867, 1874, 1884). The Pedrocchi Club in Padua removed this article from a projected statute in 1872, only to reinstate it in a subsequent document. See *Progetto di Statuto e Regolamento interno per la Società del Casino Pedrocchi* (Padua: Prosperini, 1872) and *Regolamento del Casino Pedrocchi* (Padua: Prosperini, 1875), as well as the other statutes and regulations found in Archivio dello Stato di Padova, *Società Pedrocchi*, b. 1.

13 Some Pedrocchi Club members carried more than one title. All told, 202 of the 476 members were titled (Società del Casino Pedrocchi, *Elenco dei Soci* [Padua: Guerini, 1858]). In the University of Padua's yearbook for 1858–59, Giovanni Cicogna, a Pedrocchi Club member, was listed in both the law and math departments. Subtracting his double-listing means that 54 per cent (12 of 22) of the individuals making up the law and math departments were also members of the Pedrocchi Club. *Prospetto degli studj dell'imperiale regia Università di Padova per l'anno scolastico 1858–1859* (Padua: Antonelli, n.d.); *Quadro dei giornali politici, scientifici e letterarj ed elenco dei socj del Gabinetto di lettura in Padova* (Padua: Salmin, 1871).

14 In Catania (Sicily), the reading room opened in 1845 by the bookseller Ettore Fanoj allowed its five women members (out of 182) to frequent the lending library but not the reading rooms. Alfio Signorelli, "Socialità e

circolazione di idée: L'associazionismo culturale a Catania nell'Ottocento," in *Meridiana* 22–3 (January–May 1995), p. 55.

15 *Statuto della Società dei Nuovi Casinisti*, p. 12. See also *Statuto della Società del Casino* (Vicenza: 1867); and, for an example of a statute that does reserve a specific section for a discussion of women, *Regolamento per la Società del Giardino* (Milan: 1818), titolo VI. The requirement that women guests be living with a club member was also made by the Circolo dell'Unione in Florence: Raffaele Romanelli, "Il casino, l'accademia e il circolo. Forme e tendenze dell'associazionismo d'élite nella Firenze dell'Ottocento," in *Fra storia e storiografia: Studi in onore di Pasquale Villani*, ed. Paolo Macry and Angelo Massafra (Bologna: Il Mulino, 1993), p. 832. More generally, on the subject of gender and associational life, see Marco Meriggi, *Milano borghese*, pp. 196–216; Romanelli, "Il casino," pp. 819–824; and Fiorenza Taricone, *Teoria e prassi dell'associazionismo italiano nel XIX e XX secolo* (Cassino: Università degli Studi di Cassino, 2003).

16 *Regolamento della Società del Casino al Duomo*, p. 7.

17 J.H. Plumb, "The Commercialization of Leisure in Eighteenth-Century England," in Neil McKendrick, John Brewer, and J.H. Plumb, *The Birth of a Consumer Society: The Commercialization of Eighteenth-Century England* (Bloomington: Indiana University Press, 1982), pp. 265–85.

18 Morabito, "Divertimento e élites sociali," pp. 172–3.

19 On billiards and games of chance, see *Statuto della Società del Casino* (Vicenza: 1884), p. 3. On masked balls, see Morabito, "Divertimento e élites sociali" and *Statuto della Società del Casino* (Vicenza: 1867).

20 *Regolamento della Società del Casino al Duomo in Vicenza* (Vicenza: 1834), p. 3.

21 *Regolamento della Società del Casino al Duomo in Vicenza*, cover page (p. 1).

22 Maria Elisabetta Tonizzi, "Borghesi a Genova nell'Ottocento: Associazionismo ricreativo e culturale dell'élite tra la Restaurazione e l'Unità," *Contemporanea* 13:4 (2010), pp. 618–19; Signorelli, "Socialità e circolazione di idée," pp. 40–1; Cardoza, *Aristocrats in Bourgeois Italy*, pp. 50–1.

23 Giuseppe Solitro, *La "Società di cultura e di incoraggiamento" in Padova nel suo primo centenario (un secolo di vita padovana) 1830–1930* (Padua: Seminario, 1930), pp. 3–7.

24 Angelo Gambasin, *Religione e società dalle riforme napoleoniche all'età liberale: Clero, sinodi e laicato* (Padua: Liviana, 1974), pp. 16–30. An 1818 Austrian ordinance required that a school be established wherever a parish register existed. At the time the Veneto had an unusually large number of parishes (1663), double the number in Lombardy. Silvio Lanaro,

"Genealogia di un modello," in Lanaro, ed., *Storia delle regioni dall'Unità a oggi: Il Veneto* (Turin: Einaudi, 1984), p. 24.

25 Albarosa Ines Bassani, "Giovanni Antonio Farina, docente ed erudito a Vicenza prima dell'episcopato trevigiano (1827–1850)," in *Studi e ricerche di storia sociale religiosa artistica vicentina e veneta: Omaggio a Ermenegildo Reato*, ed. Gianni A. Cisotto (Vicenza: Accademia Olimpica, 1998), pp. 25–40.

26 The post-revolutionary crackdown of the 1850s did not prevent two of Vicenza's well-connected lay activists, Fedele Lampertico and Giovanni Scola, from starting a chapter of the Society of Saint Vincent de Paul, to assist the victims of the cholera outbreak of 1855, or from creating a mutual aid society and night schools for artisans a few years later.

27 The classic example of associational activity followed by repression is the remarkable series of enterprises spearheaded by the liberal aristocrat Federico Confalonieri in Milan after 1815. These included plans for an Athenaeum, where public lectures and educational programs could be organized; an association aimed at improving one of the city's theatrical companies; and a society for the promotion of "schools of mutual instruction." All of Confalonieri's plans came to an abrupt halt in 1821, when an unsuccessful plot to free Lombardy from the Austrians ushered in a period of severe Austrian repression. See the classic work by Kent Roberts Greenfield, *Economics and Liberalism in the Risorgimento: A Study of Nationalism in Lombardy, 1814–1848* (Baltimore: Johns Hopkins University Press, 1965), pp. 199–203; and Marco Meriggi, "Lo 'spirito di associazione' nella Milano dell'Ottocento (1815–1890)," *Quaderni storici* 77 (August 1991), pp. 392–7. One institution in Vicenza that followed the same chronological trajectory was the Academy of Philologists, founded in 1815 by Venceslao Loschi and suspended by the Austrians in 1821. See Emilio Franzina, *Vicenza: Storia di una città* (Vicenza: Neri Pozza, 1980), p. 647. On the effects of the revolution of 1848 and the subsequent return of the Austrians to power on the Society for the Encouragement of Agriculture in Padua, see Giuseppe Solitro, *La "Società di cultura e di incoraggiamento,"* pp. 120–1.

28 Alberto Mario Banti, *Terra e denaro: Una borghesia padana nell'Ottocento* (Venice: Marsilio, 1989), pp. 131–2.

29 Carlo Cattaneo, *Scritti politici*, vol. 1, ed. Marco Boneschi (Florence: Le Monnier, 1964), pp. 174–6.

30 *Regolamento della Società del Casino al Duomo in Vicenza* (1834), p. 3; *Statuto della Società dei Nuovi Casinisti* (1858), p. 4.

31 This was true, for example, of Vicenza's reading room, which was more or less refounded with the help of several other local institutions in 1869. The

Olympic Academy and the Agrarian Association (Comizio Agrario) agreed
to pay the reading room's expenses, and a third body, the Professional Institute, provided a meeting place. In effect, for several years the reading
room served as little more than a library for students attending the Professional Institute. See *Regolamento pel gabinetto di lettura istituito in comune
dall'Accademia Olimpica, dal Comizio Agrario e dall'Istituto professionale
di Vicenza* (Vicenza: 1869), and *Statuti del Gabinetto di lettura discussi ed
approvati nell'assemblea generale dei soci tenuta il 25 settembre 1874* (Vicenza: 1874). But see also Fedele Lampertico, *Ricordi academici e letterari*
(Vicenza: 1872), p. 124.

32 On the latter, see the collection of *Documenti vicentini* in the manuscripts
room of the Biblioteca Bertoliana in Vicenza, b. Do 40: *Associazioni in Vicenza*, fasc. Società dei Camaleonti (1845–1851).

33 See, for example, Article IX of the 1830 statute of Padua's reading room:

> IX. - The Reading room is destined for the exclusive use of its Mem-
> bers. With the exception of the Heads of the Public Authorities who
> may honour the Reading room with their presence whenever they
> please, all other persons living or staying in Padua cannot enter.

This document is reprinted in Solitro, La *"Società di cultura,"* pp. 255–8;
see also Solitro's comments on pp. 20–1.

34 David Laven and Lucy Riall, eds., *Napoleon's Legacy: Problems of Government in Restoration Europe* (New York: Berg, 2000). Fedele Lampertico recalled that it was spies, not the official Austrian delegates, who bothered the
members of Vicenza's Olympic Academy: *Ricordi academici*, p. 110.

35 Marco Meriggi, *Milano borghese*, pp. 32–4. Throughout Italy, government officials encouraged club leaders to censor and police members themselves. For examples from the Società del Casino in Bologna and the Circolo
dell'Unione in Florence, see Morabito, "Divertimento e élites sociali," p.
184, and Romanelli, "Il casino, l'accademia e il circolo," p. 819.

36 *Il Giornale Euganeo*, 29 January 1845, p. 103.

37 *Il Caffè Pedrocchi*, 30 July 1845.

38 Giampietro Berti, "L'ideologia liberal-moderata del 'Giornale Euganeo'
(1844–1847)," in *Padova 1814–1866: Istituzioni, protagonisti e vicende di
una città*, ed. Piero Del Negro and Nino Agostinett (Padua: Istituto per la
storia del Risorgimento italiano, Comitato di Padova, 1991), p. 99.

39 *Il Caffè Pedrocchi*, 25 January 1846, 21 March 1847, 23 May 1847, 9
January 1848. On the preservation of "patrii monumenti," which could be
understood to mean local or national (historically "Italian") monuments,

see *Il Giornale Euganeo*, 29 May 1845, p. 539, and 5 December 1845, pp. 471–2.

40 *Il Caffè Pedrocchi*, 5 May 1846; 5 July 1846; 29 November 1846; *Il Giornale Euganeo*, 30 June 1845, pp. 596–7; 31 December 1845, p. 559; March 1846, p. 272.

41 References in *Il Caffè Pedrocchi* to associational activities are, for 1846: 22 February, 10 May, 14 and 28 June, and 2 August, plus two brief announcements in the 15 November and 13 December issues. References for 1847 are: 7 and 28 February, 21 March, 6 June, 8 August, 26 September, plus brief announcements on 25 July and 19 September. There were almost as many references to the Prato della Valle in 1846 as to associations, and almost as many references to the Caffè Pedrocchi in 1847 as to associations.

42 It was hardly surprising that Padua's revolution of 1848 began at the Caffè Pedrocchi. In Turin, the liberalization of press and assembly laws in late 1847 accentuated the cafe's political importance. Men gathered there daily to read and discuss the news. See Umberto Levra, "Salotti, circoli, caffè," in *Milleottocentoquarantotto: Torino, l'Italia, l'Europa*, ed. Levra Roccia and Rosanna Roccia (Turin: Archivio storico della Città di Torino, 1998), pp. 108–9; and Maria Malatesta, "Il caffè e l'osteria," in *I luoghi della memoria: Strutture ed eventi dell'Italia unita*, ed. Mario Isnenghi (Rome: Laterza, 1997), pp. 60–1.

43 Carlo Leoni, *Cronaca segreta de' miei tempi* (Cittadella: Rebellato, 1976), pp. 351, 365, 371, 380, 739.

44 Leoni, *Cronaca segreta*, pp. 412, 433, 505, 650–1.

45 Leoni, *Cronaca segreta*, pp. 385–6. On the Austrians' efforts to keep theaters open and make Carnevale celebrations look festive, see pp. 372, 385, 452–3, 491–4; on the incident in the Duse Theater, p. 494.

46 Marco Meriggi has usefully described this shift in associational orientation as one from "proximity" associations (for example, social clubs), which assumed that members knew one other and met together frequently, to "programmatic" associations (for example, encouragement societies), which depended not on members' regular attendance at meetings or active participation but simply on their "adhesion" to an agreed-upon program of goals and initiatives. See *Milano borghese*, pp. 117–41. On the European debate on pauperism, and its impact in Italy, see Stuart Woolf, "The Poor and How to Relieve Them: The Restoration Debate on Poverty in Italy and Europe," in *Society and Politics in the Age of the Risorgimento: Essays in Honour of Denis Mack Smith*, ed. John A. Davis and Paul Ginsborg (New York: Cambridge University Press, 1991), pp. 49–69.

47 Leoni, *Cronaca segreta*, pp. 138–9, 350.

48 Accademia patavina di scienze, lettere ed arti, *Rivista periodica dei lavori*, vol. 3 (1855), pp. 176–177.

49 Leoni, *Cronaca segreta*, pp. 55 (on night schools), 353 (on peasants), 443, 494 (on university students).

50 *Il Caffè Pedrocchi*, 29 March 1846, 2 August 1846, 21 March 1847, 11 April 1847, 6 June 1847, 8 August 1847. In 1846, *Il Giornale Euganeo* printed an essay by the Milanese liberal Gottardo Calvi on the scientific congresses, in which Calvi criticized the host cities' wasteful practice of throwing parties for their guests. See *Il Giornale Euganeo*, August 1846, p. 106.

51 Angelo Gambasin, *Parroci e contadini nel Veneto alla fine dell'Ottocento* (Rome: Edizioni di storia e letteratura, 1973), pp. 25–44, 58–9, 141.

52 *Atti della prima distribuzione de' premj eseguita dalla Società d'Incoraggiamento per l'agricoltura e l'industria in Padova il giorno VIII settembre MDCCCLI nell'Aula Magna dell'I. R. Università* (Padua: Sicca, 1852), pp. 27–9; Solitro, *La "Società di cultura,"* p. 100.

53 *Il Raccoglitore*, a. I (Padua: 1852), a. II (Padua: 1853), and a. III (Padua: 1854). Other topics covered in these volumes included a series of geographical, climatological, and astronomical reports; discussions of rural hygiene, land reclamation, the cultivation of linen, and a statistical overview of local governments in the province. Giuseppe Solitro found some evidence to confirm that both the *Almanacco Popolare* and the first volume of *Il Raccoglitore* received a relatively wide distribution, approximately fifteen hundred copies of the former and one thousand copies of the latter (*La "Società di cultura,"* pp. 120–1, 130–4). In 1863, *Il Raccoglitore* became a true periodical, coming out every other month.

54 These words are quoted by Carlo Leoni in "Società di mutuo soccorso degli avvocati e notai in Venice," *Il Giornale Euganeo*, July 1847, p. 91.

55 *Il Giornale Euganeo*, February 1847, pp. 157–62.

56 *Il Raccoglitore* (1852), pp. 197–204. The proponents of associations often kept their frustration with government delays and restrictions to themselves, but not always. See, for example, the expectant references to Padua's as yet unapproved Mutual Aid Society of Doctors, Surgeons, and Pharmacists in *Il Giornale Euganeo*, 30 June 1845, p. 644, and in *Il Caffè Pedrocchi*, 1 March 1846.

57 On Lampertico, see Emilio Franzina, "Introduzione," in *Fedele Lampertico, Carteggi e diari 1842–1906*, vol. 1, A–E, ed. Franzina (Venice: Marsilio, 1996), pp. 3–70; Renato Camurri, "Introduzione," in *Fedele Lampertico, Carteggi e diari 1842–1906*, vol. 2, F–L, ed. Camurri (Venice: Marsilio, 1998), pp. xix–lvii; Renato Camurri, ed., *La scienza*

moderata: Fedele Lampertico e l'Italia liberale (Milan: Franco Angeli, 1992). On Lampertico and Paolo Lioy, see Silvio Lanaro, *Società e ideologie nel Veneto rurale (1866–1898)* (Rome: Edizioni di storia e letteratura, 1976). On Morpurgo, a figure deserving greater study, the place to start is Renato Camurri, "Tradizione e innovazione nel pensiero di Emilio Morpurgo," in *La scienza moderata*, ed. Camurri, pp. 339–75. On Luzzatti, see Pier Luigi Ballini and Paolo Pecorari, eds., *Luigi Luzzatti e il suo tempo: Atti del convegno internazionale di studio (Venezia, 7–9 novembre 1991)*, 2 vols. (Venice: Istituto Veneto di scienze, lettere ed arti, 1994); and Paolo Pecorari, *Luigi Luzzatti e le origini dello "statalismo" economico nell'età della destra storica* (Padua: Signum, 1983). On Zanella and his former students, including Lampertico, Lioy, and Luzzatti, see Emilio Franzina, *Il poeta e gli artigiani: Etica del lavoro e mutualismo nel Veneto di metà '800* (Padua: Poligrafo, 1988).

58 Letter of Luigi Luzzatti to Fedele Lampertico, Venice, 9 March 1863, in Biblioteca Bertoliana di Vicenza, *Carte Lampertico.*

59 *Statuto della Società di mutuo soccorso degli artigiani sotto l'invocazione di San Giuseppe* (Vicenza: 1858), p. 5.

60 See the manifesto entitled "Agli Artigiani Vicentini!" (Vicenza: 1857), from the first of two volumes of documents relevant to the Società Generale in the Biblioteca Bertoliana in Vicenza (Gonz. 347.2).

61 Letter of Luigi Luzzatti to Fedele Lampertico, [April 1863], in Biblioteca Bertoliana di Vicenza, *Carte Lampertico.*

62 Letter of Fedele Lampertico to Luigi Luzzatti, [s.l.] 25 April 1863, in *Archivio Luzzatti*, b. 23 (Corrispondenza: Lampertico, Fedele).

63 Lampertico to Luzzatti, 25 April 1863.

64 Letter of Fedele Lampertico to Luigi Luzzatti, [s.l.] 16 May 1862, in *Archivio Luzzatti*, b. 23 (Corrispondenza: Lampertico, Fedele).

65 *Rivista Euganea*, 29 April 1858; *Il Comune* (1864), pp. 77–9.

66 Letter of Luigi Luzzatti to Antonio Tolomei, [Milano] Direzione del giornale *Il Lombardo*, summer 1864, in *Archivio Luzzatti*, b. 46 (Corrispondenza: Tolomei, Antonio e Giampaolo).

67 Letter of Luigi Luzzatti to Fedele Lampertico, [April 1863], in Biblioteca Bertoliana di Vicenza, *Carte Lampertico.*

68 Letter of Fedele Lampertico to Luigi Luzzatti, [s.l.] 22 March 1862, in *Archivio Luzzatti*, b. 23 (Corrispondenza: Lampertico, Fedele).

69 See, for example, Alberto Mario Banti and Marco Meriggi (eds.), "Élites e associazioni nell'Italia dell'Ottocento," *Quaderni storici* 77 (1991), which includes essays by Meriggi and Cardoza; and Maria Malatesta, ed., "Sociabilità nobiliare, sociabilità borghese," *Cheiron* 5:9–10 (1988).

70 *Discorsi e documenti relativi alla festa commemorativa del lavoro celebratasi in Padova il giorno 10 ottobre 1869 alla Società di mutuo soccorso degli artigiani, negozianti e professionisti* (Padua: Randi, 1869), p. 3.
71 George Simmel, "Sociability," in Simmel, *On Individuality and Social Forms: Selected Writings*, ed. Donald N. Levine (Chicago: University of Chicago Press, 1971), pp. 127–34. Simmel's essay was first published in Germany in 1910. See also the illuminating discussion of the poet Guido Gozzano's wistful ode, written in 1907, to the intimacy of bygone salons, in Levra, "Salotti," pp. 111–12.
72 "Liberia," *Il Comune*, 15 September 1864, in Antonio Tolomei, *Scritti vari* (Padua: Draghi, 1919), p. 103.

2 Poetry and Prose in the Risorgimento

1 For brief accounts of Hermann Schulze-Delitzsch and his popular banks in Germany, see James J. Sheehan, *German History 1770–1866* (New York: Oxford University Press, 1989), pp. 885–8; Theodore S. Hamerow, *The Social Foundations of German Unification 1858–1871: Ideas and Institutions* (Princeton: Princeton University Press, 1969), pp. 230–1. On Italy's popular banks, see Alessandro Polsi, *Alle origini del capitalismo italiano: Stato, banche e banchieri dopo l'Unità* (Turin: Einaudi, 1993), and Paolo Pecorari, ed., *Le banche popolari nella storia d'Italia* (Venice: Istituto Veneto di scienze, lettere ed arti, 1999).
2 The material in this and the following two paragraphs regarding Luzzatti's activities in the summer and fall of 1866 is drawn from Luigi Luzzatti, *Memorie autobiografiche e carteggi*, vol. 1 (Bologna: Zanichelli, 1931), pp. 207–14.
3 Carlo Leoni, *Cronaca segreta de' miei tempi*, ed. Giuseppe Toffanin, Jr (Padua: Rebellato, 1976), pp. 593–4.
4 Letter of Angelo Messedaglia to Luigi Luzzatti, Verona, 16 October 1866, reproduced by Angelo's son, Luigi Messedaglia, in *L'opera politica di Angelo Messedaglia nel 1866: Contributo alla storia delle liberazione del Veneto con lettere e documenti inediti* (Venice: Accademia di Agricoltura, Scienze e Lettere di Verona, 1921), pp. 890–1. Part of this letter also appears in Luzzatti, *Memorie*, vol. 1, p. 209.
5 In his memoirs, Luzzatti suggests that he and Messedaglia understood Alvisi to be their "enemy." Luzzatti cites the passage from Messedaglia's letter of 16 October 1866 that immediately followed the quotation cited above – "If the enemy attempts any serious operation of approach against the work of the piazza, I will notify the General quarters. It is absolutely necessary that

the quadrilateral remain ours" – and, in a footnote, adds: "The enemy was Alvisi, the sponsor of another system" (*Memorie*, vol. 1, p. 209). In his partial reproduction of this letter, Luzzatti places no break between Messedaglia's discussion of the popular bank and its supporters in Verona, and his comment about the "enemy" and "General quarters." In Luigi Messedaglia's full reproduction, however, the second of these topics is treated in a separate paragraph. And the younger Messedaglia goes on to argue that the "enemy" to which his father referred was, in fact, the recently departed Austrian troops. Luigi Messedaglia, *L'opera politica di Angelo Messedaglia*, pp. 894–5.

6 Villari's article appears, in translation, in the compendium of documents edited by Denis Mack Smith, *The Making of Italy 1796–1870* (New York: Walker, 1968), pp. 392–6.

7 *Il Giornale di Padova*, 1 September 1866, cited in Angelo Ventura, *Padova* (Rome-Bari: Laterza, 1989), pp. 13–14. Ventura points out that liberal newspapers in Padua echoed, or rather anticipated, Villari's famous statement in a series of articles that began to appear soon after the city's liberation. In early August, a month before Villari's article appeared in *Il Politecnico*, the Paduan *Bollettino del popolo* presented not only the same question, "Whose fault is it?," but a similar answer:

> It is important to recognize, and may this be a lesson for the future, that an army of heroes can emerge suddenly from the viscera of a great country, but that without very advanced industries, without tireless and profound studies, without long amassed fortunes, even such an army can encounter unexpected difficulties ... We must study and work; and when these studies and work, for their diligence, are such as to render us as learned and rich as our soldiers were intrepid in battle, [then] we will have little or nothing to envy of America and Prussia. (*Bollettino del Popolo*, 5 August 1866, cited in Ventura, *Padova*, p. 11)

8 Thus, it was possible for a book published in 1962, with the title *Political Currents in the Veneto ... 1859–1866*, to do without even a single reference to Luigi Luzzatti. Letterio Briguglio, *Correnti politiche nel Veneto dopo Villafranca 1859–1866* (Rome: Edizioni di storia e letteratura, 1965).

9 Fedele Lampertico, "La Società di mutuo soccorso degli artigiani," *Il Berico*, 12 December 1858; Lampertico, *Relazione per gli anni 1858 e 1859 della Società di Mutuo Soccorso degli Artigiani Vicentini* (Vicenza: 1860); Lampertico, *Dei vantaggi che la poesia puo conseguire dall'economia politica e questa da quella* (Padua: Bianchi, 1854); Lampertico, *Commemorazione funebre di Valentino Pasini letta nel Teatro Olimpico il 5 Maggio 1864*

(Vicenza: Paroni, 1864); Lampertico, "Di alcuni scritti sulle Società di mutuo soccorso in Italia. Relazione," *Atti dell'I. R. Istituto Veneto di scienze, lettere ed arti*, t. 10, s. 3 (November 1864–October 1865), pp. 729–30; Jacopo Cabianca and Fedele Lampertico, *Vicenza e il suo territorio* (Milan: Corona e Caimi, 1861).

10 In his study of the "French generation of 1820," Alan B. Spitzer writes: "The evidence for the generation's existence is to be sought in forms of collective behavior, in networks of personal relationships, in shared assumptions that underlay an ideology and attitudes that constitute a mentalité, in everything that comprised a common response to contemporary experience distinguishing the cohort from its contemporaries." Although, as we shall see, Fedele Lampertico, Luigi Luzzatti, and friends possessed "a sense of collective self-confidence and mutual regard" comparable to Spitzer's French generation of 1820, I am not trying to argue, as Spitzer does so convincingly, that the young Venetians of the 1860s saw themselves or, in turn, were believed by others to be "a privileged cohort, set apart by its talents and its coherence from older and younger contempories." Spitzer, *The French Generation of 1820* (Princeton: Princeton University Press, 1987), pp. xiii–xiv, 4. Recent historians of Risorgimento nationalism have also addressed the topic of generational cohorts. See, for example, Roberto Balzani, "I giovani del Quarantotto: Profilo di una generazione," *Contemporanea* 3 (2000), pp. 403–16.

11 Emilio Morpurgo, *Il proletariato e le società di mutuo soccorso* (Padua: Bianchi, 1859); Morpurgo, *Di alcune questioni intorno alla carità* (Rovereto: Catuno, 1863); Luigi Luzzatti, *La diffusione del credito e le banche popolari* (Padua: Sacchetto. 1863); Paolo Lioy, *Sulle scuole serali gratuite istituite dall'Accademia olimpica di Vicenza. Discorso* (Vicenza: Apollonio, 1863). Alberto Errera's and Antonio Tolomei's early published works are discussed below.

12 Letter of Emilio Morpurgo to Fedele Lampertico, Padua, 7 September 1863, BBV, CLa, s. I, b. 42, quoted in Renato Camurri, "Tradizione e innovazione nel pensiero di Emilio Morpurgo," in *La scienza moderata*, ed. Camurri, p. 345. Five months earlier, Luzzatti began a letter to Lampertico: "My Fedele, Thank you for your beautiful letter; it is very helpful, but I cannot insist enough that you do me two favors; a copy of the Statutes of your mutual aid society and the [book by E.] Laurent [*Le pauperisme et les sociétés de prévoyance* (1859)]." Fedele Lampertico, *Carteggi e diari 1842–1906*, vol. 2, ed. Renato Camurri (Venice: Marsilio, 1998), p. 646.

13 The contingent of *istriani* and *trentini* at the university added to the political importance of Padua during the Risorgimento, and made it the region's leading centre of irredentism after unification. Ventura, *Padova*, pp. 43–4.

14 Even Paolo Lioy, who never completed his degree, later reminisced about the centrality of the University of Padua, comparing the institution to "a nest" from which baby birds "eager for larger horizons" first took flight. "Giuseppe Pertile. Ricordi. Lettura del Comm. Paolo Lioy nella tornata del 15 gennaio 1878," *Atti dell'Accademia Olimpica di Vicenza. Primo Semester 1878* (Vicenza: 1878), p. 25.

15 In 1858, for example, no fewer than twenty-one people associated with the university, including seven of the Academic Senate's ten members, belonged to the city's Reading Room. Including a nineteen-member staff of librarians and custodians, the University of Padua employed eighty-seven people in 1858. Thus, approximately one of four university employees were also members of the Reading Room. Excluding the staff, the percentage is higher: twenty-one of sixty-nine, or close to one of three. Finally, if we take only the university's full professors into consideration, the figures are fourteen of thirty-six, or 39 per cent. *Prospetto degli studj dell'imperiale regia Università di Padova per l'anno scolastico 1858–1859* (Padua: Antonelli, n.d.); *Quadro dei giornali politici, scientifici e letterarj ed elenco dei socj del Gabinetto di lettura in Padova* (Padua: 1858). On the significance of the Caffe Pedrocchi, see chapter 1.

16 Maria Cecilia Ghetti, "L'università," in *Padova 1814–1866: Istituzioni, protagonisti e vicende di una citta*, ed. Piero Del Negro e Nino Agostinetti (Padua: 1991), pp. 65–71.

17 Luzzatti, *Memorie*, vol.1, pp. 22–3.

18 Letter of Luigi Luzzatti to Fedele Lampertico, Venice, 20 August 1862, in Lampertico, *Carteggi*, vol. 2, pp. 631–4.

19 Letters of Emilio Morpurgo to Luigi Luzzatti, Padua, 5, 12, 14, 27 June 1862; 5 July 1862; 19, 30 August 1862; in *Archivio Luzzatti*, b. 30 (Corrispondenza: Morpurgo).

20 Letters of Emilio Morpurgo to Luigi Luzzatti, Padua, 5, 12, 14, 27 June 1862, *Archivio Luzzatti*, b. 30 (Corrispondenza: Morpurgo).

21 Letters of Enrico Castelnuovo to Fedele Lampertico, Venice, 11, 19 September 1864, in Fedele Lampertico, *Carteggi e diari 1842–1906*, vol. 1, ed. Emilio Franzina (Venice: Marsilio, 1996), pp. 481–5.

22 For example, Alberto Errera, *Le industrie nel Veneto* (Milan: 1868); *Il primo anno di libertà nelle province venete. Annuario delle istituzioni popolari* (Venice: 1869); *Annuario industriale e delle istituzioni popolari.*

II: 1868–1869 (Venice: 1869); *Storia e statistica delle industrie venete e accenni al loro avvenire* (Venice: 1870); *Le nuove istituzioni economiche del XIX secolo* (Milan: 1874).

23 For the main period and areas in question, see Margherita Piva, ed., *La visita pastorale di Federico Manfredini nella diocesi di Padova (1859–1865)*, vol. 1 (Rome: 1971); and Gianni A. Cisotto, ed., *La visita pastorale di Giovanni Antonio Farina nella diocesi di Vicenza (1864–1871)* (Rome: 1977).

24 Silvana Patriarca, *Numbers and Nationhood: Writing Statistics in Nineteenth-Century Italy* (New York: 1996), especially chap. 7, "A Map of the New Nation," pp. 176–209.

25 *Annuario scientifico industriale. Anno Primo* (Milan: 1865), pp. 497–531.

26 Giacomo Zanella, "Religione e lavoro," reproduced in Franzina, *Il poeta e gli artigiani*, pp. 113–19.

27 *Discorso del Prof. Luigi Luzzatti all'inaugurazione della Banca Popolare di Asola* (Venice: 1864), in Luigi Luzzatti, *Opere*, vol. 4, *L'Ordine sociale* (Bologna: 1952), pp. 243–55.

28 Although Giacomo Zanella recognized the advantages of mutual aid societies, he warned Luzzatti not to offend the public with sarcastic, dismissive comments about religious corporations. See his letter to Fedele Lampertico, Padua, 5 September 1866, in Franzina, *Il poeta e gli artigiani*, p. 210.

29 See Letterio Briguglio, ed., *Carteggio Volpe-Cavalletto (1860–1866)* (Padua: 1963), pp. vii–xxix. Angelo Volpe, an ordained priest from the Venetian province of Belluno, wrote one of the most famous anti-temporalist pamphlets of the Risorgimento, *La questione romana e il clero veneto* (1862).

30 Letter of Luigi Luzzatti to Fedele Lampertico, 1863, in Lampertico, *Carteggi*, vol. 2, pp. 653–5. This long tirade of a letter, which has no subject other than the failings of academies, was apparently prompted by a request by Lampertico for Luzzatti's opinion on the matter. See also Lampertico's request that Luzzatti "not be so impatient with the [Olympic] Academy," in his letter to Luzzatti, s. l., 3 September 1863, in AL, b. 23 (Corrispondenza: Lampertico, Fedele). Another example of Luzzatti's anti-academic position is the following comment, in a letter to Antonio Tolomei: "The care with which in France and Germany one follows the cooperative movement in every country in the world makes for a curious contrast with certain Milanese and especially *Venetian* academies and institutions" (Luzzatti's emphasis) (Letter of Luigi Luzzatti to Antonio Tolomei, Milan, 28 March 1865, in *Archivio Luzzatti*, b. 46 [Corrispondenza: Tolomei, Antonio]).

31 Lampertico, *Ricordi academici*, p. 124; Franzina, *Il poeta e gli artigiani*, p. 69.

32 Lampertico, *Ricordi academici*, pp. 83–4.

33 Lampertico, "Di alcuni scritti," pp. 729–30.

34 It was not until 1911 that the association's use of the phrase "Christian brotherhood" in its official statute was called into question by the membership. See the list of statute reform proposals from 1911 included in the second of two volumes of documents relevant to the Società Generale in *Biblioteca Bertoliana di Vicenza*, Gonz. 347.3.

35 See, for example, *Discorso del Prof. Luigi Luzzatti all'inaugurazione della Banca Popolare di Asola*, pp. 248–9. In a series of charts documenting the proliferation after 1866 of new workers' associations in the Veneto, Alberto Errera put the substitution theory on brilliant display. The charts make it appear that newly created mutual aid societies, popular banks, cooperatives, popular libraries, and night schools were the commoner's best, if not only, hope. Running along the top of each chart was a small box in which all "other institutions useful for the people" were to be listed. A hospital, an orphanage, an infant nursery, and two others came close to filling this space on the province of Treviso's chart; no "other" institutions at all appeared on the charts for Vicenza and Rovigo. Errera simply made the old regime disappear. See Errera, *Il primo anno di libertà nelle province venete; Annuario industriale e delle istituzioni popolari*; and *Le nuove istituzioni economiche del XIX secolo*. On the persistence of the Catholic Church's institutions and the failure of reform efforts, see Giovanna Farrell-Vinay, *Povertà e politica nell'Ottocento: Le opere pie nello stato liberale* (Turin: Scriptorium, 1997).

36 *Discorso del Prof. Luigi Luzzatti all'inaugurazione della Banca Popolare di Asola*, pp. 247–8, 250; "Sul credito popolare per l'Italia," originally published in the Milanese newspaper *La Perseveranza*, 7 January 1864, reprinted in Luzzatti, *Opere*, vol. 4, p. 233; Luzzatti, *La diffusione del credito*, pp. 87–90. The basic elements of Luzzatti's historical contrast of France and Germany in 1848 were present in the university thesis he wrote in 1863, but did not come together to form a "story" until he left the Veneto to begin promoting the creation of popular banks in Lombardy. For an especially forceful statement of the Franco-German comparison, see "Introduzione di Luigi Luzzatti all'Opera di Schulze-Delitzsch: *Delle Unioni di Credito, Ossia delle Banche Popolari*," (Venice: 1871), in Luzzatti, *Opere*, vol. 4, pp. 271–2.

37 Steven C. Hughes, *Crime, Disorder, and the Risorgimento: The Politics of Policing in Bologna* (Cambridge: Cambridge University Press, 1995), pp. 249–53.

38 The three-volume series on united Italy's "realms of memory," inspired by Pierre Nora's enormously influential French series by the same title, pays relatively little attention to institutions. Mario Isnenghi, ed., *I luoghi della*

memoria, 3 vols. (Rome: 1996–7). See also Steven C. Soper, "La svolta man-
cata: Il 1848 e il Risorgimento italiano nella storiografia americana," in
Renato Camurri, ed., *Memoria, rappresentazioni e protagonisti del 1848
italiano* (Verona: Cierre, 2006), pp. 83–94.

39 Letter of Fedele Lampertico to Luigi Luzzatti, 16 May 1862, in *Archivio
Luzzatti*, b. 23 (Corrispondenza: Lampertico, Fedele).

40 Letter of Giacomo Zanella to Fedele Lampertico, Padua, 5 January 1864,
in Franzina, *Il poeta e gli artigiani*, p. 202. See also, in the same collection,
Zanella's many other references to popular lectures and schools in the region: for example, Luzzatti's planned talks at the Ateneo Veneto (Giacomo
Zanella to Fedele Lampertico, Padua, 19 April 1863); Zanella's prize ceremony speech to the school of design in Padua (Giacomo Zanella to Fedele
Lampertico, Padua, 13 December 1863); Lampertico's classes in political
economy (Giacomo Zanella to Fedele Lampertico, Padua, 17 January 1864).

41 The first two letters (dated 21 March and 28 March) were written in Milan,
the third (dated 19 April) in Asola. *Archivio Luzzatti*, b. 46 (Corrispondenza:
Tolomei, Antonio e Gianpaolo).

42 Luzzatti, *Memorie*, vol. 1, pp. 147, 194, 157.

43 Luzzatti, *Memorie*, vol. 1, p. 162.

44 "In memoria di Quintino Sella," in Luigi Luzzatti, *Opere*, vol. 1, *Grandi
Italiani. Grandi sacrifici per la patria* (Bologna: Zanichelli, 1924), p. 56.
Curiously, in his memoirs, Luzzatti presented this quotation as follows:
"One person sacrificed himself on the gallows, some other gave his life in
order to restore, with [sound] finances, *the honor of the Fatherland or to
raise the moral and economic level of the reborn Nation*; and in different
ways all of them died piously" (Luzzatti, *Memorie*, vol. 1, p. 203; I have
placed the altered part of the quotation in italics). As if to confirm that his
eulogy of Sella was at least in part a self-tribute as well, in his memoirs
Luzzatti used this quotation from 1884 as the epigraph to the chapter
entitled "In the liberated Veneto," in which he described his promotion of
the region's first popular banks in 1866.

45 "Introduzione di Luigi Luzzatti," in Luzzatti, *Opere*, vol. 4, p. 270.

46 "La propaganda dell'alfabeto," *Il Comune*, a. III, n. 1 (4 January 1866),
in Antonio Tolomei, *Scritti vari* (Padua: Draghi, 1919), pp. 120–2. See also,
in the same collection, "Il nuovo anno," *Il Comune*, a. I, n. 13 (1 January
1865), and "Questioni ambigue e circolo viziosi," *Il Comune*, a. II, n. 14
(5 October 1865).

47 "Alla vigilia," *Il Comune*, a. III, n. 18 (3 May 1866), in Tolomei, *Scritti vari*,
p. 135. In his contribution to the first issue of *Il Comune*, in 1864, Tolomei used the phrase *"nuovi mezzi al risorgimento"* to describe the variety of

popular credit institutions that were just then beginning to spread throughout Italy. In the same breath, however, he also paid tribute to savings banks,
mutual aid societies, retirement homes, and consumer cooperatives. Together, these institutions constituted a "movement of regeneration" in Italy.
"La piccola possidenza e i contadini," *Il Comune*, a. I, n. 1, e. 2 (1 e 15 July
1864), in Tolomei, *Scritti vari*, p. 91.
48 Franzina, *Il poeta e gli artigiani*, p. 69.
49 One of the most controversial "purges" of suspected "Austrianists" took
place in Padua in July 1866, when the provisional representative of the Italian government, "Royal Commissar" Gioacchino Pepoli, dismissed sixteen
professors from the University of Padua. See Ventura, *Padova*, pp. 67–9.

3 A New Public

1 *Il Progresso*, 15 September 1866, p. 3.
2 "Vangelo dell'Elettore," *Bollettino Elettorale del Circolo Popolare di Padova*, n. 3 (Padua, 15 October 1866).
3 *Il Progresso*, 13 October 1866.
4 Jürgen Habermas, *The Structural Transformation of the Public Sphere: An
Inquiry into a Category of Bourgeois Society*, trans. Thomas Burger (Cambridge, MA: MIT Press, 1989); Antonio Chiavistelli, *Dallo stato alla nazione: Costituzione e sfera pubblica in Toscana dal 1814 al 1849* (Rome:
Carocci, 2006).
5 *Il Corriere di Vicenza*, 23 August 1866.
6 A brief summary of nineteenth-century liberal ideology appears in the chapter entitled "Civic Ideologies and Social Values" in Theodore S. Hamerow,
The Birth of a New Europe: State and Society in the Nineteenth Century
(Chapel Hill: University of North Carolina Press, 1983), pp. 234–40. Two
examples of the large body of recent work on Italian nationalism are Bruno
Tobia, *Una patria per gli italiani: Spazi, itinerari, monumenti nell'Italia
unita (1870–1900)* (Rome-Bari: Laterza, 1991); and Albert Russell Ascoli
and Krystyna von Henneberg, eds., *Making and Remaking Italy: The Cultivation of National Identity around the Risorgimento* (Oxford: Berg, 2001).
7 Colin Gordon, "Governmental Rationality: An Introduction," in *The Foucault Effect: Studies in Governmentality*, ed. Graham Burchell, Colin Gordon,
and Peter Miller (Chicago: University of Chicago Press, 1991), p. 14. On the
exclusions of the nineteenth-century liberal public sphere, see Dennis Sweeney, "Liberalism, the Worker and the Limits of Bourgeois *Öffentlichkeit* in
Wilhelmine Germany," *German History* 22:1 (2004), pp. 36–75; Pieter M.
Judson, *Exclusive Revolutionaries: Liberal Politics, Social Experience, and*

National Identity in the Austrian Empire, 1848–1914 (Ann Arbor: University of Michigan Press, 1996); Geoff Eley, "Nations, Publics, and Political Cultures: Placing Habermas in the Nineteenth Century," in Craig Calhoun, ed., *Habermas and the Public Sphere* (Cambridge, MA: MIT Press, 1992), pp. 289–339; Leonore Davidoff and Catherine Hall, *Family Fortunes: Men and Women of the English Middle Class, 1780–1850* (Chicago: University of Chicago Press, 1987).

8 Bruce Robbins, ed., *The Phantom Public Sphere* (Minneapolis: University of Minnesota Press, 1993).

9 On museums, see Paula Findlen, *Possessing Nature: Museums, Collecting, and Scientific Culture in Early Modern Italy* (Berkeley: University of California Press, 1994); Per Bjurstrom, ed., *The Genesis of the Art Museum in the 18th Century* (Stockholm: Nationalmuseum, 1993); Daniel J. Sherman, *Worthy Monuments: Art Museums and the Politics of Culture in Nineteenth-Century France* (Cambridge, MA: Harvard University Press, 1989); Tony Bennett, *The Birth of the Museum: History, Theory, Politics* (London: Routledge, 1995); James J. Sheehan, *Museums in the German Art World: From the End of the Old Regime to the Rise of Modernism* (New York: Oxford University Press, 2000). On zoos and, more generally, the bourgeois public sphere in nineteenth-century Germany, see David Blackbourn, "The Discreet Charm of the Bourgeoisie: Reappraising German History in the Nineteenth Century," in David Blackbourn and Geoff Eley, *The Peculiarities of German History: Bourgeois Society and Politics in Nineteenth-Century Germany* (Oxford: Oxford University Press, 1984), pp. 190–205. On England, see J.H. Plumb, "The Commercialization of Leisure in Eighteenth-Century England," in Neil McKendrick, John Brewer, and J.H. Plumb, *The Birth of a Consumer Society: The Commercialization of Eighteenth-Century England* (Bloomington, IN: Indiana University Press, 1982), pp. 265–85. A good example of the transformation of existing institutions is the reorganization of the Uffizi gallery in Florence, one of Italy's oldest art museums, in the second half of the eighteenth century. Beginning in 1769, the gallery was opened to the public on a daily basis, with a new arrangement of custodial and cleaning services and a trained museum director. Silvia Meloni Trkulja and Ettore Spalletti, "Istituzioni artistiche fiorentine 1765–1825," in Francis Haskell, ed., *Saloni, gallerie, musei e loro influenza sullo sviluppo dell'arte dei secoli XIX e XX* (Bologna: CLUEB, 1981), p. 9.

10 Plumb, "The Commercialization of Leisure," pp. 280–3; R.J. Morris, "Clubs, Societies and Associations," in *The Cambridge Social History of Britain 1750–1950*, vol. 3, *Social Agencies and Institutions*, ed. F.M.L. Thompson (New York: Cambridge University Press, 1990), pp. 402–3. As

both Plumb and Morris point out, most of these early associations had another goal besides fundraising: to devise a set of rules and regulations that
would ensure orderly conduct at events involving gambling or, as in the case
of dances, contact between the sexes. On the importance of recreation (and
order) in Italian associational life, see chapter 1 of this study.

11 Fabia Borroni Salvadori, "Riunirsi in crocchio, anche per leggere: Le origini del gabinetto di lettura a Firenze," *Rassegna storica toscana*, a. XXVII,
n. 1 (1981), pp. 11–33; Alfio Signorelli, "Socialità e circolazione di idee:
l'associazionismo culturale a Catania nell'Ottocento," *Meridiana* 22–23
(1995), pp. 42–6, 52–60; Maria Gioia Tavoni, "Tipografi, editori, lettura,"
in Aldo Berselli and Angelo Varni, eds., *Bologna in età contemporanea
1796–1914* (Bologna: Bononia University Press, 2010), pp. 740–5. On "pro-
prietary libraries" in eighteenth-century England, see Morris, "Clubs, Societies and Associations," p. 406.

12 The distinction between "sacred" and "profane" sites was a common feature of guidebooks from this period.

13 Giannantonio Moschini, *Guida per la città di Padova all'amico delle belle
arti* (Venice: 1817) (henceforth *Guida*), pp. 179–88; *Guida di Padova e della
sua provincia* (Padua: 1842), pp. 486–7, 529–31.

14 *Catalogo ed illustrazione dei prodotti primitivi del suolo e delle industrie
della provincia di Vicenza offerte alla pubblica mostra nel palazzo del museo
civico il 25 aprile 1855* (Vicenza: 1855). Turning his attention from living to
ancient flora, Cabianca made note of the six most important collections of
fossils in the province; five were the private collections of distinguished naturalists, and the sixth belonged to Vicenza's newly created Civic Museum.
Cabianca did not fail to express his confidence in the lone public collection's
future growth, but he also warned that anything less than diligent oversight
of its precious collection would make people question the wisdom of remov-
ing objects from their original locations.

15 Moschini, *Guida*, pp. 235–47; Krzysztof Pomian, "Collezionisti d'arte e di
curiosità naturali," in *Storia della cultura veneta*, vol. 5, *Il settecento*, part 2,
ed. Girolamo Arnaldi and Gianfranco Folena (Vicenza: Neri Pozza, 1986),
pp. 6–7. Technically, as Pomian suggests, the first public museum of natural
history in the Veneto was Padua's botanical garden, created in 1545. It, too,
was affiliated with the university.

16 In the dedication of his guidebook to Girolamo Da Rio, Moschini made a
point of thanking his friend for "the festive welcomes you gave me each time
I came to visit, and the desire, that your House might also be mine" (Moschini, *Guida*, pp. iii–iv). Particularly lyrical is the appreciation of the Treves
garden that Pietro Selvatico contributed to the guide published in 1842. This

garden, one of several designed by Giuseppe Jappelli, Padua's leading architect, was bounded by one of the canals running through the city and dramatically situated near the churches of Sant'Antonio and Santa Giustina. It
contained enough trees, grottoes, and rocks, Selvatico noted, to make "the
spectator believe that he or she was far away from the city and among the
wildest sites in hills," but also "Chinese pagodas and Greek temples, light
bridges, arabesque cells with the cabalistic symbols of the ancient alche-
mists, a small equestrian area, spatious greenhouses where exotic plants,
procured at great expense, are conserved, and, most beautiful condiment to
so many qualities, the courteous hospitality of the owners" (*Guida di Padova e della sua provincia*, pp. 274–5). The convention of opening private
galleries to the public is mentioned in Pietro Selvatico, *Guida di Padova e
dei principali suoi contorni* (Padua: 1869), pp. 238–9.

17 For a discussion of the relationship between private and public art collections in late-eighteenth- and early-nineteenth-century London, see Giles
Waterfield, "The Development of the Early Art Museum in Britain," in Bjurstrom, ed., *Genesis of the Art Museum*, pp. 81–111. During the middle and
later part of the eighteenth century aristocratic picture collections in London
flourished. Among potential visitors, some expectation did exist that such
collections could be visited by those able to arrange minimal introductions,
and this information was published in guides to London (pp. 89–90).

18 The various articles by Antonio Keller include "Dell'Agricoltura nelle Provincie Venete, in relazione all'opera di Heuze sull'Agricoltura dell'Italia
Settentrionale," *Rivista periodica dei lavori dell'Academia di scienze, lettere ed arti in Padova*, vol. 15 (Padua: 1866), pp. 45–103; "Relazione sulla
statistica dei Vini del Distretto di Padova dell'anno 1867 letto il 15 gennaio
all'Adunanza generale del Comizio Agrario nella Sala Verde Municipale dal
Dott. Antonio Keller," *Il Raccoglitore*, s. II, a. VI, n. 8 (16 July 1869), pp.
136–43; "Tentativi fatti in Provincia per attivare un podere modello," *Il
Raccoglitore*, s. II, a. IV, n. 9 (1 February 1867), pp. 133–43. For examples
from the Agrarian Association of Vicenza, including praise for elite studies,
travels, and machinery purchases, see *Bollettino del Comizio Agrario di Vicenza*, a. I, f. III (1868), pp. 65–72, and a. I, f. IV (1868), pp. 105–13. For
two reports on excursions to large estates, see *Il Raccoglitore*, s. II, a. IV,
n. 15 (1 June 1867), pp. 225–7, and *Bollettino del Comizio Agrario di Vicenza*,
a. IX, f. VI (June 1876), pp. 183–5. On courses taught at private homes, see
Bartolo Clementi, "Relazione sull'operato dal Comizio nell'anno 1870–71,"
Bollettino del Comizio Agrario di Vicenza, a. IV, f. I (April 1871), pp. 4–5.

19 Giuseppe Solitro, *La "Società di cultura e di incoraggiamento" in Padova
nel suo primo centenario (un secolo di vita padovana) 1830–1930* (Padua:

Seminario, 1930), pp. 207–13; Sebastiano Rumor, *Il Palazzo della Banca Popolare già dei conti di Thiene a Vicenza. Note di storia e d'arte* (Vicenza: Arti Grafiche Vicentine, 1912), pp. 39–48. On the theme of liberalism and architecture, traditional and modern, see Carl Schorske's discussion of the Ringstrasse in *Fin-de-siècle Vienna: Politics and Culture* (New York: Knopf, 1981).

20 Many Italians felt that the territories of Trent, Trieste, and Dalmatia, to the north and east of the Veneto, should have been annexed to the Italian state in 1866. In a variety of ways, the more politically active members of this group tried to keep the attention of public opinion and the government on the plight of this "unredeemed land" (*terra irredenta*, in Latin). From the Latin phrase, the term *irredentist* entered united Italy's political vocabulary. Not surprisingly, the Veneto was an important centre of irredentism after unification. During the Risorgimento, the University of Padua had already begun to attract a large number of students from Trent, Trieste, and Dalmatia; from this nucleus an Associazione Trentina-Istriana was formed in the late 1860s. For a general history of the Club Alpino Italiano, see Alessandro Pastore, *Alpinismo e storia d'Italia: Dall'Unità alla Resistenza* (Bologna: Il Mulino, 2003).

21 Club Alpino Italiano, Sezione di Vicenza, *Bollettino. Anno 1877* (Vicenza: 1878), pp. 229–52; *Anno 1878* (Vicenza: 1879), pp. 53–60.

22 Club Alpino Italiano, Sezione di Vicenza, *V° Bollettino (1879–1880)* (Vicenza: 1880), pp. 170–6. Predictably, the anonymous author of this article made a special appeal to the wealthier members of the club regarding the tradition of collecting.

23 Moschini, *Guida*, pp. iii–iv; *Prima mostra*, pp. 55, 60–1. In her recent book on associations in nineteenth-century France, Carol Harrison makes a number of interesting connections between masculine identity and amateur science, two of which, in particular, parallel my own argument: first, she notes that the men who belonged to provincial learned societies distinguished between the collection of art, which because it was "market" driven could appear to be feminine, and the collection of scientific objects ("pot shards, birds' nests, and biological curiosities"), which allowed for collecting "in an altogether more heroic mode than female consumerism"; second, she makes the larger point that the male members of provincial learned societies in France defined themselves not so much by the diplomas or degrees they possessed as by "a general capacity for local leadership." Carol E. Harrison, *The Bourgeois Citizen in Nineteenth-Century France: Gender, Sociability, and the Uses of Emulation* (New York: Oxford University Press, 1999), pp. 80–1, 52. See also Pastore, *Alpinismo e storia d'Italia*, p. 19.

24 *Il Giornale Euganeo*, vol. 3 (1846), pp. 360–5. Ettore Fanoj's reading room in Catania (f. 1845) was divided into two rooms for light reading and two rooms for studying. Alfio Signorelli, "Socialità e circolazione di idee," p. 56.

25 Alessandro Cecere, "Le biblioteche popolari scolastiche in Terra di Lavoro nel primo ventennio unitario," *Rivista di Terra di Lavoro. Bollettino on-line dell'Archivio di Stato di Caserta* 1:2 (April 2006); Rossella Santolamazza, "L'archivio della Società generale di mutuo soccorso fra gli artisti e gli operai di Perugia," in *Le società di mutuo soccorso italiane e i loro archivi. Atti del seminario di studio: Spoleto, 8–10 novembre 1995* (Rome: Ministero per i beni e le attività culturali, Ufficio centrale per i beni archivistici, 1999), p. 191; Tavoni, "Tipografi, editori, lettura," pp. 746–7.

26 Paolo Lioy, *Sulle biblioteche popolari* (Verona: Apollonio, 1870). But see also, on the popular library in Venice, *La Biblioteca popolare della provincia di Venezia e le letture in commune. Relazione dei promotori e parole d'inaugurazione del prof. Busoni, del dott. Alberto Errera e dei sigg. Senatore Torelli prefetto e G.B. Giustinian sindaco di Venezia* (Venice: Antonelli, 1867). On other popular libraries in the Veneto, in Italy, and in Europe and the United States, see Alberto Errera, *Il primo anno di libertà nelle province venete. Annuario delle istituzioni popolari* (Venice: 1868); Errera, *Annuario industriale e delle istituzioni popolari. II: 1868–1869* (Venice: 1869), parte IIᵃ; Errera, *Le nuove istituzioni economiche nel secolo XIX* (Milan: Treves, 1874), pp. 328, 346–7. On popular libraries in Prato and Siena, see Luciano Banchi, *Per l'inaugurazione della Società promotrice delle biblioteche popolari nella Città e Provincia di Siena* (Siena: 1867); and Antonio Bruni, *Delle biblioteche e dei libri popolari* (Florence: 1869).

27 *La Biblioteca popolare della provincia di Venezia*, pp. 25–8; Alberto Errera, *Le nuove istituzioni economiche nel secolo XIX* (Milan: 1874), pp. 328, 346–7; *Annuario industriale e delle istituzioni popolari. II: 1868–1869*, parte IIᵃ, "Le istituzioni popolari a Venezia," p. 7.

28 Antonio Tolomei, "Per l'inaugurazione del Museo Civico di Padova (IV dicembre MDCCCLXXX)," and "Per l'inaugurazione della biblioteca popolare di Padova" (the latter originally published in *Il Giornale di Padova*, 6 and 7 November 1867), both in Antonio Tolomei, *Scritti vari* (Padua: Draghi, 1919), pp. 239–50, 221–9.

29 *La Biblioteca popolare della provincia di Venezia*, p. 16.

30 *La Biblioteca popolare della provincia di Venezia*, pp. 3–4, 11; Errera, *Il primo anno di libertà*, pp. 60–1.

31 Banchi, *Per l'inaugurazione della Società promotrice delle biblioteche popolari*, p. 7.

32 See, for example, *Il Raccoglitore*, s. II, a. IV, n. 7 (1 June 1867), pp. 108–110.

33 *Bollettino del Comizio Agrario di Vicenza*, a. I, f. I (1868), p. 9; a. II, f. III (June 1869), pp. 65–76; a. III, f. I (April 1870), pp. 1–13.

34 *Bollettino del Comizio Agrario di Vicenza*, a. II, f. XI (February 1870), pp. 335–42; a. III, f. V (August 1870), pp. 140–4.

35 For a description of the quite similar process of association-formation in early nineteenth-century England, see Davidoff and Hall, *Family Fortunes*, p. 421.

36 Many of the workers' associations that proliferated in Italy after unification were not moderate liberal but democratic and republican in political orientation; however, in many provincial cities, including Padua and Vicenza, moderate liberal leadership in all categories of associational life, including associations of workers, went largely unchallenged until the late 1870s or early 1880s. Challenges to moderate liberal dominance in Padua and Vicenza are the subject of chapters 5–7.

37 Santolamazza, "L'archivio della Società generale di mutuo soccorso fra gli artisti e gli operai di Perugia," p. 189. For similar rules in Milan, Viterbo, and Catania, see Marco Meriggi, *Milano borghese: Circoli ed élites nell'Ottocento* (Venice: Marsilio, 1992), pp. 196–216; Gilda Nicolai, *Lavoro, Patria e Libertà: Associazionismo e solidarismo nell'alto Lazio lungo l'Ottocento* (Viterbo: Sette città, 2008), p. 208; and Signorelli, "Socialità e circolazione di idee," pp. 62–3. On the male nature of associational meetings in England, see Davidoff and Hall, *Family Fortunes*, p. 416.

38 *Regolamento Annesso allo Statuto della Società Volontari Veterani 1848–49 Residente in Padova*, in Legnazzi, *La Società Volontari-Veterani* (Padua: 1893), p. 84.

39 Social clubs and political associations were the most likely to prefer personal invitations to public announcements. On the issue of publicity and political associations, see chapter 5.

40 *Il Giornale della Provincia di Vicenza*, 5 December 1876. Newspapers often simply posted the information handed to them by association leaders; however, it was not uncommon for newspapers to put announcements in their own, editorial voice, urging members to "turn out in large numbers" at particularly important meetings, and reporting cases of low attendance with critical disappointment.

41 *Il Giornale di Padova*, 3 February 1868. This piece on the Popular Bank was followed by a similarly detailed report on the meeting of a local political association, the Liberal Union.

42 Usage of these phrases and conventions was so widespread that it is point-
less to assemble a partial list of examples; however, for the purposes of comparison with the article from *Il Giornale di Padova*, cited above, see the very
efficient account of a veterans' association meeting, not long after its foundation, in *Il Corriere di Vicenza*, 11 October 1876.

43 Società di Mutuo Soccorso degli artigiani, negozianti e professionisti di Padova, *Discorso ... dal Vice-Presidente Jacopo Mattieli*, pp. 9–10.

44 These events will be discussed in chapter 5.

45 *Il Bacchiglione*, 25 October, 2 November 1876.

46 *Il Bacchiglione*, 2 November 1876. For one of many comparable examples
from the progressive press in Vicenza, see the description of the Vicentine
Progressive Society's inaugural meeting in *Il Progresso* (9 August 1877).

47 Michel Foucault, *Discipline and Punish: The Birth of the Prison*, trans. Alan
Sheridan (New York: Vintage, 1977); Pierre Bourdieu, *Outline of a Theory
of Practice* (Cambridge: Cambridge University Press, 1977); Michel de Certeau, *The Practice of Everyday Life*, trans. Steven Rendall (Berkeley: University of California Press, 1984).

48 Although assorted cultural and scientific associations often sponsored periodicals, these publications rarely drew the kind of focused, dynamic attention we associate with news. The link between Gian Pietro Vieusseux's
reading room in Florence and the influential journal *Antologia* constitutes
an important exception. For the impact of this association and journal on
elites in Catania, see Signorelli, "Socialità e circolazione di idee," pp. 48–52.

49 Gabriele De Rosa, *Il movimento cattolico in Italia: Dalla Restaurazione
all'età giolittiana* (Rome-Bari: Laterza, 1976), p. 51. The quotation comes
from a Catholic youth group in 1868.

50 Cited in Angelo Gambasin, Religione e società dalle riforme napoleoniche
all'età liberale: *Clero, sinodi e laicato cattolico in Italia* (Padua: Liviana,
1974), p. 94.

51 See, for example, on Vicenza's Collegio Convitto (f. 1868), Francesco De
Vivo, "Educazione e scuola nei congressi cattolici tra Lodi e Vicenza (spunti
di riflessione)," in *Studi e ricerche di storia sociale religiosa artistica vicentina e veneta: Omaggio a Ermenegildo Reato*, ed. Gianni A. Cisotto (Vicenza: Accademia Olimpica, 1998), p. 142.

52 *La Sveglia*, 5 August 1870, cited in Mantese, *Memorie storiche*, vol. 5, pp.
242–3. The Catholic Youth Circle in Vicenza went on to attract a respectable
number of members: sixty-seven by 1874, seventy-nine by 1879, and ninety-
three by 1885. See Ermenegildo Reato, *Le origini del movimento
cattolico a Vicenza* (Vicenza: Accademia Olimpica, 1971), p. 162. The expression of concern regarding the group's "meagre number of members"

comes from a letter from Antonio Marzotto to Alfonso Rubbiani, dated 16 April 1869, cited in Reato, *Le origini del movimento cattolico*, p. 160. The national organization's aims are cited in *Il Circolo S. Giuseppe di Vicenza della Gioventù Cattolica Italiana: Memorie* (Vicenza: 1887), p. 7. Gilda Nicolai describes a similar situation in Viterbo, where the Catholic organizers of a new lending library preferred to wait until they had gathered an impressive number of books before making a public announcement. See *Lavoro, Patria e Libertà*, pp. 148–9. For an unusually comprehensive regional study of Catholic associational life, see Mario Casella, *L'associazionismo cattolico a Roma e nel Lazio dal 1870 al primo Novecento* (Galatina: Congedo, 2002).

53 Nino Agostinetti, *L'Opposizione di carta: La stampa cattolica padovana dell'Ottocento dagli Austriaci ai massoni* (Padua: Libreria Gregoriana, 1986); Gianni A. Cisotto, *Quotidiani e periodici vicentini (1811–1926)* (Vicenza: Accademia Olimpica, 1986). As Agostinetti rightly points out (on p. 24), the local items featured in weekly newspapers were often old news before they made it into print. In addition, Catholic periodicals were often smaller in size than liberal newspapers. See, for example, the detailed information in Cisotto's book. The published minutes of a meeting of the Catholic Youth Circle of Vicenza in 1881 appear in Mariano Nardello's valuable book, *Il primo cinquantennio dell'Azione cattolica vicentina: Dalla protesta alla proposta. Storia dell'Azione cattolica vicentina, Vol. 1: 1869–1922* (Padua: Messaggero, 2010), pp. 117–21.

54 See, for example, David I. Kertzer, *The Kidnapping of Edgardo Mortara* (Boston: Knopf, 1997), chap. 22, "The Rites of Rulers," pp. 238–46.

55 *Il Giornale di Padova* (1867).

56 Letter of Giacomo Zanella to Luigi Luzzatti, Vicenza, 18 September 1866, in *Carte Zanella* 10, b. 23, in the Biblioteca Bertoliana di Vicenza, reprinted in Emilio Franzina, *Il Poeta e gli artigiani: Etica del lavoro e mutualismo nel Veneto di meta '800* (Padua: Poligrafo, 1988), pp. 195–6. Portions of this letter also appear in Luzzatti, *Memorie*, vol. 1, pp. 217–18.

57 *Il Giornale di Padova*, 9 July 1867.

58 Meriggi, *Milano borghese*, p. 182.

59 For two examples, see *Il Giornale di Padova*, 13, 17 January 1868, and 22 June 1869. Significantly, it was the larger of the two demonstrations – triggered by the mysterious assault of Cristiano Lobbia, a member of the parliamentary left who brought a state tobacco monopoly scandal to light – that inspired Padua's leading moderate liberal newspaper to write that the local "population" not only did not participate in these events but "does not understand them." Privately, moderate liberals did not hesitate to identify student demonstrators as a problem. When Alberto Cavalletto, a member of

Parliament in Florence, got news of the disruption students at the University of Padua had caused at a local celebration of the papal jubilee in 1871, he wrote to his sister: "It displeases me that those hoodlum imposters of students made such a racket, offending the religious liberty of those who believe in the Pope ... If in Padua there were a more vigilant prefect, [such] actions which dishonor the student body, the city, and the name of Italy would not be permitted. Foolish and unpredictable is the prefecture, stupid and sad those students who study nothing and come to the university to be idlers and troublemakers." Cited in Giuseppe Calore, *L'attività politica di Alberto Cavalletto dopo il 1866*, tesi di laurea, Università di Padova, Facolta di Magistero, relatore Angelo Ventura, a. a. 1968–1969, pp. 85–7.

60 For a brief introduction to this figure, see Giuseppe Toffanin, "Andrea Cittadella Vigodarzere," in *Padova 1814–1866: Istituzioni, protagonisti e vicende di una città*, ed. Piero Del Negro and Nino Agostinetti (Padua: Istituto per la storia del Risorgimento italiano, 1991), pp. 55–64.

61 *Il Giornale di Padova*, 28 March 1870. The coupling of women with "the people," but also with children, as marginal observers of public events was a standard feature of newspaper reports. For an example that pairs women and children, and that offers an explanation for their remove, see the coverage of the liberal democrat Giuseppe Bacco's funeral in *Il Corriere di Vicenza*, 24 May 1877, p. 1: "The crowd was immense ... The windows and terraces were full of people. Especially women and boys who prefered to avoid the pushing and crushing of the crowd – compact especially at the outlets of the streets."

62 *Cenni sopra la vita di Sua Eccelenza il conte Andrea Cittadella Vigodarzere* (Padua: 1870). All of the materials relating to Cittadella Vigodarzere's funeral belong to a collection, found at the Biblioteca Civica di Padova, entitled *Raccolta di quanto fu pubblicato in morte del conte Andrea Cittadella Vigodarzere*. (Unless indicated otherwise, the documents discussed in this and the following paragraphs come from this collection.) Of course, it is impossible to estimate how complete this sample of documents really is. Describing the city on the day of the funeral, the *Giornale di Padova* noted that "inscriptions affixed to doors and walls celebrated the virtues of the deceased, and portraits of his likeness at different ages were, with a kind and pious thought, exposed in a great many places." *Il Giornale di Padova*, 28 March 1870.

63 Funerals also provided flashpoints in the struggle between liberal and conservative Catholic groups. Major public funerals were staged in Vicenza for two deceased liberal Catholics, Giovanni Battista Dalla Valle (d. 1868) and Giacomo Polatti (d. 1874). See Giovanni Mantese, *Il Seminario e la vita*

religiosa vicentina negli ultimi cent'anni. Per la commemorazione centenario del seminario vescovile di Vicenza (Vicenza: Istituto S. Gaetano, 1954), pp. 75–82.

64 Calore, *L'attività politica di Alberto Cavalletto*, pp. 74–8.

65 Mariano Fogazzaro to Fedele Lampertico, Oria, 18 September 1870, in Fedele Lampertico, *Carteggi e diari 1842–1906*, vol. 2, ed. Renato Camurri (Venice: Marsilio, 1998), p. 162.

66 *Il Bacchiglione*, 31 May 1877. See also the enthusiastic account of the 1869 Festa dello Statuto in Vicenza, by the president of the local Agrarian Association, in *Bollettino del Comizio Agrario di Vicenza*, a. II, f. IV (1869). Recent studies of these and other festivities include Marco Fincardi and Maurizio Ridolfi, eds., *Le trasformazioni della festa: Secolarizzazione, politicizzazione e sociabilità nel XIX secolo (Francia, Italia, Spagna)*, a special issue of *Memoria e Ricerca 5* (July 1995); and Ilaria Porciani, *La festa della nazione. Rappresentazione dello stato e spazi sociali nell'Italia unita* (Bologna: Il Mulino, 1997). Gilda Nicolai documents the intensity of liberal and Catholic public festivities in *Lavoro, Patria e Libertà*.

67 Annual patriotic celebrations must not have attracted such large crowds, for by the 1870s local Venetian newspapers were barely reporting on them at all.

68 *Il Giornale della Provincia di Vicenza*, 14 September 1868 (Supplemento al N. 110), 15, 17 September 1868. Count Oddo Arrigoni of Padua was a guest of the noble Ascanio Pajello (residing at number 2346 on the Corso, Vicenza's historic main street); Quintino Sella, the influential moderate liberal politician from Piedmont, was a guest of the meeting's president, Paolo Lioy; and several notable visitors from outside the region stayed with the local nobles Jacopo Stecchini and Luigi Milan Massari.

69 Mariantonietta Picone Petrusa, Maria Raffaela Pessolano, and Assunta Bianco, *Le grandi esposizioni in Italia 1861–1911: La competizione culturale con l'Europa e la ricerca dello stile nazionale* (Naples: Liguori, 1988); Tobia, *Una patria per gli italiani*, pp. 68–89; Cristina Della Coletta, *World's Fairs Italian Style: The Great Exhibitions in Turin and Their Narratives, 1860–1915* (Toronto: University of Toronto Press, 2006).

70 Representatives of every major city in the Veneto met in 1871 to determine the order in which all future regional exhibitions would take place, so as to avoid conflicts and give each city a chance to organize its own exhibition. It was decided that regional exhibitions would be held every other year, and the rotation of host cities would go as follows: Treviso (1872), Udine (1874), Venice (1876), Rovigo (1878), Verona (1880), Padua (1884), Belluno (1886), and Vicenza (1888). *L'Esposizione Regionale Veneta*, n. 7

(14 October 1871), n. 12 (8 December 1871), n. 13 (20 December1871), n. 14 (24 February 1872), and n. 15 (1 May 1872). Of course, this schedule of regional exhibitions did not preclude the organization of municipal or provincial exhibitions.

71 See the *Regolamento per la Esposizione Agricola, Industriale e di Belle Arti che avrà luogo in Padova nel 1869*, in *L'Esposizione agricola industriale e di belle arti della provincia di Padova* (Padua: 1869), pp. 6–8.

72 For the criticisms registered at the meeting of the Ministry of Agriculture, Industry and Commerce, see *Bollettino del Comizio Agrario di Vicenza*, a. 4, f. 9 (December 1871), pp. 273–4. The same publication contains a pair of statements defending the proliferation of local exhibitions and calling for even greater proliferation, respectively: *Bollettino del Comizio Agrario di Vicenza*, a. 3, f. 9 (October/November 1870), pp. 193–201, and a. 10, f. 1/2 (January/February 1877), p. 49. The contrast between local and national exhibitions was made by a contributor to *L'Esposizione Regionale Veneta*, n. 13 (20 December 1871), p. 98.

73 *L'Esposizione agricola industriale e di belle arti della provincia di Padova* (Padua: 1869), pp. 10–11.

4 Popular Capitalism

1 Alberto Errera, *Annuario industriale e delle istituzioni popolari. II: 1868–1869* (Venice: Ripamonti-Ottolini, 1869), parte II^a, "Le istituzioni popolari a Venezia," pp. 1–2. Errera's first volume was entitled *Il primo anno di libertà nelle provincie venete. Annuario delle istituzioni popolari* (Venice: Antonelli, 1868).

2 Alessándro Rossi, *Dell'arte della lana in Italia e all'estero giudicata all'esposizione di Parigi 1867* (Florence: Barbera, 1869), pp. 220–1.

3 For Rossi's own accounts of the institutions he created, see his *Questione sociale e questione operaia* (Turin: Roux e Favale, 1879) and *Memoria sulle istituzioni morali, private e colletive fondate dal Senatore Alessandro Rossi* (Schio: Marin, 1884). Historians' accounts of these institutions abound. See the various relevant essays in Giovanni L. Fontana, ed., *Schio e Alessandro Rossi: Imprenditorialità, politica, cultura e paesaggi sociali nel secondo Ottocento*, 2 vols. (Rome: Edizioni di storia e letteratura, 1984); and Lucio Avagliano, *Alessandro Rossi e le origini dell'Italia industriale* (Naples: Libreria scientifica, 1970), pp. 45–63.

4 Vera Zamagni, *The Economic History of Italy 1860–1990* (New York: Clarendon, 1993), p. 104.

5 *Il Berico*, 1 January 1867, 3 March 1867; *Il Giornale di Vicenza*, 12 September 1868.

6 *L'Osservatore Euganeo. Annuario del Giornale di Padova. Anno I: 1878* (Padua: 1878), pp. 78–85; *L'Osservatore Veneto. Annuario-Guida del 1884. Anno IV* (Padua: 1884), pp. 210–11. It was not until 1895 that a guide to Padua – general, commercial, or otherwise – created a separate category of "industrialists" in which to list enterprises such as Breda's. See *Guida pratica della città di Padova* (Padua: 1895), pp. 36–7.

7 *Il Caffè Pedrocchi*, 5 May 1846, 10 May 1846, and 29 November 1846.

8 *Catalogo ed illustrazione dei prodotti primitivi del suolo e delle industrie della provincia di Vicenza offerte alla pubblica mostra nel palazzo del museo civico il 25 aprile 1855* (Vicenza: 1855), pp. 5–20, 114–15.

9 See, for example, *Il Giornale Euganeo*, 22 December 1846. By the late 1850s, readers of Padua's newest periodical, *Rivista Euganea*, could see lists of the names of recent donors to the Civic Museum and descriptions of the objects they donated. See *Rivista Euganea*, 17 May 1858.

10 Luzzatti described popular banks in such terms in innumerable speeches and publications, in particular during the 1860s, when he first began to promote the banks in Italy. For two good examples, see the series of brief articles he wrote for the Milanese newspaper *La Perseveranza* in the winter of 1864, and the speech he gave later that year to inaugurate the Popular Bank of Asola, all in Luigi Luzzatti, *Opere*, vol. 4, *L'Ordine sociale* (Bologna: Zanichelli, 1952), pp. 229–40, 243–55.

11 Banca mutua popolare di Padova, *Elenco dei soci* (Padua: 1870); *Elenco degli azionisti* (Padua: 1873, 1875, 1879).

12 See, for example, the impassioned defense of the small shareholder's rights within large corporations that the Piedmontese statesman Matteo Pescatore delivered on the floor of the Italian Senate in 1875. *Atti parlamentari Senato – Discussioni*. Legislatura XII, Sessione 1874–75, 27 April 1875, p. 1332. I will return to the topic of shareholders' meetings and rights in the next chapter.

13 *Atti dell'adunanza generale del Comizio Agrario del primo distretto della Provincia di Padova tenuta il 15, 16, 25 Gennajo 1869 nella Sala Verde municipale gentilmente accordata* (Padua: 1869).

14 Avagliano, *Alessandro Rossi e le origini dell'Italia industriale*, pp. 26–44.

15 *L'Esposizione regionale veneta*, n. 11 (26 November 1871), pp. 81–3; n. 12 (8 December 1871), pp. 89–91; n. 13 (20 December 1871), pp. 97–8. Rossi's essay was originally published in *Atti del R. Istituto Veneto*, s. 3, t. 11 (1865–1866), pp. 535–56.

16 *L'Esposizione veneta regionale*, n. 15 (1 May 1872), p. 119.

17 Fedele Lampertico, letter to Luigi Luzzatti, s. l., 22 November 1862, in *Archivio Luzzatti*, b. 23 (Corrispondenza: Lampertico, Fedele); Fedele Lampertico, "Ricordi academici e letterarii," in *Scritti storici e letterarii*, vol. 1 (Florence: 1883), pp. 288–92, 301–3, 310–11; Luigi Luzzatti, *Memorie autobiografiche e carteggi*, vol. 1 (Bologna: Zanichelli, 1931), pp. 104, 163–70. On Paolo Lioy's night school classes and speeches, see "Le scuole serali e le società di mutuo soccorso," *Museo di famiglia*, a. III, n. 35 (20 August 1863), pp. 545–8, and Emilio Franzina, *Il poeta e gli artigiani: Etica del lavoro e mutualismo nel Veneto di metà '800* (Padua: Poligrafo, 1988). On Morpurgo's activities in Padua, see Giuseppe Solitro, *La "Società di cultura e di incoraggiamento" in Padova nel suo primo centenario (un secolo di vita padovana) 1830–1930* (Padua: Seminario, 1930), pp. 70–2.

18 For an example of the moral didacticism featured in many popular periodicals, see the fictional dialogue between two artisans in *Il Raccoglitore*, a. II (1853), pp. 221–31. This pocket-sized publication, which appeared once a year between 1852 and 1856, was sponsored by Padua's Society for the Encouragement of Agriculture, Commerce and Industry. On the schools in Tuscany, see *Guida per le scuole di reciproco insegnamento* (Florence: 1830); *Adunanza annuale della Società formatosi per la diffusione delle scuole di reciproco insegnamento, tenuta in Firenza il dì 9 marzo 1832* (Florence: 1832); *Rapporto fatto alla Società per la diffusione delle scuole di reciproco insegnamento di Firenza dal suo Comitato del Metodo nella seduta del dì 26 settembre 1834, intorno ai manoscritti presentati al concorso aperto col programma del dì 28 marzo 1833* (Florence: 1834). In general, see Guido Verucci, *L'Italia laica prima e dopo l'Unità 1848–1876: Anticlericalismo, libero pensiero e ateismo nella società italiana* (Rome: Laterza, 1981), pp. 65–178.

19 Cited in Luzzatti, *Memorie*, vol. 1, p. 170.

20 Emilio Morpurgo, *Saggi statistici ed economici sul Veneto* (Padua: Prosperini, 1868), pp. 367–443. By 1876, for example, one out of every five people attending an elementary school or program in the province of Vicenza was in a night or weekend school. The figures were as follows: public elementary schools, 34,668; private elementary schools, 2,581; night or weekend schools, 8,835; nurseries, 1,077; design schools, 363. Luigi Conte, "Delle condizioni dell'istruzione primaria nella Provincia di Vicenza, rispettivamente al 1866," *Atti dell'Accademia Olimpica di Vicenza* (1877), pp. 46–7. Note that, as far as figures go, the real divide was not between public and private elementary schools but between elementary schools and night or weekend schools. Moreover, these figures are for the entire province of Vicenza and therefore include many rural towns that would have had an elementary school but not a night school, the latter being limited to significant

urban populations. Thus, the ratio of night school students to elementary school students in just the city (not the province) of Vicenza was undoubtedly much higher than one to four. With regard to the various programs mentioned above, it should also be noted that, while it was often agrarian associations that promoted popular lectures on agricultural topics, and mutual aid societies that concerned themselves with artisans, there were also many initiatives that involved several associations at once, bringing them together for the cause of popular education.

21 Morpurgo, *Saggi statistici*, p. 442, 428–9.

22 Luigi Luzzatti, *La diffusione del credito e le banche popolari* (Padua: Prosperini, 1863), reprinted in *Attualità di Luigi Luzzatti*, ed. Francesco Parrillo (Milan: Giuffrè, 1964), p. 321; Alberto Errera, *L'Istruzione pubblica a Venezia: Proposte e riforme* (Venice: Gazzetta, 1866), 6–7, 23.

23 Alberto Errera, *Annuario II*, parte IIª, "Tabella statistica delle istituzioni popolari esistenti nel 1868 nel comune di Vicenza"; and identical tables for other townships in the Veneto. For Errera's views on good and bad popular readings, in the same volume, see "Le istituzioni popolari a Venezia," pp. 4–5. His account of the group reading in Venice appears in *Le nuove istituzioni economiche*, pp. 346–7. See also Paolo Lioy, *Sulle biblioteche popolari* (Verona: Apollonio, 1870).

24 Carlo Leoni, *Libro pegli operaji* (Padua: Naratovich, 1866).

25 Cesare Cantù, *Portafoglio d'un operaio*, ed. Carlo Ossola (Milan: Bompiani, 1984), pp. 76–8, 82–7, 100–3. An influential group of Venetian Catholics supported this cautious but thoughtful embrace of modern science and industry. During the 1860s, the priest and poet Giacomo Zanella composed odes to modern labour, commerce, and industry (the last dedicated to and inspired by his nephew, Alessandro Rossi), and touched on the same themes in the many speeches he gave to artisans in mutual aid societies and night schools. By the mid-1870s, even the combative conservatives in charge of Vicenza's leading Catholic newspaper, *Il Berico* (f. 1876), demonstrated their acceptance, if not active support, of a range of modern economic institutions, including local industries and banks. See, for example, "La Cassa di Risparmio," *Il Berico*, 29 May 1876; and "Industrie," *Il Berico*, 13 July 1876.

26 Cantù, *Portafoglio*, p. 148.

27 Samuel Smiles, *Self-Help* (London: IEA Health and Welfare Unit, 1996), pp. xiv–xv, 1. On this point, see also Adriana Chemello, "Mutualismo ed associazionismo nella letteratura del 'self-help' in Italia," in *La scienza moderata: Fedele Lampertico e l'Italia liberale*, ed. Renato Camurri (Milan: Franco Angeli, 1992), pp. 61–2. For more on Smiles's career, including his activities in

Leeds, see Asa Briggs, "Samuel Smiles and the Gospel of Work," in Briggs, *Victorian People: A Reassessment of Persons and Themes 1851–67* (Chicago: University of Chicago Press, 1975), pp. 116–39.

28 Cantù, *Portafoglio*, pp. 235–44, 281–99.

29 Chemello, "Mutualismo ed associazionismo," pp. 61–88.

30 *Discorso del Prof. Luigi Luzzatti all'inaugurazione della Banca Popolare di Asola* (Venice: 1864), in Luzzatti, *Opere*, vol. 4, p. 252.

31 "Introduzione di Luigi Luzzatti all'opera di Schulze-Delitzsch: 'Delle unioni di credito, ossia delle banche popolari'" (Venice: 1871), in Luzzatti, *Opere*, vol. 4, p. 274.

32 Luzzatti, *Memorie*, vol. 1, pp. 114, 165, 179.

33 Thus, to cite just a few of the countless examples, in 1859 Emilio Morpurgo insisted that private donations to mutual aid societies did not constitute "a new form of charity" because these funds only benefited members who "recognized the necessity of providence and saving" (*Il proletariato*, p. 80). In 1862 Giacomo Zanella praised mutual aid society members for giving "alms to yourselves" (Franzina, *Il poeta e gli artigiani*, p. 121). And in 1869 Alberto Errera wrote that "science has given a big help to philanthropy" (Errera, *Annuario industriale e delle istituzioni popolari*, parte II^a: "Le istituzioni di Padova," p. 44.

34 Leo Morabito and Emilio Costa, eds., *L'Universo della solidarietà: Associazionismo e movimento operaio a Genova e Provincia. Mostra storica: Genova, Loggia della Mercanzi, 25 novembre 1995–31 gennaio 1996* (Genoa: Provincia di Genova, 1995), plate 72, p. 14. Speaking to the members of Padua's Mutual Aid Society of Artisans, Merchants and Professionals, in 1872, Emilio Morpurgo made explicit this process of institutional substitution: paying weekly dues to a mutual aid fund meant avoiding the hospital "on the day of sickness," and to pay those dues it was necessary to stay away from "the pub [*bettola*] and the lotto stand." Società di mutuo soccorso degli artigiani, negozianti e professionisti, *Relazione dell'anno 1872* (Padua: 1872), p. 12.

35 For an example of Lioy's advice to artisans, see "Le scuole serali." For Giacomo Zanella's speeches, see Franzina, *Il poeta e gli artigiani*.

36 See the collection of statutes and other documents pertaining to the General Mutual Aid Society of Vicentine Artisans in the Biblioteca Bertoliana in Vicenza (Gonz. 347.2–3). See also Annalisa Gianello, *La Società Generale di mutuo soccorso in Vicenza (1858–1888)*, tesi di laurea in lettere, Università di Padova, facoltà di lettere e filosofia, anno scolastico 1985–86, relatore Angelo Ventura. Some mutual aid societies depended on institutional benefactors. This was true, for example, of Perugia's Mutual Aid Society of

Artists and Workers (f. 1861), which got as much as one-third of its annual income from a range of local entities, including the municipal government, the Savings Bank (Cassa di Risparmio), and a Catholic hospital. See Rossella Santolamazza, "L'archivio della Società generale di mutuo soccorso fra gli artisti e gli operai di Perugia," in *Le società di mutuo soccorso italiane e i loro archivi. Atti del seminario di studio: Spoleto, 8–10 novembre 1995* (Rome: Ministero per i beni e le attività culturali, Ufficio centrale per i beni archivistici, 1999), p. 189–90. From one mutual aid society to the next, the ratio of honorary to ordinary members varied considerably. In the town of Senigallia in the Marche region, the local workers' society (f. 1860) began its existence with 123 honorary members and approximately 500 ordinary members. Tiziana Casavecchia, "Aspetti del mutuo soccorso a Senigallia tra Otto e Novecento," in *"Uniti e solidali": L'associazionismo nelle Marche tra Otto e Novecento*, ed. Paolo Giovannini (Ancona: Il lavoro, 2002), p. 57.

37 At annual meetings, the liberal leaders of mutual aid societies routinely focused on two sets of numbers: membership statistics (including the variable health of different groups of members, especially women and older men) and budget figures. For mutual aid society leaders' concerns regarding the health of women members in Viterbo, see Gilda Nicolai, *Lavoro, Patria e Libertà: Associazionismo e solidarismo nell'alto Lazio lungo l'Ottocento* (Viterbo: Sette città, 2008), p. 208.

38 *Discorso del Prof. Luigi Luzzatti all'inaugurazione della Banca Popolare di Asola*, pp. 294–7.

39 Luigi Luzzatti, "Casse di risparmio postali" (speech given to the Camera dei Deputati on 19 April 1875), in Luzzatti, *Opere*, vol. 4, pp. 301–9.

40 Luzzatti, "Casse di risparmio postali," pp. 306–7.

41 For one of the most detailed accounts of the Luzzatti-Ferrara debate, see Paolo Pecorari, *Luigi Luzzatti e le origini del "statalismo" economico nell'età della destra storica* (Padua: Signum, 1983).

42 Silvana Patriarca, *Numbers and Nationhood*; Roberto Romani, "Romagnosi, Messedaglia, la 'scuola lombardo-veneta': La costruzione di un sapere sociale," in *La Scienza moderata: Fedele Lampertico e l'Italia liberale*, ed. Renato Camurri (Milan: Franco Angeli, 1992), pp. 177–210.

43 Fedele Lampertico, *Economia dei popoli e degli stati*, vol. 1, *Introduzione* (Milan: Treves, 1874).

44 See, among many examples, Alessandro Rossi, *Questione sociale e questione operaia*, pp. 38, 190–1.

45 Ferruccia Cappi Bentivegna, *Alessandro Rossi e i suoi tempi* (Florence: Barbèra, 1955), pp. 71–2.

46 Luigi Luzzatti, letter to Fedele Lampertico, s. l., 26 April, s.a. [1876], in Fedele Lampertico, *Carteggi e diari*, vol. 2, F–L, ed. Renato Camurri (Venice:
Marsilio, 1998), pp. 690–2; Fedele Lampertico, letters to Luigi Luzzatti, Vicenza, 16, 23, and 27 January 1876, in *Archivio Luzzatti*, b. 23 (Corrispondenza: Lampertico, Fedele).

47 Alessandro Rossi, "Del credito popolare," *Nuova Antologia* (December
1878), pp. 720, 746–7.

48 Banca popolare di Vicenza, *Resoconto dell'esercizio dell'anno 1878 e
dell'assemblea generale statutaria degli azionisti* (Vicenza: 1879), pp. 3–10;
*Relazione e proposte della Commissione nominata nell'Assemblea generale
dei soci 27 aprile 1879 per la revisione dello Statuto* (Vicenza: 1879). The
reformed statutes included a formal disavowal of speculative banking and
created more specific rules for the extension and approval of large loans,
but otherwise did little to specify how the bank was or was not "popular,"
let alone what that term meant in terms of local economic and associational
life. See *Statuto della Banca popolare in Vicenza colle modificazioni portate
dalla Relazione della Commissione 2 Dicembre 1879* (Vicenza: 1879).

49 Banca mutua popolare di Padova, *Resoconto dell'anno 1879* (Padua: 1879),
pp. 34–5.

50 Luzzatti, *Opere*, vol. 4, pp. 323, 356, 370.

51 Luzzatti, *Opere*, vol. 4, p. 358.

52 Luzzatti, *Opere*, vol. 4 – speeches, 1876–1882.

53 Revealing are the individual bank profiles included as an appendix to
MAIC, *Statistica delle banche popolari* (Rome: 1882), pp. 89–145. On
the situation in Bologna, see Fiorenza Tarozzi, *Il risparmio e l'operaio: La
Banca Operaia di Bologna dalle origini al secondo dopoguerra* (Venice:
Marsilio, 1987).

54 The quotations about homeowning come from the summary of the Popular
Bank of Caiazzo's activities in 1881, in MAIC, *Statistica delle banche popolari* (1882), p. 138. During the 1880s, the number of popular banks in
southern Italy increased from 27 to 377. See Brian A'Hearn, "Could Southern Italians Cooperate? Banche Popolari in the Mezzogiorno," *Journal of
Economic History* 60:1 (March 2000), p. 72.

55 Alessandro Rossi, *Questione sociale e questione operaia*, pp. 175–6.

5 Notable Politics

1 The electoral reform of 1882 extended the franchise to approximately 7 per
cent of Italians, and the electoral reform of 1913 established universal manhood suffrage in Italy. On Venetian politicians' short stays in Parliament, see

Silvio Lanaro, "Dopo il '66. Una regione in patria," in *Storia d'Italia. Le re-gioni dall'Unità a oggi. Il Veneto*, ed. Silvio Lanaro (Turin: Einaudi, 1984), p. 434.

2 Max Weber, *Economy and Society: An Outline of Interpretive Sociology*, vol. 2, ed. Guenther Roth and Claus Wittich, trans. Ephraim Fischoff et al. (Berkeley: University of California Press, 1978), pp. 948–52. Two important views of the crisis of German liberalism are: James J. Sheehan, "German Liberalism and the City in Nineteenth-Century Germany," *Past & Present* 51 (May 1971), pp. 119–20; and Geoff Eley, "Notable Politics, the Cri-sis of German Liberalism, and the Electoral Transition of the 1890s," in *In Search of a Liberal Germany: Studies in the History of German Liberalism from 1789 to the Present*, ed. Konrad H. Jarausch and Larry Eugene Jones (New York: St. Martin's, 1990), pp. 187–216. On the tactical liberal re-sponse to the challenge of democracy, see the influential collection of essays *The Invention of Tradition*, ed. Eric Hobsbawm and Terence Ranger (New York: Cambridge University Press, 1983), but also Eric Hobsbawm, "The Politics of Democracy," chap. 4 in *The Age of Empire, 1875–1914* (New York: Pantheon, 1987), pp. 84–111. On the fin-de-siècle crisis of Italian lib-eralism, see David Roberts, *The Syndicalist Tradition and Italian Fascism* (Chapel Hill: University of North Carolina Press, 1979), esp. chap. 2, "The Politics of Pessimism," pp. 25–48.

3 Two special issues of Italian periodicals stand out in this revisionist litera-ture: *Quaderni storici*, n.s. 69 (December 1988), "Notabili Elettori Elezioni: Rappresentanza e controllo elettorale nell'800," ed. Antonio Annino and Raffaele Romanelli; and *Abruzzo contemporaneo* 10–11 (2000): "Le Italie dei notabili: il punto della situazione," ed. Luigi Ponziani. I thank Marco Meriggi for bringing the latter to my attention. But see also Emilio Franzina, "Le strutture elementari della clientela," in *La transizione dolce: Storie del Veneto tra '800 e '900* (Verona: Cierre, 1990), pp. 105–70.

4 For a general overview, see Hartmut Ullrich, "L'Organizzazione politica dei liberali italiani nel Parlamento e nel paese," in *Il liberalismo in Italia e in Germania dalla rivoluzione del '48 alla prima guerra mondiale*, ed. Rudolf Lill and Nicola Matteucci (Bologna: Il Mulino, 1980), pp. 403–50. But see also Paolo Pombeni, *All'origine della 'forma partito' contempora-nea: Emilia-Romagna, 1876–1892: Un caso di studio* (Bologna: Il Mulino, 1984).

5 *Il Corriere di Vicenza*, 23 August 1866, p. 1.

6 See chapter 1.

7 Letter of Fedele Lampertico to Luigi Luzzatti, [s. l.], 22 March 1862, in *Ar-chivio Luzzatti*, b. 23 (Corrispondenza: Lampertico).

8 Complaints about the delays or inactivity of political associations were voiced early and often by the press. The 24 January 1868 issue of the moderate liberal *Giornale di Padua*, for example, comments on the failure of the Liberal Union to prepare for the election in Cittadella. The 27 May 1877 issue of Padua's leading progressive liberal newspaper, *Il Bacchiglione*, contains a complaint about too much secrecy within political associations.

9 In the early 1870s, in Padua and Vicenza, newspapers shared this task with each city's leading social club: the Casino dei nobili (the Nobles' Club) in Vicenza and the Casino dei negozianti (the Merchants' Club) in Padua. For the administrative elections of 1873 in Vicenza, a group of associations – the Casino dei nobili, the association of lawyers and doctors, and two cultural clubs, the Concordia, and the Union Club – joined forces to create a makeshift electoral committee, which held a public meeting at the Casino (*Il Corriere di Vicenza*, 12 July 1873). In Padua, the Casino dei negozianti, a combination social club and political association, played a similar role, functioning as a kind of third party (after the moderate liberal and the progressive liberal groups) in the early 1870s. See Lucio Avagliano, *Alessandro Rossi e le origini dell'Italia industriale* (Naples: Libreria scientifica, 1970), appendix 1, "Le elezioni amministrative e il sorgere del socialismo della cattedra a Padova," pp. 307–17.

10 An example of an electoral meeting featuring the lists of candidates prepared by newspapers is discussed in *Il Corriere di Vicenza*, 21 June 1874. The instances of newspapers publishing lists without meetings are too numerous to mention.

11 In addition to the works by Ullrich and Pombeni cited above, see Fulvio Cammarano, *Il progresso moderato. Un'opposizione liberale nella svolta dell'Italia crispina (1887–1892)* (Bologna: Il Mulino, 1990); and Fulvio Conti, *I notabili e la macchina della politica. Politicizzazione e trasformismo fra Toscana e Romagna nell'età liberale* (Rome-Bari: Piero Lacaita, 1994).

12 For example, Vincenzo Stefano Breda, *Agli elettori del II collegio di Padova (Firenze: 1867); Resoconto agli elettori del II collegio di Padova* (Florence: 1868).

13 Letter of Fedele Lampertico to Paolo Lioy, Vicenza, 5 February 1871, in *Carte Lioy*, b. 9, in the Biblioteca Bertoliana di Vicenza.

14 Letter of Emilio Broglio to Fedele Lampertico, [s. l.] 22 March 1871, in *Carte Lampertico, Epistolario*, Iᵃ s., b. 37. It also appears in Fedele Lampertico, *Carteggi e diari 1842–1906*, vol. 1, A–E, ed. Emilio Franzina (Venice: Marsilio, 1996), pp. 365–6, as an undated letter from 1871.

15 Letter of Emilio Broglio to Fedele Lampertico, [s. l.] 16 May 1871, in *Carte Lampertico, Epistolario*, I^a s., b. 37; and in Lampertico, *Carteggi e diari*, vol. 1, A–E, pp. 364–5.

16 The election results of 1880 appear in the Archivio Luzzatti, b. 222: fasc. Collegio di Oderzo 1892–1926, on a handwritten sheet in a packet of materials on the 1880 election. The 1909 election results appear in Archivio Luzzatti, b. 221: fasc. Collegio di Oderzo 1908–1909, in a document entitled *Prospetto dimostrante i risultati delle votazioni nei Comuni costituenti il Collegio elettorale di Oderzo, nel giorno 7 Maggio 1909 per la elezione del Deputato al Parlamento*, signed by a local election official. Cavalletto's defeat in 1866 in Padua is discussed in a number of histories of the period. See, for example, Angelo Ventura, *Padova* (Rome-Bari: Laterza, 1989), pp. 71–4.

17 Letter of Luigi Luzzatti to Quintino Sella, Crespano, 24 September 1876, cited in Luzzatti, *Memorie autobiografiche e carteggi*, vol. 2 (Bologna: Zanichelli, 1931), pp. 17–18.

18 Letter of Emilio Morpurgo to Ida Morpurgo, 13 June [1879?], cited in Lanaro, "Dopo il '66," p. 434.

19 *Il Giornale di Vicenza*, 22 November 1866. Of course, for some men a political career could mean an opportunity to leave behind a tragic or unpleasant domestic situation. Antonio Tolomei confessed as much in his letter to Luigi Luzzatti, Torreglia, 9 October 1874, Archivio Luzzatti, b. 46 (Corrispondenza: Tolomei).

20 It is easy to dismiss such statements as empty rhetoric, or worse. Silvio Lanaro, for example, describes Lampertico's claim to tend to his sick mother as a "puerile excuse" for leaving Parliament in 1870 (Lanaro, "Dopo il '66," p. 434). But the importance of Mrs Lampertico not only to her son's personal life but to his every political decision was a well-known fact at the time. Quintino Sella, for one, was shocked by Lampertico's decision but not by his mother's involvement in it; on the contrary, he understood that a reversal of this decision meant convincing "Lampertico and his mother" of the need to remain Vicenza's representative in Parliament (Letter of Quintino Sella to Alessandro Rossi, Florence, 31 January 1870, in Quintino Sella, *Epistolario*, vol. 2, p. 34). For his part, Rossi too was surprised at Lampertico's decision, but added that "his mother is a unique woman" (Letter of Alessandro Rossi to Quintino Sella, Schio, 2 February 1870, in Quintino Sella, *Epistolario*, vol. 2, p. 35). In the fall of 1882, when the novelist Antonio Fogazzaro declined to run for Parliament in the first district of Vicenza, he confessed his "heart-felt repugnance" for politics to his parents; his uncle Mariano, a former MP, was overjoyed with the news (Letter of Antonio Fogazzaro to the

signori Fogazzaro, Montegalda, 23 October 1882, cited in Donatella and Luigi Piccioni, *Antonio Fogazzaro* [Turin: UTET, 1970], pp. 184–5). The Piccionis question the seriousness of Fogazzaro's excuse.

21 Luzzatti's speech (of 3 August 1865) was reported in the newspaper *L'Alleanza*; portions of it are reprinted in Luzzatti's memoirs. See Luzzatti, *Memorie*, vol. 1, pp. 177–8.

22 He said much the same in his letter inviting Paolo Lioy and Mariano Fogazzaro to represent the Società Generale at the counter-congress: "it being firmly understood that the congress, according to the direction already taken, will absolutely stay outside of the political field."Annalisa Gianello, *La Società Generale di mutuo soccorso in Vicenza (1858–1888)*, tesi di laurea in lettere, Università degli studi di Padova, facoltà di lettere e filosofia, anno accademico 1985–86, relatore Angelo Ventura, pp. 153–61; Gianello, "Le origini della Società Generale di Mutuo Soccorso di Vicenza e la presidenza Lampertico (1858–1888)," in *La scienza moderata: Fedele Lampertico e l'Italia liberale*, ed. Renato Camurri (Milan: Franco Angeli, 1992), pp. 109–11.

23 On the relationship between agricultural associations and the state, see Maria Malatesta, *I signori della terra: L'organizzazione degli interessi agrari padani (1860–1914)* (Milan: Franco Angeli, 1989), pp. 33–50.

24 *Resoconto degli argomenti piu importanti pertrattati dalla Camera di Commercio ed Arti di Padova nel quadrennio 1869-70-71-72 (fatto dal suo presidente Cav. Moise Vita Jacur* (Padua: 1873), pp. 5–7. See also *Bollettino mensile della Camera di Commercio ed Arti di Vicenza*, a. VII, n. 4 (1 April 1875), p. 4.

25 *Bollettino mensile della Camera di Commercio ed Arti di Vicenza*, a. VII, n. 4 (1 April 1875), p. 5.

26 Even Vicenza's Catholic newspaper, *Il Berico*, took an interest in the elections held by the city's popular bank. See *Il Berico*, 24 April and 1 May 1879; 6, 10, 17, and 24 June 1880.

27 Both facts – low voter turnout at commercial elections and the failure to form and sustain a political association – the *Corriere* saw as symptomatic of a wider civic indifference, characterized by associations that were "supported by three hundred members, attended by twenty," and by residents whose credo seemed to be "*it doesn't concern me, I don't want to be bothered*" (italics in original). *Il Corriere di Vicenza*, 7 December 1872.

28 *Il Giornale della Provincia di Vicenza*, 6, 9, 11, 13, and 14 June 1880. This particular election was unusual because it was called to choose all eighteen members of the bank's administration, following a series of reforms in the bank's statute the previous year. As was the case with many large

associations, and the offices of local government, popular bank elections were generally partial elections. Each year, on a rotating basis, some portion – usually between one-third and one-half – of the bank's leadership would be elected, or re-elected. Thus, the 1880 election of the Popular Bank of Vicenza was the first complete election to be held since the bank's very first administrative elections in December 1866. For examples of the rules pertaining to popular bank elections, see Banca Popolare di Vicenza, *Statuti* (Vicenza: [s.d. but 1866–67], 1870, 1874, 1879 1890, 1913).

29 *Bollettino del Comizio Agrario di Vicenza*, a. II, f. IX (December 1869), pp. 257–62.

30 The leaders of agricultural associations often registered a similar concern: how to make it easier for busy landowners to travel what were often long and rough roads to the urban centres where meetings and elections occurred.

31 "Introduzione di Luigi Luzzatti all'opera di Schulze-Delitzsch: 'Delle unioni di credito, ossia delle banche popolari,'" in Luigi Luzzatti, *Opere*, vol. 4, p. 288.

32 When a law on commercial enterprises came before the Italian Senate in 1875, the Piedmontese jurist and law professor Matteo Pescatore showed his concern and respect for Italy's humble shareholders. "Discorso intorno al progetto di legge sulle societa ed associazioni commerciali," in *Atti Parlamentari Senato – Discussioni*, Legislatura XII, Sessione 1874–75, 27 April 1875, p. 1339.

33 Associazione costituzionale di Padova, *Elenco dei soci* (Padua: 1876); Banca mutua popolare di Padova, *Resoconto* dell'anno 1873 e Atti delle assemblee generali di azionisti tenute al 16 febbraio e 2 marzo 1879 (Padua: Sacchetto, 1879), pp. 28–2, 51–3.

34 See chapter 4.

35 *Il Bacchiglione*, 28 July 1879.

36 Banca Mutua Popolare di Padova, *Resoconto dell'anno 1881 e Atti dell'adunanza generale di azionisti tenuta il 20 febbraio 1881* (Padua: 1881).

37 Letter of Carlo Tivaroni to Luigi Luzzatti, Padua, 30 August 1883, *Archivio Luzzatti*, b. 46 (Corrispondenza: Tivaroni, Carlo). The one to go, Tivaroni insisted, was himself: "I, who for some time have been considering resignation because of an absolute lack of time and have remained only so as not to leave free the position to one of the majority."
  See also Angelo Ventura, *Padova*, p. 179.

38 Even in private, elites made an effort not to appear too partisan; thus, in the last lines of his letter to Luzzatti, cited above, Tivaroni reaffirmed his loyalty to the Popular Bank, "an Institution which is good and which with little effort can improve even more, adopting at least some of your

reforms which are the convictions of us all." Padua was not the only city where opposition groups set their sights on positions of leadership in popular banks. In 1887, the prefect of Forlì (a small city in the Romagna) noted that republicans there hoped to make gains by "prevailing in political and administrative elections, in the administration of municipal and charitable organizations, in popular credit institutions and wherever they can make their presence pay off." Cited in Paolo Pombeni, "All'origine dell'organizzazione dei partiti: Il caso dell'Emilia-Romagna (1876–1892)," in *Ravenna 1882: Il socialismo in parlamento*, ed. Alessandro Roveri (Ravenna: 1985), pp. 94–5.

39 Letter of Antonio Tolomei to Luigi Luzzatti, Torreglia, 1 October 1883, in *Archivio Luzzatti*, b. 46 (Corrispondenza: Tolomei, Antonio e Giampaolo).

40 In his insightful discussion of the Risorgimento roots of *trasformismo*, Raymond Grew says this about the ruling liberals' limited and limiting concept of politics: "Politics, after unification just as before, carried grave risks. Elections continued to be – in the tradition of the plebiscites – an occasion for ensuring a general mandate rather than for presenting the population with controversial problems." Grew, "Il trasformismo: Ultimo stadio del Risorgimento," in *Il trasformismo dall'Unità ad oggi,* ed. Giampiero Carocci (Milan: Unicopli, 1992), p. 58. On the impact of professional and technical expertise on politics and social policy, see Maria Malatesta, *Society and the Professions in Italy, 1860–1914* (New York: Adrian Belton, 1995), and on Britain during the same period, Lawrence Goldman, *Science, Reform, and Politics in Victorian Britain: The Social Science Association, 1857–1886* (New York: Cambridge University Press, 2002). On the broader significance of administrative concepts of democracy in nineteenth-century Europe, see Nadia Urbinati, *Mill on Democracy: From the Athenian Polis to Representative Government* (Chicago: University of Chicago Press, 2002), and Pierre Rosanvallon, *The Demands of Liberty: Civil Society in France since the Revolution* (Cambridge, MA: Harvard University Press, 2007).

41 Società di S. Giuseppe pel mutuo soccorso degli artigiani, *Ufficio del socio visitatore* (Vicenza: 1857), in the first of two volumes of documents relevant to the Società Generale in the Biblioteca Bertoliana di Vicenza [Gonz. 347.2].

42 Administrative arrangements varied from one city to the next. For example, in Padua's Mutual-Aid Society of Artisans, Merchants and Professionals, the "council" that mediated between leaders and members was a mixed body made up of honorary as well as ordinary members, which grew in size over the years, from four in 1864 to eight in 1867, twelve in 1871, and twenty-four in 1879.

43 The letter, which appears in the archives of the Società Generale in Vicenza, is cited in Gianello, *La Società Generale*, pp. 171–3.

44 Cited in Gianello, *La Società Generale*, pp. 178–81.

45 In 1882, for example, forty members protested the "disgraceful and provocative behaviour of certain members," but also, more specifically, "the rude phrases and malicious suggestions hurled at the Distinguished Leadership of the Society, which from the moment it was first constituted has always been a zealous and astute guide." *Protesta* (Vicenza: 1882), in the second volume of documents relevant to the Società Generale in the Biblioteca Bertoliana di Vicenza [Gonz. 347.3].

46 *L'Amico del Popolo*, 24 May 1882.

47 *L'Amico del Popolo*, 27 August 1882.

48 *L'Amico del Popolo*, 24 and 27 August 1882. Emphasis in original.

49 *L'Amico del Popolo*, 24 August 1882.

50 Gianello, *La Società Generale*, pp. 86–102; 182–3.

51 Letter of Fedele Lampertico to Luigi Luzzatti, Montegaldella, 2 October 1882, in *Archivio Luzzatti*, b. 23 (Corrispondenza: Lampertico).

52 Letter of Fedele Lampertico to Luigi Luzzatti, Montegaldella, 8 October 1882, in *Archivio Luzzatti*, b. 23 (Corrispondenza: Lampertico).

53 Gianello, *La Società Generale*, pp. 70–2, 100–4.

54 Renato Camurri, "Un 'piccolo Nathan' nella roccaforte del moderatismo Veneto: L'esperienza politica e amministrativa di Riccardo Dalle Mole," in *Il Comune democratico: Riccardo Dalle Mole e l'esperienza delle giunte bloccarde nel Veneto giolittiano (1900–1914)*, ed. Camurri (Venice: Marsilio, 2000), pp. 75–87.

6 The Death of a Generation

1 Adriano Navarotto, *Ottocento vicentino* (Padua: Istituto veneto di arti grafiche, 1937), pp. 459–76. Navarotto noted the involvement of women in the brawl atop Mount Berico: "the enraged contenders did not pay attention to the targets they hit nor measured their blows, and there were contusions and ripped clothes even among the women, a few of whom ... punched like lionesses." See also Giovanni Mantese, "Liberali e cattolici a Vicenza tra il 1870 e il 1895," in *Cattolici e liberali veneti di fronte al problema temporalistico. Atti del II° Convegno di Studi risorgimentali. Vicenza, 2–3 Maggio 1870*, ed. Ermenegildo Reato (Vicenza: Istituto per la storia del Risorgimento, 1972), pp. 124–30; 143–51. Following the events of June 10, 1897, the Prime Minister of Italy, Antonio di Rudinì dissolved the Zileri government in Vicenza.

2 Bruno Tobia, *Una patria per gli italiani: Spazi, itinerari, monumenti nell'Italia unita (1870–1900)* (Rome-Bari: Laterza, 1991), p. viii. See also Umberto Levra, *Fare gli italiani: Memoria e celebrazione del Risorgimento* (Turin: Comitato di Torino dell'Istituto per la storia del Risorgimento, 1992), and Lucy Riall, *Garibaldi: Invention of a Hero* (New Haven: Yale University Press, 2008).

3 On veterans' associations, see Gianni Isola, "Un luogo di incontro fra erercito e paese: Le associazioni dei veterani del Risorgimento (1861–1911)," in *Esercito e città dall'Unità agli anni Trenta* (Rome: Ministero per i Beni Culturali, 1989), pp. 499–519; Fulvio Conti, "Con il culto della patria: Le società di veterani e reduci del Risorgimento nella Toscana postunitaria," in *L'Italia dei democratici: Sinistra risorgimentale, massoneria e associazionismo fra Otto e Novecento* (Milan: Ministero per i Beni Culturali, 2000), pp. 193–229; Eva Cecchinato, *Camicie rosse: I garibaldini dall'Unità alla Grande Guerra* (Rome: Laterza, 2009), pp. 205–26. On sharpshooters, see Gilles Pécout, "Les sociétés de tir dans l'Italie unifiée de la seconde moitié du XIXe siècle. La difficile mise en place d'une sociabilité institutionnelle entre volontariat, loisir et apprentissage civique," *Mélanges de l'École française de Rome. Italie et Méditerranée* 102:2 (1990), pp. 533–676.

4 *Il Corriere di Vicenza*, 11 October 1876.

5 *Il Bacchiglione*, 20 February 1877.

6 *Il Bacchiglione*, 2–3 December 1878.

7 *Il Paese*, 19 September 1878.

8 The moderates' dominance of public life in Vicenza was reflected in the choice of the 10th of June and Mount Berico as the date and place for the inauguration of a monument to "the men who died for Italian independence." See Antonio Ciscato, *Guida di Vicenza* (Vicenza: Paroni, 1871), p. 111.

9 *Il Berico*, 8 September 1881, "Al Berico! Al Berico!" For the timing of the federal festivals, see the special tenth anniversary publication *Le X feste federali* (Vicenza: n.d. [1898]).

10 *L'Amico del Popolo*, 8 June 1882.

11 *L'Amico del Popolo*, 27 August 1882.

12 *L'Amico del Popolo*, 8 June 1882, p. 3.

13 *L'Amico del Popolo*, 8 June 1882. The authors of the circular were Anna Maria Piccoli Cariolato, Teresa Boschetti Confortini, Maddalena Schiavo Fabrello, and Maria Casalini Cavalli. Three of the four – Cariolato, Fabrello, and Cavalli – were married to influential members of the city's progressive and democratic opposition.

14 *Il Paese*, 28 July 1878. On the list of donors were Anna Maria Piccoli Cariolato and Maddalena Schiavo Fabrello, two of the four women responsible for the 1882 Garibaldi circular. Also on the list were several women with family ties to the city's most influential moderate liberals, including Elisa Lampertico, Carolina Colleoni, Teresa Clementi, Maria Bonin, and Elena Trissino. In several respects, this initiative to help out the sharpshooting association seemed to anticipate the visit of the royal family a few weeks later, an event which brought together many of the same women.

15 *L'Amico del Popolo*, 8 June 1882.

16 Whereas the Catholic lists were provided exclusively by *Il Berico*, the lists of Garibaldi's supporters were published not only in *L'Amico del Popolo*, but also in the *L'Elettore Amministrativo*. By the end of the first week of September, the list of women who supported *Il Berico* was in its twelfth installment.

17 *L'Amico del Popolo*, 28 October 1882, p. 3: "Offerte per gl'inondati." All told, there were fifty-seven names on the list for a total of 44.5 lire. In a statement, the group noted that one reason why the total was so low was that "many workers [*lavoranti*] are not from Vicenza and that among those damaged [by the floods] in other towns are their families, to whom they had to send their savings, fruit of their labours."

18 The use of the term "Savoy" marked a departure in the naming practices of Venetian political associations. During the years 1866–1882, the vast majority of political associations adopted the generic titles of Popular Circle, Liberal Union, Constitutional Association, Progressive Association, and so on. In the 1880s and 1890s, however, a series of more explicitly national and commemorative names began to appear: in Padua alone, in addition to the Popular Savoy Association, there was the Italy Circle, the Benedetto Cairoli Circle, and the Camillo Cavour Association.

19 Tobia, *Una patria per gli italiani*, p. 108. For some of the figures regarding the number of signatures collected – over thirty thousand from Milan, twenty-six times the number of "pilgrims"; about fifty thousand from Naples; over ten thousand from Vicenza; about thirteen thousand from Perugia – see p. 134. See also Catherine Brice, *Monarchie et identité nationale en Italie (1861–1900)* (Paris: Éditions de l'École des hautes etudes en sciences sociales, 2010), and Denis Mack Smith, *Italy and Its Monarchy* (New Haven: Yale University Press, 1989).

20 *La Libertà*, a. III, n. 10–12 (31 December 1888), pp. 65–6: "Il Principe di Carignano"; a. IV, n. 2–3 (February–March), pp. 9–12: "Il Duca Ferdinando di Genova"; a. III, n. 1–5 (1 May 1888), pp. 2–3: "Il sentimento nazionale in Italia e la casa di Savoia"; a. III, n. 8–9 (1 September 1888), pp. 50–2:

"Carolina di Savoia. Canzone popolare piemontese." This sample does not include the Savoy Association's own commemorations of the royal family, for an example of which see *La Libertà*, a. III, n. 10–12 (31 December 1888), p. 90.

21 *La Libertà*, a. IV, n. 1 (9 January 1889), pp. 1–3.

22 *La Libertà*, a. II, n. 2 (15 January 1887), p. 5. The speaker was Antonio Favoron, vice-president of the Society of Volunteer Veterans of 1848–49 in Padua.

23 Antonio Tolomei, "Per l'inaugurazione dell'orfanotrofio *Vittorio Emanuele II*," in Tolomei, *Scritti vari* (Padua: Draghi, 1919), pp. 254–5. Tolomei also used the phrase "Immortal One" in his speech inaugurating the Victor Emmanuel monument in Padua in June 1882: "We draw close together around You, o Immortal One, with the flags of the trades and the banners of the people ... while the standards of your young army file in front of You."

      "Inaugurazione del monumento a Vittorio Emanuele II eretto in Padova per sottoscrizione cittadina (XVIII Giugno MDCCCLXXXII)," in *Scritti vari*, p. 253.

24 Legnazzi, *La Società Volontari-Veterani 1848–49 di Padova*, p. 16. As the official guardians of the Victor Emmanuel monument in Padua, the Society of Volunteer Veterans of 1848–49 took the initiative of creating a collection of these crowns at the association's headquarters, a short distance from the monument.

25 Catherine Brice, "'The King Was Pale': Italy's National-Popular Monarchy and the Construction of Disasters, 1882–1885," in *Disastro!: Disasters in Italy since 1860: Culture, Politics, Society*, ed. John Dickie, John Foot, and Frank M. Snowden (New York: Palgrave McMillan, 2002), pp. 61–79.

26 See, for example, the plaque on the bell tower in the town of Bovolenta, near Padua, which was inaugurated on Constitution Day in 1883 along with plaques to Victor Emmanuel II and Garibaldi. The inscription on the plaque notes that Umberto "climbed this tower" and "piously" looked over the flood damage in the surrounding area. *L'Osservatore Veneto. Annuario-Guida del 1884. Anno IV* (Padua: 1884), pp. 67–8.

27 *L'Euganeo*, 12 June 1882. Due to an illness, Tolomei could not attend the ceremony in person; instead, he asked another city official to read his speech for him.

28 *L'Osservatore Veneto. Anno IV* (1884), pp. 65–116.

29 Società di Mutuo Soccorso di Artigiani, Negozianti e Professionisti, *Statuto* (Padua: 1867), Titolo XII, Art. 44, appended to *Resoconto della adunanza generale, tenuta nel teatro Sociale di Padova, il 29 settembre 1867 dalla Società di Mutuo Soccorso di Artigiani, Negozianti e Professionisti* (Padua: 1876), p. 18. For two of many examples of Italian mutual aid societies that

paid considerable attention to funerary rites and benefits, see Gilda Nicolai, *Lavoro, Patria e Libertà: Associazionismo e solidarismo nell'alto Lazio lungo l'Ottocento* (Viterbo: Sette città, 2008), pp. 210–13; and Michele Durante, "Le società di mutuo soccorso a Taranto: Cenni su alcuni sodalizi sorti tra il XIX e il XX secolo," in *Le società di mutuo soccorso italiane e i loro archivi. Atti del seminario di studio: Spoleto, 8–10 novembre 1995* (Rome: Ministero per i beni e le attività culturali, 1999), pp. 246–7. Statistics from 1885 on the number of mutual aid societies that provided funeral benefits appear in Franco Della Peruta, "Il Mutuo Soccorso dagli inizi dell'800 al 1885, " in *Il mutuo soccorso: Lavoro e associazionismo in Liguria (1850–1925)*, ed. Leo Morabito (Genoa: Istituto Mazziniano, 1999), p. 48; statistics from 1895 appear in Ulisse Gobbi, *Le società di mutuo soccorso* (Milan: Società editrice libraria, 1901), p. 69.

30 On the Popular Savoy Association's funerary rules, see *La Libertà* (1886), pp. 42, 54–6; (1887), pp. 7–8, 75–6. For an example of heroic commemoration, see the discussion of the Popular Savoy Association's project to assemble an album of veterans from the city and province of Padua who "died for the Fatherland" in *La Libertà* (1886), p. 32. For examples of humble obituaries of Popular Savoy Association members, see *La Libertà* (1886), p. 36; (1887), p. 16. On the Workers' Society in Monselice, see *La Libertà* (1888), pp. 38–9; on the Workers' Society in Montagnana, *La Libertà* (1889), pp. 5–7.

31 *La Libertà* (1886), p. 54; (1888), pp. 83–4; (1889), pp. 15, 19, 54.

32 *La Libertà* (1888), pp. 30, 61; (1889), p. 19; (1890), p. 9.

33 Società Operaia di mutuo soccorso degli artigiani, negozianti e professionisti, *Relazione e esercizio dell'anno 1889* (Padua: 1890), pp. 3–7, 9–10. *La Libertà* (1889), pp. 43, 54; (1890), p. 1.

34 *Annuario biografico universale. Raccolta dei piu illustri contemporanei compilato sotto la direzione del Professore Attilio Brunialti da distinti scrittori italiani e stranieri, anno I: 1884–85* (Turin: 1885), p. 465.

35 Antonio Tolomei, "Cenni necrologi letti nella seduta 23 marzo 1881 del Consiglio Comunale," in *Scritti vari*, p. 287.

36 *Il Giornale di Padova*, 1 March 1881, in the collection of commemorative material *Ferdinando Coletti* (Padua: 1882), p. 16. See also, in the same volume, the commemoration read by E.N. Legnazzi, president of the Society of Volunteer Veterans of 1848–49, which described Coletti's clandestine activities during the Risorgimento, and ended with the comment, "The best men are abandoning us; Marzolo, Bellavitis, Coletti ..."

37 Antonio Tolomei, "Sulla bara di Francesco Piccoli," in *Scritti vari*, pp. 303–4.

38 Francesco Molon, *Ricordi* (Vic: 1886).
39 See, however, Axel Körner, *Politics of Culture in Liberal Italy: From Unification to Fascism* (New York: Routledge, 2009), pp. 179–96; Massimo Baioni, "Identità nazionale e miti del Risorgimento nell'Italia liberale. Problemi e direzioni di ricerca," *Storia e problemi contemporanei* 22 (December 1998), pp. 29–31; and, on France, William Cohen, "Symbols of Power: Statues in Nineteenth-Century Provincial France," *Comparative Studies in Society and History* 31:3 (July 1989), pp. 491–513; on Germany, Alon Confino, *The Nation as a Local Metaphor: Württemberg, Imperial Germany, and National Memory, 1871–1918* (Chapel Hill: University of North Carolina Press, 1997).
40 Lionello Puppi and Giuseppe Toffanin, *Guida di Padova: Arte e storia tra vie e piazze* (Trieste: Lint, 1985), pp. 318–9, 467; Tolomei, *Scritti vari*, pp. 250–5, 269–71, 291–2. This list of public monuments does not include commemorative plaques (*lapidi*), the full range of which I have not been able to chronicle. Among Tolomei's many commemorative acts as mayor, for example, was the inauguration of a plaque to the liberal democrat Roberto Marin, a veteran of several Risorgimento wars, in 1887 (Tolomei, *Scritti vari*, pp. 271–5). Among the monuments erected after the turn of the century were the statues of Alberto Cavalletto (1902), Giuseppe Mazzini (1903), and a monument to the Italian state's occupation of Rome on 20 September 1870 (1912) (Puppi and Toffanin, *Guida di Padova*).
41 Franco Barbieri, *Guida di Vicenza* (Vicenza: Eretenia, 1956). Other monuments that followed included the statues of Fedele Lampertico (1924) and Antonio Fogazzaro (1936). It should be noted that, compared to Padua, Vicenza lost fewer of its leading notables during the 1880s, and no one of the political stature of Piccoli or Morpurgo. Among the exceptional figures in Vicenza who did die in the 1880s were Lodovico Bonin, Francesco Molon, Mariano Fogazzaro, and Giacomo Zanella. Other notables like Fedele Lampertico and Paolo Lioy survived this first, pivotal moment of mourning and commemoration.
42 Antonio Caccianiga, *Feste e funerali* (Treviso: 1889). Yearbooks from the period like the *Osservatore Veneto* also began to note the deaths of minor local notables.
43 Gaetano Sorgato, *Memorie funebre antiche e recenti*, vol. 6 (Padua: 1862), pp. 249–50.
44 In his massive *Historical Bibliography of the City and Province of Vicenza*, which appeared in 1916, Sebastiano Rumor listed one hundred "funereal collections" published in Vicenza between unification and 1916, with the following chronological distribution: 1866–1876 (six); 1876–1886

(fourteen); 1886–1896 (thirty); 1896–1906 (twenty-six); 1906–1916 (twenty-four). Many of these publications were dedicated to the city's political elite, but as time went on more of them paid tribute to humbler men and women. Rumor listed only collections published in the city of Vicenza, excluding the dozens of collections published in nearby provincial cities such as Bassano del Grappa and Schio. Even for just the city of Vicenza, Rumor's list is probably not complete, but it is certainly the best source I know of from which to sketch the trajectory of this publishing trend. Regarding the collections dedicated to women, Rumor's list offers the following numbers: three of the fifteen (20 per cent) published between 1866 and 1884, twenty-three of the seventy-four (31 per cent) published between 1884 and 1914. No such list exists for Padua in this period. Nevertheless, the trend towards more elaborate public commemoration can be deduced from the following contrast: whereas the materials pertaining to the funeral in 1870 of one of Padua's most powerful noblemen, Andrea Cittadella Vigodarzere, were assembled and loosely placed in a folder by an archivist at the city's Civic Museum, the documents regarding the funerals of Coletti (d. 1881), Piccoli (d. 1883), Morpurgo (d. 1885), and Cavalli (d. 1888), among others, were bound and published. Rumor, *Bibliografia storica della città e provincia di Vicenza* (Vicenza: S. Giuseppe, 1916).

45 *L'Osservatore Veneto: Annuario-Guida del 1884. Anno IV* (Padua: 1884), pp. 25–7

46 *Relazione dello stato morale ed economico della Società Volontari Vicentini del 1848 ed anni successivi dall'aprile al dicembre 1883 e I° semestre 1884* (Vicenza: 1884), p. 11; Associazione dei volontari vicentini del 1848 ed anni successivi, *Relazione sullo stato economico e morale della Società nell'esercizio dell'anno 1887 letta nell'assemblea generale del 15 aprile 1888 dal Presidente Cav. Arch. Antonio Ciscato Negrin* (s. l [Vicenza]: s.d. [1888]), p. 3. Some Italian veterans' associations solved the problem of generational decline by admitting retired soldiers, regardless of whether they fought in a war. For this practice in Tuscany, see Conti, "Con il culto della patria." For more examples from several regions, see Cecchinato, *Camicie rosse*, p. 222.

47 E.N. Legnazzi, *La Società Volontari-Veterani 1848–49 di Padova* (Padua: 1893), pp. 7–9, 17, 28–9; 32–3. The association's statute dictated that as soon as the membership dropped in number to twenty, the association would be formally dissolved. With the membership averaging between sixty-four and seventy-five years of age, Legnazzi estimated that this "fatal" event would occur within twelve years. At the twenty-fifth anniversary celebration, Legnazzi told the crowd that the veterans had already decided to

leave their collection of internal documents and Risorgimento memorabilia – "arms, books, autographs, coins," and so on – to the city's Civic Museum upon the association's dissolution. See also Andrea Moschetti, *Il Museo Civico di Padova* (Padua: Prosperini, 1903).

48 Antonio Fogazzaro, "Commemorazione dei soci usciti di vita nell'anno 1891 tenuta dal presidente dell'Accademia nella tornata dell'8 gennaio 1891 [*sic*]," in *Minime. Studi, discorsi, pensieri* (Milan: Baldini & Castoldi, 1908), pp. 79–100. Writing about one of the eight deceased, Antonio Pazienti (1819–1891), a professor and scholar who refused to seek "offices and honours" for himself, Fogazzaro stated that he almost felt as if he were commemorating "not a dead person but a dead virtue." "Commemorazione," pp. 92–3.

49 A table indicating the number of years each member had belonged to the association appears in Società Operaia di mutuo soccorso degli artigiani, negozianti e professionisti, *Relazione e resoconto dell'anno 1888* (Padua: 1889), pp. 22–3. On the disturbingly high rate of sickness among suburban members, see president Giovanni Battista Fiorioli della Lena's remarks in Società Operaia di mutuo soccorso degli artigiani, negozianti e professionisti, *Relazione e esercizio dell'anno 1890* (Padua: 1891), pp. 8–9. Fiorioli della Lena reported that the association's suburban members, who represented one-seventh of the total membership, accounted for 90 of the 151 members who received sickness payments in 1890. The president went so far as to suggest that the association consider limiting the admission of workers from the city's most dangerous professions (often located in the suburbs, he noted) and from residents outside of the city's walls.

50 "Per la bandiera della Società dei macellai," in Tolomei, *Scritti vari*, pp. 265–7.

7 Unknown Territory

1 *L'Osservatore Euganeo. Annuario del Giornale di Padova. Anno I* (Padua: 1878).

2 *L'Osservatore Veneto. Annuario del 1883. Anno III* (Padua: 1883); *L'Osservatore Veneto. Annuario-Guida del 1884. Anno IV* (Padua: 1884).

3 *Guida pratica della città di Padova* (Padua: 1895).

4 Ottone Brentari, *Guida di Padova* (Bassano: 1891), pp. 5–11.

5 *L'Osservatore Euganeo. Anno I* (1878), pp. 12–28, 61–9, 78–85; *Guida pratica della città di Padova*, pp. 22–3, 34, 38–9, 56–7. In making these comparisons, one has to allow for varying degrees of completeness and consistency in the two guides. For example, among the list of "various

associations" in the *Guida pratica* were three political associations, a form
of association that the *Osservatore Euganeo* of 1878 did not take into consideration; likewise, the *Cassa di risparmio* (Savings Bank) appeared under
the category of "charitable institutions" in the *Osservatore Euganeo*, but
not in the *Guida pratica*, where instead it appeared on a list of the city's
banks. Nevertheless, in most cases the numbers even out, and the respective
lists are complete enough to suggest the basic pattern of growth.

6 Emilio Morpurgo, *Le condizioni dei contadini nel Veneto, in Atti della Gi-
unta per la inchiesta agraria sulle condizioni della classe agricola*, vol. 4
(Rome: 1882).

7 Giulio Monteleone, *Economia e politica nel padovano dopo l'Unità. 1860–
1900* (Venice: Deputazione di storia patria per le Venezie, 1971), pp. 46–82.

8 *L'Osservatore Veneto. Anno IV* (1884), pp. 65–74.

9 The proliferation of associations of all kinds in the late nineteenth and early
twentieth centuries poses a significant methodological problem: to conduct
a detailed study of every association listed in the *Osservatore Euganeo* of
1878 would be difficult; to do so with the associations catalogued in the
Guida pratica of 1895 would be next to impossible.

10 *La Libertà*, a. III, n. 7 (1 July 1888), pp. 34–5. In fact, this was only one in
a series of very limited solutions to the problem of low-income housing in
Padua. The Riello Foundation for Worker Housing needed five years and
and more than one large private donation in order to break ground. The result: six apartments at a minimum rent of 240 lire per year, modest enough
to attract six skilled artisans and their families, but not the "poor workers"
for whom the foundation was created. In fact, the first large-scale construction of low-income housing in Padua did not occur until after 1900, when
control of the city government passed from the moderate liberal "establishment" to the "popular" coalition of radicals, republicans, and socialists.
L'Osservatore Veneto. Anno III (1883), pp. 93–9; Monteleone, *Economia e
politica*, pp. 73–7; Margherita Carniello, *Padova democratic: Politica e amministrazione negli anni del blocco popolare (1900–1905)* (Padua: Regionale
Veneta, 1989).

11 *La Libertà*, a. II, n. 3 (1 February 1887), p. 11; n. 5 (1 March 1887), p. 18;
n. 6 (15 March 1887), p. 24; n. 7 (1 April 1887), pp. 27–8.

12 Ermenegildo Reato, *Le origini del movimento cattolico a Vicenza (1860–
1891)* (Vicenza: Accademia Olimpica, 1971), pp. 118–19.

13 Fulvio Conti, *L'Italia dei democratici: Sinistra risorgimentale, massoneria e
associazionismo fra Otto e Novecento* (Milan: Ministero per i Beni Culturali, 2000), pp. 236–8, which describes the situation in Mantua.

14 *La Libertà*, a. II, n. 4 (15 February 1887), p. 14.

15 The name "rural bank" (*cassa rurale*) refers specifically to the network of credit cooperatives that were modelled after the institutions developed in Germany by Friedrich Wilhelm Raiffeisen. See Anna Maria Preziosi, "Appunti sulla origine e sulla diffusione delle casse rurali nel padovano," in *Un secolo di cooperazione di credito nel Veneto: Le casse rurali ed artigiane 1883–1983*, ed. Giovanni Zalin (Padua: Signum, 1985), pp. 123–46; and Laura Stancari, "La nascita delle casse rurali nel Veneto," in *Il movimento cooperativo nella storia d'Italia 1854–1975*, ed. Fabio Fabbri (Milan: Feltrinelli, 1979), pp. 375–86.

16 *La Libertà*, a. III, n. 6 (1 June 1888), pp. 24–6: "Le Casse rurali di prestiti nella provincia di Padova."

17 These figures appear among a series of statistical tables in Angelo Gambasin, *Il movimento sociale nell'Opera dei Congressi (1874–1904). Contributo per la storia del cattolicesimo sociale in Italia* (Rome: Università Gregoriana, 1958), pp. 734–41.

18 Of the 784 Catholic workers' associations in 1897, the four northern regions of Piedmont (118), Lombardy (217), the Veneto (243), and Liguria (105) accounted for 573, or 73 per cent. In the Veneto, the diocese with the heaviest concentration of workers' associations was Vicenza, with 119 associations in 1897. This figure was only matched by the Lombard diocese of Bergamo, with 130 workers' associations in 1897. The next highest figures were reported by Genoa (82), Bagnorea, a diocese in the central Italian region of Latium, near Rome (70), Turin (48), and Pavia (40). Gambasin, *Il movimento sociale*, pp. 734–41.

19 Reato, *Le origini del movimento cattolico a Vicenza*, pp. 266–73 and, among the appendices, pp. 424–5. Nationally, the most impressive figures were once again registered in northern Italy, only this time with a more even distribution..

20 Thus, in the diocese of Vicenza, the years 1879–1883 marked a period of intense activity among local leaders of the Opera dei Congressi, which resulted in the creation of dozens of parish committees. Figures are provided by Reato in *Le origini del movimento cattolico a Vicenza*; to see how these dates and figures compare with other dioceses in the Veneto and Italy, see Gambasin, *Il movimento sociale*.

21 "Relazione del Prefetto di Vicenza per il 1890," reproduced in the documentary appendix to Reato, *Le origini del movimento cattolico a Vicenza*, pp. 328–30.

22 Reato, *Le origini del movimento cattolico a Vicenza*, pp. 169 (on the Vicenza Youth Circle's meeting place), 375–8 (on Bertolini's report from 1887); Mariano Nardello, *Il primo cinquantennio dell'Azione cattolica*

vicentina: Dalla protesta alla proposta. Storia dell'Azione cattolica vicentina, vol. 1, *1869–1922* (Padua: Messaggero, 2010), pp. 158–62, 208–9.

23 Maria Malatesta, *I signori della terra: L'organizzazione degli interessi agrari padani (1860–1914)* (Milan: Franco Angeli, 1989), pp. 177–214, 311–52. On Alessandro Rossi and the leaders of the protectionist campaign in the province of Vicenza, see Silvio Lanaro, *Società e ideologie nel Veneto rurale (1866–1898)* (Rome: Edizioni di storia e letteratura, 1976), pp. 82–93.

24 For example, between 1859 and 1865, Bishop Federico Manfredini visited 82 of the 303 parishes in the area surrounding the city of Padua. Margherita Piva, ed., *La visita pastorale di Federico Manfredini nella diocesi di Padova (1859–1865),* vol. 1 (Padua: Edizioni di storia e letteratura, 1971), p. xv.

25 See the documents on this project assembled in Biblioteca Bertoliana di Vicenza, Sala Manoscritti, Do. 36, fasc. Monografia della Provincia di Vicenza.

26 Needless to say, the precise administrative boundaries of the province do not simplify the task of assessing the meaning of provincial identity or the relative historical importance of the province as a political or geographical entity. As recent historians of Italian regions and regionalism have demonstrated, subregional (and supraprovincial) zones such as the lower Po Valley have played an especially important role in modern Italian history. See, for example, Giorgio Mori, "Dall'unità alla guerra: Aggregazione e disaggregazione di un'area regionale," in *Storia d'Italia. Le regioni dall'Unità a oggi: La Toscana,* ed. Giorgio Mori (Turin: Einaudi, 1986), pp. 51–5; Emilio Franzina, *La trasizione dolce: Storie del Veneto tra '800 e '900* (Verona: Cierre, 1990), pp. i–iii; Carl Levy, "Introduction: Italian Regionalism in Context," p. 6, and Adrian Lyttelton, "Shifting Identities: Nation, Region and City," p. 34, both in Carl Levy, ed., *Italian Regionalism: History, Identity and Politics* (Washington, DC: Berg, 1996); Axel Körner, *Politics of Culture in Liberal Italy: From Unification to Fascism* (New York: Routledge, 2009), pp. 165–6.

27 *La Libertà,* a. III, n. 1–5 (1 May 1888), pp. 8–9; a. III, n. 8-9 (1 September 1888), pp. 55–6. On the importance of the *verbale* as an expression of liberal "publicity," see chapter 2.

28 *La Libertà,* a. III, n. 6 (1 June 1888), pp. 24–5.

29 *La Libertà,* a. V, n. 1–2 (January–February 1890), pp. 4–5.

30 *La Libertà,* a. III, n. 6 (1 June 1888), pp. 25–6, on the banks of S. Angelo di Piove, Montemerlo, and Castelbaldo; a. III, n. 8–9 (1 September 1888), pp. 55–7 on the bank in Abano. The two members of the bank in Abano who were also familiar names in Padua's *Comizio Agrario* were Giuseppe Sette and Antonio Rebustello.

31 *La Libertà,* a. IV, n. 2–3 (February–March 1889), p. 18. Another phrase used to describe the pool of likely founding members was "the most notable

persons in the town [*le persone più ragguardevoli del Comune*]." See, for example, the description of the Rural Bank of Abano's origins in *La Libertà*, a. III, n. 6 (1 June 1888), p. 26.

32 Among the donors to the Workers' Society of Camposampiero were Paolo Camerini (the association's honorary president), Gino Cittadella Vigodarzere, and Carlo Maluta, three of Padua's leading political figures. *La Libertà*, a. IV, n. 6–8 (June–August 1889), p. 52.

33 The members of the Workers' Society of Montagnana hoped to involve "the best cyclists, whose fame would assure a large turnout of spectators." *La Libertà*, a. III, n. 8–9 (1 September 1888), p. 57. For the meeting of the Association of Artisans, Workers, and Small Merchants of Cervarese S. Croce, see *La Libertà*, a. IV, n. 2–3 (February–March 1889), p. 17. I discuss liberal attitudes towards celebrations in chapter 3.

34 *La Libertà*, a. III, n. 10–12 (31 December 1888), pp. 79–80.

35 *La Libertà*, a. II, n. 21–22 (1, 15 December 1887), p. 83.

36 Margaret Kohn, *Radical Space: Building the House of the People* (Ithaca, NY: Cornell University Press, 2003), pp. 78–9.

37 See, for example, Tiziana Casavecchia's discussion of the Mutual Aid Society of Scapezzano, a small town in the Marche, in "Aspetti del mutuo soccorso a Senigallia tra Otto e Novecento," in *"Uniti e Solidali": L'Associazionismo nelle Marche tra Otto e Novecento*, ed. Paolo Giovannini (Ancona: Il lavoro, 2002), pp. 101–2. In his brief study of mutual aid societies, published in 1901, Ulisse Gobbi notes the correlation between small localities and the need to form general associations. See Gobbi, *Le società di mutuo soccorso* (Milan: 1901), p. 87.

38 *Il Comune*, 22, 23 October 1892.

39 *Il Comune*, 2 November 1892.

40 *Il Comune*, 31 October 1892.

41 *Il Comune* often refered to the actions of "the principal electors" of a town. In Feltre, a district centre in the province of Belluno, *Il Comune* reported that Marco Donati, a Paduan notable running for election there, was greeted at the train station by "the most conspicuous citizens" of the town. *Il Comune*, 23 October 1892.

42 *La Provincia di Vicenza*, 31 October 1892.

43 *Il Giornale della Provincia di Vicenza*, 29 October 1876. For an example of an event for which the presence of mayors and local notables was highlighted, see the same newspaper's account of Pasquale Antonibon's speech and banquet in the small town of Sandrigo, 26 September 1876.

44 Luca Pes, "Elezioni a sistema maggioritario. Breve guida alle leggi elettorali politiche dell'Italia liberale (1860–1918)," in *Il sistema maggioritario italiano (1860–1918): Elezioni, collegi e deputati nel Veneto liberale*, ed. Pes (Verona: Cierre, 1994), p. 16.

45 *La Provincia di Vicenza*, 14, 19 November 1890. Mazzoni was introduced to the gathering at Barbarano by Cav. Carampin, the town's mayor.

46 *La Provincia di Vicenza*, 16 May 1895. For a similar comment about Luigi Cavalli, Felice Piovene's opponent in Vicenza in 1892, see *La Provincia di Vicenza*, 28 October 1892.

47 *La Provincia di Vicenza*, 31 October 1892.

48 Letter of Lelio Bonin to Fedele Lampertico, undated (but, in all likelihood, 1892), in Biblioteca Bertoliana di Vicenza, *Carte Lampertico. Epistolario.* 2^a serie, b. 74.

49 Letter of Pietro Rigoni to Luigi Luzzatti, Padua, 26 August 1908, in *Archivio Luzzatti*, b. 37. Rigoni told Luzzatti that if he did not accept the Workers' Society of Abano's invitation to inaugurate its flag with a speech and a banquet, the organinzers of the event "will turn to others." Rigoni also told Luzzatti that he really had to follow through on his plans to give a speech in the town of Albignasego; not to do so, he said, would upset the mayor and the population. Local notables made their own "tours" of the district on behalf of Luzzatti, as is clear from the telegram sent to Luzzatti by Giovanni Migliorati on 26 May 1895, in *Archivio Luzzatti*, b. 222, f.: *Persone e questioni del Collegio di Padova (1895–96)*.

50 Letters of Francesco Gasparinetti to Luigi Luzzatti, Oderzo, 21 June, 4 September, 13 October 1909, in *Archivio Luzzatti*, b. 222, f.: *Collegio di Oderzo 1908–1909*; telegram of (Francesco) Gasparinetti to Luigi Luzzatti, Oderzo, 6 April 1913, in *Archivio Luzzatti*, b. 222, f.: *Collegio di Oderzo 1892–1926*.

51 Francesco Barbagallo, "Da Crispi a Giolitti. Lo Stato, la politica, i conflitti sociali," in *Storia d'Italia*, vol. 3, *Liberalismo e democrazia*, ed. Giovanni Sabbatucci and Vittorio Vidotto (Rome: Laterza, 1995), pp. 103–11.

52 See, for example, Frank M. Snowden, *Naples in the Time of Cholera, 1884–1911* (New York: Cambridge University Press, 1997); Maria Sophia Quine, *Italy's Social Revolution: Charity and Welfare from Liberalism to Fascism* (New York: Palgrave McMillan, 2002); Carl Ipsen, *Italy in the Age of Pinocchio: Children and Danger in the Liberal Era* (New York: Palgrave McMillan, 2006). See also Alberto Caracciolo's classic study *Stato e società civile: Problemi dell'unificazione italiana* (Turin: Einaudi, 1960).

Conclusion

1 Robert D. Putnam, *Making Democracy Work: Civic Traditions in Modern Italy* (Princeton: Princeton University Press, 1993), p. 97; Putnam, "Bowling Alone: America's Declining Social Capital," *Journal of Democracy* 6 (1995), pp. 65–78. Putnam revised and greatly expanded his essay on American civic life to produce a five-hundred-page book, *Bowling Alone: The Collapse and Revival of American Community* (New York: Simon & Schuster, 2000). See also Alexis de Tocqueville, *Democracy in America* (New York: Harper Collins, 1988).

2 Putnam, *Making Democracy Work*, pp. 137–42.

3 Alberto Mario Banti, *La nazione del Risorgimento: Parentela, santità e onore alle origini dell'Italia unita* (Turin: Einaudi, 2000); Alberto Mario Banti and Paul Ginsborg, eds., *Storia d'Italia, Annali*, vol. 22, *Il Risorgimento* (Turin: Einaudi, 2007); Christopher Duggan, *The Force of Destiny: A History of Italy since 1796* (Boston: Houghton Mifflin, 2008); Emilio Gentile, *La Grande Italia: The Myth of the Nation in the Twentieth Century*, trans. Suzanne Dingee and Jennifer Pudney (Madison: University of Wisconsin Press, 2009).

4 Banti, *La nazione del Risorgimento*.

5 Fulvio Conti, *L'Italia dei democratici: Sinistra risorgimentale, massoneria, e associazionismo fra Otto e Novecento* (Milan: Ministero per i Beni Culturali, 2000); Alessandro Pastore, *Alpinismo e storia d'Italia: Dall'Unità alla Resistenza* (Bologna: Il Mulino, 2003); Gilles Pécout, "Les sociétés de tir dans l'Italie unifiée de la seconde moitié du XIXe siècle. La difficile mise en place d'une sociabilité institutionnelle entre volontariat, loisir et apprentissage civique," *Mélanges de l'Ecole française de Rome. Italie et Méditerranée 100*:2 (1990), pp. 533–676.

6 Raffaele Romanelli, *Il commando impossibile: Stato e società nell'Italia liberale* (Bologna: Il Mulino, 1988).

7 Michael Burawoy and Katherine Verdery, eds., *Uncertain Transition: Ethnographies of Change in the Postsocialist World* (Lanham, MD: Rowman & Littlefield, 1999); Gordon White, *In Search of Civil Society: Market Reform and Social Change in Contemporary China* (New York: Clarendon, 1996); Philip Oxhorn, *Organizing Civil Society: The Popular Sectors and the Struggle for Democracy in Chile* (University Park, PA: Pennsylvania State University Press, 1995); Jillian Schwedler, ed., *Toward Civil Society in the Middle East? A Primer* (Boulder, CO: L. Rienner, 1995); Marvin B. Becker, *The Emergence of Civil Society in the Eighteenth Century: A Privileged Moment in the History of England, Scotland, and France*

(Bloomington, IN: Indiana University Press, 1994); Victor Pérez-Díaz, *The Return of Civil Society: The Emergence of Democratic Spain* (Cambridge, MA: Indiana University Press, 1993). In the opening paragraph of *Making Democracy Work*, Putnam writes that "the former communist nations of Eurasia find themselves having to build democratic systems of governance from scratch" (p. 3).

8 Among many examples, see Sven Eliaeson, ed., *Building Democracy and Civil Society East of the Elbe: Essays in Honour of Edmund Mokrzycki* (London: Indiana University Press, 2006); Sarah L. Henderson, *Building Democracy in Contemporary Russia: Western Support for Grassroots Organizations* (Ithaca, NY: Cornell University Press, 2003); Larry Diamond, *The Spirit of Democracy: The Struggle to Build Free Societies throughout the World* (New York: Henry Holt, 2008); Daniel Robert Dechaine, *Global Humanitarianism: NGOs and the Crafting of Community* (Lanham, MD: Lexington Books, 2005). Theda Skocpol has reminded historians of associational life in the United States of the state's important role. See especially *Diminished Democracy: From Membership to Management in American Civil Life* (Norman, OK: University of Oklahoma Press, 2003).

9 Even Tocqueville's America has undergone this shift in perspective. See Johann N. Neems, *Creating a Nation of Joiners: Democracy and Civil Society in Early Massachusetts* (Cambridge, MA: Harvard University Press, 2008). Cutting against this trend is Pamela Radcliff's important new study of grassroots associations in Spain, *Making Democratic Citizens in Spain: Civil Society and the Popular Origins of the Transition, 1960–78* (New York: Palgrave Macmillan, 2011). On the challenge of studying the democratic content and potential of the civil society concept in a way that is critical without being cynical, see Jeffrey Alexander, *The Civil Sphere* (New York: Oxford University Press, 2006), and Margaret R. Somers, *Genealogies of Citizenship: Markets, Statelessness, and the Right to Have Rights* (New York: Cambridge University Press, 2008).

10 Giorgio Roverato, "La terza regione industriale," in *Storia d'Italia. Le regioni dall'Unità a oggi: Il Veneto*, ed. Silvio Lanaro (Turin: Einaudi, 1984), pp. 165–230; Silvio Lanaro, "Genealogia di un modello," in *Storia d'Italia*, ed. Lanaro, 5–96. The Veneto is today considered part of the so-called Third Italy, a zone of relatively successful small- and medium-sized firms and "industrial districts" stretching from Tuscany in central Italy to the Veneto and Fruili regions in the northeast. See Marco Bellandi, "'Terza Italia' e 'distretti industriali' dopo la seconda guerra mondiale," in *Storia d'Italia, Annali, vol. 15: L'industria*, ed. Franco Amatori, Duccio Bigazzi, Renato Giannetti, and Luciano Segreto (Turin: Einaudi, 1999), pp. 843–91.

Bibliography

Archival Sources

Padua

ARCHIVIO DI STATO DI PADOVA

Comitato politico centrale veneto
Gabinetto Prefettura
Società dei veterani del 1848–1849
Società del casino Pedrocchi
Teatro dei concordi
Teatro Verdi

BIBLIOTECA CIVICA DI PADOVA

Archivio di Alberto Cavalletto
Elezioni polìtiche
Francesco Piccoli, Scritti del medesimo
Raccolta di quanto fu pubblicato in morte del
    conte Andrea Cittadella-Vigodarzere

Venice

ISTITUTO VENETO DI SCIENZE, LETTERE ED ARTI

Archivio Luzzatti
Corrispondenza: b. 1–49
Trattati economici e politici, b. 100
Banche, b. 172
Politica nazionale ed internazionale, b. 221–2

Vicenza

ACCADEMIA OLIMPICA DI VICENZA
Archivio dell'Accademia Olimpica di Vicenza
s. (Attività accademiche), b. 1–3

BIBLIOTECA BERTOLIANA DI VICENZA
Carte Lampertico
Epistolario (1ᵃ e 2ᵃ serie), b. 36–141
Carte Lioy
Documenti vicentini, b. Do 40: Associazioni in Vicenza
Scritti politici di Fedele Lampertico (Gonz. 101.9)
Società Generale di Mutuo Soccorso degli artigiani vicentini, two volumes of documents (Gonz. 347.2–3)

Newspapers

L'Amico del Popolo, Vicenza, 1881–1882
L'Aurora, Padua, 1869
Il Bacchiglione, Padua, 1874–1882
Il Berico, Vicenza, 1867
Il Berico, Vicenza, 1876–1895
Il Caffè Pedrocchi, Padua, 1845–1847
Il Comune, Padua, 1864–1866
Il Comune, Padua, 1892
Il Corriere di Vicenza, 1866
Il Corriere di Vicenza, 1872–1877
L'Elettore Amministrativo, Vicenza, 1882
L'Euganeo, Padua, 1882
La Gazzetta di Vicenza, 1866
Il Giornale della Provincia di Vicenza, 1876–1882
Il Giornale di Padova, 1866–1870, 1876–1882
Il Giornale di Vicenza, 1866–1876
Il Giornale Euganeo, Padua, 1844–1848
La Libertà, Padua, 1885–1890
Il Paese, Vicenza, 1878
Il Progresso, Vicenza, 1866
La Provincia di Vicenza, 1890–1895
La Rivista Euganea, Padua, 1858

Periodicals

Bollettino del Club Alpino Italiano, Sezione di Vicenza, 1876–1882
Bollettino del Comizio Agrario di Vicenza, 1866–1882
Bollettino Elettorale del Circolo Popolare di Padova, 1866–1870
Bollettino mensile della Camera di Commercio ed Arti di Vicenza, 1872–1876
L'Esposizione Regionale Veneta, Vicenza, 1871–1872
Il Raccoglitore, Padua, 1852–1854

Published Associational Records

Associazione dei volontari vicentini del 1848 ed anni successivi. *Relazione sullo stato economico e morale della Società nell'esercizio dell'anno 1887 letta nell'assemblea generale del 15 aprile 1888 dal Presidente Cav. Arch. Antonio Caregaro Negrin.* n.p. [Vicenza]: Burato, n.d. [1888].
Associazione Popolare Savoia. *Padova e le sue industrie. Relazione letta ed approvata nell'assemblea generale del 6 Dicembre 1883.* Padua: Prosperini, 1883.
Atti dell'adunanza generale del Comizio Agrario del primo distretto della Provincia di Padova tenuta li 15, 16, 25 Genajo 1869 nella Sala Verde municipale gentilmente accordata. Padua, 1869.
Atti della prima distribuzione de' premj eseguita dalla Società d'Incoraggiamento per l'agricoltura e l'industria in Padova il giorno VIII settembre MDCCCLI nell'Aula Magna dell' I. R. Università. Padua: Sicca, n.d. [1852].
Banca mutua popolare di Padova. *Elenco degli azionisti.* Padua: Penada, 1873, 1875; Padua: Salmin, 1879.
Banca mutua popolare di Padova, *Elenco dei soci.* Padua: Crescini, 1870.
Banca mutua popolare di Padova. *Resoconti.* Padua: Sacchetto, 1867–82.
Banca mutua popolare di Padova. *Statuti.* Padua: Sacchetto, 1864; 1867; 1871; 1879.
Banca popolare di Vicenza. *Relazione e proposte della Commissione nominata nell'Assemblea generale dei soci 27 aprile 1879 per la revisione dello Statuto.* Vicenza: Burato, 1879.
Banca popolare di Vicenza. *Resoconti.* Vicenza: Burato, 1867–95.
Banca popolare di Vicenza. *Statuti.* Vicenza: Burato, [n.d. but 1866–67]; 1870; 1874; 1879; 1890; 1913.
Discorsi e documenti relativi alla festa commemorativa del lavoro celebratasi in Padova il giorno 10 ottobre 1869 dalla Società di mutuo soccorso degli artigiani, negozianti e professionisti. Padua: Randi, 1870.

*Discorso per la generale adunanza degli artigiani, negozianti e profession-
isti di Padova pronunciato nel Teatro Garibaldi il 19 aprile 1868 dal vice-
presidente Jacopo Mattieli.* Bassano, 1868.

Progetto di Statuto e Regolamento interno per la Società del Casino Pedrocchi.
Padua: Prosperini, 1872.

*Prospetto degli studj dell'imperiale regia Università di Padova per l'anno scolas-
tico 1858–1859.* Padua: Antonelli, n.d.

*Quadro dei giornali politici, scientifici e letterarj nel Gabinetto di lettura in Pa-
dova pel nuovo anno MDCCCXXXVII unitovi l'elenco dei socj attuali ordi-
narj e forestieri.* Padua: Minerva, 1836.

*Quadro dei giornali politici, scientifici e letterarj ed elenco dei socj del Gabi-
netto di lettura in Padova.* Padua: Salmin, 1871.

Regolamento della Società del Casino al Duomo in Vicenza. Vicenza: Tremeschin, 1834.

Regolamento pel Casino Pedrocchi. Padua: Prosperini, 1875.

*Regolamento pel gabinetto di lettura istituito in comune dall'Accademia Olim-
pica, dal Comizio Agrario e dall'Istituto professionale di Vicenza.* Vicenza:
Paroni, 1869.

*Relazione dello stato morale ed economico della Società Volontari Vicentini del
1848 ed anni successivi dall'aprile al dicembre 1883 e I° semestre 1884.* Vicenza: Burato, 1884.

*Relazione dello stato morale ed economico della Società dei Volontari Veterani
del 1848 ed anni successivi letta nell'Assemblea generale del 28 aprile 1883
dal Presidente cav. Antonio Negrin Caregaro.* Vicenza: Burato, 1883.

*Resoconto degli argomenti piu importanti pertrattati dalla Camera di Commer-
cio ed Arti di Padova nel quadrennio 1869–70–71–72 (fatto dal suo presidente Cav. Moise Vita Jacur).* Padua: Penada, 1873.

Società di mutuo soccorso degli artigiani, negozianti e professionisti in Padova.
Relazioni. Padua: Randi, 1868–1895.

*Statuti del Gabinetto di lettura discussi ed approvati nell'assemblea generale dei
soci tenuta il 25 settembre 1874.* Vicenza: Paroni, 1874.

Statuto del Casino dei negozianti in Padova. Padua: Penada, 1876.

*Statuto della Banca popolare in Vicenza colle modificazioni portate dalla Re-
lazione della Commissione 2 Dicembre 1879.* Vicenza: Burato, 1879.

Statuto della Società dei Nuovi Casinisti al Duomo. Vicenza: Paroni, 1858.

Statuto della Società del Casino in Vicenza. Vicenza: Burato, 1867; 1874; 1884.

Statuto della Società del Casino Pedrocchi. Padua: Prosperini, 1857.

*Statuto e Regolamento della Associazione dei Volontari 1848–49 residente in
Padova approvati nella convocazione generale del 14 maggio 1871.* Padua:
Sacchetto, 1871.

Other Published Sources

Agulhon, Maurice. *Le cercle dans la France bourgeoise 1810–1848: Étude d'une mutation de sociabilité*. Paris: A. Colin: École des hautes études en sciences sociales, 1977.

---. *The Republic in the Village: The People of the Var from the French Revolution to the Second Republic*. Trans. Janet Lloyd. New York: Cambridge University Press, 1982.

A'Hearn, Brian. "Could Southern Italians Cooperate? Banche Popolari in the Mezzogiorno." *Journal of Economic History* 60:1 (March 2000): 67–93.

Alexander, Jeffrey. *The Civil Sphere*. New York: Oxford University Press, 2006.

Annino, Antonio, and Raffaele Romanelli, eds. "Notabili Elettori Elezioni: Rappresentanza e controllo elettorale nell'800." *Quaderni storici* 69:3 (December 1988).

Arnaldi, Girolamo, and Gianfranco Folena, eds. *Storia della cultura veneta*. Vol. 6, *Dall'età napoleonica alla prima guerra mondiale*. Vicenza: Neri Pozza, 1986.

Ascoli, Albert Russell, and Krystyna von Henneberg, eds. *Making and Remaking Italy: The Cultivation of National Identity around the Risorgimento*. Oxford: Berg, 2001.

Ashley, Susan A. *Making Liberalism Work: The Italian Experience, 1860–1914*. Westport, CT: Praeger, 2003.

Atti della esposizione agricola industriale e di belle arti tenuta in Padova nell'ottobre 1869. Padua: Prosperini, 1870.

Augello, Massimo M., and Marco E.L. Guidi, eds. *Associazionismo economico e diffusione dell'economia politica nell'Ottocento: Dalle società economico-agrarie alle associazioni di economist*. 2 vols. Milan: Franco Angeli, 2000.

Avagliano, Lucio. *Alessandro Rossi e le origini dell'Italia industriale*. Naples: Libreria scientifica, 1970.

Banchi, Luciano. *Per l'inaugurazione della Società promotrice delle biblioteche popolari nella Città e Provincia di Siena*. Siena: Mucci, 1867.

Ballini, Pier Luigi, and Paolo Pecorari, eds. *Luigi Luzzatti e il suo tempo: Atti del convegno di studio (Venezia, 7–9 novembre 1991)*. 2 vols. Venice: Istituto Veneto di scienze, lettere ed arti, 1994.

Banti, Alberto Mario. *La nazione del Risorgimento: Parentela, santità e onore alle origini dell'Italia unita*. Turin: Einaudi, 2000.

---. "Public Opinion and Associations in Nineteenth-Century Italy." In *Civil Society before Democracy: Lessons from Nineteenth-Century Europe*, ed. Philip Nord and Nancy Bermeo (pp. 43–59). Lanham, MD: Rowman & Littlefield, 2000.

---. *Storia della borghesia italiana: L'età liberale (1861–1922)*. Rome: Donzelli, 1996.

---. *Terra e denaro: Una borghesia padana nell'Ottocento*. Venice: Marsilio, 1989.

Banti, Alberto Mario, and Roberto Bizzochi, eds. *Le immagini della nazione nell'Italia del Risorgimento*. Rome: Carocci, 2002.

Banti, Alberto Mario Banti, and Paul Ginsborg, eds. *Storia d'Italia. Annali*. Vol. 22, *Il Risorgimento*. Turin: Einaudi, 2007.

Banti, Alberto Mario, and Marco Meriggi. "Premessa." *Quaderni Storici* 77:2 (August 1991): 357–62.

Barbagallo, Francesco. "Da Crispi a Giolitti. Lo Stato, la politica, i conflitti sociali." In *Storia d'Italia*. Vol. 3, *Liberalismo e democrazia*. Ed. Giovanni Sabbatucci and Vittorio Vidotto. Rome: Laterza, 1995.

Barbieri, Franco. *Guida di Vicenza*. Vicenza: Eretenia, 1956.

Becker, Marvin B. *The Emergence of Civil Society in the Eighteenth Century: A Privileged Moment in the History of England, Scotland, and France*. Bloomington, IN: 1994.

Bellandi, Marco. "'Terza Italia' e 'distretti industriali' dopo la seconda guerra mondiale." In *Storia d'Italia, Annali*. Vol. 15, *L'Industria*. Ed. Franco Amatori, Duccio Bigazzi, Renato Giannetti, and Luciano Segreto (pp. 843–91). Turin: Einaudi, 1999.

Bennett, Tony. *The Birth of the Museum: History, Theory, Politics*. New York: Routledge, 1995.

Berengo, Marino. *L'agricoltura veneta dalla caduta della Repubblica all'Unità*. Milan: Banca Commerciale Italiana, 1963.

Bermeo, Nancy, and Philip Nord, eds. *Civil Society before Democracy: Lessons from Nineteenth-Century Europe*. Lanham, MD: Rowman & Littlefield, 2000.

Berti, Giampietro. *Censura e circolazione delle idee nel Veneto della Restaurazione*. Venice: Deputazione, 1989.

---. "L'ideologia liberal-moderata del 'Giornale Euganeo' (1844–1847)." In *Padova 1814–1866: Istituzioni, protagonisti e vicende di una città*, ed. Piero Del Negro and Nino Agostinetti. Padua: Istituto per la storia del Risorgimento italiano, Comitato di Padova, 1991.

Bevilacqua, Piero. *Breve storia dell'Italia meridionale: Dall'Ottocento a oggi*. Rome: Donzelli, 1993.

La Biblioteca popolare della provincia di Venezia e le letture in comune. Relazione dei promotori e parole d'inaugurazione del prof. Busoni, del dott. Alberto Errera e dei sigg. Senatore Torelli prefetto e G. B. Giustinian sindaco di Venezia. Venice: Antonelli, 1867.

Bjurstrom, Per, ed. *The Genesis of the Art Museum in the 18th Century.* Stockholm: Nationalmuseum, 1993.

Borroni Salvadori, Fabia. "Riunirsi in crocchio, anche per leggere: Le origini del gabinetto di lettura a Firenze." *Rassegna storica toscana* 27:1 (1981): 11–33.

Bourdieu, Pierre. *Outline of a Theory of Practice.* Cambridge: Cambridge University Press, 1977.

Bradley, Joseph. *Voluntary Associations in Tsarist Russia: Science, Patriotism, and Civil Society.* Cambridge, MA: Harvard University Press, 2009.

Breda, Vincenzo Stefano. *Agli elettori del II collegio di Padova.* Florence: Botta, 1867.

---. *Resoconto agli elettori del II collegio di Padova.* Florence: Botta, 1868.

Brentari, Ottone. *Guida di Padova.* Bassano: Pozzato, 1891.

Brice, Catherine. "'The King Was Pale': Italy's National-Popular Monarchy and the Construction of Disasters, 1882–1885." In *Disastro! Disasters in Italy since 1860: Culture, Politics, Society,* ed. John Dickie, John Foot, and Frank M. Snowden (pp. 61–79). New York: Palgrave McMillan, 2002.

---. *Monarchie et identité nationale en Italie (1861–1900).* Paris: Éditions de l'École des hautes etudes en sciences sociales, 2010.

Briggs, Asa. "Samuel Smiles and the Gospel of Work." in *Victorian People: A Reassessment of Persons and Themes 1851–67.* Chicago: University of Chicago Press, 1975.

Briguglio, Letterio. *Correnti politiche nel Veneto dopo Villafranca 1859–1866.* Rome: Edizioni di storia e letteratura, 1965.

Bruni, Antonio. *Delle biblioteche e dei libri popolari.* Florence: Botta, 1869.

Burawoy, Michael, and Katherine Verdery, eds. *Uncertain Transition: Ethnographies of Change in the Postsocialist World.* Lanham, MD: 1999.

Burchell, Graham, Colin Gordon, and Peter Miller, eds. *The Foucault Effect: Studies in Governmentality, with Two Lectures and an Interview with Michel Foucault.* Chicago: University of Chicago Press, 1991.

Caccianiga, Antonio. *Feste e funerali.* Treviso: Zoppelli, 1889.

Caglioti, Daniela Luigia. *Associazionismo e sociabilità d'élite a Napoli nel XIX secolo.* Naples: Liguori, 1996.

---. "Associazionismo e volontariato nell'Italia del XX secolo: Alcune ricerche." *Annali di Storia moderna e contemporanea* 4 (1998): 521–35.

Calhoun, Craig, ed. *Habermas and the Public Sphere.* Cambridge, MA: MIT Press, 1992.

Calore, Giuseppe. *L'attività politica di Alberto Cavalletto dopo il 1866.* Thesis, Università di Padova, Facoltà di Magistero, 1969.

Cammarano, Fulvio. *Il progresso moderato. Un'opposizione liberale nella svolta dell'Italia crispina (1887–1892).* Bologna: Il Mulino, 1990.

---. *Storia politica dell'Italia liberale: l'età del liberalismo classico, 1861–1901.* Rome: Laterza, 1999.

Camurri, Renato, *Attilio Brunialti: un deputato dell'Italia liberale. Scienza e politica tra il 1868 e il 1920.* Thesis, Università di Bologna, Facoltà di Scienze Politiche, 1986.

---. "Istituzioni, associazioni e classi dirigenti dall'Unità alla Grande Guerra." In *Storia di Venezia: L'Ottocento e il Novecento,* ed. Mario Isnenghi and Stuart Woolf (pp. 225–303). Rome: Istituto della Enciclopedia Italiana, 2002.

---, ed. *La scienza moderata: Fedele Lampertico e l'Italia liberale.* Milan: Franco Angeli, 1992.

---. "La "seconda società": L'associazionismo borghese nel Lombardo-Veneto (1848–1866)." In *Memoria, rappresentazioni e protagonisti del 1848 italiano,* ed. R. Camurri (pp. 249–76). Verona: Cierre, 2006.

---. "Un 'piccolo Nathan' nella roccaforte del moderatismo Veneto: L'esperienza politica e amministrativa di Riccardo Dalle Mole." In *Il Comune democratico: Riccardo Dalle Mole e l'esperienza delle giunte bloccarde nel Veneto giolittiano (1900–1914),* ed. R. Camurri (pp. 65–129). Venice: Marsilio, 2000.

Camurri, Renato, and Marco Fincardi, eds. "Spazi laici: Strutture e reti associative tra Ottocento e Novecento." *Venetica* 2 (2004).

Cantù, Cesare. *Portafoglio d'un operaio,* ed. Carlo Ossola. Milan: Bompiani, 1984.

Cappi Bentivegna, Ferruccia. *Alessandro Rossi e i suoi tempi.* Florence: Barbèra, 1955.

Caracciolo, Alberto. *Stato e società civile: Problemi dell'unificazione italiana.* Turin: Einaudi, 1960.

Cardoza, Anthony L. *Aristocrats in Bourgeois Italy: The Piedmontese Nobility, 1861–1930.* New York: Cambridge University Press, 1997.

---. "Tra caste e classe. Clubs maschili dell'élite torinese, 1840–1914." *Quaderni Storici* 77:2 (August 1991): 363–88.

Carniello, Margherita. *Padova democratica: Politica e amministrazione negli anni del blocco popolare (1900–1905).* Padua: Regionale Veneta, 1989.

Casalena, Maria Pia. *Per lo stato, per la nazione. I congressi degli scienziati in Francia e in Italia.* Rome: Carocci, 2008.

Casavecchia, Tiziana. "Aspetti del mutuo soccorso a Senigallia tra Otto e Novecento." In *"Uniti e solidali": L'associazionismo nelle Marche tra Otto e Novecent,* ed. Paolo Giovannini. Ancona: Il lavoro, 2002.

Casella, Mario. *L'associazionismo cattolico a Roma e nel Lazio dal 1870 al primo Novecento.* Galatina: Congedo, 2002.

Catalogo ed illustrazione dei prodotti primitivi del suolo e delle industrie della provincia di Vicenza offerte alla pubblica mostra nel palazzo del museo civico il 25 agosto 1855. Vicenza: Paroni, 1855.

Cattaneo, Carlo. *Scritti politici*. Vol. 1. Ed. Marco Boneschi. Florence: Le Monnier, 1964.

Cecchinato, Eva. *Camicie rosse: I garibaldini dall'Unità alla Grande Guerra.* Rome: Laterza, 2009.

Cecere, Alessandro. "Le biblioteche popolari scolastiche in Terra di Lavoro nel primo ventennio unitario." *Rivista di Terra di Lavoro. Bollettino on-line dell'Archivio di Stato di Caserta* 1:2 (April 2006): 135–48.

Cenni sopra la vita di Sua Eccelenza il conte Andrea Cittadella Vigodarzere. Padua: Crescini, 1870.

Cerasi, Laura. "Identità sociali e spazi delle associazioni. Gli studi sull'Italia liberale." *Memoria e Ricerca* 10 (1997): 123–45.

Cherubini, Arnaldo. *Il problema sociale e il mutuo soccorso nella stampa senese (1860–1893).* Siena: Accademia Senese degli Intronati, 1967.

Chiavistelli, Antonio. *Dallo stato alla nazione: Costituzione e sfera pubblica in Toscana dal 1814 al 1849.* Rome: Carocci, 2006.

Choate, Mark I. *Emigrant Nation: The Making of Italy Abroad.* Cambridge, MA: Harvard University Press, 2008.

Il Circolo S. Giuseppe di Vicenza della Gioventù Cattolica Italiana: Memorie. Vicenza: S. Giuseppe, 1887.

Ciscato, Antonio. *Guida di Vicenza.* Vicenza: Paroni, 1871.

---. *Il Vecchio Casino dei Nobili. Per le nobili nozze Arrigoni-Mugani.* Vicenza: Paroni, 1874.

Cisotto, Gianni A., ed. *Quotidiani e periodici vicentini (1811–1926).* Vicenza: Accademia Olimpica, 1986.

---. *La visita pastorale di Giovanni Antonio Farina nella diocesi di Vicenza (1864–1871).* Rome: Edizioni di storia e letteratura, 1977.

Confino, Alon. *The Nation as a Local Metaphor: Württemberg, Imperial Germany, and National Memory, 1871–1918.* Chapel Hill: University of North Carolina Press, 1997.

Conti, Fulvio. *L'Italia dei democratici: Sinistra risorgimentale, massoneria, e associazionismo fra Otto e Novecento.* Milan: Franco Angeli, 2000.

---. *I notabili e la macchina della politica: Politicizzazione e trasformismo fra Toscana e Romagna nell'età liberale.* Manduria: Piero Lacaita, 1994.

Davidoff, Leonore, and Catherine Hall. *Family Fortunes: Men and Women of the English Middle Class, 1780–1850.* Chicago: University of Chicago Press, 1987.

Davis, John A. *Conflict and Control: Law and Order in Nineteenth-Century Italy.* Atlantic Highlands, NJ: Humanities Press International, 1988.

---. "Modern Italy: Changing Historical Perspectives since 1945." In *Companion to Historiography*, ed. Michael Bentley (pp. 591–619). New York: Routledge, 1997.

---. *Naples and Napoleon: Southern Italy and the European Revolutions (1780–1860)*. New York: Oxford University Press, 2006.

---. "Remapping Italy's Path to the Twentieth Century." *Journal of Modern History* 66:2 (June 1994): 291–320.

de Certeau, Michel. *The Practice of Everyday Life*. Trans. Steven Rendall. Berkeley: University of California Press, 1984.

Dechaine, Daniel Robert. *Global Humanitarianism: NGOs and the Crafting of Community*. Lanham, MD: Lexington Books, 2005.

Della Coletta, Cristina. *World's Fairs Italian Style: The Great Exhibitions in Turin and Their Narratives, 1860–1915*. Toronto: University of Toronto Press, 2006.

Della Peruta, Franco. "Il Mutuo Soccorso dagli inizi dell'800 al 1885." In *Il mutuo soccorso: Lavoro e associazionismo in Liguria (1850–1925)*, ed. Leo Morabito. Genoa: Istituto Mazziniano, 1999.

Del Negro, Piero, and Nino Agostinetti, eds. *Padova 1814–1866: Istituzioni, protagonisti e vicende di una città*. Padua: Istituto per la storia del Risorgimento italiano , 1991.

De Rosa, Gabriele. *Giuseppe Sacchetti e la pietà veneta*. Rome: Studium, 1968.

---. *Il movimento cattolico in Italia: Dalla Restaurazione all'età giolittiana*. Rome-Bari: Laterza, 1976.

Diamond, Larry. *The Spirit of Democracy: The Struggle to Build Free Societies throughout the World*. New York: Henry Holt, 2008.

Dickie, John. *Darkest Italy: The Nation and Stereotypes of the Mezzogiorno, 1860–1900*. New York: St. Martin's Press, 1999.

Il 10 Giugno. Raccolta di documenti e di scritti che illustrano i fatti del 1848. Numero unico. Vicenza: 1881.

Le X feste federali. Vicenza: S. Giuseppe, n.d. [1898].

Duggan, Christopher. *The Force of Destiny: A History of Italy since 1796*. Boston: Houghton Mifflin, 2008.

---. *Francesco Crispi, 1818–1901: From Nation to Nationalism*. New York: Oxford University Press, 2002.

Durante, Michele. "Le società di mutuo soccorso a Taranto: Cenni su alcuni sodalizi sorti tra il XIX e il XX secolo." In *Le società di mutuo soccorso italiane e i loro archivi. Atti del seminario di studio: Spoleto, 8–10 novembre 1995*. Rome: Ministero per i beni e le attività culturali, 1999.

Eley, Geoff. "Notable Politics, the Crisis of German Liberalism, and the Electoral Transition of the 1890s." In *In Search of a Liberal Germany: Studies in the History of German Liberalism from 1789 to the Present*, ed. Konrad H. Jarausch and Larry Eugene Jones. New York: St. Martin's, 1990.

Eley, Geoff, and David Blackbourn. *The Peculiarities of German History: Bourgeois Society and Politics in Nineteenth-Century Germany*. New York: Oxford University Press, 1984.

Eliaeson, Sven, ed. *Building Democracy and Civil Society East of the Elbe: Essays in Honour of Edmund Mokrzycki*. London: Indiana University Press, 2006.

Errera, Alberto. *Annuario industriale e delle istituzioni popolari*, II: 1868–1869. Venice: Ripamonti-Ottolini, 1869.

---. *La Biblioteca popolare della provincia di Venezia e le letture in commune. Relazione dei promotori e parole d'inaugurazione del prof. Busoni, del dott. Alberto Errera e dei sigg. Senatore Torelli prefetto e G.B. Giustinian sindaco di Venezia*. Venice: Antonelli, 1867.

---. *Le industrie nel Veneto*. Milan: n.p., 1868.

---. *L'Istruzione pubblica a Venezia: Proposte e riforme*. Venice: Gazzetta, 1866.

---. *Le nuove istituzioni economiche nel secolo XIX*. Milan: Treves, 1874.

---. *Il primo anno di libertà nelle province venete. Annuario delle istituzioni popolari*. Venice: Antonelli, 1868.

---. *Storia e statistica delle industrie venete e accenni al loro avvenire*. Venice: Antonelli, 1870.

L'Esposizione agricola industriale e di belle arti della provincia di Padova. Padua: Prosperini, 1869.

Fincardi, Marco, and Maurizio Ridolfi, eds. "Le trasformazioni della festa: Secolarizzazione, politicizzazione e sociabilità nel XIX secolo (Francia, Italia, Spagna)." *Memoria e Ricerca* 3:5 (September 1995).

Findlen, Paula. *Possessing Nature: Museums, Collecting, and Scientific Culture in Early Modern Italy*. Berkeley: University of California Press, 1994.

Fogazzaro, Antonio. *Minime. Studi, discorsi, pensieri*. Milan: Baldini & Castoldi, 1908.

Fontana, Giovanni L., ed. *Schio e Alessandro Rossi: Imprenditorialità, politica, cultura e paesaggi sociali nel secondo Ottocento*. 2 vols. Rome: Edizioni di storia e letteratura, 1984.

Foucault, Michel. *Discipline and Punish: The Birth of the Prison*. Trans. Alan Sheridan. New York: Vintage, 1977.

Francesco Piccoli. Padua: Prosperini, n.d. [1884].

Franzina, Emilio, ed. *Movimento cattolico e sviluppo capitalistico: Atti del convegno su movimento cattolico e sviluppo capitalistico nel Veneto*. Venice: Marsilio, 1974.

---. *Il poeta e gli artigiani: Etica del lavoro e mutualismo nel Veneto di metà '800*. Padua: Poligrafo, 1988.

---. "Le strutture elementari della clientele." In *La scienza moderata: Fedale Lampertico e l'Italia liberale*, ed. Renato Camurri (pp. 377–430). Milan: Franco Angeli, 1992.

---. *La transizione dolce: Storie del Veneto tra '800 e '900*. Verona: Cierre, 1990.

---. *Vicenza: Storia di una città*. Vicenza: Neri Pozza, 1980.

Fumian, Carlo. *La città del lavoro: Un'utopia agroindustriale nel Veneto contemporaneo*. Venice: Marsilio, 1990.

Gambasin, Angelo. *Il movimento sociale nell'Opera dei Congressi (1874–1904). Contributo per la storia del cattolicesimo sociale in Italia*. Rome: Università Gregoriana, 1958.

---. *Parroci e contadini nel Veneto alla fine dell'Ottocento*. Rome: Edizioni di storia e letteratura, 1973.

---. *Religione e società dalle riforme napoleoniche all'età liberale: Clero, sinodi e laicato cattolico in Italia*. Padua: Liviana, 1974.

Garibaldi e Vicenza. Vicenza: Tip. Comm., n.d. [1887].

Gemelli, Giuliana, and Maria Malatesta. *Forme di sociabilità nella storiografia francese contemporanea*. Milan: Feltrinelli, 1982.

Gentile, Emilio. *La Grande Italia: The Myth of the Nation in the Twentieth Century*. Trans. Suzanne Dingee and Jennifer Pudney. Madison: University of Wisconsin Press, 2009.

Ghisalberti, Carlo. *Storia costituzionale d'Italia, 1849–1948*. Bari: Laterza, 1974.

Gianello, Annalisa. *La Società Generale di mutuo soccorso in Vicenza (1858–1888)*. Thesis, Università di Padova, Facoltà di lettere e filosofia, 1986.

Ginsborg, Paul. *Daniele Manin and the Venetian Revolution of 1848–49*. New York: Cambridge University Press, 1979.

Giovannini, Paolo, ed. *"Uniti e solidali": L'associazionismo nelle Marche tra Otto e Novecento*. Ancona: Il lavoro, 2002.

Gobbi, Ulisse. *Le società di mutuo soccorso*. Milan: Società editrice libraria, 1901.

Goldman, Lawrence. *Science, Reform, and Politics in Victorian Britain: The Social Science Association, 1857–1886*. New York: Cambridge University Press, 2002.

Gordon, Colin. "Governmental Rationality: An Introduction." In *The Foucault Effect: Studies in Governmentality*, ed. Graham Burchell, Colin Gordon, and Peter Miller. Chicago: University of Chicago Press, 1991.

Gozzini, Giovanni. *Il segreto dell'elemosina: Poveri e carità legale a Firenze 1800–1870*. Florence: Olschki, 1993.

Greenfield, Kent Roberts. *Economics and Liberalism in the Risorgimento: A Study of Nationalism in Lombardy, 1814–1848*. Baltimore: Johns Hopkins University Press, 1965.

Grew, Raymond. "The Paradoxes of Nineteenth-Century Italy's Political Culture." In *Revolution and the Meanings of Freedom in the Nineteenth Century*, ed. Isser Woloch (pp. 212–45). Stanford: Stanford University Press, 1996.

---. *A Sterner Plan for Italian Unity*. Princeton: Princeton University Press, 1963.

---. "Il trasformismo: Ultimo stadio del Risorgimento." In *Il trasformismo dall'Unità ad oggi,* ed. Giampiero Carocci. Milan: Unicopli, 1992.

Guenzi, Alberto, Paola Massa, and Fausto Piola Castelli, eds. *Guilds, Markets and Work Regulations in Italy, 16th–19th Centuries.* Brookfield, VT: Ashgate, 1998.

Guida di Padova e della sua provincia. Padua: Seminario, 1842.

Guida indispensablile per la città di Padova. Anno I: 1868. Padua: Sacchetto, 1868.

Guida indispensablile per la città di Padova. Anno II: 1870. Padua: Sacchetto, 1870.

Guida pratica della città di Padova. Padua: Salmin, 1895.

Habermas, Jürgen. *The Structural Transformation of the Public Sphere: An Inquiry into a Category of Bourgeois Society.* Trans. Thomas Burger. Cambridge, MA: MIT Press, 1989.

Hamerow, Theodore S. *The Birth of a New Europe: State and Society in the Nineteenth Century.* Chapel Hill: University of North Carolina Press, 1983.

---. *The Social Foundations of German Unification 1858–1871: Ideas and Institutions.* Princeton: 1969.

Harrison, Brian. *Peaceable Kingdom: Stability and Change in Modern Britain.* New York: Oxford University Press, 1982.

Harrison, Carol E. *The Bourgeois Citizen in Nineteenth-Century France: Gender, Sociability, and the Uses of Emulation.* New York: Oxford University Press, 1999.

Henderson, Sarah L. *Building Democracy in Contemporary Russia: Western Support for Grassroots Organizations.* Ithaca, NY: Cornell University Press, 2003.

Hobsbawm, Eric. *The Age of Empire, 1875–1914.* New York: Pantheon, 1987.

Hobsbawm, Eric, and Terence Ranger, eds. *The Invention of Tradition.* New York: Cambridge University Press, 1983.

Hoffmann, Stefan-Ludwig. *Civil Society, 1750–1914.* New York: Palgrave McMillan, 2006.

---. "Democracy and Associations in the Long Nineteenth Century: Toward a Transnational Perspective." *Journal of Modern History* 75 (June 2003): 269–99.

---. *The Politics of Sociability: Freemasonry and German Civil Society, 1840–1918.* Ann Arbor: University of Michigan Press, 2007.

Holt, Thomas C. *The Problem of Freedom: Race, Labor, and Politics in Jamaica and Britain, 1832–1938.* Baltimore: Johns Hopkins University Press, 1992.

Hughes, Steven C. *Crime, Disorder, and the Risorgimento: The Politics of Policing in Bologna.* New York: Cambridge University Press, 1995.

Ipsen, Carl. *Italy in the Age of Pinocchio: Children and Danger in the Liberal Era.* New York: Palgrave McMillan, 2006.

Isabella, Maurizio. *Risorgimento in Exile: Italian Émigrés and the Liberal International in the Post-Napoleonic Era.* New York: Oxford University Press, 2009.

Isnenghi, Mario. *L'Italia in piazza: I luoghi della vita pubblica dal 1848 ai giorni nostril.* Milan: Mondadori, 1994.

Isola, Gianni. "Un luogo di incontro fra erercito e paese: Le associazioni dei veterani del Risorgimento (1861–1911)." In *Esercito e città dall'Unità agli anni Trenta: Atti del convegno di studi: Perugia, 11–14 maggio 1988* (pp. 499–519). Rome: Ministero per i Beni Culturali, 1989.

Jacob, Margaret C. *Living the Enlightenment: Freemasonry and Politics in Eighteenth-Century Europe.* New York: Oxford University Press, 1991.

Jensen, Richard Bach. *Liberty and Order: The Theory and Practice of Italian Public Security Policy, 1848 to the Crisis of the 1890s.* New York: Garland, 1991.

Judson, Pieter M. *Exclusive Revolutionaries: Liberal Politics, Social Experience and National Identity in the Austrian Empire, 1848–1914.* Ann Arbor: University of Michigan Press, 1996.

Kertzer, David I. *The Kidnapping of Edgardo Mortara.* Boston: Knopf, 1997.

Körner, Axel. *Politics of Culture in Liberal Italy: From Unification to Fascism.* New York: Routledge, 2009.

Koshar, Rudy. *Social Life, Local Politics, and Nazism: Marburg, 1880–1935.* Chapel Hill: University of North Carolina Press, 1986.

Lampertico, Fedele. *Carteggi e diari 1842–1906.* Vol. 1. Ed. Emilio Franzina. Venice: Marsilio, 1996.

---. *Carteggi e diari 1842–1906.* Vol. 2. Ed. Renato Camurri. Venice: Marsilio, 1998.

---. *Commemorazione funebre di Valentino Pasini letta nel Teatro Olimpico il 5 Maggio 1864.* Vicenza: Paroni, 1864.

---. *Dei vantaggi che la poesia puo conseguire dall'economia politica e questa da quella.* Padua: Bianchi, 1854.

---. "Di alcuni scritti sulle Società di mutuo soccorso in Italia. Relazione." *Atti dell'I. R. Istituto Veneto di scienze, lettere ed arti* 3:10 (November 1864–October 1865).

---. *Economia dei popoli e degli stati.* 5 vols. Milan: Treves, 1874–1878.

---. *Relazione per gli anni 1858 e 1859 della Società di Mutuo Soccorso degli Artigiani Vicentini.* Vicenza: 1860.

---. *Ricordi academici e letterari.* Vicenza: 1872.

---. *Scritti storici e letterarii.* 2 vols. Florence: Le Monnier, 1882–1883.

Lampertico, Fedele, and Jacopo Cabianca. *Vicenza e il suo territorio.* Milan: Corona e Caimi, 1859.

Lanaro, Silvio. *L'Italia nuova: Identità e sviluppo 1861–1988.* Turin: Einaudi, 1988.

---. "Genealogia di un modello." In *Storia d'Italia. Le regioni dall'Unità a oggi: Il Veneto,* ed. Silvio Lanaro (pp. 5–96). Turin: Einaudi, 1984.

---, ed. *Movimento cattolico e sviluppo capitalistico: Atti del Convegno su movimento cattolico e sviluppo capitalistico nel Veneto.* Padua: Marsilio, 1974.

---, ed. *Le regioni nella storia d'Italià: Il Veneto.* Turin: Einaudi, 1984.

---. *Società e ideologie nel Veneto rurale (1866–1898).* Rome: Edizioni di storia e letteratura, 1976.

---, ed. *Storia d'Italia. Le regioni dall'Unità a oggi: Il Veneto.* Turin: Einaudi, 1984.

Laven, David. *Venice and Venetia under the Habsburgs 1815–1835.* New York: Oxford University Press, 2002. .

Laven, David, and Lucy Riall, eds. *Napoleon's Legacy: Problems of Government in Restoration Europe.* New York: Berg, 2000.

Legnazzi, E.N. *La Società Volontari-Veterani 1848–49 di Padova.* Padua: Crescini, 1893.

Leoni, Carlo. *Cronaca segreta de' miei tempi.* Ed. Giuseppe Toffanin, Jr. Padua: Rebellato, 1976.

---. *Libro pegli operaji.* Venice: Naratovich, 1866.

Levra, Umberto. *Fare gli italiani: Memoria e celebrazione del Risorgimento.* Turin: Comitato di Torino dell'Istituto per la storia del Risorgimento, 1992.

---. "Salotti, circoli, caffè." In *Milleottocentoquarantotto: Torino, l'Italia, l'Europa,* ed. Levra Roccia and Rosanna Roccia (pp. 101–12). Turin: Archivio storico della Città di Torino, 1998.

Levy, Carl, ed. *Italian Regionalism: History, Identity and Politics.* Washington, DC: Berg, 1996.

Lioy, Paolo. *Sulle biblioteche popolari.* Verona: Apollonio, 1870.

---. *Sulle scuole serali gratuite istituite dall'Accademia olimpica di Vicenza. Discorso.* Vicenza: Paroni, 1863.

Lumley, Robert, and Jonathan Morris. *The New History of the Italian South: The Mezzogiorno Revisited.* Exeter: University of Exeter Press, 1997.

Luzzatti, Luigi. *La diffusione del credito e le banche popolari.* Padua: Prosperini, 1863. Reprinted in *Attualità di Luigi Luzzatti,* ed. Francesco Parrillo. Milan: Giuffrè, 1964.

---. *Memorie autobiografiche e carteggi.* 2 vols. Bologna: Zanichelli, 1931.

---. *Opere.* 6 vols. Bologna: Zanichelli, 1924–1966.

Mack Smith, Denis. *Italy and Its Monarchy.* New Haven: Yale University Press, 1989.

---. *The Making of Italy 1796–1870.* New York: Walker, 1968.

Malatesta, Maria. "Il caffè e l'osteria." In *I luoghi della memoria: Strutture ed eventi dell'Italia unita,* ed. Mario Isnenghi. Rome: Laterza, 1997.

---. *I signori della terra: L'organizzazione degli interessi agrari padani (1860–1914).* Milan: Franco Angeli, 1989.

---, ed. "Sociabilità nobiliare, sociabilità borghese." *Cheiron* 5:9–10 (1988).

---, ed. *Society and the Professions in Italy, 1860–1914.* Trans. Adrian Belton, New York: Cambridge University Press, 1995.

Mantese, Giovanni. "Liberali e cattolici a Vicenza tra il 1870 e il 1895." In *Cattolici e liberali veneti di fronte al problema temporalistico. Atti del II° Convegno di Studi risorgimentali. Vicenza, 2–3 Maggio 1870,* ed. Ermenegildo Reato. Vicenza: Istituto per la storia del Risorgimento, 1972.

---. *Memorie storiche della Chiesa vicentina.* Vol. 5, *Dal Risorgimento ai nostri giorni.* Vicenza: Istituto S. Gaetano, 1954.

---. *Il Seminario e la vita religiosa vicentina negli ultimi cent'anni. Per la commemorazione centenario del seminario vescovile di Vicenza.* Vicenza: Istituto S. Gaetano, 1954.

Marino, Giuseppe Carlo. *La formazione dello spirito borghese in Italia.* Florence: La Nuova Italia, 1974.

Marucco, Dora. *Mutualismo e sistema politico: Il caso italiano (1862–1904).* Milan: Franco Angeli, 1981.

Meriggi, Marco. "Associazionismo borghese tra '700 e '800. Sonderweg tedesco e caso francese." *Quaderni Storici* 71:2 (August 1989): 589–627.

---. *Milano borghese: Circoli ed élites nell'Ottocento.* Venice: Marsilio, 1992.

---. *Il Regno Lombardo-Veneto.* Turin: UTET, 1987.

---. "Società, istituzioni e ceti dirigenti." In *Storia d'Italia.* Vol. 1, *Le premesse dell'Unità: Dalla fine del Settecento al 1861.* Ed. Giovanni Sabbatucci and Vittorio Vidotto (pp. 119–228). Rome: Laterza, 1994.

---. "Lo 'spirito di associazione' nella Milano dell'Ottocento (1815–1890)." *Quaderni Storici* 77:2 (August 1991): 389–417.

---. "Vita di circolo e rappresentanza civica nella Milano liberale." In *Memoria e progetto per la Milano italiana 1870–1900 e il caso Bagatti-Valsecchi,* ed. C. Mozzarelli and R. Pavoni. Milan: Guerini, 1991.

Messedaglia, Angelo, and Luigi Messedaglia. *Opere scelte di economia e altri scritti.* 2 vols. Vicenza: Rumor, 1920–1.

Messedaglia, Luigi. *L'opera politica di Angelo Messedaglia nel 1866: Contributo alla storia delle liberazione del Veneto con lettere e documenti inediti.* Venice: Accademia di Agricoltura, Scienze e Lettere di Verona, 1921.

Moe, Nelson. *The View from Vesuvius: Italian Culture and the Southern Question.* Berkeley: University of California Press, 2002.

Monteleone, Giulio. *Economia e politica nel padovano dopo l'Unità. 1866–1900.* Venice: Deputazione di storia patria per le Venezie, 1971.

Montobbio, Luigi. *Vincenzo Stefano Breda (con un carteggio inedito 1896–1902).* Padua: Fondazione V.S. Breda, 1987.

Morabito, Leo, and Emilio Costa, eds. *L'Universo della solidarietà: Associazionismo e movimento operaio a Genova e Provincia. Mostra storica: Genova, Loggia della Mercanzi, 25 novembre 1995–31 gennaio 1996.* Genoa: Provincia di Genova, 1995.

Mori, Giorgio. "Dall'unità alla guerra: Aggregazione e disaggregazione di un'area regionale." In *Storia d'Italia. Le regioni dall'Unità a oggi: La Toscana,* ed. Giorgio Mori. Turin: Einaudi, 1986.

Morpurgo, Emilio. *Di alcune questioni intorno alla carità.* Rovereto: Catuno, 1863.

---. *Il proletariato e le società di mutuo soccorso.* Padua: Bianchi, 1859.

---. *Saggi statistici ed economici sul Veneto.* Padua: Prosperini, 1868.

---. *La statistica e le scienze sociali.* Florence: Le Monnier, 1872.

Morris, R.J. *Class, Sect and Party: The Making of the British Middle Class, Leeds 1820–1850.* New York: Manchester University Press, 1990.

---. "Clubs, Societies and Associations." In *The Cambridge Social History of Britain 1750–1950.* Vol. 3, *Social Agencies and Institutions.* Ed. F.M.L. Thompson (pp. 395–443). New York: Cambridge University Press, 1990.

---. "Introduction: Civil Society, Associations and Urban Places: Class, Nation and Culture in Nineteenth-Century Europe." In *Civil Society, Associations and Urban Places: Class, Nation and Culture in Nineteenth-Century Europe,* ed. Graeme Morton, Boudien de Vries, and R.J. Morris. Aldershot, UK: Ashgate, 2006.

Morton, Graeme, Boudien de Vries, and R.J. Morris, eds. *Civil Society, Associations and Urban Places: Class, Nation and Culture in Nineteenth-Century Europe.* Aldershot, UK: Ashgate, 2006.

Moschetti, Andrea. *Il Museo Civico di Padova.* Padua: Prosperini, 1903.

Moschini, Giannantonio. *Guida per la città di Padova all'amico delle belle arti.* Venice: Gamba, 1817.

Nardello, Mariano. *Il primo cinquantennio dell'Azione cattolica vicentina: Dalla protesta alla proposta. Storia dell'Azione cattolica vicentina.* Vol. 1, *1869–1922.* Padua: Messaggero, 2010.

Navarotto, Adriano. *Ottocento vicentino.* Padua: Istituto veneto di arti grafiche, 1937.

Neems, Johann N. *Creating a Nation of Joiners: Democracy and Civil Society in Early Massachusetts.* Cambridge, MA: Harvard University Press, 2008.

Nicolai, Gilda. *Lavoro, Patria e Libertà: Associazionismo e solidarismo nell'alto Lazio lungo l'Ottocento*. Viterbo: Sette città, 2008.

Nord, Philip. "Introduction." In *Civil Society before Democracy: Lessons from Nineteenth-Century Europe*, ed. Nancy Bermeo and Philip Nord. Lanham, MD: Rowman & Littlefield, 2000.

---. *The Republican Moment: Struggles for Democracy in Nineteenth-Century France*. Cambridge, MA: Harvard University Press, 1995.

L'Osservatore Euganeo. Annuario del Giornale di Padova. Anno I. Padua: Sacchetto, 1878.

L'Osservatore Veneto. Annuario del 1883. Anno III. Padua: Sacchetto, 1883.

L'Osservatore Veneto. Annuario-Guida del 1884. Anno IV. Padua: Sacchetto, 1884.

Oxhorn, Philip. *Organizing Civil Society: The Popular Sectors and the Struggle for Democracy in Chile*. University Park, PA: 1995.

Palazzolo, Maria Iolanda. *I salotti di cultura nell'Italia dell'800. Scene e modelli*. Milan: Franco Angeli, 1985.

Pastore, Alessandro. *Alpinismo e storia d'Italia: Dall'Unità alla Resistenza*. Bologna: Il Mulino, 2003.

Patriarca, Silvana. *Italian Vices: Nation and Character from the Risorgimento to the Republic*. New York: Cambridge University Press, 2010.

---. *Numbers and Nationhood: Writing Statistics in Nineteenth-Century Italy*. New York: Cambridge University Press, 1996.

Pecorari, Paolo, ed. *Le banche popolari nella storia d'Italia*. Venice: Istituto Veneto di scienze, lettere ed arti, 1999.

---. *Luigi Luzzatti e le origini dello "statalismo" economico nell'età della destra storica*. Padua: Signum, 1983.

Pécout, Gilles. "Les sociétés de tir dans l'Italie unifiée de la seconde moitié du XIXe siècle. La difficile mise en place d'une sociabilité institutionnelle entre volontariat, loisir et apprentissage civique." *Mélanges de l'École française de Rome. Italie et Méditerranée* 102:2 (1990): 533–676.

Pérez-Díaz, Victor. *The Return of Civil Society: The Emergence of Democratic Spain*. Cambridge, MA: 1993.

Pes, Luca. "Elezioni a sistema maggioritario. Breve guida alle leggi elettorali politiche dell'Italia liberale (1860–1918)." In *Il sistema maggioritario italiano (1860–1918): Elezioni, collegi e deputati nel Veneto liberale*. Verona: Cierre, 1994.

---. "Sei schede sulle società di mutuo soccorso a Venezia. 1849–1881." *Cheiron* 7:12–13 (1989–90): 115–45.

Piccioni, Luigi. *Antonio Fogazzaro*. Turin: UTET, 1970.

Picone Petrusa, Mariantonietta, Maria Raffaella Pessolano, and Assunta Bianco. *Le grandi esposizioni in Italia 1861–1911: La competizione culturale con l'Europa e la ricerca dello stile nazionale.* Naples: Liguori, 1988.

Piva, Margherita, ed. *La visita pastorale di Federico Manfredini nella diocesi di Padova (1859–1865).* Vol. 1. Rome: Edizioni di storia e letteratura, 1971.

Plumb, J.H. "The Commercialization of Leisure in Eighteenth-Century England." In *The Birth of a Consumer Society: The Commercialization of Eighteenth-Century England,* ed. Neil McKendrick, John Brewer, and J.H. Plumb. Bloomington: Indiana University Press, 1982.

Polsi, Alessandro. *Alle origini del capitalismo italiano: Stato, banche e banchieri dopo l'Unità.* Turin: Einaudi, 1993.

Pombeni, Paolo. *All'origine della 'forma partito' contemporanea: Emilia-Romagna, 1876–1892: Un caso di studio.* Bologna: Il Mulino, 1984.

Ponziani, Luigi, ed. "Le Italie dei notabili: Il punto della situazione." *Abruzzo contemporaneo* 10–11 (2000).

Porciani, Ilaria. *La festa della nazione. Rappresentazione dello stato e spazi sociali nell'Italia unita.* Bologna: Il Mulino, 1997.

Preziosi, Anna Maria. "Appunti sulla origine e sulla diffusione delle Casse rurali nel padovano." In *Un secolo di cooperazione di credito nel Veneto: Le casse rurali ed artigiane 1883–1983,* ed. Giovanni Zalin. Padua: Signum, 1985.

Puppi, Lionello, and Giuseppe Toffanin, Jr. *Guida di Padova: Arte e storia tra vie e piazze.* Trieste: Lint, 1985.

Putnam, Robert D. "Bowling Alone: America's Declining Social Capital." *Journal of Democracy* 6:1 (1995): 65–78.

---. *Bowling Alone: The Collapse and Revival of American Community.* New York: Simon & Schuster, 2000.

---. *Making Democracy Work: Civic Traditions in Modern Italy.* Princeton: Princeton University Press, 1993.

Quine, Maria Sophia. *Italy's Social Revolution: Charity and Welfare from Liberalism to Fascism.* New York: Palgrave McMillan, 2002.

Radcliff, Pamela. *Making Democratic Citizens in Spain: Civil Society and the Popular Origins of the Transition, 1960–78.* New York: Palgrave Macmillan, 2011.

Reato, Ermenegildo, ed. *Cattolici e liberali veneti di fronte al problema temporalistico e alla questione romana. Atti del II° Convegno di Studi risorgimentali. Vicenza, 2–3 Maggio 1870.* Vicenza: Comune di Vicenza, 1972.

---. *Le origini del movimento cattolico a Vicenza (1860–1891).* Vicenza: Accademia Olimpica, 1971.

Riall, Lucy. *Garibaldi: Invention of a Hero*. New Haven: Yale University Press, 2007.

---. *The Italian Risorgimento: State, Society and National Unification*. New York: Routledge, 1994.

---. *Risorgimento: The History of Italy from Napoleon to Nation-State*. New York: Palgrave McMillan, 2009.

Riall, Lucy, and David Laven, eds. "The New History of Risorgimento Nationalism." *Nations and Nationalism* (special issue) 15:3 (2009).

Ridolfi, Maurizio. *Il circolo virtuoso: Sociabilità democratica, associazionismo e rappresentanza politica nell'Ottocento*. Florence: Centro editoriale toscano, 1990.

Robbins, Bruce, ed. *The Phantom Public Sphere*. Minneapolis: University of Minnesota Press, 1993.

Roberts, David. *The Syndicalist Tradition and Italian Fascism*. Chapel Hill: University of North Carolina Press, 1979.

Roberts, M.J.D. *Making English Morals: Voluntary Association and Moral Reform in England, 1787–1886*. New York: Cambridge University Press, 2004.

Romanelli, Raffaele. "Il casino, l'accademia e il circolo. Forme e tendenze dell'associazionismo d'élite nella Firenze dell'Ottocento." In *Fra storia e storiografia: Scritti in onore di Pasquale Villani*, ed. Paolo Macry and Angelo Massafra (pp. 809–51). Bologna: Il Mulino, 1994.

---. *Il commando impossibile: Stato e società nell'Italia liberale*. Bologna: Il Mulino, 1988.

---. "Political Debate, Social History, and the Italian Borghesia: Changing Perspectives in Historical Research." *Journal of Modern History* 63:4 (December 1991): 717–39.

Rosanvallon, Pierre. *The Demands of Liberty: Civil Society in France since the Revolution*. Cambridge, MA: Harvard University Press, 2007.

Rossi, Alessandro. *Dell'arte della lana in Italia e all'estero giudicata all'esposizione di Parigi 1867*. Florence: Barbera, 1869.

---. *Memoria sulle istituzioni morali, private e colletive fondate dal Senatore Alessandro Rossi*. Schio: Marin, 1884.

---. *Questione sociale e questione operaia*. Turin: Roux e Favale, 1879.

Roverato, Giorgio. "La terza regione industriale." In *Storia d'Italia. Le regioni dall'Unità a oggi: Il Veneto*, ed. Silvio Lanaro. Turin: Einaudi, 1984.

Rumor, Sebastiano. *Bibliografia storica della città e provincia di Vicenza*. Vicenza: S. Giuseppe, 1916.

---. *Il Palazzo della Banca Popolare già dei conti di Thiene a Vicenza. Note di storia e d'arte*. Vicenza: Arti Grafiche Vicentine, 1912.

---. *Gli scrittori vicentini dei secoli decimottavo e decimono*. 3 vols. Venice: Emiliana, 1905–1909.

---. *La vita e le opere di Fedele Lampertico*. Vicenza: S. Giuseppe, 1907.

Ryan, Mary P. *Cradle of the Middle Class: The Family in Oneida County, New York, 1790–1865*. New York: Cambridge University Press, 1981.

Santolamazza, Rossella. "L'archivio della Società generale di mutuo soccorso fra gli artisti e gli operai di Perugia." In *Le società di mutuo soccorso italiane e i loro archivi. Atti del seminario di studio: Spoleto, 8–10 novembre 1995*. Rome: Ministero per i beni e le attività culturali, Ufficio centrale per i beni archivistici, 1999.

Sarti, Roland. *Mazzini: A Life for the Religion of Politics*. Westport, CT: Praeger, 1997.

Schorske, Carl. *Fin-de-siècle Vienna: Politics and Culture*. New York: Knopf, 1981.

Schwedler, Jillian, ed. *Toward Civil Society in the Middle East? A Primer*. Boulder, CO: 1995.

Selvatico, Pietro. *Guida di Padova e dei principali suoi contorni*. Padua: Sacchetto, 1869.

Sewell, William H., Jr. *Work and Revolution in France: The Language of Labor from the Old Regime to 1848*. New York: Cambridge University Press, 1980.

Sheehan, James J. *German History 1770–1866*. New York: Oxford University Press, 1989.

---. *Museums in the German Art World: From the End of the Old Regime to the Rise of Modernism*. Oxford: New York: Oxford University Press, 2000.

Sherman, Daniel J. *Worthy Monuments: Art Museums and the Politics of Culture in Nineteenth-Century France*. Cambridge, MA: Harvard University Press, 1989.

Signorelli, Alfio. "Socialità e circolazione di idée: L'associazionismo culturale a Catania nell'Ottocento." *Meridiana* 22–23 (1995): 39–65.

Simmel, George. "Sociability." In *On Individuality and Social Forms: Selected Writings*, ed. Donald N. Levine. Chicago: University of Chicago Press, 1971.

Skocpol, Theda. *Diminished Democracy: From Membership to Management in American Civil Life*. Norman, OK: University of Oklahoma Press, 2003.

Smiles, Samuel. *Self-Help*. London: IEA Health and Welfare Unit, 1996.

Snowden, Frank M. *Naples in the Time of Cholera, 1884–1911*. New York: Cambridge University Press, 1997.

Le società di mutuo soccorso italiane e i loro archivi. Atti del seminario di studio: Spoleto, 8–10 novembre 1995. Rome: Ministero per i beni e le attività culturali, 1999.

Soldani, Simonetta. "La mappa delle società di mutuo soccorso in Toscana fra l'Unità e la fine del secolo." In *Istituzioni e borghesie locali nell'Italia liberale*, ed. Mariapia Bigaran (pp. 247–92). Milan: Franco Angeli, 1986.

---. "Vita quotidiana e vita di società in un centro industrioso." In *Storia di Prato*. Vol. 3, *Il tempo dell'industria (1815–1953)*. Ed. Giorgio Mori (pp. 663–806). Prato: Comune di Prato, 1988.

Soldani, Simonetta, and Gabriele Turi. *Fare gli italiani: Scuola e cultura nell'Italia contemporanea*. 2 vols. Bologna: Il Mulino, 1993.

Solitro, Giuseppe. *La "Società di cultura e di incoraggiamento" in Padova nel suo primo centenario (un secolo di vita padovana) 1830–1930*. Padua: Seminario, 1930.

Somers, Margaret R. *Genealogies of Citizenship: Markets, Statelessness, and the Right to Have Rights*. New York: Cambridge University Press, 2008.

Sorgato, Gaetano. *Memorie funebre antiche e recenti*. 11 vols. Padua: Seminario, 1856–1862.

Stancari, Laura. "La nascita delle casse rurali nel Veneto." In *Il movimento cooperativo nella storia d'Italia 1854–1975*, ed. Fabio Fabbri. Milan: 1979.

Sweeney, Dennis. "Liberals, the Worker, and the Limits of Bourgeois Öffentlichkeit in Wilhelmine Germany." *German History* 22:1 (2004), pp. 36–75.

Taricone, Fiorenza. *Teoria e prassi dell'associazionismo italiano nel XIX e XX secolo*. Cassino: Università degli Studi di Cassino, 2003.

Tarozzi, Fiorenza. *Il risparmio e l'operaio: La Banca Operaia di Bologna dalle origini al secondo dopoguerra*. Venice: Marsilio, 1987.

Tavoni, Maria Gioia. "Tipografi, editori, lettura." In *Bologna in età contemporanea 1796–1914*, ed. Aldo Berselli and Angelo Varni. Bologna: Bononia University Press, 2010.

Tobia, Bruno. *Una patria per gli italiani: Spazi, itinerari, monumenti nell'Italia unita (1870–1900)*. Rome: Laterza, 1991.

de Tocqueville, Alexis. *Democracy in America*. Ed. J.P. Mayer. Trans. George Lawrence. New York: Harper Collins, 1988.

Toffanin, Giuseppe, Jr. *La Camera di Commercio in 175 anni di economia padovana 1811–1987*. Padua: Programma, 1988.

Tolomei, Antonio. *Scritti vari*. Padua: Draghi, 1919.

Tonizzi, Maria Elisabetta. "Borghesi a Genova nell'Ottocento: Associazionismo ricreativo e culturale dell'élite tra la Restaurazione e l'Unità." *Contemporanea (Bologna, Italy)* 13 (2010): 609–32.

Trentmann, Frank, ed. *Paradoxes of Civil Society: New Perspectives on Modern German and British History*. New York: Berghahn, 2000.

Trkulja, Silvia Meloni, and Ettore Spalletti. "Istituzioni artistiche fiorentine 1765–1825." In *Saloni, gallerie, musei e loro influenza sullo sviluppo dell'arte dei secoli XIX e XX*, ed. Francis Haskell. Bologna: CLUEB, 1981.

Ullrich, Hartmut. "L'Organizzazione politica dei liberali italiani nel Parlamento e nel paese." In *Il liberalismo in Italia e in Germania dalla rivoluzione del '48 alla prima guerra mondiale,* ed. Rudolf Lill and Nicola Matteucci (pp. 403–50). Bologna: Il Mulino, 1980.

Urbinati, Nadia. *Mill on Democracy: From the Athenian Polis to Representative Government.* Chicago: University of Chicago Press, 2002.

Ventura, Angelo. *Padova.* Rome: Laterza, 1989.

Vergani, Raffaele. "Elezioni e partiti a Padova dopo l'Unita (1866–1870)." *Rassegna storica del Risorgimento* 54:2–3 (July–September 1967): 237–68, 410–37.

Verucci, Guido. *L'Italia laica prima e dopo l'Unità 1848–1876: Anticlericalismo, libero pensiero e ateismo nella società italiana.* Rome: Laterza, 1981.

Vicenza-Garibaldi, XXI Agosto MDCCCLXXXVII. n.p. [Vicenza]: Burato, n.d. [1887].

Vicenza nel 1848. X Giugno nel cinquantesimo anniversario della gloriosa epopee. Vicenza: Giuliani, 1898.

Weber, Max. *Economy and Society: An Outline of Interpretive Sociology.* Vol. 2. Ed. Guenther Roth and Claus Wittich. Trans. Ephraim Fischoff et al. Berkeley: University of California Press, 1978.

White, Gordon. *In Search of Civil Society: Market Reform and Social Change in Contemporary China.* New York: 1996.

Woolf, Stuart. "The Poor and How to Relieve Them: The Restoration Debate on Poverty in Italy and Europe." In *Society and Politics in the Age of the Risorgimento: Essays in Honour of Denis Mack Smith*, ed. John A. Davis and Paul Ginsborg. New York: Cambridge University Press, 1991.

Yeo, Stephen. *Religion and Voluntary Organisations in Crisis.* London: Croom Helm, 1976.

Zamagni, Vera. *The Economic History of Italy 1860–1990.* New York: Clarendon, 1993.

Zanella, Giacomo. *Scritti varii di Giacomo Zanella.* Florence: Le Monnier, 1877.

Index

academies, 68, 218n4, 230n30
adult education, 4, 120–1, 208. *See also* night schools; popular libraries
Agrarian Association of Padua, 85, 116–17, 194
Agrarian Association of Thiene, 93, 109
Agrarian Association of Vicenza, 92–3, 150, 152, 222n31
agrarian associations (*comizi agrari*), 83, 85, 87–8, 106, 202
Agrarian Defense League (Turin), 192
agricultural associations, 40, 64, 149, 150, 192, 255n30
Agulhon, Maurice, 9–10, 15
alpine clubs, 87–8, 149, 207
Alvisi, Gian Giacomo, 54, 70, 226n5
Arts and Crafts Room for engineers, artists, and artisans (Padua), 48–9
Association for the Progress of Economic Science, 130
Association of Italian Popular Banks, 135–8, 192, 193, 202
associations: 1840s as turning point, 11, 24, 215n20; annual reports of, 12; in Austria-Hungary, 7; banners and flags of, 175–6, 184;

and businesses, 113; celebrations, 47, 175–6, 184, 195–7; and civil society, 5; collections and museums in, 87–93; and commemoration, 174–6; distinction between honorary and ordinary members, 69, 127, 154, 249n36; elections of leaders and administrators, 7, 150–7, 193; in France, 7; in Germany, 7; in Great Britain, 7; historical profiles of, 65–71; historiography, general, 5, 7, 231n10; historiography, Italian, 7, 14; and Italian liberalism, 11–12, 160, 162–3, 192–3, 206; meetings of, 7, 81, 95–100, 153–4, 193–5; and middle class, 5, 8–9; and newspapers, 4, 12, 96–100; and philanthropy, 93, 126, 248n33, 248n36; and politics, 149–50, 163; and public culture, 11–12, 35–9, 87–9, 93–4, 99–100, 109, 162, 195, 207–8; in Russia, 7; as sites of civic education, 6; statistics and, 61–2; statutes and regulations of, 7, 27–32, 94–6, 97; unification as turning point, 10–13, 79; and unification of Italy, 3–4,

166, 169, 240n52, 242n63; rural
banks, 190; strength in Vicenza,
17, 19; ties with moderate liberals
in Vicenza, 168
Catholic Workers' Association (Vi-
cenza), 188–9
Catholic Youth Circle of Vicenza,
100, 191, 240n52
Cattaneo, Carlo, 33, 119
Cavalletto, Alberto, 55, 56, 105,
147–8, 241n59, 262n40
Cavalli, Ferdinando, 42, 180, 263n44
Cavalli, Maria Casalini, 258n13
Cavour, Camillo Benso di, 121; commemoration of, 173–4, 178–9;
leader of agricultural association in
Turin, 31, 64; Risorgimento hero, 54
Chamber of Commerce of Padua,
150–1
chambers of commerce, 149, 150–1
Chemello, Adrianna, 125
cholera, 188–9, 221n26
Cibele, Nicolo, 93
Circolo dell'Unione (Florence),
221n15, 222n35
circulating libraries, 88, 93, 191,
202. See also popular libraries
Cittadella, Giovanni, 40–1, 84, 178
Cittadella Vigodarzere, Andrea, 21,
42, 80, 84; death and commemoration of, 104–5, 178, 263n44
Cittadella Vigodarzere, Antonio, 195
Civic Museum of Padua, 91, 263n44,
264n47
Civic Museum of Vicenza, 235n14
civil society: and associations, 5–6;
definitions of, 215n19; historiography of, 5, 208–9; in Venetian historiography, 19; Venetian liberals'
conception of, 6, 205, 208

Club Alpino Italiano, 16, 64, 86–7
Coletti, Domenico, 174
Coletti, Ferdinando: commemoration
of Francesco Marzolo, 176; death
and commemoration of, 176–7,
178, 179, 180, 181–2, 263n44;
founder of Venetian marine
hospice, 179, 181–2; organized
opposition to Austrian rule, 55,
261n36
Colleoni, Carolina Giustiniani Ban-
dini, 171, 259n14
Colleoni, Guardino, 170, 200
comizi agrari. See agrarian associations
Confalonieri, Federico, 119, 221n27
Confortini, Teresa Boschetti, 258n13
confraternities, 6, 10, 32, 43, 65, 69
Congresses of Italian Scientists, 21–2,
58, 69, 79, 224n50
Constitutional Association (Padua), 99
Constitutional Association (Vicenza),
199
Constitution Day, 102, 106, 149,
173, 196; disputed by Catholics in
Vicenza, 168, 169
cooperatives: in Alessandro Rossi's
factory complex in Schio, 111,
138; as example of popular association, 4, 12–13, 55, 56, 110, 115,
124, 125, 126, 144, 209, 231n35,
233n47; novelty of, 1, 2, 12, 76,
79, 110, 119, 126, 233n47; as part
of network of popular associations,
7, 111, 135–8, 188; in provincial
Venetian towns, 189; and public
works contracts, 202; in Robert
Putnam's *Making Democracy
Work*, 206. *See also* rural banks
(*casse rurali*)

189; in provincial Venetian towns, 187, 189, 190, 195, 197; sponsors of popular libraries, 89–90; ties with popular banks, 136–7, 202; and workers' self-help, 118, 120, 123, 125–6

Mutual Aid Society of Artisans, Merchants and Professionals (Padua): administration, 256n42; commemoration of Emilio Morpurgo, 176; "festival of work" (1869), 50, 195; lack of funeral benefits, 175; leadership of Emilio Morpurgo, 127, 183; newspaper coverage of meetings, 98; speeches to members by Emilio Morpurgo, 248n34; statistical information on age and sickness rates of members, 264n49; ties to Popular Bank of Padua, 137; twenty-fifth anniversary celebration, 176

Mutual Aid Society of Artists and Workers (Perugia), 89, 96, 248n36

Mutual Aid Society of Doctors, Surgeons, and Pharmacists (Padua), 25, 36, 43–4, 224n56

Mutual Aid Society of Lawyers and Notaries (Venice), 43

Mutual Aid Society of Loreggia, 193

Naples, 16, 215n20
Nardi, Giuseppe, 87
nationalism: in associations, 167; Italian historiography, 14–15, 178, 206; public celebrations, 102, 103–4, 105–6; and public culture, 81, 206
Navarotto, Adriano, 164–5
nazione del Risorgimento, La, 14–15, 33, 207
Negri, Eleonoro, 195

Negrin, Antonio Caregaro, 182
newspapers: and associations, 4, 12, 35–9, 96–100, 167, 239n40; and elections, 145–6, 151, 197–201, 252nn9–10; reporting on businesses, 112–15; reporting on nationalist celebrations, 106; reporting on public demonstrations, 104
NGOs (non-governmental organizations), 205
night schools: as example of popular association, 10, 12, 42, 110, 111, 137, 209, 231n35; as part of network of popular associations, 111, 188; promoted before unification, 41; ties with popular banks, 202; Venetian liberals' involvement in, 118–19, 120; 246n20; in Vicenza, 48, 57, 221n26, 246n20
Nobles' Club (Vicenza), 28, 252n9
Nord, Philip G., 7, 215n19

O'Connor, Sandra Day, 204–5, 208
Oderzo (Treviso), 148, 201
Olympic Academy of arts and sciences (Vicenza): co-sponsor of Reading Room of Vicenza, 221n31; as form of association, 45, 183, 218n4; as host of night schools, 44, 57, 73, 76–7, 119; as public meeting place, 27–8, 86; in speeches and writings of Fedele Lampertico, 68–9, 72, 222n34

Paduan Academy of Science, Letters, and the Arts, 40
Panozzo, Giovanni, 162
Papafava dei Carraresi, Francesco, 194, 195
Parolini, Alberto, 88
Pasini, Eleonoro, 117